Library Information Systems

Recent Titles in
Library and Information Science Text Series

Library Information Systems

Second Edition

Joseph R. Matthews and Carson Block

Library and Information Science Text Series

 LIBRARIES UNLIMITED®

An Imprint of ABC-CLIO, LLC

Santa Barbara, California • Denver, Colorado

Library of Congress Cataloging-in-Publication Data

Names: Matthews, Joseph R., author. | Kochtanek, Thomas R. Library information systems. | Block, Carson, 1963- author.
Title: Library information systems / Joseph R. Matthews and Carson Block.
Description: Second edition. | Santa Barbara, California : Libraries Unlimited, 2020. | Series: Library and information science text series | Includes bibliographical references and index.
Identifiers: LCCN 2019028068 (print) | LCCN 2019028069 (ebook) | ISBN 9781440851940 (paperback) | ISBN 9781440851957 (ebook)
Subjects: LCSH: Libraries—Automation. | Library information networks. | Integrated library systems (Computer systems) | Information storage and retrieval systems. | Information technology.
Classification: LCC Z678.9 .K59 2020 (print) | LCC Z678.9 (ebook) | DDC 025.00285—dc23
LC record available at https://lccn.loc.gov/2019028068
LC ebook record available at https://lccn.loc.gov/2019028069

ISBN: 978-1-4408-5194-0 (paperback)
       978-1-4408-5195-7 (ebook)

24 23 22 21 20   1 2 3 4 5

This book is also available as an eBook.

Libraries Unlimited
An Imprint of ABC-CLIO, LLC

ABC-CLIO, LLC
147 Castilian Drive
Santa Barbara, California 93117
www.abc-clio.com

This book is printed on acid-free paper ∞

Manufactured in the United States of America

Contents

Preface: A Word of Caution

> Modern technology was designed to empower us and set us free.
> So why do we often feel more like its slaves than its masters?
> —Michelle Weil and Larry Rosen[1]

Too often library board members, stakeholders, customers, and some staff members will ask why aren't we using a particular technology (you can pick the hot technology de jour) in our library. And many libraries, unfortunately, immediate go about the process of acquiring and trying to learn to use the new technology, without a clue of how the new technology will benefit the library's customers. Such an approach has been described by Michael Stephens as "technolust"—the creation or adoption of technologies simply for their own sake, based on the assumption that there is great demand for them.[2] Michael goes on to suggest that other states exist in which a library might find itself—technostress, technodivorce, technoshame, and technophobia.

Not surprisingly, the author does not recommend embracing "technolust," but rather takes the view that any tool, including information technologies, is a means to an end. As Stephen Covey is apt to remind us in his books and seminars, "Begin with the end in mind." Have a clear understanding of how a specific technology will be of real value to the library's customers. Technology decisions should be grounded in real insight into the actual characteristics, needs, and behaviors of various groups (often called market segments). Moreover, it is also important to understand how library programs, services, and collections will likely assist the larger organization achieve its goals and objectives. Char Booth in her report *Informing Innovation: Tracking Student Interest in Emerging Library Technologies at Ohio University* illustrates the reality of technolust in one library setting as well as detailing how library staff members achieved a greater understanding of those whom they served.[3]

It may be that a specific technology, such as a social media site, is already being frequently used by a specific customer segment of the library. If the library were to embrace a new technology that is already being heavily used *and* the library is able to add content or context from which the users of the technology will clearly benefit, then the new technology is likely one the library should embrace and utilize.

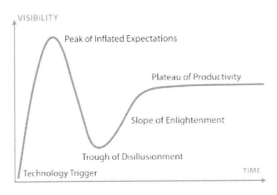

FIGURE P.1. Gartner Hype Cycle
Source: https://www.gartner.com/en/research/methodologies/gartner-hype-cycle.

It doesn't take too long to recognize that change is a constant within the realm of information and digital technologies. Tools change and morph over time, and the way people use a specific tool will also change over time. Gartner, an international consulting firm, developed the Technology Hype Cycle to illustrate how technologies evolve over time, as shown in Figure P.1.[4]

If a library is willing to take risk, then the benefits have to be quite high as an early adopter. Others will wait (and lower their risk) and implement a technology at some point after the benefits have been proven in several settings. The Hype Cycle phases include the following:

- **Technology trigger**—Vendors introducing a new technology often rely on press stories and white papers articulating the possible benefits, but actual customers are either nonexistent or few in number.

- **Peak of inflated expectations**—Some customers emerge using the new technology, and the successes often match the number of failures.

- **Trough of disillusionment**—Interest wanes, as the technology failures become better known. The technology will fail to advance unless some consistent success stories emerge.

- **Slope of enlightenment**—More instances of how the technology benefits the customers are articulated as second- and third-generation products emerge. Yet conservative customers remain cautious.

- **Plateau of productivity**—Greater numbers of customers embrace the technology, to the point that any risk is minimized. There is general market acceptance of the technology.

Discussion of how a specific technology will best "fit" is focused on the technology rather than on the benefits that may derive to the user of the technology. Too often an organization or institution such as a library will provide a tool and expect a user to "get it." And if users don't "get it" or "get it" in the way libraries expect, then libraries will often provide remedial instruction. And every tool clearly has a life cycle that must be recognized and planned for.

Lorcan Dempsey, in his talks and writings, has noted that although libraries of a decade or two ago used to be the center of the information universe, today what is in short supply is attention. And it's just not attention and what people spend their time focused on, but people themselves are being changed by this plethora of digital devices that we use each and every day. Have we carefully considered and thought about how having access to digital devices and information technology anytime, anywhere is changing our daily lives? If you are like most people, probably not to any great degree. In what ways are teaching, learning, and research being impacted and changed (often in radically short periods of time) by the accessibility of digital information resources and digital technologies?

It is also important to acknowledge that libraries are facing real competition that is disrupting traditional library services. Henry Lucas has warned in his book *The Search for Survival* that there are eight warning signs that an organization is failing in the face of disruption:[5]

1. **Denial**—Denying that a disruption has either occurred or is important.

2. **History**—Believing that a library will always be a key provider of information and thus falling a victim of history.

3. **Resistance to change**

4. **Mind-set**—Having little recognition that the status quo is failing

5. **Brand**—Relying on brand—for example, believing the library is *the* place for high-quality resources—without acknowledging that people's perception of the library brand is changing

6. **Sunk costs**—Refusing to invest in new systems and services because of the high costs the library has already made (for years) in an existing service

7. **Profitability**—Maintaining that a library may continue to receive gifts and grants to digitize its content but not invest in improving the tools that provide access to this digital content, which suggests the library has the wrong focus

8. **Lack of imagination**

Some libraries have enthusiastically embraced an open-source integrated library system (ILS), whereas others are fearful that moving to an open-source solution will bring unacceptable risks. The open-source option, along with a host of others, will be explored in this book.

Rather than focusing on tools and the enabling power of information technology and all things digital, let us rather focus on people and, in particular, the people that libraries are serving and should be serving. One of the more important underlying questions we should be asking is "What does physical and virtual engagement look like?" (and engagement is likely to be different for various customer segments).

Libraries are in the process of moving beyond traditional information (text-based) technologies so that they can implement and support a variety of technologies, including 3D printing, virtual reality, managing large data sets, providing visualization tools, providing geographic information systems (GISs), providing content to learning management systems, and oh so much more. The narrow focus of a system manager is broadly expanding—seemingly at warp speed!

Thus, what needs to be extracted from this book are the core concepts on how to evaluate technology for suitability in meeting the larger goals of the organization. It is the larger goals of the organization that always have to serve as the framework for understanding and applying technology solutions that might be available.

Notes

1. Michelle Weil and Larry Rosen. *TechnoStress: Coping with Technology @Work, @Home, @Play* (New York: Wiley, 1997), 76.

2. Michael Stephens, "Taming Technolust: Ten Steps for Planning in a 2.0 World," *Reference and User Services Quarterly* 47, no. 4 (2008), 314–17.

3. Char Booth, *Informing Innovation: Tracking Student Interest in Emerging Library Technologies at Ohio University* (Chicago: Association of College & Research Libraries, 2009).

4. More about the Gartner Hype Cycle is available at "Gartner Hype Cycle: Interpreting Technology Hype," *Gartner* (n.d.), http://www.gartner.com/technology /research/methodologies/hype-cycle.jsp.

5. Henry Lucas, *The Search for Survival: Lessons from Disruptive Technologies* (Santa Barbara, CA: Praeger, 2012).

Acknowledgments

A number of individuals, with their unique and diverse backgrounds and experience, were instrumental in developing library automation. The intent of the library automation tree, shown in Figure A.1, is to illustrate the "roots" from which the field of library automation emerged and the branches that, in part, shaped each individual's perspective and contributions.

Pauline Atherton Cochrane was a professor at Syracuse University iSchool and was the president of the American Society of Information Science and Technology in 1971. She is well known for a study demonstrating the value of "enhanced" bibliographic records for information retrieval.

Henriette Avram was a systems analyst at the Library of Congress when she led the team that developed the machine-readable cataloging (MARC) format in 1968. She is often referred to as the "mother of MARC."

Joseph Becker designed the Library/USA exhibit for the 1964 World's Fair and worked on developing a national information network. Becker and Robert Haynes provided library and computer network consulting services.

Kenneth Bierman spent forty years automating libraries, including an early CLSI system at the Tucson Public Library and Network Operator Trouble Information System (NOTIS) at the Oklahoma State University library. He was active as a speaker and writer, and an expert in preparing unit cost analysis of various library operations.

Abraham Bookstein was a professor at the University of Chicago Graduate Library School (the school closed in 1989) and is best known for his work in operations research.

Christine Borgman, a librarian, is the Distinguished Professor and Presidential Chair in Information Studies at University of California, Los Angeles. Her early worked focused on user studies, especially studies of children interacting with an online catalog. Perhaps her most well-known book is *From Gutenberg to the Global Information Infrastructure* (2000).

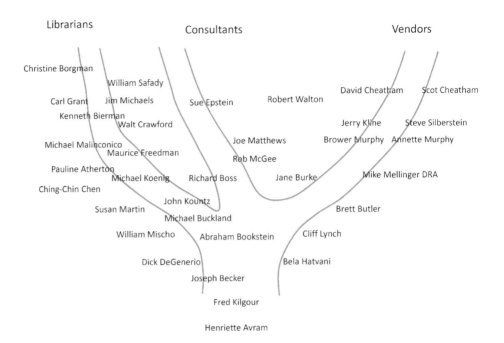

FIGURE A.1. Library Automation Pioneers Tree

Richard Boss was an early library automation consultant who wrote numerous articles and books. Perhaps Dick's best-known book is *The Library's Manager's Guide to Automation* (1981).

Michael Buckland is an emeritus professor and former dean of the University of California Berkeley School of Information. Two of Michael's more influential books are *Redesigning Library Services* (1992) and *Information and Information Systems* (1991).

Jane Burke worked as a Computer Library Systems Inc. (CLSI) sales representative and later became president of NOTIS Systems, Endeavor Information Systems. She also worked in market development for ProQuest and Ex Libris.

Brett Butler was an entrepreneur who pioneered the development of electronic content and was the founder and publisher of Information Access Company.

David Cheatham was the founder of Data Trek (later named EOS International), which developed microcomputer-based systems for special libraries.

Scot Cheatham, brother of David, became the president of EOS International and pioneered the cloud-based integrated library system.

Ching-Chin Chen, a professor emeritus of Simmons College, had a long career as an educator, consultant, speaker, and writer in the field of digital information management.

Walter Crawford is a well-known librarian and writer and for many years worked as a senior analyst for the Research Libraries Group in Palo Alto. He is well known for his blog *Walt at Random,* and wrote (with Michael Gorman) *Future Libraries: Dreams, Madness & Reality* (1995).

Carlos Cuadra assisted in the development of software for personal computers and in the development of the large ORBIt and SDC search services.

Richard DeGenerio, an early pioneer of information technology, was library director at the University of Pennsylvania, the New York Public Library, and Harvard College. He was an active early member of the Library Information Technology Association (LITA), a division of the American Library Association (ALA).

Sue Baerg Epstein is a longtime library consultant who has assisted numerous libraries with various aspects of system selection, contract negotiations, and implementation.

Maurice (Mitch) Freedman published numerous articles, reports, and books about library automation and information technology. Mitch was active in ALA (former ALA president) and LITA and was a longtime director of the Westchester (NY) Library System.

Carl Grant is the Associate Dean for Knowledge Services and the Chief Technology Officer at the University of Oklahoma Libraries. Previously Carl worked at the Virginia Tech Libraries and has held senior management positions in Ex Libris and Data Research Associates. Carl is well known for his thoughtful blog *Thoughts from Carl Grant.*

Béla Hatvani was a pioneer in library automation and the information industry and founded CLSI and Silver Platter Information Ltd. Bela received the National Federation of Advanced Information services Miles Conrad Award in 2000.

Frederick Kilgour, former director of the Yale Medical Library, was the founding director of OCLC (Online Computer Library Center), was active in LITA, and wrote extensively about library automation.

Jerry Kline began his career at the University of California Berkeley library, developing software, and was a cofounder of Innovative Interfaces, Inc. (III); he also created SkyRiver Technology Solutions.

John Kountz worked as a systems analyst for the Orange County (CA) Library System before becoming the director of Systemwide Library Automation for the California State Universities.

Clifford Lynch has been the director of the Coalition for Networked Information (CNI) since 1997. Previously, Cliff worked at the University of California's Library Automation center.

Michael Malinconico is the EBSCO Professor at the School of Library and Information Science, University of Alabama, Tuscaloosa, and was for many years responsible for automation at the New York Public Library.

Susan Martin started her automation career at the University of California, Berkeley; was active in LITA, and was the university librarian at Georgetown University for more than ten years.

Rob McGee worked on library automation projects at the University of Chicago before becoming a library consultant. Rob's firm, RMG Consultants, has helped more libraries automate than any other consulting firm.

Michael Mellinger was the founder of Data Research Associates (DRA), a library automation pioneer, headquartered in St. Louis.

Jim Michaels, a librarian, was an early DRA employee who worked tirelessly as an advocate for standards to promote interoperability among diverse library automation products.

William Mischo is the dean of the Grainger Engineering Library Information Center and a professor at the University of Illinois, Urbana-Champaign. He is a prolific author and has worked on several digital library research projects.

Annette Murphy is the cofounder and president/CEO of The Library Corporation (TLC) that provides automation technology for libraries and school districts.

Brower Murphy, a cofounder of TLC, developed BiblioFile, a CD-ROM cataloging product in 1985.

William Safady, author and tenured university professor, wrote detailed studies dealing with various aspects of library automation. These studies were published in *Library Technology Reports* from the 1980s until 2000. Since that time, his work has focused on records and automation management.

Steve Silberstein was one of the first computer programmers at the University of California, Berkeley library and was the cofounder of Innovative Interfaces, Inc. (III).

Robert Walton got his start at the Texas State Library, was a library consultant for many years, and then became the chief financial officer for Innovative Interfaces, vice president for Finance and Business at the College of Wooster, and CEO of the National Association for College Stores.

Introduction to the Revised Edition: A Word of Hope

What, me worry?

—Alfred E. Neuman[1]

The library technology landscape in 2019 has more churn than ever before—and although wishing that it would settle out a bit is a common feeling among library people, we have some news that is both good and bad: our wild technological ride is really just beginning. We think that is mostly good.

This book offers an overview of the key technology systems used in modern libraries and offers a clear sense of how technology has formed and adapted to ultimately serve patrons. A good number of these technology systems—many with roots in pre-internet computing—were first designed to digitally replicate our physical analog systems that have served libraries well. Many of these traditional systems were mostly static (no need to change things that are successful).

As the internet and Web grew, our entire context for using technology passed through a gateway into a new world. Although traditional library goals of access, equity, education, enlightenment, and public service remain, the manner in which we achieve those goals in a digital age has changed—and continues to change—drastically and often. This ongoing change—sometimes referred to as "churn"—is a hallmark of the digital age.

How is this mostly good news? When things change, it's our human nature to mourn what we have lost. Mourning is a form of healthy respect for the good people and things no longer with us. Mourning can be a gateway to connect us with our values, especially when we ask ourselves the "why?" questions, such as "Why do I miss the old ways so much?"

When mourning, however, we also have the chance to see what new opportunities are brought by change. This is the good news. The habit and skill of spotting opportunities in the midst of chaos is one of the factors fueling technology changes in so many fields. Often referred to as "disruption," there is rarely a day that passes where some new technological development offers an opportunity that didn't exist before. For libraries closely in touch with their missions (of access, equity, public service, and more) the modern technological age presents an ever-refreshing cornucopia of options to serve patrons—and to run the library operations in ways that are both more efficient and kinder to staff.

As you read this book, it's our hope that by understanding where we came from—and where we are today—you will be able to lead us into the future. In the information age (and as information providers), libraries have maintained a unique position of trust with patrons. It is essential that as we embrace change to pursue new opportunities, we do it in a way that doesn't just maintain but further strengthens that bond of trust.

Happy reading—and we hope you will join us in looking forward to what's next!

Joe Matthews
Carson Block

Note

1. Alfred E. Neumann, *Wikipedia*, https://en.wikipedia.org/wiki/Alfred_ E._Neuman.

Part I

The Broader Context

Two chapters comprise Part I of this book. Chapter 1 provides a historical perspective about the library information systems marketplace and the evolution of computer hardware and software.

Chapter 2 explores in greater detail the various segments and options of the library information systems marketplace as well as the expanding electronic resources (eResources) marketplace.

1
The Evolution of Information Technology

This chapter presents an overview of the evolution of information technology and its impact on the application of computing systems in libraries. Beginning with the first rudimentary card-based sorting systems and their eventual evolution into what is broadly acknowledged as a catchall phrase—integrated library systems (ILS), information technologies have had a wide-ranging impact on libraries of all types. Systems evolved with the development of stand-alone experimental systems that were developed by innovative teams in a number of libraries until commercial vendors slowly awoke to the possibilities of an automated systems marketplace.

Origins of Library Information Systems

As library collections and the associated card catalog grew, libraries sought to provide better and more cost-effective solutions to the access and control of their collections. The roots of using technology to assist a library in its operations predated the early digital computers and relied on either *manual sorting* (using needles) or *mechanized sorting* of 80-column punch cards. The card sorting systems developed by libraries in the 1940s and 1950s typically included rudimentary circulation control systems as well as producing recent acquisition lists (sorted in any number of ways).

The phrase *library automation* has been generally accepted within the profession to encompass early automation activities in the 1960s and 1970s. The professional journal dealing with libraries and information technology was called *The Journal of Library Automation*, or *JOLA*.[3] In the 1980s, as information technology systems moved beyond single-function systems, the term *integrated library system (ILS)* or *integrated online library system (IOLS)* began to appear in the literature. And although the journal *Library Hi Tech* has a focus on technology in libraries, today almost every library professional journal publishes articles dealing with the many aspects of technology in libraries, especially information technology.

In addition, over the course of time, every library school introduced into their curriculum one or more technology classes that primarily focused on selecting and implementing "library information systems" (LISs). These LIS classes recognized that technology is having a pervasive and long-lasting effect on the profession and the ways in which libraries deliver services to their users. The evolution of the integrated library system was a slow and painful process both for the vendors and for their customer libraries. Developing a comprehensive module that includes acquisitions, serials control, circulation, metadata/cataloging, and the online public access catalog was no small undertaking. In addition to integrated library systems, the focus was on the blossoming field of online databases, as well as on building and maintaining attractive library websites. In the meantime, technology has become integrated into most—if not all—library operations in either a supporting role or as a service unto itself.

Several libraries began experimenting with information technology in the 1960s, and their offspring are still with us today. Consider that the National Library of Medicine's efforts to begin to control and provide access to an ever-increasing deluge of journal articles led to the development of *Medline* and the Web's *PubMed*. And a team from the US Library of Congress, led by Henriette Avram, developed the machine-readable cataloging (MARC) record standard in 1968. Even a cursory examination of MARC (now called the MARC 21) format reveals that the MARC structure is closely linked to magnetic tape technology, and although bibliographic records would shortly move from magnetic tape to rotating disk drives, the MARC structure itself did not change for decades. Recently, at the behest of the Library of Congress, the library community is moving to a linked data model for the description of bibliographic information called BIBFRAME.[4] The goal is to make bibliographic data more useful to those inside and outside the library community.

Historical Perspectives

Other early pioneering efforts focused on automating all or parts of a single-functional area with the library. Consider early circulation control systems that used punch-card systems to track borrowing and automated the production of paper notices. Slowly over time these single-solution systems evolved into the integrated library system found in many libraries today, so that the ILS provides access to acquisition, cataloging, materials booking, reserve room, serials control, and an online catalog.

During the 1990s and early 2000s, the library information systems field has been marked by the development of a number of solutions to problems that left the integrated library system as a single silo that addressed a few concerns but did not become a platform for integrating other digital solutions. For example, many libraries have had to manage multiple computer systems that also operate as silos—consider electronic resource management systems (ERMSs), link resolvers, authentication systems, digital repositories, and media content, among others.

A number of authors, including Michael Buckland, Lluís Anglada, Christine Borgman, and Cliff Lynch, have looked back over time and have organized the evolution of library information systems into groups or categories.

Michael Buckland,[5] a wonderful librarian and former Dean of the Library School at the University of California Berkeley, suggested that libraries could be considered to fall into three distinctive periods:

- **The paper library**—Paper is a predominant example of the hard-copy media library, and the library catalog also uses a form of paper—cards—to provide access to the collection. The paper library is inherently inflexible and provides real challenges in terms of providing storage and access.

- **The automated library**—An automated library refers to a hard-copy media collection, but many of the library's internal procedures have been computerized. Automated systems used the MARC record and the Z39.50 search-and-retrieval standard. Given the increasing amount of the library's budget devoted to people, computer systems were seen as a way of improving service while maintaining or reducing personnel costs, as seen in Figure 1.1.

Michael Gorman suggested that efficient libraries followed three principles:

- Nothing should be done by a professional that can be done by a technician.

- Nothing should be done by a technician that can be done by a clerk.

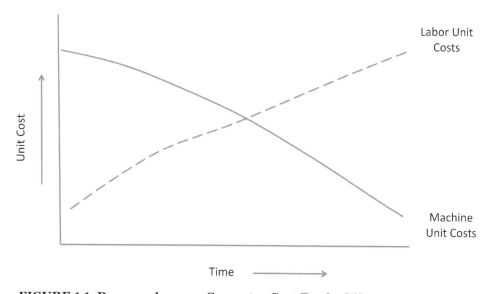

FIGURE 1.1. Personnel versus Computer Cost Trade-Offs
Source: Michael Buckland. *Redesigning Library Services: A Manifesto.* Chicago: American Library Association, 1992, figure 3.2.

- Nothing should be done by a human being that can be done by a machine.[6]

It was during this time period that the Online Computer Library Center (OCLC) experienced its tremendous growth.

- ***The electronic library***—The content of collections are "digitized" and stored in a digital format in the electronic library. In addition, libraries license access to electronic (digital) resources, including journals, magazines, newspapers, and eBooks. Given the widespread availability of the internet, about 92 percent of the world's population have immediate anytime, anywhere access to digital content using their smartphones (and the percentage is growing every day).[7] Mobile phones account for 54 percent of all web pages served, and laptops and desktop computers account for 41 percent of all web traffic.

Lluís Anglada has suggested that technology in libraries can be divided into three stages: mechanization, automation (or computerization stage), and digitization.[8] In a similar vein, Christine Borgman has argued that the evolution of technology has also gone through three stages:

- Efficiency of internal operations
- Access to local library collections
- Access to resources outside the library[9]

Cliff Lynch, the long-time executive director of the Coalition for Networked Information, has divided forty years of libraries and information technology into three "ages."[10]

- **The first age, computerizing library operations**, focused on making existing manual process more efficient and controlling costs. Of particular note was the development of shared copy-cataloging systems such as OCLC and RLIN.
- **The second age, the rise of public access**, built on the foundation of machine-readable cataloging records to create public access online catalogs (to replace the card catalog). At the same time, abstracting and indexing services were moving to provide online access to their content (these services were initially very expensive and required trained intermediaries to conduct a search). With the benefit of hindsight, we now take online access to a staggering amount of content via the internet for granted.
- **The third age, automation, when print content went electronic**, has meant that the end user is increasingly demanding access to all content, print and electronic, in very short time frames (most often, the end user defines a "short period of time" as "immediate"). Thus, library catalogs and other online services were pushed to the side in favor of internet-based search engines such as Google.

In our view, the development of library information systems can be chronicled by looking at six overlapping eras of development, as seen in Figure 1.2.

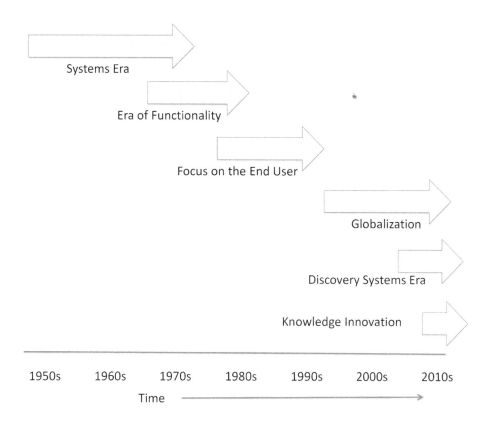

FIGURE 1.2. Evolution of Library Information Systems

The *Systems Era* lasted from the 1950s to the 1970s and was exemplified by the development of software applications that replicated existing library procedures and processes, with heavy emphasis on technology being on center stage. This was a period of experimentation and pioneering. The most frequently developed application was circulation control, with particular emphasis on the identification of overdue materials.

The *Era of Functionality* moved to systems being developed by the commercial sector, and these "turnkey vendors" provided a package solution of computer hardware and parameter-driven software that extended the depth of functionality available to the library. A library would typically automate one area within the library, and as the marketplace matured, the library would add more modules—cataloging, acquisitions, serials control, materials booking, circulation control, and other modules. In the 1980s, vendors introduced the online catalog that in its earliest incarnations only provided rudimentary electronic access to the collections for end users. Rather than taking advantage of a much larger surface on a cathode-ray tube (CRT) screen, the earliest form of the online catalog replicated the card catalog format, with all of its inherent limitations because of the restrictions imposed by a 3 x 5–inch card. This provides a great illustration of how information technology can be disappointing if the status quo is automated rather than rethinking and reconsidering what needs to be accomplished from the customer's perspective. As Roy Tennant observed:

> I wish I had known that the solution for needing to teach our
> users how to search our catalog was to create a system that
> didn't need to be taught . . . I wish I had known that we would
> come to pay the price of our folly by seeing our users flock to
> commercial companies like Google and Amazon.[11]

The focus on the *end user*, especially in today's digital world, means that libraries are recognizing that they must provide services that provide real value, using devices that the end user is engaged with, seemingly 24/7. Acknowledging that it is no longer necessary for people to visit the library, the systems that libraries provide must be able to deliver content (both digital and analog) wherever they are located (the local library, nearby libraries, libraries across the nation and around the world).

The *Globalization of Information Resources* acknowledges that libraries are increasingly licensing digital content (rather than purchasing content) from a variety of vendors located around the world. The vendors provide access to a wide variety of electronic resources, including academic journal articles, newspapers, popular magazines, historical content, photographs, and eBooks, among a variety of other content.

The *Era of Discovery Systems* began about 2010. A discovery system is an index that combines all of the records from the library's own online catalog and provides access to electronic journal articles (and in some cases additional electronic resources) that the library has licensed or owns. This new index is maintained by a commercial vendor in the cloud and typically replaces the library's online catalog. In some cases, the discovery service was able to add records for digital objects as well as for eBooks. The discovery service must partner with content providers to deliver licensed content (citation metadata and/or full text of each journal article).

Starting in the 2010's, the vendors that provide the traditional ILS have been moving to a new model that attempts to consolidate many library automation silos into one platform. Marshall Breeding coined a term for this new platform—the "library services platform"—in 2011, and Ken Chad, a UK-based library technology consultant, began calling the new platform a "library management platform" in 2012.

The creation of *Knowledge Innovation* environments moves libraries toward realizing that discovery systems are coming to a close, and because libraries need to differentiate themselves from Google Scholar, Bing, and so on, this is forcing us to create a new "value triangle" above the various silos offered for discovery. This value triangle is where we're creating new ways to analyze existing knowledge; compare, contrast, and correlate what we find there; and then derive and build new meaning. This is accomplished by using tools such as 3D printing, virtual reality, and the Open Journal System (OJS) for creating open access and peer-reviewed scholarly works that, once published, move into the repository as new knowledge (created), and the cycle begins anew.

Regardless of the era, libraries have adopted computer-based technology at different rates. Some of the possible adoption patterns, as shown in Figure 1.3, can be categorized as:

Bleeding edge—Some organizations are more willing to accept risk and thus are willing to experiment (or be the "guinea pigs"). This type of organization may bear a few scars, but it has staff that have the skills and personality to endure more than a few arrows stuck in their back. This type of library is willing to use beta software.

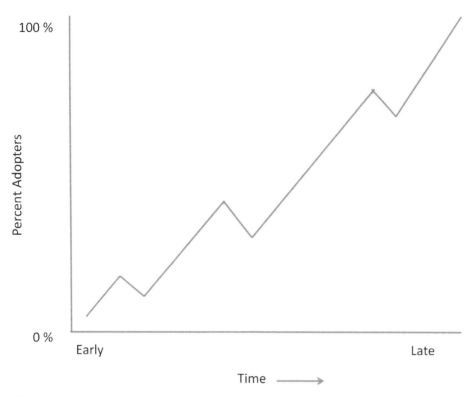

FIGURE 1.3. Percentage of Adopters

Leading edge—These libraries acknowledge that risk exists with early versions of software, so they typically wait to install the release immediately preceding the "latest and greatest." This type of library will adopt new technologies on a systematic and incremental basis.

In the wedge—A majority of libraries will wait to install new technologies when they are proven to be stable and well tested. This type of organization is risk averse, to say the least.

Trailing edge—A small percentage of libraries are true laggards and continue to use older technologies and software well past the time when they should have migrated to newer products. These organizations bemoan the fact that the vendor no longer supports the software that they are using—and they can't understand why they have problems!

Developments Impacting Library Information Systems

Developments in the domains of hardware, software, and telecommunications all have had an impact on the evolution LISs. The following overview describes the developments in each of these areas.

Hardware: From Mainframes to Ubiquitous Computing

In the beginning were large, clunky mainframe computers, and they required a good deal of handholding and care in order to make them operate well. The capabilities of these systems were quite limited, and they were very expensive to purchase and operate; thus only larger organizations, for example, research universities and large corporations, could afford such systems. The dominant mainframe supplier was IBM, although a group of competitors were affectionately referred to as the BUNCH (Burroughs, Univac, National Cash Register, Control Data Corporation, and Honeywell). These mainframe systems operated in a host configuration, whereby a single set of computer processing units were accessed in a batch processing mode using keypunch cards or in an online mode using expensive cathode-ray tubes with keyboards, often referred to as character-based "dumb terminals." In a host or shared configuration, all computing resources were centrally maintained under the careful control of a select few.

Starting in the mid 1960s, an innovation in hardware emerged, called the minicomputer. This is a classic example of what Clayton Christensen calls "disruptive innovation" in that the established mainframe computer manufacturers dismissed the minicomputer as an insignificant competitive threat given its reduced processing capabilities.[12] First pioneered by Digital Equipment Corporation (DEC) and other manufacturers, these machines were smaller than their mainframe counterparts, but they were significantly less costly to acquire and maintain ($1 million and up for a mainframe and generally less than $100,000 for a minicomputer). Individual libraries could now afford to purchase solutions based on these new minicomputer-based systems. These minicomputers allowed vendors to develop stand-alone systems (purchasing the hardware and software as a package) to a library as a total system (often referred to as a "turnkey system" or a "turnkey solution").

In the later 1970s and early 1980s, the emergence of low-cost personal desktop devices from Apple Computer and IBM (and a host of IBM clone manufacturers) opened up even more doors for libraries to automate various library processes. And their even lower cost meant that smaller school, special, public, and academic libraries could now purchase automated solutions.

Today, the lines between computing devices are quite blurred, due in no small part to Moore's law. Gordon Moore, one of the cofounders of Intel, predicted that the processing power of integrated circuits (the foundation on which all digital devices are built) would effectively double every eighteen months, whereas the price would stay the same or decline. Thus, computing power is widely distributed in the devices we use on a daily basis—consider, for example, smartphones, the Apple watch, Fitbit, the iPad, the iPod, tablets, and oh so many more.

The implications of Moore's law is that not only does the price/performance of computer systems continue to improve each year, but the computer chips are reduced in size, allowing the chips to be embedded in a host of other products. These products range from handheld personal digital assistants, cellular phones that interact with the internet, pagers, and other "net appliances," to the chips being embedded in automobiles, vending machines, household appliances, DVRs, routers, and clothing. Many analysts suggest that by the year 2020, more than 20 billion connected objects will be in use. Collectively, all of these objects are called the Internet of Things (IoT).[13]

The End of Moore's Law

Moore's law states that the processing power of integrated circuits doubles every eighteen months while the price remains constant or declines. This increase in processing capacity is accomplished by shrinking the size of the transistor in order to double the number of silicon transistors with each new generation of chip. As it turns out, Moore's law proved true over a period of time, but in 2019 has not kept such an ambitious pace, though performance of computing power continues to improve in other ways. Intel has announced that it will stop introducing new generations of computer chips by 2022.[14] In addition to the physical realities of physics, the end of Moore's law is also about economics. Each new generation of computer chip requires a new generation of fabrication lab. The costs to build the next generation of fabrication labs are several billion dollars (that's a "billion," not million).

The end of Moore's law does not mean the end of the computer processing power to accomplish a wide variety of tasks. Among the many things that will likely happen to extend the annual innovations in the information technology arena are these:

- Better algorithms and software

- Custom specialized computer processors

- Large computational tasks being moved to the cloud

- New materials that replace silicon chips

- New types of computers, such as "quantum computing"

- Stuff that has not even been considered yet.[15]

Early computers used large expensive CRT terminals (often called dumb terminals because they contained very little memory) that were connected to a computer, as shown in Figure 1.4A. Customers were able to rent computer processing power and storage space (time sharing), which was less expensive than owning and operating a mainframe computer. Over time, these character-based, dumb terminals were replaced by desktop computers, and as these desktop computers matured over time, they assumed some of the tasks or workload, often presenting the data and supporting information in an application using a graphical user interface (GUI) to the user, as shown in Figure 1.4B. This latter, distributed application structure is often called a *client-server model*. The server may run one or more application programs that share their resources with the clients.

Eric Schmidt, when he was chief technology officer of Sun Microsystems in 1993, foretold the future when he suggested that when the network becomes as fast as the processor, the computer hollows out and spreads across the network, which led to the notion that "the network is the computer." This insight is sometimes known as Schmidt's law.

The server may perform a wide range of functions, such as serving web pages (web server), providing access to a set of files (file server), and so forth. Obviously the server needs to be sized appropriately (memory, number of processors, and data storage) so that it can service the expected workload. Clients and servers exchange request-response messages, and if these messages become formalized, the result is an application programming interface, or API. The use of an API facilitates the communication of messages and

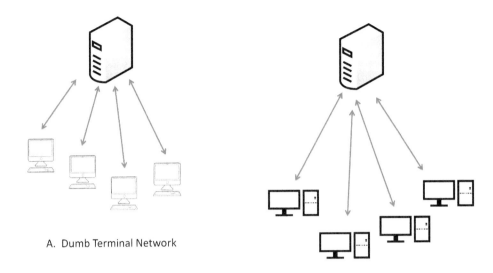

A. Dumb Terminal Network

B. Client-Server Model

FIGURE 1.4. Network Architecture

data across different computer manufacturers. Gordon Bell, an engineer at Digital Equipment Corporation, suggested that every decade a hundredfold drop in the price of processing power engenders a new computer architecture. This insight became known as Bell's law.

As the server capabilities increased, vendors were able to partition a single server into several parts so that the server could handle the workload from several customer libraries—each of whom might have a hundred of more desktop computers connected to the library application. Using the partition approach, separate copies of the application software operate for each customer using the server.

The development of the web browser software, with its graphical user interface, allowed users to quickly locate and download content from around the world. As mass storage costs became more affordable and web applications matured, the availability of cloud computing became a reality. With computer resources located in the cloud, it no longer mattered where a server was physically located.

The "cloud" is really immense data centers composed of massive systems of computer processors and data storage linked together by miles of fiber-optic lines consuming lots of electrical power. Given people's desire not to have to wait for any system, the various components must be physically close to one another to improve response times. The actual limit to the speed of light, a pulse of light traveling down a fiber-optic line, is actually 9 inches in a billionth of a second. These data centers are comprised of aisle after aisle of columns or racks of computers that look like horizontal books in a futuristic library of tomorrow.

Popular applications from the past, such as Hotmail, were developed with a single copy of the software serving all customers (millions) and are typically referred to as *multitenant software*. Multitenant software enables multiple customers who are using the same software application, for example, a library services platform, to operate on the same server running the same operating system. Customers do not see other customers' data but do have the ability to control the software, using parameters and other settings.

Multitenant software allows vendors to save money by being able to simplify the release of new software to all customers, and customers typically see any bugs or problems fixed and the software released on a faster time schedule. Carl Grant has suggested that multitenant software architecture is very important to libraries and that some, but not all, of the new library services platform products, such as Sierra, Worldshare, and Alma, are not using true multitenant software.[16]

Although hardware is an important component in the mix to deliver services to end users, it is the software that delivers the real value.

Software Ranging from Proprietary to Open Systems

Software can be broken down into two broad categories: *systems software* and *applications software.* Systems software includes such categories as device operating systems (Microsoft Windows, MacOS, Linux, and Google's Android), programming languages/environments (such as C++, Java, SQL—Structured Query Language, Hypertext Preprocessor [PHP], Ruby, Python), and communications software (the internet's TCP/IP, the World Wide Web [WWW] protocols, wireless standard protocols), among others. Application software includes programs that perform specific tasks such as word processing, database management, spreadsheets, presentations, graphics, library circulation control, an integrated library system, an app [short for application], and so forth.

Vendors who provided the initial library turnkey systems relied on proprietary software (typically provided by the hardware manufacturer). The turnkey vendor selected the hardware manufacturer, operating system, programming language, and database management system, and then wrote specific programming software code to perform library-related processes and procedures.

As the software development process matured, the vendors in almost every industry found that better financial results were achieved if they moved from proprietary solutions to industry-standard products such as relational databases from Oracle, Informix, SQL Server, and so forth.

It is possible to identify that integrated library systems have moved through three eras or ages: (1) the character-based user interface, (2) the graphical user interface using Windows or Macintosh computers, and (3) the internet web browser user interface. And as systems have moved to the web browser, library systems can take advantage of using other internet-based services. For example, a library system might provide the end user the ability to pay fines and fees, using a credit card. Rather than developing unique code to accomplish this activity, the vendor or library can implement this request/response service. This service-oriented architecture (SOA) provides a specific service to other applications, using a communications protocol over a network. Use of SOA allows for the delivery of a wide range of services that can be used independent of specific products, technologies, and vendors.

The World Wide Web Consortium (W3C) defines the framework around which SOA services can be developed and delivered. SOA services can be implemented using a variety of technologies such as these:

- Simple Object Access Protocol, or SOAP, provides specifications for the exchange of structured information (XML format), typically using the Hypertext Transfer Protocol (HTTP).

- Web services description language (WSDL) describes the functionality offered by a web service.

- Representational State Transfer (REST) allows requesting systems to access and manipulate text resources, using a set of predefined set of stateless operators.

Three entities are involved in the use of an SOA-based service:

- **Service provider**—creates and maintains a specific service

- **Service registry**—a discovery service that maintains a database of available services for potential requesters

- **Service requester**—integrates one or more web services into an application.

Microservices, specific implementations of service-oriented architecture, have been available since 2014 and communicate with other services, using a network to fulfill a specific objective.

Telecommunication Developments

Developments relating to telecommunications can best be viewed by examining four phases or periods of innovation:

- Mechanization period—prior to the 1940s

- Host period—1940 to 1970

- The network period—1970 to 1990

- The end-user period—1990 to now

During the *host-centric period*, a single computer processing unit (CPU) provided all of the processing, and users were connected to this device (typically using leased telephone lines), using dumb terminals. Dumb terminals were keyboards connected to a CRT, and the terminal had little or no memory or processing power. The user pressed a key, and a signal was sent to the central computer, which then returned a signal to the device that then displayed the character related to the key pressed by the user. The focus was definitely on the computer as the object of attention, not the user.

These centralized systems were generally proprietary in nature. The same manufacturer made all the equipment, including the host computer and all the peripherals. To connect to IBM mainframes, one needed IBM terminals and printers. The same was true in connecting to Hewlett Packard or DEC minicomputers: one had to purchase HP or DEC terminals and printers. The proprietary nature not only drove the price of technology up but stifled competition within the technology realm. It was considered natural to expect such proprietary designs, as this was the best means of guaranteeing that everything would work together properly.

During the *network-centric phase*, the emphasis shifted to connectivity rather than proprietary designs. A more open design of network architectures and computing platforms meant that a variety of terminals and other devices could be connected to a computer system. As computing platforms—both mainframe and minicomputer-based systems—became cheaper while their processing power was increasing every eighteen months or so, the spread of networks reached across the nation and in some cases around the world.

What's Old Is New Again

The *network-centric* phase may have passed, but it's core concepts are being used in virtual desktop infrastructure (VDI) systems. Typically in libraries, VDI (a term coined by the company VMWare but often used generically to describe similar systems from a number of different companies) allows for the use of older and/or lower-powered desktop computers—or even devices that are much like the "dumb terminals" of the past (now often called "thin clients")—and leverage computing and sometimes even graphics power from a powerful server or servers to service multiple end-user machines. The advantage of VDI systems in libraries comes in the consistency of the computer workstation for each user and the ease of management and maintenance for the IT Department. For the best performance, VDI systems require robust internal networks—poor or inconsistent network performance can hinder VDI systems. And despite the impression that VDI saves money on hardware (because lower-powered PCs and less-expensive thin clients can be used), the expense of a VDI system compared to individual PCs can be a wash—or even a little more expensive on the VDI system side. However, when factoring in the staff hours saved by the management; maintenance advantages; and the consistent computing experience for users (patrons and staff alike), many have determined VDI to be a worthy investment.

The development of the personal computer or the microcomputer became more widespread in the 1980s and 1990s, and led to the most recent era of computing, the *end user–centric period*. Users are distributed across vast geographic distances and are connected to resources stored on multiple computer processing units called servers. The internet is a prime example of a distributed network environment that is capable of connecting both people and resources together, regardless of location. A simple click of the mouse enables one to download a file or watch a video that is stored on a server located halfway around the world. The amazing growth of the internet means more people are truly connected and rely less on the traditional information-rich institutions known as libraries. As can be seen in Figure 1.5, by June 2018 about 51 percent of the world's population has an internet connection using a computer, and some 92 percent have access to the internet via their smartphone.[17]

Clearly the development of the World Wide Web (and its associated graphical user interface) by Tim Berners-Lee and others has led billions of people to use the internet in order to be connected to interesting content (that is made accessible using a variety of standards, including HTML—hypertext markup language).

More recently the stability and reliability of the internet has meant that where computing resources are located has become less important. Thus, libraries have the option of providing access to computing resources and services that are "in the cloud" as a less expensive option than housing and managing computing resources locally. Thousands of libraries are now using cloud-based computing services rather than having the server for their ILS being in the library or housed in a municipal or campus computer center.

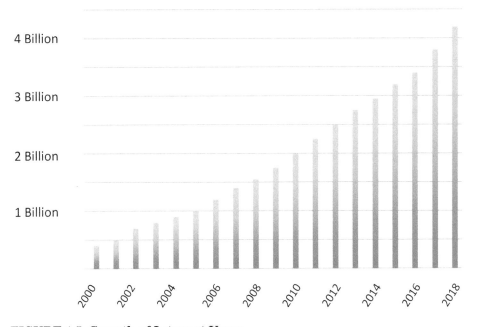

FIGURE 1.5. Growth of Internet Users
Source: "Global Statshot: Digital in Q3 2017," *Hootsuite*, October 7, 2018 https://
www.slideshare.net/wearesocialsg/global-digital-statshot-q4-2018.

End users are less likely to concern themselves with boundaries between disparate offerings and are more interested in accessing information from distributed locations, any time of the day, any day of the week. End users prefer one-stop, convenient desktop solutions as well as handheld solutions for accessing information resources. And with the growing popularity of social media, users are spending more time online. Lorcan Dempsey, vice-president for research and strategic planning at OCLC, calls this kind of behavior "operating at the network level." This reality of an abundance of information resources and scarcity of attention to focus on all this content has been called the *Dempsey Paradox* (in the good old days, people were required to take the time to visit the library to use the local collections).[18]

Today, the de facto telecommunications standard is the internet protocol (TCP/IP) and other web-based authoring environments, allowing end users to be located anywhere they can access the internet and run their web browsers.

Summary

The evolution of technology and the subsequent application of that technology to library situations have led to the development of several market-places that collectively address the information needs of the end user, including the following:

- Integrated library systems
- Online databases

- Digital library collections
- eBooks and eResources
- Digital repositories

An increasing amount of a library's budget is being spent on the care and feeding of automating the library (with its many needed systems) as well as on licensing digital content. As is shown in later chapters, this increasing emphasis on all things digital is going to take an ever-increasing role in the services provided to library customers. Thus, this book provides some guidance and advice on how to best manage digital content and services for any type of library while meeting the overall organizational objectives.

Questions to Consider

- Does the phrase *library automation* encompass the entirety of the use of information technology in libraries today? If not, what phrase would you use?

- Do you find Michael Buckland's view of three distinctive periods in the use of information technology to be a helpful way of thinking about technology evolving and maturing over time?

- Cliff Lynch has divided forty years of libraries and information technology into three "ages." Do you think we are now entering the fourth age? What would mark the transition into a fourth age?

- Can you articulate the differences between a library services platform and an integrated library system?

- Is your library in the bleeding edge, leading edge, in the wedge, or in the trailing edge of technology?

- What are some of the possible implications of Moore's law for libraries over the next five years?

- How is your library moving to interacting with customers who are found at the network level?

- Are you reactive or proactive in terms of engaging library customers in the social media arena?

Notes

1. Kathy Dempsey, "Lankes' Library Survival Plan: Ease Control, Invite Input," *Marketing Library Services* 26, no. 6 (November/December 2012).

2. Elayne Boosler, quoted in Karen O'Connor, *My Senior Moments Have Gone High-Tech* (Eugene, OR: Harvest House Publishers, 2016), 84.

3. The first issue of *JOLA* was published in March 1968 and in early 1982, *JOLA* was renamed *Information Technology & Libraries* (a journal of the Library Information & Technology Association, a division of the American Library Association).

4. For more information about BIBFRAME, visit "Bibliographic Framework Initiative," Library of Congress, accessed August 2, 2019, https://www.loc.gov/bibframe.

5. Michael Buckland, *Redesigning Library Services: A Manifesto* (Chicago: American Library association, 1992).

6. Michael Gorman, "The Organization of Academic Libraries in the Light of Automation," *Advances in Library Automation and Networking* 1 (1987): 152.

7. "Global Statshot: Digital in Q3 2017," Hootsuite, August 7, 2017, https://www.slideshare.net/wearesocialsg/global-digital-statshot-q3-2017.

8. Lluís Anglada, "Are Libraries Sustainable in a World of Free, Networked, Digital Information?," *El profesional de la información* 23, no. 6 (November–December 2014): 603–11.

9. Christine Borgman, "From Acting Locally to Thinking Globally: A Brief History of Library Automation," *Library Quarterly* 67 (July 1997): 215–49.

10. Cliff Lynch, "From Automation to Transformation: Forty Years of Libraries and Information Technology in Higher Education," *EDUCAUSE Review* (January–February 2000): 60–68.

11. Jim Hahn, "The Internet of Things: Mobile Technology and Location services in Libraries," *Library Technology Reports* 53, no. 1 (January 2017): 1–28.

12. Roy Tennant, "Digital Libraries: What I Wish I Had Known," *Library Journal* November 15, 2005.

13. Clayton Christensen, *The Innovator's Dilemma: When New Technologies Cause Great Firms to Fail (Management of Innovation and Change)* (Cambridge, MA: Harvard Business Review Press, 2016).

14. Tom Simonite, "Moore's Law is Dead. Now What?," *MIT Technology Review*, May 13, 2016, https://www.technologyreview.com/s/601441/moores-law-is-dead-now-what/.

15. Luke Dormehl, "Computers Can't Keep Shrinking, But They'll Keep Getting Better. Here's How," *Digital Trends*, March 17, 2018, https://www.digitaltrends.com/computing/end-moores-law-end-of-computers/.

16. Carl Grant, "Introduction and Definitions/Descriptions," *Thoughts from Carl Grant* (blog), October 22, 2012, http://thoughts.care-affiliates.com/2012/10/impressions-of-new-library-service.html.

17. "Global Statshot: Digital in Q3 2017,"; and "Internet Growth Statistics: Today's Road to e-Commerce and Global Trade Internet Technology Reports," *Internet World Stats*, accessed August 2, 2019, https://www.internetworldstats.com/emarketing.htm.

18. Lorcan Dempsey, "Thirteen Ways of Looking at Libraries, Discovery, and the Catalog: Scale, Workflow, Attention," *Educause Review Online*, December 10, 2012, http://www.educause.edu/ero/article/thirteen-ways-looking-libraries-discovery-and-catalog-scale-workflow-attention.

2
The Library Information Systems Marketplace

Products considered innovative or pioneering two years ago
must now be ready for routine operational implementation
in order for these products to succeed...

—Marshall Breeding[1]

Sources of Software

Third-party companies, referred to as independent software vendors (ISVs), in the 1970s through the 1990s started developing computer software that they could license and support. In the 1970s and 1980s, these programs were not expensive, especially when compared to the price of a mainframe computer. The ISV had to make an important decision about which hardware platform its software would run on, as the computer equipment and operating system were proprietary. These systems were typically minicomputer-based networks of dumb terminals.

The larger and more powerful computer firms maintained their hold over customers by the proprietary nature of the computer equipment, operating systems, utilities, and programming language compilers. Information technology (IT) staff within an organization are familiar with the tools and capabilities of a particular set of hardware and software programs. Effectively this "locked in" the customer because the switching costs to move from manufacturer A to manufacture B were so high that the vast majority of customers would not change, and computer manufacturers were able to charge very high prices for system support and upgrades.

However, there were three factors affecting the marketplace:

1. The constant state of price/performance improvements, as illustrated by Moore's Law, which states that the performance of a computer chip will double every 18 months while price remains constant.

2. Starting with the personal computer, but moving into the mainframe and minicomputer arena, as organizations migrated to client/server architecture, computer equipment became more like a commodity. And with a commodity, the customer is able to make a selection based almost solely on price. People rarely talk about the name of the computer manufacturer today, but rather they focus on the number, size, and processing power of the servers that are needed to accomplish a particular task.

3. Customers' increasing demand that computer hardware and software be developed that embrace and support open standards.

The net impact of these trends was that the customer is empowered with choice! However, with the consolidation in the marketplace because of mergers and buyouts, there is less choice today than there was in the 1990s.

Another group of companies came into existence to help an organization integrate computer hardware, networking software, and application(s) software. Within the library community, examples include Innovative Interfaces, SirsiDynix, and The Library Corporation, among others. These vendors guaranteed that their combination of hardware and software would work as advertised and meet the performance expectations in the marketplace. In fact, few individuals really appreciate the complexity and sophistication embodied in an integrated library system, or ILS, as exemplified by the size of the programming source code.

Commercial firms make an investment when developing a software product or application. The source code for this operating system, software application, or utility is considered a valuable asset. In some cases, the software may receive a patent, but in almost all cases, the software is copyrighted to protect its intellectual property. Customers purchase a license that gives them the right to use, but not own, the software. Also, customers typically purchase software support and maintenance, which entitles the customer to receive bug fixes and assistance from the vendor, to resolve a problem or learn how to use a particular software feature. After a software product has been through a number of releases, it is not unusual for as much as 75 percent of available programming resources to be spent on maintenance.

For obvious business reasons, a vendor wants to develop software that appeals to a large group of potential customers. For the customer, a large network of other customers means more choices in the software (in terms of features, options, etc.) and more opportunities for support. Customers often receive greater value when they are able to use a dominant technology because those technologies tend to equate to de facto "standards" offering customers more options than technologies that exist in a figurative silo. This does present a common dilemma: although it's true that customers are in fact locked in to the Microsoft ecosystem when (for instance) using a Windows-based solution, they do have more options when using a dominant technology such as word processing software because Microsoft Word is currently the de facto "standard" for word processing across the globe—although this is beginning to change.

The vast majority of automation vendors clearly understand that they need to listen carefully to their customers so product enhancements are included in future releases and the software better meets the needs of their customers. Similarly, the vendor must also provide software that has been thoroughly tested and released with as few bugs as possible (fewer bugs means fewer support calls received by the vendor).

Given that a majority of libraries are now using cloud-based products that have embraced multi-tenant architecture platforms, vendors are now able to provide new software releases much faster to all customers (which lowers the costs for vendors while improving customer satisfaction).[2] Marshall Breeding estimates that at the start of 2019, slightly more than half of all academic library systems are in the cloud, whereas only about a third of public library systems are in the cloud.[3]

Complexity of Commercial Software

The complexity of commercial software, as expressed by the number of specific functional features, setup options, or the total lines of programming code can be considerable. For example, library automation vendors have systems that run on minicomputers or larger servers, and the total lines of code range from 500,000 to more than 1 million.[4] The learning curve for any new programmer to learn and understand the structure of the source code, database table structures, and the workflow associated with a given set of functional features can be considerable—in most cases, probably more than six to twelve months. Thus, an automation vendor needs to have a team of programmers that is able to assume the responsibility for continually enhancing the product as well as fixing the bugs that crop up on a continuing basis.

The complexity of the products can also be understood by the increased scope of the functionality included in today's automated library system—the traditional ILS modules plus an electronic resources management system, a repository, and a knowledge base, among a number of other possible components.

Size of the Commercial Library Automation Marketplace

The library automated system marketplace, with estimated annual revenues of some $440 million (US share of the marketplace), is very small in terms of global spending on information technology products, but relatively large given library budgets.[5] The annual library automation marketplace article that appears in *Library Journal* or *American Libraries* typically identifies some twenty-five to thirty vendors who are active in the market. Usually the market is segmented by type of library—academic, public, school, and special libraries.

In this chapter, the origins of the marketplace are explored to provide an overview of the current status of the marketplace.

The Integrated Library Systems Marketplace

An overview of the integrated library systems marketplace has been published annually in the April issues of *Library Journal* since 1982.[6] In Chapter 1, we noted that the pioneering era, the period before an ILS marketplace was established, was a time of exploration and innovation. This period ended with the beginning of the ILS marketplace, which began in 1971 when Computer Library Systems, Inc. (CLSI) offered its first circulation control system, the LIBS 100, as a turnkey option for libraries. CLSI was soon joined by companies such as Data Research Associates, Sirsi, DataPhase, and others to form the initial ILS marketplace. By 1982, this marketplace had revenues of approximately $50 million annually and was growing at a rapid pace as libraries selected from among the circulation control systems provided by the vendor market. During this time CLSI offered its first version of a turnkey online public access catalog, and others soon followed suit. By 1990, there were more than thirty distinct vendors participating in the marketplace, which had collective revenues of $178 million.

During the next few years, several vendors were bought, sold, and merged, and a period of vendor instability ensued. Add to that the number of changes in the top management positions within those companies, and one can see that this had become big business for these competitive vendors. Each vendor sought to claim its portion of the overall growing marketplace for integrated library systems solutions. By 2016, the US share of the ILS marketplace had grown to a point where annual revenues hovered around $500 million.

After fifty years of establishing a marketplace for integrated library systems, there appear to be some common themes. The current status of the ILS marketplace can be characterized by the following properties:

- It exhibits rich functionality.

- The majority of libraries have installed automated systems

- Newer installations are based on multitenant technologies, based in the cloud, using a Web-based user interface design.[7]

The current marketplace strives to extend the physical library into the global, digital environment where information and commerce takes on new forms. The major challenge confronting a library is to provide integrated access to collections, both physical and electronic resources—wherever they may be located. In addition, libraries are no longer the place where discovery happens—it's happening up at the network level, using Google and social media. All of this suggests that the library community is tackling another period of serious change.

System Architectures

System architectures have certainly changed over the years as well. Mentioned earlier, many so-called legacy systems are being phased out, to be replaced by client-server solutions based on distributed networking models of operation. These legacy systems include solutions based on:

- Mainframes: NOTIS, DOBIS

- Minicomputer-based systems: DRA Classic, Sirsi, Dynix

- Microcomputer-based systems: Follett, Sagebrush

- Platform-based systems: Ex Libris Alma, the Online Computer Library Center (OCLC) WorldShare Management System

Mergers and Acquisitions

As is typically the case with legacy systems, development has ceased, but support continues because revenues are still derived from support that is renewed each year. In fact, some ILS vendors have acquired other vendors, which generate continued revenues from support and maintenance, and offer possibilities for future system migration. The acquisition of Polaris by

Innovative Interfaces and the merging of Sirsi and Dynix are examples of growth by acquisition.

Current System Architectures

Figure 2.1 provides an overview of the system architecture for the typical integrated library systems. Notice that each module operates as a separate silo, although each module has access to any of the necessary data files as and when needed. In some cases, the staff interface might be Windows-based or Web-based while the user of the online catalog uses the Web-based interface.

In terms of system architectures for library systems—integrated or otherwise, it appears that:

- Client/server solutions prevail in the public library sector.

- Graphical user interfaces dominate.

- Web-based online public access catalog (OPACs) are the norm.

- Modern database technologies are being incorporated (e.g., many vendors incorporate Oracle and Microsoft's SQL Server into their systems designs).

- Sophisticated indexing tools such as SOLR and Elasticsearch may be employed.

- Academic libraries for the most part rely on services-oriented architecture systems.

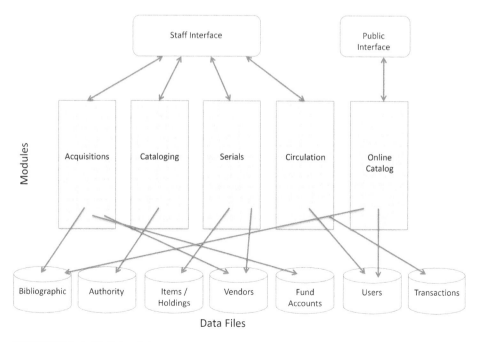

FIGURE 2.1. ILS Architecture

As mentioned earlier, many ILS vendors began in an era when host computing was predominant. Although they still support and possibly continue to develop those markets, many have moved forward to develop distributed computing solutions based on the client-server model. In these environments, the end user accesses the applications from any remote location (within the library or from home, office, or hotel room) using a personal computer and/or a smartphone plus a connection to the internet. The library develops its applications and stores a variety of content on one or more servers connected together so as to support an array of end-user requests. The key is that the end user is empowered with processing capabilities, can access the system around the clock from any location, and may even be able to manipulate retrieved content directly on their desktop devices. This results in a convenient, flexible connection to an array of digital resources secured by library for end-user access.

The Web browser (often Microsoft Edge, Firefox, Safari, or Chrome) acts on behalf of the user as the client software, using an interface developed for the library, to interact with server-side software provided by the ILS vendor. As libraries move to include richer media, including sound and video, expect to see Web-based applications continually refined to support end-user access.

Operating Systems

Software choices are decisions faced by vendors when developing any new venture. Today's solutions seem to be based on two popular operating systems: software environments and several database programming environments.

When it comes to the choice of operating systems, we often see variations of Linux and Microsoft Windows Servers for implementations of very large systems.

Database Environments

As for database environments, Oracle and Microsoft's SQL are often popular choices, and MySQL and PostgreSQL are popular open-source database technologies.

Choosing network protocols has been the easiest for vendors. Only TCP/IP (transmission control protocol/internet protocol,) called "internet protocol" is tolerated. What were once proprietary networked solutions have migrated directly to this type of network connectivity. Those offering proprietary versions of network protocols often find themselves last on the list of choices by libraries seeking to develop next-generation ILS solutions.

On the client side, Web-based interfaces are becoming the norm. There are some Macintosh developments and some java clients running Windows or Linux or both. SirsiDynix Workflows and Innovative's Millennium and Sierra clients are all using Java Runtime Environment.

Summary

Clearly, the library systems market has grown over the last twenty years. Yet, as the vendors move to provide innovative new products, such as providing access to personalized content delivery using a library's online catalog, libraries will see an increasing amount of their budget flowing to these marketplaces.

Questions to Consider

- Do you have a rough idea of how many lines of software code are needed to run your library's automated system (the higher the number, the more complex the software)?

- What are the trade-offs for deciding to use an OPAC that is different from that provided by your vendor's automated system?

- What are the concerns that fewer firms are in the library automation marketplace? What are the risks for your library?

- The annual costs to license eResources for your library is not likely to decline anytime soon. What options are available to a library interested in stretching their eResources budget?

- Does your library face constraints from a local government or campus information technology department that dictates hardware or software choices? What options are available to the library to explore or use other alternatives?

Notes

1. Marshall Breeding, "Library Systems Report 2015: Operationalizing Innovation," *American Libraries* (May 2015): 29.

2. Marshall Breeding, "Library Systems Report 2018," *American Libraries* 49, no. 5 (May 2018): 22–35.

3. Marshall Breeding, email message to author, February 2, 2019.

4. Breeding, "Library Systems Report 2018," 30.

5. Breeding, email message to author.

6. Joseph R. Matthews, "Automated Library System Marketplace: 1981: Active and Heating Up," *Library Journal* 107, no. 3 (February 1, 1982): 233–35.

7. Stuart Ferguson and Rodney Hebels, *Computers for Librarians: An Introduction to the Electronic Library* (London: Chandos, 2003).

Part II
The Technologies

This part of the textbook is focused on the underlying technologies and is comprised of five chapters. Chapter 3 is concerned with a variety of standards and standards organizations. Chapter 4 explores telecommunication and network standards and technologies (both hardware and software).

Chapter 5 considers the strengths and weaknesses of proprietary library systems. Chapter 6 explores the open source library systems and its attendant risks and rewards. And finally Chapter 7 considers all of the other automated systems, often called silos, which a library may need to implement and maintain.

3
Standards and Standards Organizations

The nice thing about standards
is that there are so many to choose from.

—Andrew S. Tanenbaum[1]

This chapter addresses the role and importance of information standards, organizations that support the development and dissemination of standards, and how standards are instituted. Library classification systems, such as the Dewey Decimal system or the Library of Congress system, are clear examples of procedures and tools that were developed in a nonstandardized fashion.

In recent years, emerging library information systems (LISs) have spawned the need for highly technical standards for retrieving information from remote sources in a complex networked environment. The information standards included in this chapter illustrate the useful capabilities of the more prominent library information systems, and how applying these standards might affect the direction of technology usage and vice versa.

Besides discussing library standards, this chapter also profiles the various organizations that support the continued development of such standards. Additional organizations and selected emerging standards that are relevant to the practical implementation of online information systems standards in libraries are also discussed. The chapter closes with an argument as to why librarians must take an active role in the standards development process.

Standards

Libraries have been a part of the standards process for many years. Early on, libraries developed formal standards for physical components used within the library, such as the brass pulls on the card catalog drawers. Later, as libraries began incorporating technology, the focus turned first to bibliographic standards, then to communications standards, and later to search and retrieval standards. This chapter focuses on formal library standards related to technological development. Formal standards are developed under rigorous review and validation, while industry or de facto standards are often developed through the dominance of a particular company or agency. There are many formal standards within librarianship that address topics such as preservation, format of print documents, and so forth that are not covered here. Efforts in standards developments are occurring outside of libraries and information agencies, and have significant impact on how libraries operate in the distributed networked world, both of which are also discussed.

Standards are criteria against which entries may be judged for consistency or uniformity. To standardize generally means to create or modify all entries to conform to a single pattern or format. According to the International Standards Organization (ISO), standardization "creates documents that provide requirements, specifications, guidelines or characteristics that can be used consistently to ensure that materials, products, processes and services are fit for their purpose."[2]

Walt Crawford suggests that there are several benefits that arise through using standards.[3] Among these are the following:

- **A common language**—Consistent and agreed-upon definitions of terminology improve the communication process among and between various parties (e.g., librarians, vendors, and computer programmers).

- **Stability**—Once a standard has been adopted, it provides the assurance that others can supply and support products that encompass the standard.

- **Cooperation and competition**. Adopting a standard eases the entry for new suppliers into a marketplace. The standard also encourages existing suppliers to become more competitive and improve production efficiencies. Even vendors who are competitors often cooperate on developing new standards or enhancing an existing standard.

- **Saving money**—The presence of a standard means that a supplier does not need to support two (or more) software solutions to interface two (or more) systems, which would cost more than working with a single standard.

- **Self-regulation**—The marketplace has a wonderful, positive impact on standards. Those that work are embraced, supported, and in most cases enhanced over time. Those standards that do not work are dropped.

Why do we need standards in libraries? Imagine if all original cataloging were done in every library using locally determined structures. Each cataloger could pick and choose which fields were to be cataloged, what elements might go in each field, what the format of those fields should be, and so forth. Although this might work well in that individual library, this "uniqueness" inhibits the ability to share bibliographic data, and hence bibliographic objects, among libraries that are attempting to cooperate in programs such as interlibrary loan and collection development. If these libraries were to agree on a standardized bibliographic structure, along with guidelines and rules for completing those bibliographic records, then cooperation across libraries would be enhanced. In fact, original cataloging could be shared as well. This is the rationale behind conforming to various bibliographic standards and to standards in general. The key point is inter-institutional cooperation.

How are standards used to design a library information system? Although libraries have agreed on a wide array of standards, not all of these are directly related to technological developments. Standards associated with an integrated library system (ILS) include bibliographic standards, communications standards, and standards that support the search and retrieve functions across libraries with disparate computing platforms, separated by geographic distances.

Not all standards are created equal. Some standards are formal, whereas others may be de facto, ad hoc, or industry standards. There are also government standards. The distinction is important. Formal standards are those that have been through a rigorous submission and review process by a community of volunteers who seek to establish a consensus on that particular topic. Formal standards are those "blessed" by an accredited standardizing body at the national or international level. The standards are reviewed periodically and are continually updated. The key is that these formal standards are developed and maintained through a process involving a consensus of practicing professionals and concerned experts.

Industry standards, on the other hand, are often developed through the dominance of a particular corporation or institution. For example, the size of the cards in a card catalog is the result of an industry standard and as such is not a formal standard. Outside of librarianship, although it is true that the Microsoft's Windows™ operating system is a proprietary product, its market dominance means that it is a de facto standard. Industry or ad hoc standards arise out of a consensus of use and are not necessarily subject to debate or control by a formal standards accrediting agency. There are instances where industry standards have been formally adopted using a consensus process. It is not unusual for an industry standard to evolve into a formal standard. Such is the case of what is often referred to as Ethernet, a protocol for assembling packets of bits to be transmitted across a telecommunications system. Ethernet was developed cooperatively by corporate and research partners, but after the protocol took hold worldwide as a popular networking solution, that informal or industry standard was made formal at an international level and eventually became an Institute of Electrical and Electronics Engineers (IEEE) standard (IEEE 802.3).

This chapter focuses on formal standards and the processes and organizations that support their development. Industry standards can be powerful forces as well, although they are beyond the control of the rigors of consensus. Technology innovation often outpaces the slower, more carefully paced developments of formal standards. Well-developed industry standards are needed in an environment that is fast paced, as many technologic enterprises fight to remain front-runners in innovation and development.

Official Standards Organizations

Who decides what a standard is and how it is going to be enforced? For the most part, adopting a standard is voluntary. Representatives from both the private and public sectors, through a process involving voluntary consensus, develop formal standards. Most organizations involved with standards are nonprofit, receiving financial support from the communities they serve and intellectual support from professionals within that community.

> **Tip!** You might ask your library systems vendor to explain its participation in making standards. Some may send representatives; some may support the organization with donations; and some may even participate in the administrative aspects of an organization like National Information Standards Organization (NISO), which presides over standards associated with libraries and related information agencies.

The American National Standards Institute (ANSI) serves as the administrator of the US voluntary standardization efforts. Founded in 1918 by five engineering societies and three government agencies as a nonprofit organization, ANSI is a member of the International Standards Organization (ISO). The organization promotes US standards internationally in an effort to have them adopted by other countries.

Although ANSI is a rather broad-based standards agency reaching beyond libraries and information services, one of its domains covers libraries, publishers, government agencies, and information-based businesses. NISO is a nonprofit association accredited as a standards developer by ANSI. NISO was originally formed in 1939 as the American National Standards Committee Z39. NISO is responsible for developing and maintaining standards and Recommended Practices for library and information science and related publishing practices. All NISO standards are numbered beginning with Z39.

> **Tip!** Two of the more important NISO Z39 standards are Z39.2, which formed the basis for online shared cataloging, and Z39.50, which forms the basis for shared access to remote databases.

NISO publishes Recommended Practices as "guidelines" or "best practices" for materials, methods, or practice to provide guidance to the user. Typically a Recommended Practice is a leading edge or proven industry practice, and its use is optional. Examples of a Recommended Practice that have been published by NISO include altmetrics (measuring the impact of scholarly research), the transfer of journal content metadata, improving OpenURL, and so forth.

One of the few US government organizations involved with establishing standards is the National Institute of Standards and Technology (NIST). Congress formed this organization in 1901 as the National Bureau of Standards. Over the years, NIST has been recognized worldwide for its standards development. In 1989, NIST was transferred to the US Department of Commerce's Technology Administration.

These three organizations (NISO, ANSI, and NIST) are the main standards formulation entities within the United States. They rely on the public and private sectors to adopt the standards they articulate. Because most standards are not made into law, these groups can do very little without the participation of those who will use the standards.

On a global scale, the primary standards organizations include ISO, IEEE, and CCITT. The ISO is a global federation of national standards bodies from one hundred countries. It is also a nongovernmental organization, first established in 1947 to help develop an international set of standards involving trade and to help promote worldwide cooperation worldwide in the sciences. The IEEE focuses primarily on standards to support electrical and computer engineering and the information and communications technologies. Founded in 1884, IEEE is a nonprofit technical professional society of more than 350,000 members in more than 150 countries. One of IEEE's responsibilities is to develop and promote international standards that affect its membership.

CCITT is an abbreviation for the **C**omité **C**onsultatif **I**nternational **T**élé**phonique** et **T**élégraphique, which is an organization that sets international communications standards and is now known as International Telecommunication Union (ITU).

The ITU is an intergovernmental organization that encourages public and private organizations in the development of telecommunication standards. As a United Nations agency, it is responsible for international treaties, regulations, and standards governing telecommunications.

Standards Important to Libraries

Standards that address technology-based product development and service provision are those of interest to libraries. The ISO's standards definition stipulates that each standard contains specific criteria to be applied consistently to its respective function. These standards must also be accepted and used on a universal basis before their benefits to automated library systems can be realized. Standards relevant to libraries are designed "to achieve compatibility and therefore interoperability between equipment, data, practices, and procedures so information can be made easily and universally available."[4] Thus, interoperability is the key to data retrieval, and these "standards make it possible to integrate hardware, software, and communications systems and to exchange information across boundaries of different systems."[5]

Important standards for libraries are organized into seven broad categories as shown in Figure 3.1. Some of the more important standards and frameworks are identified here, although there are a host of others that the reader might encounter.

Conceptual Model

Conceptual model frameworks include the following:

International Standard Bibliographic Description (ISBD)—ISBD creates a bibliographic description in a standard form for use in a bibliography or a library catalog. The ISBD defines nine areas of description and standardized punctuation (colons, semicolons, dashes, slashes, commas, and periods) used to identify and separate the content. The International Federation of Library Associations and Institutions (IFLA) maintains the ISBD specifications.

Resource Description Framework (RDF)—RDF is a World Wide Web (WWW) Consortium (W3C) initiative to support the use and exchange of metadata on the Web. RDF provides a standard means for designating metadata, creating the potential for conducting high-quality searches on the Web. Libraries benefit from this in that they are able to search more effectively for resources outside their own collections. Cataloging in particular may benefit from the enhanced content description and

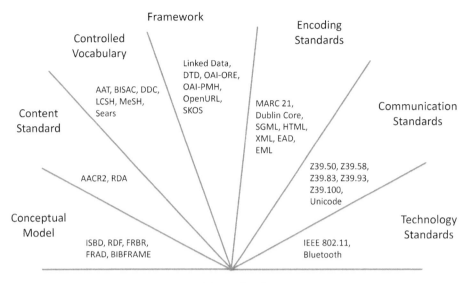

FIGURE 3.1. Broad Categories of Standards

relationships of a particular website that RDF makes possible. As an application, RDF is coded in XML, which complements RDF as a standardized metadata structure. The basic RDF data model consists of the following:

Resources—anything described by RDF expressions (can be a web page, part of a web page, or even printed books)

Properties—specific characteristics, attributes, or relations used to describe a resource

Statements—a Resource + Property + a Value = a Statement

RDF allows various interest groups to use certain defined schemas. For example, libraries could use Dublin Core vocabulary by including it in the RDF tagging.[6]

As more software solutions incorporate metadata standards, they will be required to recognize multiple formats. To enable this, crosswalks or similar mapping techniques will need to be developed across various combinations of standards, such as the Dublin Core/MARC crosswalk. This crosswalk document maps MARC 21 fields to Dublin Core elements; there are separate sections for unqualified and qualified Dublin Core. The alternate mapping, Dublin Core to MARC, is also available.[7]

RDF is used as a general method to model information that is implemented in the Web environment. Typically entity-relationship diagrams or class diagrams are used to assist in understanding the content. W3C maintains the RDF specifications.

Functional Requirement for Bibliographic Records (FRBR)—FRBR uses a entity-relationship model information retrieval and access issues related to bibliographic databases. FRBR was developed by the International Federal of Library Associations and institutions (IFLA) and is comprised of groups of entities:

- Group 1 entities are work, expression, manifestation, and item—products of intellectual or artistic expression.

- Group 2 entities include person, family, and corporate bodies that are responsible for Group 1 entities.

- Group 3 entities are concepts, objects, events, and places.

Functional Requirement for Authority Data (FRAD)—FRAD is a conceptual entity-relationship model for library authority data that is maintained by IFLA.

Bibliographic Framework (BIBFRAME)—BIBFRAME is a bibliographic description data model, designed to replace the MARC 21 standards, using linked data principles. BIBFRAME uses the RDF entity-relationship model with three models of abstraction, as shown in Figure 3.2:

- **Work**—Work is considered the highest level of abstraction and reflects the essence of the item (author, language and subject content).

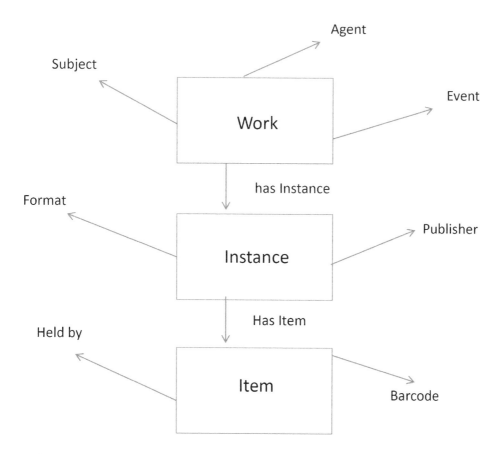

FIGURE 3.2. BIBFRAME Framework
Source: Adapted from BIBFRAME 2.0 Model found at https://www.loc.gov /bibframe/docs/bibframe2-model.html.

- **Instance**—A work may have one or more material formats and is reflected in an instance (publisher, place and format).

- **Item**—Item is the actual physical or electronic copy of an instance (location, shelf mark, barcode, or radio-frequency identification [RFID] tag)

The Online Computer Library Center (OCLC) and a number of other organizations and libraries are conducting experiments to determine the issues and challenges of using BIBFRAME as the basis for creating a linked library data.[8] The Linked Data for Libraries (LD4L) group has suggested that all of these activities can be gathered into six groups:[9]

- Bibliographic + curation data
- Bibliographic + personal data
- Leveraging external data (including authority data)
- Leveraging the deeper graph
- Leveraging usage data
- Three-site services (a mash-up of data from multiple sources)

Content Standards

Standards in this area include the following:

Anglo-American Cataloging Rules (AACR2)—AACR2 rules include the description and provision of access points for materials in a library collection. AACR2 has since been superseded by RDA—Resource Description and Access code.

Resource Description and Access (RDA)—RDA is a descriptive cataloging standard and is organized based on FRBR creating a hierarchy of relationships using bibliographic data.

Controlled Vocabularies

Standards for controlled vocabularies include the following:

Art and Architecture Thesaurus (AAT)—The AAT has a structured vocabulary of terms, concepts, descriptions related to art and architecture.

Book Industry Standards and Communications (BISAC)—BISAC subject headings are used by bookstores to organize their materials, and some libraries have embraced BISAC subject heading as a replacement for the Dewey Decimal Classification system.

Dewey Decimal Classification (DDC)—Developed by Melvil Dewey in 1876, the DDC organizes materials by subject, using three-digital Arabic numerals for main classes.

Library of Congress Subject Headings (LCSH)—LCSH is a controlled vocabulary of subject headings for use in bibliographic records.

Medical Subject Headings (MeSH)—MeSH is a controlled vocabulary for subject headings for materials in the life sciences developed by the National Library of Medicine to improve indexing and searching for information.

Sears Subject Headings—Sears is a simplification of the Library of Congress Subject headings developed by Minnie Earl Sears.

Framework

Among the standards in this area are these:

Linked data—Linked data use web technologies to publish structured data so it can be linked and more easily "read" by computers.

Document type definition (DTD)—DTD defines the structure of a document as a part of a Standard Generalized Markup Language (SGML) family of markup languages (XML, HTML, SGML).

Open Archives Initiative Objects Reuse and Exchange (OAI-ORE)— OAI-ORE is a standard for the description and exchange of web resources to expose content to support deposit, exchange, reuse, visualization, and preservation.

Open Archives Initiative Protocol for Metadata Harvesting (OAI-PMH)—OAI-PMH uses the Dublin Core to facilitate harvesting metadata descriptions of materials in an archive.

OpenURL—OpenURL is a standard (Z39.88) for encoding a description of a resource within a uniform resource locator (URL) and is used by libraries to connect people to books, articles and other materials held in a library's collection.

Simple Knowledge Organization System (SKOS)—SKOS, developed by W3C, is designed to facilitate use of thesauri, classification systems, taxonomies and other types of controlled vocabularies as linked data.

Encoding Standards

Metadata is "data about data." Librarians think of metadata in terms of bibliographic descriptions, where professional catalogers create secondary records and indexers identify and describe primary sources. Metadata also covers topics such as the administration, legal requirements, technical functionality, use and usage, and preservation aspects relating to those primary resources. Among the encoding standards are these:

MARC 21—The most prominent bibliographic standard is the **MA**chine **R**eadable **C**ataloging, or MARC, format used by librarians worldwide. The NISO equivalent is referred to as Z39.2–1994 and is called the Information Interchange Format (reaffirmed March 24, 2016). Internationally, this standard is known as ISO 2709. The MARC format has been referred to as a communications standard because it supports the sharing of bibliographic content across different library institutions, but here we consider it a bibliographic standard. Its usage is so pervasive that we often overlook other bibliographic standards that are important as well. There exists a set of NISO standards that also describes the bibliographic structure of the patron record (Z39.70) and the holdings

statement (Z39.71), which specifies holdings statements display requirements for bibliographic items. MARC is now typically referred to as
MARC 21—Format for Bibliographic Data.

The strength of the MARC format is that hundreds of millions of records have been created using this standard format that have created enor-
mous benefit for libraries. Yet, this standard is anchored in the formats
when it was created in 1968—catalog cards and magnetic tapes. The basic
MARC record consists of three main components: a leader, directory, and
variable fields.

A number of MARC critics called for the modernization of MARC into a
new format. Among the criticisms of MARC are the following:[10]

- A format designed for magnetic tapes
- Lack of standardized statements/declarations when those would be
  useful
- Inability to unambiguously encode important characteristics.
- Over-reliance on punctuation for semantic purposes
- Some ambiguous MARC fields
- Some information presented redundantly
- Needless complexity to MARC
- Lack of sufficient granularity
- Formatting requirements for some MARC free-text fields
- Punctuation in free-text fields sometimes meaningful, sometimes not
- Hidden assumptions coded in some MARC fields
- Semantic complexity in some MARC fields
- Lack of easy extensibility
- Technical marginalization (MARC is isolated to the library
  community)
- Long tail in MARC—while the standard has many tags, most are
  rarely used

Dublin Core—The Dublin Core, NISO Z39.85–2001, is a set of fifteen elements designed to help catalog internet resources. In 1995, a group of
fifty-two librarians, archivists, and scholars met at an OCLC-sponsored
workshop in Dublin, Ohio, and tried to come up with a standard descriptive record for items on the internet. The idea was to improve public
access to information. The fifteen data elements include title, author or
creator, subject and keywords, description, publisher, other contributor,
date, resource type, format, resource identifier, source, language, rela-
tion, coverage, and rights management.

The Dublin Core is a metadata element set that works with MARC records. It is not expected to meet everyone's needs.

BIBFRAME—Short for Bibliographic Framework, BIBFRAME uses linked
data principles to make the resulting data more useful. BIBFRAME,

expressed using the Resource Description Framework or RDF (a W3C specification), is based on three categories of abstraction (work, instance, item), with three additional modifiers (agent, subject, and event).[11] A comparison of a MARC record to a BIBFRAME record is shown in Table 3.1.

Standard Generalized Markup Language (SGML)—This standard is recognized by both NISO and the ISO (ISO 8879) and is used by many commercial and governmental agencies in the online environment. The ANSI/NISO/ISO designation is 12083–1995 Electronic Manuscript Preparation and Markup, which is in complete conformance with ISO 8879 (SGML). ANSI/NISO/ISO 12083 provides a toolkit for developing customized SGML applications. Four distinct Document type definitions (DTDs) are specified for books, serials, articles, and mathematics.

SGML is a digital encoding system that preserves the logical structure of the text in its entirety as it is transferred through different operating systems. In a sense, SGML can be categorized as "descriptive" for its distinction between the components in a text, such as a paragraph, and by its system of structural "tags" that define the boundaries of each part.[12]

For the Web, SGML has manifested itself as hypertext markup language (HTML). HTML is a DTD of SGML, an example of a use of SGML. The current version of HTML (version 5.0) is not a formal standard on its own, but rather a DTD of SGML. As such, HTML can be considered a de facto or industry standard, popularized by the rise in the use of the World Wide Web.

Hypertext Markup Language (HTML)

Simple ASCII-based HTML documents began appearing in 1991, shortly after Tim Berners-Lee created the hypertext transfer protocol (the "http://" portion of the address you used to have to enter in the Open field of a web browser). With the release of a graphical user interface (GUI) web browser in early 1993 (developed by Marc Andreesen and others at the National Center for Supercomputing Applications (NCSA) site at the University of Illinois and originally called "Mosaic"), the potential for internet delivery of hypertext dawned on a host of net users. Currently HTML is the lingua franca for publishing hypertext on the World Wide Web. It is a nonproprietary format based on SGML and can be created and processed by a wide range of tools, from simple plain text editors to sophisticated "what you see is what you get" (WYSIWYG) authoring tools.

The concepts of HTML were based on notions of hypertext that had been floating around in computer science and other fields for some time. In 1945, Vannevar Bush first wrote an article, published in the *Atlantic Monthly*, entitled "As We May Think," where, among other things, he planted the notion of retrieving knowledge records by "associative trails" and actually used the word *web* in his text. In 1965, J.C.R. Licklider wrote a book entitled *The Future of Libraries*, in which he referred to a sort of digital library of the future, based on bits, not atoms. In 1977, another pioneer, Theodor Nelson, was the first to articulate a vision for personal computers. In his book *The Home Computer Revolution*, Nelson envisioned the world's knowledge being available to all persons via desktop devices. He called his ambitious project "Xanadu." Nelson is usually credited with inventing hypertext in the 1960s.

TABLE 3.1. Comparison of MARC to BIBFRAME

Sample MARC Record

```
01035cam a2200325 a 4500
001    5226
005    20081223095049.0
008    940817s1983  nyua  j  000 1 eng
010    $a  82060878
020    $a0394856309
035    $9(DLC)  82060878
040    $aDLC$cDLC$dDLC
042    $alcac
050 00 $aPZ7.F598295$bSn 1993
082 00 $a[E]$220
100 1 $aFlanagan, Terry.
245 10 $aSnoopy on wheels /$c[designed by Terry Flanagan].
260    $a[New York] :$bRandom House,$cc1983.
300    $a1 v. (unpaged) :$bcol. ill. ;$c88 mm.
490 0 $aA chunky book
500    $a"Based on the Charles M. Schulz characters"--P. 4 of cover.
500    $aOn board pages.
650    0 $aMiniature books$vSpecimens.
650    1 $aWheels$vFiction.
650    1 $aDogs$vFiction.
650    1 $aMiniature books.
700    1 $aSchulz, Charles M.$q(Charles Monroe),$d1922-2000.
906    $a7$bcbc$corignew$d2$eopcn$f19$gy-gencatlg
922    $aco
955    $auc   **-**-93 to Cat.; lb14 08-17-94; lb01 03-28-95; lb15 03-30-95
```

Sample BIBFRAME Record

```
@prefix bf: <http://id.loc.gov/ontologies/bibframe/>.
@prefix bflc: <http://id.loc.gov/ontologies/bflc/>.
@prefix madsrdf: <http://www.loc.gov/mads/rdf/v1#>.
@prefix rdf: <http://www.w3.org/1999/02/22-rdf-syntax-ns#>.
@prefix rdfs: <http://www.w3.org/2000/01/rdf-schema#> .
@prefix xml: <http://www.w3.org/XML/1998/namespace>.
@prefix xsd: <http://www.w3.org/2001/XMLSchema#>.
@prefix zs: <http://docs.oasis-open.org/ns/search-ws/sruResponse>.

<http://bibframe.example.org/5226#Item050-12> a bf:Item ;
   bf:itemOf <http://bibframe.example.org/5226#Instance> ;
   bf:shelfMark [ a bf:ShelfMarkLcc ;
       rdfs:label "PZ7.F598295 Sn 1993" ;
       bf:source <http://id.loc.gov/vocabulary/organizations/dlc>].
```

(continued)

TABLE 3.1. (continued)

Sample BIBFRAME Record

<http://bibframe.example.org/5226#Topic650-22> a bf:Topic,
    madsrdf:ComplexSubject ;
  rdfs:label "Wheels--Fiction." ;
  bf:source [a bf:Source ;
    bf:code "lcshac"] ;
  madsrdf:authoritativeLabel "Wheels--Fiction." ;
  madsrdf:componentList ([a madsrdf:Topic ;
     madsrdf:authoritativeLabel "Wheels"] [a madsrdf:GenreForm ;
     madsrdf:authoritativeLabel "Fiction"]) ;
  madsrdf:isMemberofMADSScheme <http://id.loc.gov/authorities/childrens
Subjects>,
    <http://id.loc.gov/authorities/subjects>.

<http://bibframe.example.org/5226#Work> a bf:Text,
    bf:Work ;
  rdfs:label "Snoopy on wheels /" ;
  bf:adminMetadata [a bf:AdminMetadata ;
    bflc:encodingLevel [a bflc:EncodingLevel ;
     bf:code "f"] ;
    bf:changeDate "2008-12-23T09:50:49"^^xsd:dateTime ;
    bf:creationDate "1994-08-17"^^xsd:date ;
    bf:descriptionAuthentication <http://id.loc.gov/vocabulary/marcauthen
/lcac> ;
    bf:descriptionConventions [a bf:DescriptionConventions ;
     bf:code "aacr"] ;
    bf:descriptionModifier [a bf:Agent ;
     rdfs:label "DLC"] ;
    bf:identifiedBy [a bf:Local ;
     bf:source <http://id.loc.gov/vocabulary/organizations/dlc> ;
     rdf:value "5226"] ;
    bf:source [a bf:Agent,
      bf:Source ;
     rdfs:label "DLC"],
    [a bf:Agent,
      bf:Source ;
     rdfs:label "DLC"] ;
   bf:status [a bf:Status ;
     bf:code "c"]] ;
  bf:classification [a bf:ClassificationDdc ;
    bf:classificationPortion "[E]" ;
    bf:edition "20",
     "full" ;

(continued)

TABLE 3.1. (continued)

Sample BIBFRAME Record

bf:source <http://id.loc.gov/vocabulary/organizations/dlc>],
  bf:source <http://id.loc.gov/vocabulary/organizations/dlc>] ;
  [a bf:ClassificationLcc ;
    bf:classificationPortion "PZ7.F598295" ;
    bf:itemPortion "Sn 1993" ;
bf:contribution [a bflc:PrimaryContribution,
    bf:Contribution ;
  bf:agent <http://id.loc.gov/authorities/names/n82247773> ;
  bf:role <http://id.loc.gov/vocabulary/relators/ctb>],
  [a bf:Contribution ;
    bf:agent <http://id.loc.gov/authorities/names/n79021850> ;
    bf:role <http://id.loc.gov/vocabulary/relators/ctb>] ;
bf:genreForm <http://id.loc.gov/vocabulary/marcgt/fic> ;
bf:hasInstance <http://bibframe.example.org/5226#Instance> ;
bf:intendedAudience <http://id.loc.gov/vocabulary/maudience/juv> ;
bf:language <http://id.loc.gov/vocabulary/languages/eng> ;
bf:subject <http://bibframe.example.org/5226#Topic650-22>,
    <http://id.loc.gov/authorities/subjects/sh2008102051>,
    <http://id.loc.gov/authorities/subjects/sh85085643>,
    <http://id.loc.gov/authorities/subjects/sh85085644> ;
bf:title [a bf:Title ;
  rdfs:label "Snoopy on wheels /" ;
  bflc:titleSortKey "Snoopy on wheels /" ;
  bf:mainTitle "Snoopy on wheels"].

<http://id.loc.gov/authorities/names/n79021850> a bf:Agent,
    bf:Person ;
  rdfs:label "Schulz, Charles M. (Charles Monroe), 1922-2000." ;
  bflc:name00MarcKey "7001 $aSchulz, Charles M.$q(Charles
    Monroe),$d1922-2000." ;
  bflc:name00MatchKey "Schulz, Charles M. (Charles Monroe), 1922-2000." .

<http://id.loc.gov/authorities/names/n82247773> a bf:Agent,
    bf:Person ;
  rdfs:label "Flanagan, Terry." ;
  bflc:name00MarcKey "1001 $aFlanagan, Terry." ;
  bflc:name00MatchKey "Flanagan, Terry." ;
  bflc:primaryContributorName00MatchKey "Flanagan, Terry." .

<http://id.loc.gov/authorities/subjects/sh2008102051> a bf:Topic,
    madsrdf:ComplexSubject ;
  rdfs:label "Dogs--Fiction." ;
  bf:source [a bf:Source ;
      bf:code "lcshac"] ;

(continued)

TABLE 3.1. (continued)

Sample BIBFRAME Record

madsrdf:authoritativeLabel "Dogs--Fiction." ;
madsrdf:componentList ([a madsrdf:Topic ;
  madsrdf:authoritativeLabel "Dogs"] [a madsrdf:GenreForm ;
  madsrdf:authoritativeLabel "Fiction"]) ;
madsrdf:isMemberofMADSScheme <http://id.loc.gov/authorities
/childrensSubjects>,
  <http://id.loc.gov/authorities/subjects> .

<http://id.loc.gov/authorities/subjects/sh85085643> a bf:Topic,
  madsrdf:Topic ;
rdfs:label "Miniature books." ;
bf:source [a bf:Source ;
  bf:code "lcshac"] ;
madsrdf:authoritativeLabel "Miniature books." ;
madsrdf:isMemberofMADSScheme <http://id.loc.gov/authorities
/childrensSubjects>,
  <http://id.loc.gov/authorities/subjects> .

<http://id.loc.gov/authorities/subjects/sh85085644> a bf:Topic,
  madsrdf:ComplexSubject ;
rdfs:label "Miniature books--Specimens." ;
bf:source [a bf:Source ;
  bf:code "lcsh"] ;
madsrdf:authoritativeLabel "Miniature books--Specimens." ;
madsrdf:componentList ([a madsrdf:Topic ;
  madsrdf:authoritativeLabel "Miniature books"] [a
  madsrdf:GenreForm ;
  madsrdf:authoritativeLabel "Specimens"]) ;
madsrdf:isMemberofMADSScheme <http://id.loc.gov/authorities/subjects>.

<http://id.loc.gov/vocabulary/countries/nyu> a bf:Place.
<http://id.loc.gov/vocabulary/issuance/mono> a bf:Issuance.
<http://id.loc.gov/vocabulary/languages/eng> a bf:Language.
<http://id.loc.gov/vocabulary/marcauthen/lcac> a bf:DescriptionAuthentication.
<http://id.loc.gov/vocabulary/marcgt/fic> a bf:GenreForm ; rdfs:label "fiction".
<http://id.loc.gov/vocabulary/maudience/juv> a bf:IntendedAudience ; rdfs:label "juvenile".
<http://id.loc.gov/vocabulary/millus/ill> a bf:Illustration ; rdfs:label "illustrations".

(continued)

TABLE 3.1. (continued)

Sample BIBFRAME Record

<http://bibframe.example.org/5226#Instance> a bf:Instance ;
   rdfs:label "Snoopy on wheels /" ;
   bf:dimensions "88 mm." ;
   bf:extent [a bf:Extent ;
       rdfs:label "1 v. (unpaged)"] ;
   bf:hasItem <http://bibframe.example.org/5226#Item050-12> ;
   bf:hasSeries [a bf:Instance ;
       rdfs:label "A chunky book" ;
       bf:seriesStatement "A chunky book"] ;
   bf:identifiedBy [a bf:Lccn ;
       rdf:value " 82060878"],
    [a bf:Isbn ;
       rdf:value "0394856309"] ;
   bf:illustrativeContent <http://id.loc.gov/vocabulary/millus/ill> ;
   bf:instanceOf <http://bibframe.example.org/5226#Work> ;
   bf:issuance <http://id.loc.gov/vocabulary/issuance/mono> ;
   bf:note [a bf:Note ;
       rdfs:label "\"Based on the Charles M. Schulz characters\"--P. 4 of cover."
       ],
    [a bf:Note ;
       rdfs:label "On board pages."],
    [a bf:Note ;
       rdfs:label "col. ill." ;
       bf:noteType "Physical details"] ;
   bf:provisionActivity [a bf:ProvisionActivity,
       bf:Publication ;
      bf:agent [a bf:Agent ;
        rdfs:label "Random House"] ;
      bf:date "c1983" ;
      bf:place [a bf:Place ;
        rdfs:label "New York"]],
    [a bf:ProvisionActivity,
       bf:Publication ;
      bf:date "1983"^^<http://id.loc.gov/datatypes/edtf> ;
      bf:place <http://id.loc.gov/vocabulary/countries/nyu>] ;
   bf:provisionActivityStatement "[New York] : Random House, c1983." ;
   bf:responsibilityStatement "[designed by Terry Flanagan]" ;
   bf:title [a bf:Title ;
       rdfs:label "Snoopy on wheels /" ;
       bflc:titleSortKey "Snoopy on wheels /" ;
       bf:mainTitle "Snoopy on wheels"] .
<http://id.loc.gov/vocabulary/relators/ctb> a bf:Role.

<http://id.loc.gov/vocabulary/organizations/dlc> a bf:Source .

Licklider, who was the first head of the Advanced Research Projects Agency (ARPA) in 1962, is often credited with conceptualizing and seeding the development of what we now call the internet.

Berners-Lee created the original tags and format for HTML when he created the HTTP protocol (the web or hypertext protocol, if you will). HTML originated as an application (a DTD) of SGML. By 1995, Berners-Lee and David Connolly had completed work on version 2.0 of HTML, and this effort became the de facto standard for web-page authoring. In January 1997, the W3C released HTML version 3.2, elevating the web markup language from a crude functional beginning to a more effective authoring environment. Work continued on the standard, and version 4.0 (late 1997) brought the controversial "frames" tag and improved display and layout tags.

HTML5 is the latest evolution of HTML that provides new attributes, elements, behaviors, and a set of technologies that allows for building more powerful websites and applications.

Extensible Markup Language (XML)

Approved in October 1998 by the W3C, this new standard has caused quite a commotion, especially because, as yet, it has few full-blown applications. XML is a markup language built from the start to be extensible, meaning that the author/creator can make up any tags he or she likes (so long as they are specified in the author's XML DTD). XML is designed to enable the use of SGML on the WWW in a more robust manner than was ever possible when using HTML as a web markup language.

XML offers the following three benefits not found in HTML:

Extensibility—Because HTML is based on a DTD, HTML does not allow users to specify their own TAGS or ATTRIBUTES or otherwise semantically qualify their data. Programmers love to create new stuff that's all their own. XML supports this creativity because XML is on the same level of generality as SGML: one creates a DTD and uses whatever codes one wants. An analogy might be a palette that allows painters to create new colors out of the basic set of primary colors. Just think how boring art would be without those mixes!

Structure—HTML does not support the specification of "deep structures" needed to represent database schemas or object-oriented hierarchies. Ask any developer of a database application about their efforts to create a web-based version of that database, and you will begin to understand the difficulties.

Validation—HTML does not support the kind of language specification that allows consuming applications to check data for structural validity on importation. This is crucial in all commercial applications and important in database applications as well.

A key element of XML is that it supports Unicode (ISO 10646), the international standard two-byte character set that covers most human written languages. Thus, XML can be written in nearly any language.

SGML is very complex. It's specification manual is nearly unreadable and quite lengthy. The specifications for XML are less than thirty pages (HTML is even shorter!). The learning curve of any authoring tool is closely related to the length of these specifications!

Existing HTML documents can be converted over to XML by following certain rules for the various tags. For example, XML is case sensitive, whereas HTML is not. XML requires that *all* open tags have a closed tag as well (for those of you who code in HTML, think about paragraph <P> and line breaks <BR>). A sloppily coded HTML document is difficult to convert to XML. XML is positioned to replace HTML as the markup language of choice for developing professional web applications. As things move toward XML, we will likely see XML-compliant browsers surface that are capable of handling both HTML and XML coding. The advantages of XML in handling richer media and databases should serve end users well in future developments.

XML is a simpler version of the original and more complex SGML, but designed specifically for the Web. Organizations can define, transmit, validate, and interpret data between applications and databases. XML provides structure rather than being a presentation system. XML separates the underlying data from how the data are displayed; thus, the data can more easily organized, programmed, edited, and exchanged between websites and applications. XML and its associated DTD plays an important role in the exchange of information. Besides the rules for establishing XML entities, there are nine other key XML-related standards.

- **XML Schema Definition (XSD)** defines a standard way of describing XML document structures and adding data types to XML data fields. The intent is to facilitate cross-organizational document exchange and verification. Tools are available for converting XML DTDs to XSD that will assist in the exchange of information.

- **Simple Object Access Protocol (SOAP)** is one of the more popular XML Schema Definitions that allows applications to pass data and instructions to one another. SOAP was originally developed for distributed applications to communicate over HTTP and through corporate firewalls. SOAP defines the use of XML and HTTP to access services, objects, and servers in a platform-independent manner. SOAP itself does not define any application semantics such as a programming model or implementation-specific semantics; rather, it defines a simple mechanism for expressing application semantics by providing a modular packaging model and encoding mechanisms for encoding data within modules. This allows SOAP to be used in a large variety of systems, ranging from messaging systems to a remote procedure call.

- **Representational State Transfer (REST),** or RESTful, web services provides interoperability among computer systems on the internet, using a stateless protocol. Most web services provide access to a set of RESTful Application Programming Interfaces, or APIs.

- **BISAC** and **SISAC** have developed XSDs to facilitate ordering, acknowledging receipt of an order, claiming, and other transaction sets. These XSDs will be incorporated into applications by both the ILS vendors and the book and serials jobbers.

- **Resource Description Framework (RDF)** is an XML-based infrastructure that enables structured metadata to be encoded, exchanged, and reused. RDF allows for more than one data type to be included in the same metadata package. A group of interested parties is working on representing the Dublin Core in RDF.

Encoded Archival Description (EAD)—EAD is an XML standard for coding archival finding aids, developed and maintained by the Society of American Archivists.

Ecological Metadata Language (EML)—EML is an XML schema that provides for structured metadata within the ecology discipline.

Communication Standards

Communications standards are designed to support the interchange of information among distinctly different information systems operated by different institutions.

Standards in the communication standards area include the following:

Z39.58—the Common Command Language. The notion of developing a common set of commands that could be used in search tools (Z39.58) arose during a period prior to client-server computing, when databases were searched using command languages, not graphical-based clients. As database use proliferated, users were faced with memorizing an array of searching syntaxes that varied from system to system.

A common command language identifies a common set of functions, links a certain set of verbs directly to those functions, and uses them in all applications. This was a noble idea but became less than necessary because of several reasons. The first was the development of graphical interfaces that sheltered the end user from the specific commands within the system. Second, vendors were reluctant to implement a common command language because it would eliminate an important product differentiator—unique search capabilities. Because each NISO standard is reviewed periodically by a designated committee for updates and continuation, standards such as the Common Command Language can and do rise and fall with use and relevance in this rapidly developing technologic age.

Z39.50—the Information Retrieval Service Definition and Protocol Specifications for Library Applications. Z39.50–2003 is presently a widely used protocol enabling communication between distributed and possibly disparate computer systems. More specifically, Z39.50 is used as a sort of translator and interpreter between a searchable database, or server, and the desktop workstation, or client, issuing the search query. In practice, the client's search query is translated into the Z39.50 standard search format and is then reinterpreted into the server's format.[13] The search results are then provided to the end user in the client's particular local format, regardless of the local system's hardware or interfaces.[14]

This search and retrieve standard has helped foster the trend in client-server computing, allowing information to be retrieved through the desktop workstation from any database utilizing it. The Z39.50 protocol guidelines provide balance between both ends of the remote search interaction process. Z39.50 is a robust protocol that facilitates these:

- Restricting access to authenticated users
- Browsing indexes and thesauri

- Retrieving selected content
- Negotiating the retrieval of large search results (query refinement, limiting)
- Removing duplicates from the retrieval set
- Sorting the search results before presentation
- Searching and presenting results
- Extending services such as placing orders, updating files, saving search result sets, and exporting data (in the MARC format)[15]

Tip! One of the interesting and unintended consequences of Z39.50 is that MARC records are delivered to the requesting automated library system. These records can then be imported into the requesting library's database for use by the cataloging module.

Presently, most ILS vendors in the library community have developed a Z39.50 client module that promises access to any Z39.50-compliant database. Most vendors have also developed a Z39.50 server so a library can provide access to its collection—see Figure 3.3.

A major problem associated with implementing Z39.50 is that not all vendors or libraries that develop their own software are fully compliant with the latest version of Z39.50 (2003). To improve the compatibility level among different ILSs, several groups have defined an acceptable functional compliance level. These definitions are called "profiles," and the more prominent of these are the Bath Profile (United Kingdom), the Union Catalogue Profile (Australia), and the Z Texas Profile (United States). Several other profiles have either been defined or are in the process of being defined.

Z39.83—NISO Circulation Interchange, Part 1: Protocol (NCIP) and Part 2: Implementation Profile. Z39.83 defines a protocol that provides a standard interface between a library's circulation system and library self-service automation devices. Z39.83 has more than forty possible messages that can exhibit three types of behaviors:

- **Inquiries or lookups**. Examples: What is the name associated with patron ID #123456789? What is the mailing address for the patron with ID #123456789? How many items does the patron have checked out?
- **Actions**. Examples: Place a hold on this title. Check in the item with ID #987654321. Authenticate this patron. Check out this item.
- **Notifications**. Examples: One system informs another system that a specific item has been checked in.

Counting Online Usage of Networked Electronic Resources (COUNTER) Code of Practice. COUNTER lists a series of reports a content provider is expected to make available, as well as the metrics and format included for each report.

Z39.93—Standardized Usage Statistics Harvesting Initiative (SUSHI) Protocol. SUSHI uses a client-server model using Simple Object Access Protocol (SOAP) to enable machine-to-machine exchange of COUNTER reports. SUSHI-Lite uses the representational transfer

A. Without a "Search and Retrieve" Protocol

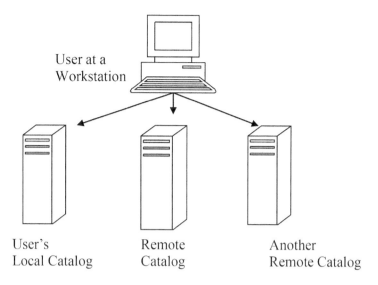

B. With a "Search and Retrieve" (Z39.50) Protocol

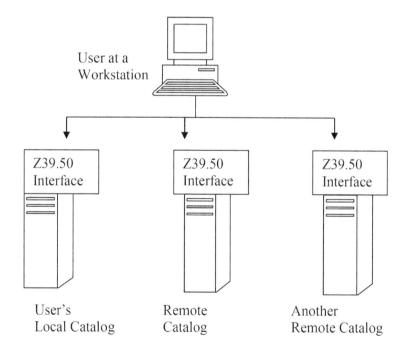

FIGURE 3.3. Z39.50 Searching

state (REST) approach to web services, using JSON (JavaScript Object Notation) formatted data rather than XML.

Z39.100—Standard Interchange Protocol (SIP). Z39.100 defines a protocol that provides a standard interface between a library's circulation system and library self-service automation devices.

Unicode. Unicode is a standard developed by the Unicode Consortium and intended to provide a unique number for every character, regardless of language, platform, or program. It should facilitate information exchange by enabling a computer to process the text of any language without needing to use numerous, sometimes contradictory, encoding systems.

One problem with the previous encoding systems was that the length of the code was too short (generally one byte, seven- or eight-bit codes) and thus could not accommodate a large number of characters across many languages. Most institutions simply chose the encoding system that accommodated most of their local needs.

Given the very low costs for disk storage today, concerns about implementing Unicode have disappeared. Unicode also has some nifty linguistic and technological features, which make it rather useful. One of those features is embedding semantics into the code to provide concept information in addition to the code for the character and how to display it.[16] For more information about Unicode, visit the Unicode website at http://www.unicode.org.

Technology Standards

Other communications standards have been created outside NISO that support interactions among computer systems. Many of these are technical, involving transferring packets of information within an information system that may or may not involve libraries. For example, IEEE 802.3 (Ethernet) and IEEE 802.2 (Token Passing) are common protocols used to support local area network (LAN) development. IEEE 802.16 is a series of wireless broadband communication standards.

The most well-known communications standard is undoubtedly TCP/IP, which the internet is based on. This standard is actually a de facto standard that underlies the internet and supports services and applications running on the internet.

Among the more notable technology standards are the following:

IEEE 802.11—The IEEE 802.16 is a family of standards that provides wireless local area networking communication, mostly commonly known as WiFi. WiFi-compatible devices can connect to the internet using a wireless access point, often called a hot spot or WiFi router, that is connected to a wide area network (connected to the internet).

Bluetooth—Bluetooth is a wireless standard for exchanging data and messages over short distances, using radio waves. The Bluetooth Special Interest Group maintains this standard.

De Facto Standards

Many content providers and websites provide access to their data using an **application programming interface** (API) that in essence is a standard. An API is a set of definitions, protocols, and tools to exchange data from one machine to another. An API specification typically provides access to routines, data structures, and variables, using a specific protocol. Access to a set of APIs is typically fairly transparent, although the vendor's of some systems may make the process challenging.

The Standards Reality

One characteristic of highly technical standards is that the various standards organizations and their voting members constantly scrutinize them to ensure that each is conducive to the realities of the information environment. Information standards are dependent on the consent of such members and their acknowledgement of the standard's relevance by implementing it on a widespread basis. Even if a standard is recognized by an official organization as furthering the exchange of information, the individual members put it into practice at their discretion—they won't do it if it does not advance their interests or seem to comply with the emerging market.

This example illustrates that implementing a national standard is a process that libraries, as primarily consumers of information, sometimes have little control over. Although standards that increase access and compatibility between computer systems are beneficial to all parties, the private sector must naturally safeguard its investments. One effort with this intention is the digital object identifier (DOI) standard, which was developed to "facilitate electronic commerce and allow publishers to maintain copyright" on information through what may be thought of as "an ISBN for electronic publishing."[17] The DOI has been mandated by the Association of American Publishers under the development of R. R. Bowker and the Corporation for National Research Initiatives. Each DOI is a number consisting of one component given by the DOI agency (Bowker) and another by the publisher for assignment to a specific online article. The DOI thereby distinguishes various forms of content by assigning each a unique number for copyright purposes.

The trend in developing metadata standards is to design structures and formats that will support the understanding and usage of information, increase the availability and accessibility of that information, and enable interoperability among different computing systems using different formats and structures. Out of necessity, this will need to occur at the local, regional, national, and international levels.

Related Organizations

Other groups contributing to the compatibility or implementation of information systems in libraries are the Coalition for Networked Information (CNI), the World Wide Web Consortium (W3C), and the Corporation for National Research Initiatives (CNRI). The CNI is a partnership of the Association of Research Libraries, the Association for Managing and Using Information Resources in Higher Education (CAUSE), and the Inter-University Communications Council (EDUCOM). The coalition was founded in March 1990 to promote the distribution of networked information on the National Research and Education Network (NREN). CNI also has numerous auxiliary members from public libraries and publishers in its Task Force to promote greater communication within higher education on information policies.[18] Although CNI does not regulate or propose standards for information technology, it does provide a forum for communicating on the range of emerging issues in networked information systems.[19]

The W3C is another potential resource that can help libraries stay abreast of trends in online information retrieval. This collection of various organizations is "vendor neutral, working with the global community to produce specifications and reference software that is made freely available throughout the world."[20] Again, W3C does not issue literal standards, but does pass recommendations that have attained "a general . . . consensus among members." Official recommendations start out as working drafts of specifications available for consideration and are then promoted to proposed recommendations by the consortium director before becoming endorsed recommendations.[21]

A final organization worth mentioning for its role in the DOI project is the CNRI. Besides its involvement in developing technologies for resolving intellectual property or copyright—as exemplified by the DOI—this nonprofit corporation works toward facilitating access to the National Information Infrastructure (NII) in general.[22]

The obvious importance of library standards requires that librarians and their representative organizations be assertive in conveying their practical priorities and values to these various standards-making organizations. Standards do much more than affect the procedures for retrieving bits of data—they unavoidably define the policies of those information agencies that use them. Therefore, it is only reasonable to conclude that libraries must communicate their concerns to groups such as CNRI if they are to promote a relatively open realm of information. As ANSI declares,

> That is why American National Standards are usually referred to as "open" standards. In this sense, "open" refers to a process used by a recognized body for developing and approving a standard. The Institute's definition of openness has many elements, but basically refers to a collaborative, balanced and consensus-based approval process. The content of these standards may relate to products, processes, services, systems or personnel."[23]

By contrast, direct involvement within the standards creation process through the above-cited organizations will continue to give librarians leadership opportunity in information access.[24]

Summary

This chapter began with a basic understanding of the role of standards in designing LISs and closed with a call for professional involvement in developing standards that affect the dissemination of content to end users in increasingly complex technological environments. National and international organizations that support the continued development of standards relating to the processes and services found in most libraries and information agencies were profiled. Seven categories of standards relating to libraries and information technology were identified and discussed. As long as libraries seek to develop and implement new information technologies, they need to be cognizant of the impact standards development has on the processes involved and the services delivered using those technologies.

Questions to Consider

- What are some of the benefits that arise from the use of standards?
- What is the relationship between the International Standards Organization (ISO) and the National Information Standards Organization (NISO)?

- Do the vendors who provide the systems in your library participate in one of more standards setting groups?

- What do you think are the three or four standards that are most important to the library community? To your library?

- Is your library moving to adopt the new BIBFRAME metadata model? If so, what are objectives for making this move?

- How is your library working to make all of its machine-readable data more visible and of value to library customers?

- Are you aware of some of the limitations of the MARC 21 bibliographic standard?

- Why are internet-based standards so important to libraries now and into the future?

Notes

1. Andrew S. Tanenbaum, *Computer Networks* (New York: Prentice Hall, 2010): 254.

2. "Standards," *ISO* (n.d.), https://iso.org/standards.html.

3. Walt Crawford, *Technical Standards: An Introduction for Librarians* (White Plains, NY: Knowledge Industry, 1986).

4. *NISO Strategic Directions 2018* (Baltimore, MD: NISO, 2018), https://groups .niso.org/apps/group_public/download.php/18972/NISO_strategic_directions_2018 .pdf.

5. Shirley M. Radack, "More Effective Federal Computer Systems: The Role of NIST and Standards," *Government Information Quarterly* 7, no. 1 (1990): 38.

6. "W3C Semantic Web Frequently Asked Questions: Questions on RDF," *W3C Semantic Web*, accessed July 31, 2019, http://www.w3.org/RDF/FAQ; "RDF/XML Syntax Specification (Revised)," *W3C*, February 10, 2004, http://www.w3.org/TR /REC-rdf-syntax/; Miloslav Nic, "RDF Tutorial—Part 1: Basic Syntax and Containers," Zvon.org, accessed July 31, 2019, http://www.zvon.org/xxl/RDFTutorial/General /book.html; Tim Bray, "RDF and Metadata," XML.com, June 9, 1998, http://www.xml .com/pub/a/98/06/rdf.html; Rachel M. Heery. "What Is . . . RDF," *Ariadne (Online)* 14, March 1998, http://www.ariadne.ac.uk/issue14/what-is/; and Ora Lassila, "Introduction to RDF Metadata," November 13, 1997, http://www.w3.org/TR/NOTE-rdf -simple-intro.

7. The crosswalk can be found at "MARC to Dublin Core Crosswalk," Library of Congress, April 24, 2008, http://www.loc.gov/marc/marc2dc.html.

8. Erik T. Mitchell, "The Current State of Linked Data in Libraries, Archives, and Museums," *Library Technology Reports* (January 2016): 1–33.

9. Simeon Warner, "LD4L Use Cases," *Linked Data for Libraries Wiki*, May 7, 2015, https://wiki.duraspace.org/pages/viewpage.action?pageId=41354028.

10. See, for example, Roy Tennant, "MARC Must Die," *Library Journal* 127, no. 17 (October 15, 2002): 26–27; Roy Tennant, "MARC Exit Strategies," *Library Journal* 127, no. 9 (November 15, 2002): 27–28; Roy Tennant, "The Post-MARC Era, Part 1: If It's Televised, It Can't Be the Revolution," *The Digital Shift* (blog), *Library Journal*, April 17, 2013; Roy Tennant, "The Post-MARC Era, Part 2: Where the Problems Lie," *The Digital Shift* (blog), *Library Journal*, May 8, 2013; and Roy Tennant, "A Bibliographic Metadata Infrastructure for the Twenty-First Century," *Library Hi Tech* 22, no. 2 (2004): 175–81.

11. Angela Kroeger, "The Road to BIBFRAME: The Evolution of the Idea of Bibliographic Transition into a Post-MARC Future," *Cataloging & Classification Quarterly* 51, no. 8 (2013): 873–890.

12. Malcolm Brown, "What Is SGML?," *Information Technology and Libraries*, March 13, 1994, 10.

13. Maribeth Ward, "Expanding Access with Z39.50," *American Libraries* 25, (July–August 1994): 640.

14. Lennie Stovel, "Sidebar 6: Zephyr: RLG's Z39.50 Implementation," *Library Hi Tech* 12, no. 2 (1994): 20.

15. "ANSI/NISO Z39.50-2003 (S2014) Information Retrieval: Application Service Definition & Protocol Specification," *NISO* (May 7, 2015), https://www.niso.org/publications/ansiniso-z3950-2003-s2014.

16. Joan M. Aliprand, "The Unicode Standard: Its Scope, Design Principles, and Prospects for International Cataloging," *Library Resources & Technical Services* 44, no. 3 (July 2000): 160–67.

17. Norman Oder, "New Online ISBN Moves Ahead," *Library Journal* 121 (October 1, 1996): 15–16.

18. John K. Lippencott, "Change and the Referent Organization: The CNI," *Journal of Library Administration* 19, no. 3–4 (1993): 250–52.

19. Lippencott, "Change and the Referent Organization," 254.

20. "About W3C," *W3C* (n.d.), http://www.w3.org/pub/WWW/consortium/.

21. "All Standards and Drafts," *W3C* (n.d.), http://www.w3.org/pub/WWW/TR/.

22. "Welcome to CNRI (Corporation for National Research Initiatives)," *CNRI* (n.d.), http://www.cnri.reston.va.us/home/cnri.html.

23. Introduction to ANSI. *ANSI* (n.d.), https://www.ansi.org/about_ansi/introduction/introduction?menuid=1.

24. Maribeth Ward, "Expanding Access with Z39.50," *American Libraries* 25 (July–August 1994): 641.

4
Telecommunications and Networks

We are all now connected by the Internet,
like neurons in a giant brain.

—Stephen Hawking[1]

This chapter presents an overview of telecommunication and network fundamentals. Networks can be broadly divided into two types: local area networks (LANs) and wide area networks (WANs). Having a basic understanding of how networks operate is central to gaining a better insight of their possible implications, especially service delivery consequences.

Telecommunications

Telecommunications generally means an electronic means of communication (analog or digital) including, but not limited to, radio, television, telephone, microwave, satellite, computer network, and the internet. Some telecommunication technologies are unidirectional (one-way), and some are bidirectional.

"Broadcast" applies to communications that take place using unidirectional technology to a large audience. Broadcast television, for example, transmits (broadcasts) a signal to everyone in a region—the signal is picked up with a television receiver (antenna). However, there is no possibility for someone watching a show to send a message back to the station, using the television. Radio is a broadcast technology that uses radio waves, whereas *DirectTV* broadcasts television signals from a satellite. Broadcast technologies efficiently distribute content to large audiences, using minimal infrastructure; however, such technology empowers the broadcaster, not the end user or recipient.

Bidirectional communications, such as those using a cell phone or the internet, allow for simultaneous two-way conversations. Bidirectional communications technologies allow for both *synchronous* (sent at the same time) and asynchronous (can only be sent in one direction at a time) messages. Interactive technologies allow individuals to make choices and determine the information to be received.

Yet the clear distinctions between various telecommunication technologies are blurring. Someone can listen to a radio station located anywhere around the world because of the ability of streaming the audio signal, using the internet. The radio station sends packets of digital information (containing the audio signal) across the internet. This internet-based audio streaming gives a radio-like experience to those who are listening, but it's not exactly radio (no radio waves are involved). The same thing applies to broadcast television and streaming video technologies.

The whole field of telecommunications is becoming quite jumbled. Telephone companies are now cable TV providers. Cable television companies also provide internet and telephone services (a package deal). Satellite television companies are now providing internet services. And cell phone companies are providing voice and data services. The reasons for this blurring of business boundaries are two: the US government has deregulated the telecommunications industry, and digital technologies make it easy to blur the lines between telephones, internet service, and television. After all, a digital "bit" can be used to represent just about anything. This blurring of boundaries among service providers is sometimes called the "confluence of technology offerings."

Networks

In general terms, a network can be defined as the interconnection of points (sometimes called nodes) for the purpose of communicating information (the message might be analog or digital). The network is the mechanism that connects the points or nodes.

Consider the post office as a network that moves messages in the form of letters, catalogs, and packages from one location to another (node). As the West was settled, the pony express network was established to move letters more quickly from one east–west location to another, using horses and riders (you had to be small and tough to ride the pony express). The introduction of the telegraph allowed brief messages to be moved about the country and then around the world.

A computer network connects any number of computers so they can exchange or communicate digital information with one another. A computer network can use a variety of media to move messages from a source location to a destination. Typically a message moves through a number of locations or intermediate stops (sometimes called hops) as it moves to its ultimate destination.

Robert Metcalfe, who invented Ethernet technology, has observed that the value of a network is equal to the square of the number of nodes or users. This observation, now known as Metcalfe's law, states that as a network grows, the value of being connected to it grows exponentially. Doubling the number of participants doubles the value to each participant while the total value of the network increases fourfold. Thus, while tens of thousands of fax machines provide some limited value, a network of a million fax machines provides tremendous value to all users.

The following sections of this chapter provide a more detailed discussion of the components of LANs and WANs.

Local Area Networks

When it was recognized that connecting desktop computers would allow an array of hardware and software to be shared, the LAN was born. A LAN, by its very definition, is limited geographically: an office, a floor of a building, an entire building, or even a campus. In almost every organization, the presence and availability of a LAN is taken for a given, and as such the LAN has become an invisible infrastructure required for the efficient operation of every organization.

The benefits of a LAN include these:

- More expensive peripheral devices, such as printers, scanners, fax machines, among others, can be shared by all users connected to the LAN. The net effect is that the organization will need to purchase fewer peripheral devices and is thus able to save money.

- As desktop and portable computing devices become more powerful and affordable, they can assume responsibilities formerly served by centralized computers or servers.

- Licenses for infrequently used computer software can be shared when needed.

- Information—data files, documents, spreadsheets, and presentations—can be placed in public directories and shared with others.

- Reliability is improved such that when one device is inoperable, other options will likely exist.

- Licensed databases and other electronic resources can be made accessible on demand to each and every desktop computer and handheld device.

- Incremental growth—computer resources can be added in an incremental manner rather than having to replace an existing system with an even larger system. Thus, the investment in information technology occurs in a more measured and affordable manner.

LAN Technologies

LANs can employ a variety of wiring media, and this wiring can be laid out in several different ways. Typically four types of transmission media may be used in a LAN: twisted-pair copper wire, coaxial cable (sometimes called an Ethernet cable), WiFi, and fiber-optic cables. The speed with which data travels is measured in bits per second (bps) and is called the data rate. Thus, Kbps is 1,000 (kilo) bits per second, Mbps is 1 million bits per second, and Gbps is 1 billion bits per second (or 1,000 Mbps). Bandwidth, however, measures the amount of information that can be transmitted simultaneously. The bandwidth of a medium is often referred to as channel capacity. Bandwidth and the data rate are interrelated, because the greater the bandwidth, the greater the data rate, as seen in Table 4.1.

Twisted-Pair Cable

Twisted-pair cable is the most ubiquitous communication medium and is easy to handle, splice, connect, and install. It has been historically used for conventional analog voice communications (the landline telephone) and for

TABLE 4.1. Transmission Characteristics of Communications Media

Medium	Data Rate	Bandwidth	Repeater Spacing
Twisted-pair cable	10 Mbps	500 KHz	100 m
Coaxial cable	500 Mbps	550 MHz	1–10 km
Optical fiber	2 Gbps	2 Gbps	10–100 km
Wireless LAN–WiFi	100–1,000 Mbps	10–100 Mbps	Varies

TABLE 4.2. Ethernet Standards

Types of Cables*					
	Cat 5	Cat 5e	Cat 6	Cat 6a	Cat 7
Cable type	Unshielded twisted pair (UTP)	UTP	UTP or shielded twisted pair (STP)	STP	Fully shielded twisted pair (F/STP)
Max transmission speed	10/100/1000 Mbps	10/100/1000 Mbps	10/100/1000 Mbps	10,000 Mbps	10,000 Mbps
Max bandwidth	100 MHz	100 MHz	250 MHz	500 MHz	600 MHz

Source: Based on data from http://ciscorouterswitch.over-blog.com/article-the-different-types-of-ethernet-cables-125299851.html.

digital data transmission. One wire of the pair carries the signal, and the other wire is grounded and absorbs signal interference.

There are two broad groups of twisted-pair wiring—unshielded and shielded. The unshielded twisted-pair (UTP) wiring, sometimes called telephone wire, is susceptible to interference from devices such as electrical motors, fluorescent lights, elevators, and other electrical equipment. Shielded wiring incorporates a layer of insulation (such as copper foil or wire braid) that blocks noise and signal interference from external devices.

Ethernet shielded wiring consists of four twisted-pairs of copper wire terminated by RJ45 connectors (jacks). Developed by the Electronics Industries Alliance and the Telecommunications Industry Association (EIA/TIA), this cable is based on the EIA/TIA 568 Communications Building Telecommunications Wiring Standard—see Table 4.2.

> **Tip!** When installing Ethernet cabling at your library, make sure the contractor tests the installed wiring and certifies that it meets the required standard for quality of the electrical signal for the category of wiring you are installing. It is not unusual for wiring to be damaged during installation. Thus, the need for testing and certification once the wiring has been installed is very important.

Fiber-Optic Cable

Optical fiber cables have a significant amount of bandwidth because they are made of glass or plastic fibers that transmit light pulses (digital signals). The diameter of an optical fiber is five times as wide as the wavelength of

TABLE 4.3. Optical Fiber Network Speeds

Fiber Technology	Wavelength per Fiber	Optical Carrier Speed
Single fiber	One wavelength	Up to 10 gigabits per second
Multiple fibers Wave division Multiplexing (WDM)	Up to four wavelengths per fiber	Up to 40 gigabits per second
Multiple fibers Dense wave division Multiplexing (DWDM)	Up to 160 wavelengths per fiber	Up to 1.6 terabits per second

infrared light (less than 2 microns), and a single fiber has a theoretical capacity as high as 25,000 gigabits per second—roughly equivalent to transmitting the contents of 3 million books per second. Optical fiber cables are not affected by magnetic or radio frequency interference and have error rates that are 10 billion times lower than twisted-pair copper wires. Optical fiber cables are now about the same price as twisted-pair or coaxial cables, although the installation price might be slightly higher because of the need for special tools and expertise in splicing fiber cables. In 2019, prices range from $1–6 per installed foot, depending on the capacity (number of individual fibers) in the cable.

In 2000, George Gilder, a noted technology author, proposed "Gilder's law," which posits that available bandwidth triples every twelve months, whereas costs decline. Optical fiber is not only being used as the backbone of the internet but is also being extended to the front doors of businesses, homes, and other organizations. Because of the increasing use of fiber-optic cables throughout the network, the available bandwidth increases at three times the rate of Moore's law for the foreseeable future. Optical fiber network speeds are shown in Table 4.3.

Not surprisingly, Google has installed fiber-optic cables in a number of US cities. The 1–10 Gbps, sometimes called "gig," fiber-optic internet connection has attracted entrepreneurial groups to the Kansas City area and other areas that have installed high-speed optical networks. In addition to for-profit firms rolling out fiber-optic networks, many cities and counties have been installing their own publicly owned next-generation networks. These networks offer very fast connections to the internet (1 gig to 10 gig for both upload and download speeds) for television, telephone, and broadband access services to all members of the community.

> **Tip!** For more information about community approaches to installing high-speed broadband networks, visit the Institute for Local Self-Reliance website at https://ilsr.org/initiatives/broadband.

Some state libraries are providing grants to encourage public libraries to become connected to the internet using 1–10 Gbps fiber-optic solutions. Academic libraries, more often than not, have had fiber-optic connection speeds for several years.

WiFi

WiFi is a radio/wireless local area networking technology based on the Institute of Electrical and Electronics Engineers (IEEE) 802.11 standards.

WiFi is used by desktop, laptop, and tablet computers; smartphones; video game consoles; digital audio players; printers; and so many more devices. A WiFi-enabled device can connect with the internet via a wide area network. The typical wireless access point or "hot spot" has a range of about 60 feet indoors and a wider range outdoors.

Perhaps a majority of libraries provide WiFi access within their facilities, and many communities provide WiFi access (a quick Google search often reveals a map of WiFi hot spots within a community) in public spaces. Many stores, such as coffee shops, provide WiFi access in order to draw customers in. It is important to periodically check to ensure that the WiFi connection to the internet has sufficient bandwidth so that communication occurs in a timely manner.

Network Design

The choice of cabling media, access method, and topology is affected by some of the following considerations:

1. Distance—What is the maximum distance of a cabling run? In most cases, LANs are limited to a few hundred feet.

2. Number of workstations or devices to be connected to the LAN.

3. Response time requirements—What are the user expectations in terms of response times? Do response times vary by type of application or by type of transaction? In almost all cases, users now expect quick (1- to 2-second response times) every time they click their mouse or request something be done.

4. Throughput requirements—What is the average and peak period volume of transactions? What type of data will be transmitted—text, audio and/or video files (streaming media), file transfers, images, and so forth. Note that the file size of audio, video, or images is considerably larger than the relatively brief messages associated with an integrated library system (ILS), and the mix of these types of files will have a major impact on the ultimate communications configuration.

Once the likely LAN configuration has been determined, bandwidth considerations must be addressed for the three components of the LAN:

- From the backbone to each device—desktop computer, printer, scanner
- The LAN backbone
- Connection to a wide area network and ultimately to the internet.

Tip! A network interface card (NIC) is a small device that allows a computer, printer, fax machine, or scanner to connect to the LAN itself. Most NICs are designed to support one speed—up to 1,000 megabits per second (Mbps) or 1 Gbps. If your organization is moving to fiber-optic cabling, especially to your desktop computer or device, then a NIC supporting 1 Gbps is a minimum requirement.

Wireless LANs

The IEEE 802.11 standard provides for interoperability between devices that have wireless modems and a LAN. Using wireless LANs, users have immediate access to file servers, printers, and databases, regardless of their location within the building. An in-building wireless network is most often comprised of multiple units containing a radio (often called an access point, or AP) that connects to client devices with WiFi capability. Each AP can support a number of simultaneous users clients (some as few as fifteen to twenty; other more complex units with multiple radios can support more than fifty, assuming adequate bandwidth of the LAN and the connection between the LAN and the internet). The principal advantage of wireless is the elimination of the physical "tether," or wiring that limits mobility with the network infrastructure. Some building construction materials may block the radio signal and thus create a "dead zone."

The original 802.11a standard enabled devices to provide data speeds of up to 11 Mbps over distances of 400 feet. Since the original standards were implemented, WiFi speed and distance continue to increase—although data speeds decline when encountering walls or metal construction materials.

One obvious advantage of wireless technology is that an individual always has connectivity, even when moving around within the building. Wireless 802.11x networks have connected LANS located in two separate buildings, in lieu of a physical cable to connect the two buildings. The library can decide whether to require the use of a password to access the wireless network or if it will simply provide the service as a "hot spot" (with no password required).

A wireless access point is connected to a LAN cable and provides users with access to the LAN (and the internet), using a radio signal. The current wireless standard is the IEEE 802.11ac, and it provides better WiFi coverage than the older WiFi standards (802.11a/b/g/n). Depending on obstacles like walls, the radio signals of most wireless routers travel up to 300 feet. In some cases, relying on one or more wireless access points (WAPs) extends the wireless router's signal range and strength and eliminates dead spots (no WiFi service).

As more people bring their own devices wherever they go, the library must ensure that its WiFi network has sufficient capacity (including bandwidth) so that each user does not experience slow response times. And the library's internet connection must also have sufficient bandwidth to support all of the physical workstations and other devices located in the library plus all of the associated data traffic on its WiFi network. When an internet connection experiences 75 percent utilization of the available bandwidth, then it is time to significantly increase the capacity of the internet connection.

Tip! Visit http://www.bandwidthplace.com to conduct a download and upload speed test.

Tip! Make sure all wireless gear supports the latest 802.11x standard.

Location-Based Service

A location-based service refers to the mapping of the geographic relationships associated with data. That is, the location-based service can digitally pinpoint the physical location of an object or individual through WiFi cellular networks, RFID, and more recently Bluetooth Beacon technology. The number of people carrying mobile devices on their persons—such as smartphones, tablets, wearables, and other devices everywhere they go—is driving the proliferation of this technology.

Location-based services offer the opportunity for libraries to provide to their customers with very specific information tailored to their very specific location within a library, allowing the delivery of personalized information. A person who happens to be near the cookbooks might learn about a cooking demonstration and presentation scheduled in the next few days. Entering the library, the customer might be informed that a book she had placed on hold was available for pickup.

Mobile app developers (such as *Capira Technologies* and *BluuBeam*, serving the library market) are using location-based services to push out event notification and news about specific library locations or collections, and enable people to pay fines or fees, take a self-guided library tour, book a study room, and checkout library materials. Clearly, location-based services open up lots of possibilities.

> **Tip!** It's a standard practice for network installers to provide documentation of the physical network—including numbered jack plates throughout the building, with corresponding numbers at the central patch panel and a document showing locations of all wiring terminations. Sadly, this crucial documentation is not always provided, and when it is, it is sometimes not updated as changes occur in the library's wiring over time. The library's system manager should keep an accurate diagram of the LAN configuration with an inventory of the devices connected to the LAN. A list of each of the cable runs should be maintained along with the identifying number of each cable and its termination point. This is an invaluable tool when attempting to troubleshoot a connectivity problem (which will inevitably occur in the future).

Wide Area Networks

A communications capability linking two or more geographically dispersed computers is called a wide area network, or WAN. Historically libraries with multiple locations (and the Online Computer Library Center [OCLC]) created and maintained a private wide area network (typically using leased telephone lines) that connected all branch locations to a central site. Today, networks for library systems are often a sophisticated mix of connectivity, with a WAN still being used for building-to-building internal communications, and different methods used for internet connectivity (including using the WAN as a point for central distribution of internet access to the entire library system, using separate internet connections at each building, or a hybrid of both.)

Optical Fiber Connections

The library may be able to use a fiber-optic cable to connect to the internet. As almost every library is providing access to a WiFi network, and more and more users come to the library with their own devices, ensuring sufficient bandwidth to handle all of the various types of internet traffic (downloading of files, streaming audio and video, visiting websites that have a lot of images and graphics) has become an expected, minimum level of service for library users across the United States. For some libraries (especially rural libraries in areas of little or no internet connectivity options), this expectation can be a challenge.

In addition to cable television companies, some communities can lease a fiber-optic cable from other providers (which will likely reduce the monthly fee). And some states have programs to encourage libraries to use fiber-optic lines at reduced rates.

> **Tip!** The bandwidth connecting the library's LAN or WAN to the internet must be regularly monitored so that the productivity of the user is not reduced because of slow response rates. There is nothing quite like the frustration experienced by users while waiting for an internet site to respond. When network slowdowns occur, it's often due to a bottleneck created when the library's available bandwidth is exceeded by the demand brought by multiple simultaneous users (who might each be using high-bandwidth services like streaming media, video conferencing, and more). Should bandwidth capacity ever exceed 75 percent at any point during the day, then you will likely need to add bandwidth to ensure good response times in your network.

Internet Protocol

The internet has four basic layers, each with a distinct function to perform. The first layer is the physical link, such as copper wires, fiber-optic cables, cellular towers and local routers, over which data are sent. The second and third layers are governed by rules or protocols that define how the data is named and routed.

The Internet Protocol (IP) is the foundational communications protocol used by the internet for moving data contained within a packet originally developed by Vint Cerf and Bob Kahn in 1974.[2] In addition to the data, the packet contains an IP address so that data moves from the source host to the destination. The companion piece of the protocol is called the Transmission Control Program (TCP), which describes how data are transferred. The two protocols are often referred to as TCP/IP and were the basis for the first interconnection of networks that we now call the internet. The fourth layer defines various protocols so that data can be displayed using internet browsers and other application programs.

The Advanced Research Projects Agency funded the development of ARPANET, the precursor of the internet. Initially ARPANET connected the University of Utah with three California-based research centers, and by the end of 1970, there were a total of thirteen nodes (some nodes located on the East Coast). In 1982, ARPANET had about one hundred nodes, including some international locations. And by 1992, the internet was dominated by nodes located in the United States and was becoming a truly global network. By the year 2000, about half of all Americans were using the internet, and by mid-2018, more than 4.2 billion people around the world were using the internet.

The design of the internet is showing that it is more than forty-five years old, and its not uncommon for a user to receive a "buffering" message while watching a video being streamed. Experiments are underway to modify the

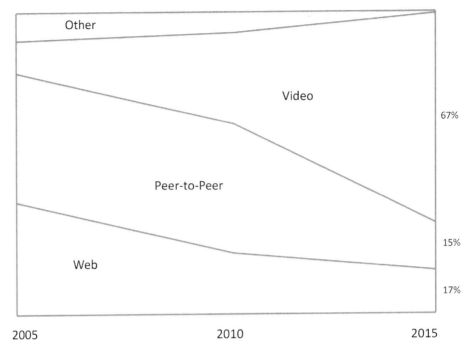

FIGURE 4.1. Proportion of Total US Internet Traffic

basic internet architecture so that it can more easily handle the volume of traffic that is expected to increase at least 20 percent per year for the foreseeable future.[3] And the type of traffic on the internet has been changing, especially over the last ten years, as noted in Figure 4.1. The amount of video streaming has been increasing at a steady pace so that in 2017 it accounts for two-thirds of all traffic in the United States—think Netflix, YouTube, Amazon, and providers of video content.

Infrastructure Implications

The ability for any library staff member to instantly connect to the library's ILS or the internet, when needed, has become such a commonplace event that we no longer think about it. Yet libraries are completely reliant on the networking and telecommunications infrastructure for their day-to-day operations, whether it be staff members performing their daily tasks, printing documents, searching the Web, or patrons using the library's online catalog or using the library's WiFi network.

Christine Borgman has noted that any infrastructure, whether it is an electrical grid, a railroad, the cell phone network, a highway system, or a computer-based telecommunications network, has several important characteristics:[4]

- Infrastructures are embedded in other structures, social arrangements, and technologies.

- Infrastructures are transparent and support tasks invisibly.

- Infrastructures are built on standards so complementary tools and services can interconnect.

- Infrastructures remain invisible until they fail to perform their function. Then everyone wants to know when the network will be operational again.

Planning for the sporadic types of communication transactions that occur with office applications and the library's ILS (and other applications), as well as the bandwidth-intensive audio and video streaming content traversing the LAN within the library, means that it is prudent to periodically reassess the available LAN bandwidth (and plan to upgrade the bandwidth to meet peak period demands—not average demand).

Summary

This chapter has provided a primer on telecommunications and technology options for LANS and WANs. The importance of having a stable and robust infrastructure to support the library's data communication needs can't be overemphasized. The next chapter focuses on standards and standards organizations and the increasing positive impacts standards have on libraries and their ability to deliver quality services to their customers.

Questions to Consider

- Has the library explored the need to change its LAN topology in the last year or two?

- Has the library assessed its current Ethernet capability and considered wiring upgrades to each computer workstation and other digital devices (printers, self-checkout machines, etc.) to ensure optimum performance?

- Is the operating performance of the library's WiFi network providing great service to customers? Are there "dead spots" that prevent WiFi access in some locations in the library?

- Does the library's system manager monitor the use of the WiFi network and the connection to the internet every month? At what point should a library consider that it needs to upgrade its connection to the internet?

- Does the library have separate, secure WiFi connections for patrons and staff use?

- Has your library considered the use of a location-based service? If not, why not?

Notes

1. Stephen Hawking, quoted on Twitter, January 2, 2016.

2. Vinton G. Cerf and Robert E. Kahn, "A Protocol for Packet Network Intercommunication," *IEEE Transactions on Communications* 22, no. 5 (May 1974): 637–48.

3. Glenn Edens and Glenn Scott, "The Packet Protector," *IEEE Spectrum* 4, no. 17 (April 2017): 42–48.

4. Christine Borgman, *From Gutenberg to the Global Information Infrastructure: Access to Information in the Networked World* (Cambridge, MA: MIT Press, 2000).

5
Proprietary Library Systems

The structures and practices of libraries will no more withstand
the technological changes we are facing than they
withstood the changes brought on by the printing press.
Change will not be instantaneous, but will be relentless.

—David W. Lewis[1]

Integrated Library Systems

An integrated library system (ILS) assists libraries in performing a majority of the processes associated with the acquisition and cataloging of materials; providing access to them via the library catalog; and the borrowing of materials (circulation). These systems have been around for some decades and have evolved and matured over time.

Originally, a plethora of vendors developed systems with a focus limited to a single module and then added modules over time. Computer Library Systems Inc. (CLSI) and DataPhase, early library automation pioneers, focused on circulation control that was marketed to public libraries. The first product Dynix and Innovative Interfaces developed was an interface between the Online Computer Library Catalog (OCLC) system and the CLSI circulation control system. Innovative Interfaces then focused on developing acquisitions and serials control modules before slowly moving to develop other modules that came to be known as an integrated library system. So, from humble beginnings, the concept of an ILS slowly evolved rather than being a grand plan from the outset.

> For the past 25 years, OPACs [online public access catalogs] have been at the center of the library world. That era is over. Ask any patron how many times a week he uses an OPAC and how many times a week he uses a Web search engine. The answer to that question should scare us.[2]

An ILS can be considered to encompass the following modules:

- Acquisitions
- Serials control
- Cataloging
- Circulation control
- Online catalog

An ILS provides a significant amount of flexibility in terms of a library choosing to use (or ignore) a variety of policies and parameters that are built into the software in order to meet the needs of all types of libraries, large and small. The development of all this flexibility means that the underlying software code is large and complex and represents a significant investment in terms of financial resources and manpower. And although many libraries, especially academic libraries will be interested in the next generation system, an ILS system will serve the needs of many libraries (of various types and sizes) for many years to come. The dominant focus of the workflow of all of the modules within an ILS is the handling of physical materials within the library's collections, principally by technical services staff members.

The growth of the ILS marketplace has slowed as it has matured, but it is still fairly active in terms of new worldwide sales and total installations, as shown in Table 5.1.

Originally ILS vendors provided both the hardware and software as a "turnkey" solution; however, as hardware became a commodity, libraries often purchased the license for the software and provided their own servers and other necessary hardware. The annual software maintenance agreement ensured that the vendor fixed any problems (bugs) that might have occurred, and provided updates (containing both fixes to the bugs as well as system enhancements). Until 2010 or so, the majority of ILS systems were installed on servers located either in the library itself or on servers located in the Information Technology department on campus or in city hall.

Over time, libraries began to embrace digital technologies, as the internet expanded, and content was increasingly only available in digital form. Vendors developed new systems such as an electronic resource management system (ERMS), a repository, an authentication system, a federated search system, a third-party discovery system, and more. These stand-alone silos often came from multiple vendors and required a great deal of staff time and expertise to manage and migrate data from one system to another.

An ERMS, sometimes called a digital collection management system, provides the tools to manage the licensing, rather than the purchasing, of electronic content—electronic journals and other digital content. An institutional repository (IR) is an online archive for collecting, preserving, and providing access to the intellectual output of an organization. Materials that might be added to an institutional repository include eBooks, journal articles, conference presentations, chapters contributed to a book, research reports, course notes, data sets, and so much more. Some of the more popular institutional repository software includes DSpace, EPrints, Digital Commons, and Fedora Commons, among other options.

Marketplace Dynamics

One of the marketplace realities is that vendors realized it was less expensive to acquire a competitor than it was to try to acquire the customers

TABLE 5.1. Worldwide ILS Sales and Installations

		2012	2013	2014	2015	2016	2017	2018	Total Systems
Auto-graphics	VERSO	19	17	21	5	7	23	4	529
Biblionix	Apollo	80	87	49	63	65	56	58	719
Book systems	Atrium	157	158	164	165	147	125	145	4,575
Civica	Spydus	0	0	0	0	0	64	105	351
Infovision software	Evolve	11	8	5	7	4	0	16	147
Ex Libris	Aleph	26	25	25	20	10	6	3	2,401
Ex Libris	Alma*	17	31	43	88	132	116	115	1,543
Innovative interfaces	Millennium	30	6	0	0	0	0	0	358
Innovative interfaces	Polaris	30	30	15	13	16	2	0	557
Innovative interfaces	Sierra	117	113	123	90	82	31	0	931
Innovative interfaces	Virtua	14	7	5	3	0	0	0	225
Library Corporation	Library Solution	13	17	65	0	12	11	14	766
Library Corporation	CARL-X	1	2	0	0	3	6	1	114
OCLC	WMS*	163	92	79	68	83	52	53	565
SirsiDynix	Symphony	122	104	118	122	143	90	107	2,498
SirsiDynix	Horizon	1	9	13	15	13	10	17	879
SirsiDynix	EOS	58	70	58	52	31	28	28	1,045
Totals		**859**	**776**	**783**	**711**	**748**	**620**	**666**	**18,203**

* Library Services Platform.
Note: Data as of April 2019.
Source: Data found at https://librarytechnology.org/products/sales/. Created by author.

of a competitor, one by one, over time. Thus, a significant market consolidation occurred in the early 2000s. Beginning with the merger of the two dominant vendors of Sirsi (which had previously purchased Data Research Associates) and Dynix in 2005, the consolidation has continued with Proquest's purchase of Ex Libris and Innovative Interface's purchase of VTLS and Polaris.

The implications of this marketplace consolidation is that there are fewer options available to a library or a consortia of libraries, making it more difficult to work with a vendor who is responsive to the needs of its customers. With fewer options in the marketplace, libraries must become much more astute in picking their technology-based partners. And a library and its automation vendor(s) truly are in a partnership, as the resulting automated system must serve library customers 24/7—without exception or interruption. With mergers and consolidations of ILS vendors, it's true that there is less choice in the marketplace than in years past. However, libraries should still strive to be good consumers with the choices that are available, and ask for things that they need in the ever-changing worlds of technology and public service.

The library technology marketplace is fairly large, with worldwide revenues of about $770 million for library automation vendors (in 2012) and aggregate revenues of about $1.8 billion when the radio-frequency identification and self-service products are included.[3] Worldwide revenues for the aggregate marketplace are estimated to be in the $2 billion range. Even so, when compared to the other technology market sectors (with the so-called "top five companies"—Apple, Amazon, Facebook, Microsoft, and Alphabet—reportedly reaching $3 trillion aggregate value in 2018), in the grand scheme of things, the library market can be considered a niche.[4]

> **Tip!** Matthew Reidsma's book *Customizing Vendor Systems for Better User Services* provides a wealth of practical suggestions of how to work with the tools provided by a vendor to customize and improve on a vendor's standard offering. Reidsma gives examples of specific programming scripts and programs using the vendor-provided APIs and other web services.[5]

Library Services Platforms

As libraries began to embrace various types of eResources (eBooks, eJournals, digitized content in repositories, etc.), librarians found that the core feature set of ILSs did not provide the functionality needed to manage these eResources. Thus, most vendors worked to develop what came to be known as electronic resource management systems (ERMSs), digital collection management systems, digital asset management systems (DAMSs), eBook platforms, link resolvers, and other types of systems to help manage electronic content, resulting in very complicated and time-consuming workflows. And managing each of these automated silo systems—and attempting to move data from one system to another or import vendor-provided bibliographic data and other types of records—also commanded a significant amount of time and effort.

Marshall Breeding proposed the term *library services platform* (LSP) in 2011 that would encompass a new or next-generation system that would provide the functionality to support both traditional physical library collections as well as the burgeoning eResources that libraries wanted to handle.[6] This term, embraced by the marketplace, avoided the various and different names each of the vendors attempted to use in an effort to differentiate their next-generation products and services. In the United Kingdom, Ken Chad (a well-known library technology consultant) has called an LSP a "library management platform." In some cases, an LSP may be referred to as a unified resource management system.

In essence, a library services platform (LSP) consolidates the workflows surrounding the management of print and electronic materials into a single solution, taking advantage of shared knowledge data files, multiple simplified workflows, and improved efficiencies, as shown in Figure 5.1. A library services platform can be characterized by the following:

- Multitenant application
- Software as a Service (SaaS)—also known as a cloud-based service

- Web-based interface
- Interoperability with other applications
- Multiple metadata formats
- Multiple workflows
- Knowledge bases
- Discovery services.

A multitenant application serves multiple individuals or organizations through a single instance of the underlying software. The majority of the data are kept separate for each organization, although some data files, often called knowledge bases, may be shared for the benefit of all. The value of multitenant platforms is that they can support really large-scale services, for example, Amazon, Gmail, Facebook, and so forth.

In the library world, multitenant platforms include the majority of eResource products (Elsevier, Emerald, Sage, Taylor & Francis, and a host of others), OCLC's WorldCat, discovery services (EBSCO Discovery Service, Summon, Primo Central), and library service platforms (Ex Libris Alma and OCLC WorldShare Management Services, among others).

The value of multitenant services for the vendor means that routine system maintenance, installation of new software releases, and bug patches can be done once and are applied for all customers at the same time. Typically this means that software releases occur much more frequently, and the

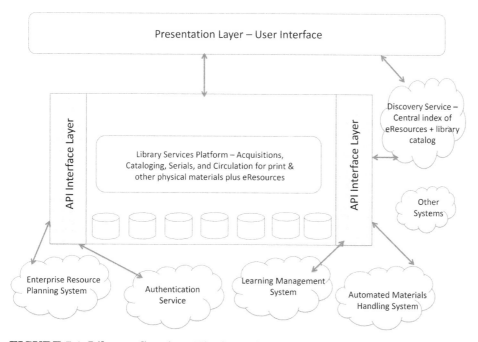

FIGURE 5.1. Library Services Platform Architecture
Source: Adapted from Marshall Breeding's Library Automation Marketplace 2/3/25 Innovative Interfaces Internal Meeting, https://slideplayer.com/slide /6653757/ (slide 24/89).

vendor needs fewer programmers and technical personnel to maintain a single instance of the software, rather than having to distribute or update hundreds or thousands of instances of the software. Clearly a multitenant platform requires that the servers be located in one or more server farms located in the cloud.

Software as a service (SaaS) is a service in which the software is licensed on a subscription basis and is centrally hosted rather than the software being hosted in a server located on the customer's premises. Using a web browser, users access SaaS applications. Customer relationship management (CRM), enterprise resource planning (ERP), computer-aided design (CAD) software, payroll, accounting, and many other applications are now typically provided using the SaaS model.

Libraries require fewer technology skilled personnel when using software as a service (SaaS), as the vendor has assumed responsibility for the hosting and maintenance of the systems.

A web-based interface is used by library services platforms, so no local software is needed in order that staff and patrons may interact with the system. One of the obvious implications of this arrangement is that the library's internet bandwidth must be sufficiently fast to handle both the volume of transactions as well as the necessary one- to two-second response time for each transaction. LSPs are browser agnostic, so any web browser will work just fine.

Interoperability allows the library services platform to interact with a campus ERP system, learning management systems, and student record management systems, among other types of systems. This interaction is facilitated through the use of an application programming interface (API) for instant transactions rather than relying on older methods such as the batch exchange of records. At the beginning of each semester, the library system can receive updated student registration information from the registrar's system. The library services platform can exchange financial transaction information with the parent organization's accounting system as well as other necessary systems.

Multiple metadata formats are supported by the library services platform so that bibliographic or authority data (MARC and other variations) for physical items, Dublin Core for digitized content, or XML-based records for eBooks and eResources can be imported and managed by library staff. New and emerging formats such as BIBFRAME and linked data can be provided as these new standards are finalized and adopted by the library community.

Multiple workflow processes will support multiple metadata formats, using the tools provided by the LSP. This means that workflow optimized for the consideration and licensing of eResources will be different from the workflows that are used to acquire, manage, and provide access to physical materials. Although the software and the user interface for digital and physical materials will be different (to accomplish different tasks), the library will achieve maximum benefits if it redesigns all existing processes and procedures so that these processes complement the capabilities provided by the software.

Knowledge bases that will benefit all libraries can be created once and shared with each customer library. For example, eResource suppliers can provide access to journal article metadata repositories, as well as the journals that are included in various subscription packages provided by the publisher or aggregator. In addition, the tracking of the printing and distribution of print journals and newspapers can be shared by each customer library, thereby reducing the need to manually track the receiving of individual issues.

Discovery services are integrated into the library services platform rather than using the traditional library online catalog as the primary user interface. Although the LSP vendor may likely provide its own discovery service, a library can choose to use another discovery service using the APIs provided by and exposed by the two vendors.

Maturing LSP Marketplace

The development of a library service platform is not for the faint of heart. An LSP, by its very design, is large and complicated and requires a considerable development effort over several years. Carl Grant has estimated that two of the LSP vendors have spent 500 person-years of programming effort to develop their respective products.[7]

The library services platform products have been in the marketplace for several years, and by the beginning of 2019, more than a thousand libraries had selected and implemented an LSP product, as shown in Table 5.2. The dominant vendor, particularly among larger academic libraries, is Ex Libris's Alma, with about 65 percent share of the market.

Given the large number of libraries that have implemented and are using an LSP product, the risk for future libraries to select this option is fairly low—provided sufficient attention is paid to the migration from the old to the new system.

> **Tip!** You can stay current about developments in the ILS and LSP marketplace by reviewing the annual articles about library automation that are published each year in *American Libraries* and *Library Journal*. Additional information, including the results from the Annual Library Automation Perceptions survey, may be found at http://libraries.org.
>
> In addition, check *Library Technology Reports* for more current information about library systems and services for more up-to-date information about ILS and LSPs.[8]

LSP Products

The major LSP products include Alma and WorldShare.

Ex Libris Alma—Ex Libris decided to start afresh and developed its LSP-based product Alma from scratch, using a multitenant architecture.

TABLE 5.2. Worldwide Library Services Platform Sales and Installations

Company	System	2011	2012	2013	2014	2015	2016	Total Installed
Ex Libris	Alma	24	17	31	43	234	203	829
OCLC	WorldShare	184	163	92	79	68	83	440
	Totals	208	180	123	122	302	286	1,269

Source: Data found at https://librarytechnology.org/products/sales/. Created by author.

Alma provides the tools so a library can manage both print and electronic resources. Data centers for Alma are located in the Netherlands, Singapore, and the United States. Boston College was the first US library to place Alma in production in 2012, and Alma is now in more than 800 libraries.

OCLC WorldShare Management System—OCLC decided to develop WorldShare using new software and multitenant architecture. The first WorldShare system became operational in 2011, and since then additional libraries (about three-fourths of WorldShare customers are academic libraries) have implemented this LSP.

Two other products, Innovative Interfaces Sierra and SirsiDynix's Blue Cloud, can be classified as hybrid products:

Innovative Interfaces Sierra—Sierra uses a new technology platform, but rather than starting afresh, Innovative migrated the functionality and features of Millennium into Sierra. Sierra provides a set of RESTful (representational state transfer web services) APIs so that other systems can interact with it. Sierra provides access to its data, which are stored in a PostgreSQL relational database management system. Rather than using modules for circulation, acquisitions, and so forth in an ILS, Sierra offers staff members access to all tools (to which they are entitled). It should be noted that Sierra is not based on a multitenant architecture, so software can be installed locally or hosted by the vendor.

SirsiDynix BLUEcloud—The BLUEcloud LSP solution is a hybrid solution in that a library must be using either a Symphony or Horizon ILS product in order to implement some of the cloud-based components. The cloud-based multitenant architecture components include eResource Central, BookMyne mobile platform, BLUEcloud Circulation, and BLUEcloud Cataloging.

Tip! Carl Grant has a number of interesting blog posts about the development of library services platform products that make for interesting and thought-provoking reading. Check them out.[9]

Table 5.3 offers a summary of the differences between an ILS and an LSP from several different perspectives. Clearly, both ILS and LSPs

TABLE 5.3. Comparing ILS and LSP Systems

Perspective	*Integrated Library System*	*Library Services Platform*
Resources	Physical	Physical, electronic
Technology	Server-based, multiple instances	Multi-tenant single instance
Server location	Library, hosted by vendor	Cloud-based SaaS
Staff interface	Desktop GUI	Browser-based
Patron interface	Browser-based	Browser-based
Procurement model	Purchase	License

Source: Adapted from Marshall Breeding's Library Automation Marketplace 2/3/25. Innovative Interfaces Internal Meeting, https://slideplayer.com/slide/6653757/ (slide 13/89).

will continue to be an active part of the library marketplace for many years to come.

Summary

Librarians have been advocating for some time the notion that each of their automated systems should be open to some degree so that one system could communicate with another—this is called interoperability. At a minimum, interoperability should include a robust set of API tools to facilitate data interchange. And although LSP vendors have exposed their APIs and even created a developer network to encourage third-party development, these efforts have gained little traction so far. As Ken Chad has noted,

> Solutions are moving to the Cloud but aren't really platforms. It is a platform-based ecosystem model that will be the "next generation" in library automation. The promise for libraries is a more flexible and cost-effective solution and for users a more improved user experience.[10]

Questions to Consider

- What are the modules that make up a standard integrated library system?

- What differentiates an electronic resource management system from an ILS serials control module?

- Is your library a candidate for a library services platform (LSP)? If you think so, what are the likely costs, and how much time would be needed to transition to a new system?

- Can you articulate the potential benefits for the library customer if the library switches to an LSP?

- Has your library considered joining a consortium to share an automated system? If not, consider preparing an analysis comparing the costs and benefits of such a move.

- Has your library considered moving its automated system to the cloud? Can you articulate the benefits of moving to the cloud?

- Has your library management team had a discussion about the topic "discovery happens elsewhere"?

Notes

1. David W. Lewis, *A Model for Academic Libraries 2005 to 2025*, Paper presented at Visions of Change Conference, California State University at Sacramento, January 26, 2007.

2. Stuart Weibel, quoted in Ron Chepesiuk, "Organizing the Internet: The 'Core' of the Challenge," *American Libraries* 31, no. 1 (January 1999): 59–63.

3. Marshall Breeding, "Automation Marketplace 2013: The Rush to Innovate," *Library Journal*, April 2, 2013, https://www.libraryjournal.com/?detailStory =automation-marketplace-2013-the-rush-to-innovate.

4. Alex Wilhelm, "Tech's 5 Biggest Players Now Worth $3 Trillion," *Tech Crunch*, March 2017, https://techcrunch.com/2017/07/19/techs-5-biggest-players-now -worth-3-trillion/.

5. Matthews Reidsma, *Customizing Vendor Systems for Better User Services: The Innovative Librarian's Guide* (Santa Barbara, CA: Libraries Unlimited, 2016).

6. Marshall Breeding, "Smarter Libraries through Technology: The Beginning of the End of ILS in Academic Libraries," *Smart Libraries Newsletter* 31, no. 8 (August 2011): 1–2.

7. Carl Grant, "FOLIO, Acronym for 'Future of Libraries Is Open'? I'd suggest 'Fantasy of Librarians Inflamed by Organization,'" *Thoughts from Carl Grant* (blog), November 28, 2016, http://thoughts.care-affiliates.com.

8. For example, consider Marshall Breeding, "Library Services Platform: A Maturing Genre of Products," *Library Technology Reports* 51, no. 4 (May/June 2015).

9. Visit *Thoughts from Carl Grant* (blog), http://thoughts.care-affiliates.com: "Impressions of the New Library Service Platforms—Part 1," October 22, 2012; "Impressions of the New Library Service Platforms—Part 2—Sierra by Innovative," October 24, 2012; "Impressions of the New Library Service Platforms—Part 3—Intota by Serials Solutions," October 29, 2012; "Impressions of the New Library Service Platforms—Part 4—WorldShare Management Services by OCLC," November 5, 2012; "Impressions of the New Library Service Platforms—Part 5—OLE by Kuali," November 8, 2012; "Impressions of the New Library Service Platforms—Part 6—Alma by Ex Libris," November 14, 2012; "Impressions of the New Library Service Platforms—Part 6a—Ex Libris & Golden Gate Capital," November 16, 2012; "Impressions of the New Library Service Platforms—Part 1," October 22, 2012; and "Impressions of the New Library Service Platforms—Part 7—Open Skies by VTLS," November 26, 2012.

10. Ken Chad, "Rethinking the Library Services Platform," Higher Education Library Technology Briefing Paper, January 2016, http://www.kenchadconsulting .com/publications/.

6
Open Source Systems

Many users of the GNU/Linux system
will not have heard the ideas of free software.
They will not be aware that we have ideas,
that a system exists because of ethical ideals,
which were omitted from ideas associated with the term "open source."
—Richard Stallman[1]

An open system, by design, contrasts sharply with solutions designed to be proprietary. The idea is that any organization will be able to "mix and match" a combination of components and deliver services that cross vendors' offerings. For example, a library might implement a couple of integrated library system (ILS) modules from one of the open source options and implement another two to three modules from another vendor while using yet another vendor's Discovery Service because it can be easily customized to provide the look and feel the library wants. Alternatively, the library may use an open source software product developed by another library or develop one or more components themselves. Clearly, such an approach requires an experienced team of talented individuals to provide the necessary integration to make this approach work well.

The issue and importance of standards are addressed in greater detail in a subsequent chapter. However, it is important to note that industry standards can embrace standards that are vendor neutral (e.g., TCP/IP as well as proprietary products such as Microsoft Office, Oracle's RDBMS, etc.). Although the prospect of building open systems (by using a mix-and-match approach) is attractive, care must be taken when open systems built on proprietary products result in limiting the library's flexibility—the use of proprietary products, even market-leading proprietary products, locks the library in to the vendor). Aside from the seemingly yearly price increases for support licenses for these products, the library system vendor or library must continually upgrade to the latest release of *both* open and proprietary products.

For example, if the system is using an Oracle database or a licensed search engine, the library (or its vendor) must stay current with the latest release of these products, as most vendors of licensed software products only support an earlier release of its product for a short period of time.

As libraries move to replace their older systems with the next-generation library services platform (LSP), the need to provide a wide range of services to their patrons means that libraries will want systems that are more open and interoperable with other technology systems that are also undergoing constant change. Libraries may want systems that can interface with a campus or parent organization's accounting system, purchasing system, student registration system, and so forth. Indeed, some libraries will want to be able to select one portion of a system from Vendor A and another portion from Vendor B and have the two systems "talk" to each other (be able to exchange a variety of data).

It is increasingly clear that for most organizations Extensive Markup Language (XML) will be the glue that binds two or more systems together. XML, which was designed specifically for web documents, is a smaller version of the older and more intricate Standard Generalized Markup Language (SGML). XML allows organizations to define, transmit, validate, and interpret data between applications and databases. XML's strength is that it provides structure to the data, yet it is not a language or a presentation system. XML separates the data themselves from how the data are displayed or used in an application. Thus, the data can then be more easily organized, programmed, edited, and exchanged between websites, applications, and devices. XML and its associated document type definition (DTD) will play an important role in exchanging information between applications of interest to libraries.

A standardized way of describing XML document structures and adding data types to XML data fields are defined using an XML Schema Definition (XSD). The XSD standard facilitates cross-organizational document exchange and data verification. Tools for converting XML DTDs to XSD assist the information exchange. The purpose of an XML Schema is to define the building blocks of an XML document:

- The elements and attributes that can appear in a document
- The number of (and order of) various elements
- Data types for elements and attributes
- Default and fixed values for elements and attributes

XML Query provides the capabilities to create queries on collections of XML files that might contain unstructured data (e.g., documents and web pages). XML Query provides a set of searching capabilities that is comparable to those found with Structured Query Language (SQL) used when searching a relational database management system (RDBMS).

Open Source Software

In real open source,
you have the right to control your own destiny.

—Linus Torvalds[2]

After the personal computer was introduced in the early 1980s, many programmers made their programs available in one of two ways: freeware and shareware.

> **Freeware** were programs that were available without charge and could be freely distributed to friends, relatives, coworkers, and others, but could not be modified. The source code is *not* included with the freeware software. If a problem developed with the freeware software, the user could wait for an update or choose another software application to replace the freeware.

> **Shareware** was software that could also be distributed freely. However, the developer typically placed a message within the program telling users that if they liked the program and used it on a regular basis, they should send a suggested contribution to the software developer. This allowed the software developer to earn a living and, in most cases, to provide support to customers who experienced a problem. Shareware is seldom accompanied by the source code and is not free software.

The concept of open source software is markedly different from other models. For some, especially those managing high-stakes systems such as the ILS, it can simultaneously be appealing and frightening to consider. Open software allows programmers to read, modify, and redistribute the source code and, as such, the software becomes a growing and evolving organism. Any number of people can fix bugs, adapt it to better meet their needs, or improve it and then share their efforts with a larger community of interested parties. Because any number of people can be involved in making enhancements, the speed with which this open software evolves and improves can be quite astonishing. Good open source software provides feedback to contributors and is thus similar to the peer review process used to ensure quality control of the scholarly communication process.

Yet, if the source code is open, then what should a library do if the software needs fixing, but no one on the staff has the talent to do so? This concern illustrates what can be a frightening aspect of open source software.

Systems built on open standards have been gaining momentum for the last 25 years, especially among those in the technical culture involved in building the internet and the World Wide Web. Thus, anyone sending and receiving emails or visiting websites is likely using open source software as well as software based on standards. In fact, there is a plethora of open or standards-based software involved in all of the possible activities on the internet.

The Open Source Initiative has developed a definition of open source that includes the following elements:

- **Free redistribution**—Open source software can be sold or given away and does not require a royalty or other fee.

- **Source code**—The program's source code and compiled code should be easily accessible, preferably by downloading it from the internet. Intentionally obfuscating source code is a no-no.

- **Derived works**—Modifications and derived works must be allowed, and these modifications can be freely distributed.

- **The integrity of the author's source code**—The license can require that modifications be uniquely identified and kept separate from the original base software.

- **No discrimination against persons or groups**.

- **No discrimination against fields of endeavor**—The type of organization or how the software would be used cannot restrict use of an open source program.

- **Distribution of license**—Additional licensees are not required as the software is redistributed.

- **License must not be specific to a product**—Use of an open source program cannot be dependent on use of other software.

- **License must not contaminate other software**—The licensee of open source software cannot place restrictions on other software.

A Creative Commons (CC) license provides public copyright licenses that enable free distribution of content based on one of several possible licenses. CC licenses are based on a combination of four conditions:

- Attribution (BY)

- Share-alike (SA)

- Noncommercial (NC)

- No derivative works (ND).

Thus, the seven possible CC licenses include:

- CC0   No restrictions
- BY   Attribution only
- BY-SA   Attribution + Share Alike
- BY-NC   Attribution + Noncommercial
- BY-ND   Attribution + No Derivatives
- BY-NC-SA   Attribution + Noncommercial + Share Alike
- BY-NC-ND   Attribution + Noncommercial + No Derivatives

If the source code is openly available for downloading, without charge, it is typically called open source software. Open source software, sometimes called free software, means that an individual is free to look at and modify the source code. And in this case, "free" is the also same as a "free kitten"—the software must be fed, cared for, and cleaned up after. Most open source software is distributed under a public copyright license that balances the traditional "all rights reserved" setting that copyright law establishes and the desire to share, distribute, edit, remix, and build on while remaining within the boundaries of copyright law.

Contributors to an open source product must earn the trust of those who are already a part of the community. The code submitted by a contributor must be good in the sense that it does what it is designed to do, is efficient, and does not introduce errors into other areas of the program. Open source ILS products are gaining functionality at a fairly rapid pace, making them a viable option for large libraries or a consortium of libraries.

Open source software is readily available for a great many purposes. A recent Gartner survey found that more than half of all commercial firms are using some open source software. Many organizations have found that open source software has higher quality and reliability as well as more flexibility, and assists in preventing vendor lock-in. Collaboration, transparency, meritocracy, generosity, proponents of standards, and innovation characterize most open source communities.

Although a great deal of open source software is available, these are perhaps the most frequently used open source software:

- **Linux**—a version of a computer operating system called Unix that runs on a variety of servers and desktop computers.

- **Apache**—Web server software. Apache controls the majority of the web server marketplace, and programmers worldwide work together on Apache so that it is continually improved. Any problems, "bugs" in programming lingo, are quickly corrected and then shared with all Apache users.

- **MySQL**—a relational database management system (SQL stands for Structured Query Language) that is used for a variety of software applications and websites.

- **Hypertext Preprocessor (PHP)**—a web development scripting language that is often used in conjunction with MySQL.

- **Perl**—another popular programming language.

These open source software components are so frequently used that the acronym LAMP is often used as a shorthand by programmers and web developers [L = Linux; A = Apache; M = MySQL; P = PHP, Perl] to identify the underlying foundation of their system.

The more active the user community is in suggesting ideas, finding bugs, contributing code, and sponsoring development, the more dynamic the resulting software can be. Open source software, not surprisingly, relies on common and open standards in order to assist with the integration and interoperability with other systems.

Some better-known open source software products include Linux, Firefox, and Apache. A range of other open source products and projects is shown in Table 6.1. The success of these products demonstrates that it is possible for some open source software projects to achieve "commercial quality."

Unless there is a large cadre of programmers willing to take on a large project, the utility of the source code probably declines with the size of the computer program. For the individual programmer, a computer program above a certain size will become incomprehensible.

To illustrate the potential of open source software, consider the success of Linux (pronounced "LYNN–ucks"). Linus Torvalds started this operating system variant of Unix while he was a student at the University of Helsinki in 1991 and, at the beginning of 2019, had more than 17.8 million lines of code and 3.3 million lines of comments in the kernel.[3] In a relatively short time, Linux has achieved real acceptance in the market because:

- It is trusted in mission critical environments.

- It's a best-of-breed variant of Unix that outperforms other commercial versions of Unix.

TABLE 6.1. Open Source Software Products

Type of Software	Products
Operating systems	Linux (GNU/Linux) Free BSD (Berkeley Standard Distribution) Open BSD NetBSD GNU/Hurd
Utilities	GNU Utilities Multi Router Traffic Grapher (MRTG) Snort intrusion detection system Junkbuster Majordomo Cron Sendmail
Languages	GNU C/C++ Perl Python Tel
Windowing Systems	X Window System
Desktop environment	GNOME (GNU Network Object Model Environment) KDE (K Desktop Environment) GNUStep Xfce
Web browser	Firefox Mozilla
Office suites	Open Office K Office
Productivity applications	ABI Word GNU IMAGE Manipulation program Jabber instant messaging
Server-type software	Samba Apache PhP
Relational database management	MySQL PostgreSQL
Object-oriented database	Zope
Library applications	Free reserves (www.lib.edu/san/freereserves) Prospero (document delivery module that complements Ariel) Jake (a journal finding aid)

- Not everything is compiled as the user is able to configure only what is needed.
- Modules are dynamically loaded when needed from the thousands available.
- Over 10,000 developers from more than 1,000 companies have contributed to the kernel over the last ten years.

- It is the only Unix operating system to gain market share in recent years.

- New versions of Linux can appear quite quickly to respond to a particular security threat or bug (typically every sixty to seventy days and involving more than 10,000 changes or patches).

Factors Influencing Open Source Software

A number of factors have an impact on the development of open source software. Among these are the following:

Piracy—Obviously, many individuals engage in the piracy of copy-protected and closed source software. For some that engage in piracy, it is the price of a product that encourages them to get it for free. For others (in the hacker community), it is the challenge to defeat the copy protection technology of a software program that offers a thrill and a sense of accomplishment. Given that piracy on the internet is a fact of life, this situation can be leveraged by simply giving away software in order to capture a dominant share of the market. This is the approach that was employed by Netscape and subsequently followed by Microsoft when they distributed their respective web browsers for free.

According to Conner and Rumelt, if a firm chooses to protect its software, profits will fall depending on the success of the pirates. The stigma of stealing falls as the number of pirates increase, lowering costs for all pirates.[4] Yet, the utility of the software increases as the number of paying customers and pirates increases. If there is a viable option to stealing (i.e., if there is an open source competing product), then pirates and paying customers will move away from the copy-protected software to the free software. Thus, Conner and Rumelt suggest making the price of the software free and consequently capturing the dominant share of the market.

With a large market comes the demand for additional complementary software and services. Marc Andreesen, one of the founders of Netscape, suggests that "If you get ubiquity, you get a lot of options . . . One of the fundamental lessons is that market share now equals revenue later. With dominant market share you can just plain win."[5]

Network connections—The existence of the internet facilitates the network of programmers that can come together to work on an open source software project. And the programmers can be individuals interested in the "techie" side of things, users of the software who are willing to invest in the project as well as selected businesses who may see their participation as leading to an economic gain. And the larger the network of participation, the fewer the bugs because more eyes are examining the source code. The proponents claim that the resulting software is best of breed because the developers and customers who are participating in the project will focus their efforts on what works well.

Thus, the internet is used to spread an open source program, and is used to maintain and improve the base source code. To some extent, the free distribution of open source software and its continuing enhancement is similar to a "gift culture" where members of the society compete by giving things away.[6] Among the participating programmers, there is both collaboration as well as competition that works to improve the software in a relatively short period of time. Those whose efforts move the project ahead ignore programmers who do not make a contribution.

An examination of the contributions of programmers to Linux is revealing. For some, the potential of many people contributing to a code base suggests images of rooms of programmers hacking away—or even a global network of dozens of people working from coffee shops, basements, coworking spaces, and apartments. According to one study, the vast majority of open source developers only work on one or two computer programs, while only four developers had made more than 20 contributions.[7] Clearly the contributions of developers to Linux are quite broad based, with slightly more than one-third being European and nearly one-fourth of the developers working for a commercial firm.

For-Profit Firms Support Open Source Software

Any automated library system, regardless of whether the software is developed and maintained by a commercial firm or if the software is open source, must offer the features that allow a library to operate efficiently, be scalable so that large libraries or a consortium of libraries can use the system, and consistently operate in a reliable manner (minimize downtime).

Initially, many libraries that embraced open source did so based on philosophical grounds, but lately libraries are basing their decisions on sound objective criteria.[8] Concerns about choosing to use the open source option for any library or group of libraries include the time, resources, and staff expertise needed in order to effect a successful implementation of the new system. Other concerns typically raised by a library include the functionality and usability of the software, the scalability of an open source ILS system, its ability to interoperate with other automated systems, and its ability to download and share records with other libraries.[9] Vendors of proprietary ILS systems, not surprisingly, have questioned the viability of open source ILS system software.[10] A comparison of the Evergreen system compared to the SirsiDynix Horizon system is available.[11]

A real challenge for any open source product is to identify an organization or group of individuals who will coordinate and guide the many different versions of the software and approve bug fixes (or patches) that have been submitted by an individual programmer or a company. The challenge is to funnel back fixes and enhancements so that the broader community of existing and new users can benefit. The coordinating group or organization takes on the role of vetting software submissions and creating new releases of the software. Not surprisingly, the vast majority of system enhancements are made by a small group of devoted programmers.

Because of the active involvement of the many open sources customers, the experiences and solutions to problems can be quickly shared should a library experience a problem. There are active email message boards as well as blogs and wikis pertaining to each open source product.

Organizations that wish to rely on open source software have three choices that they can make. They can hire one or more programmers; note that talented programmers are expensive and in demand. Second, they can band together with other libraries using the software. And third, they can contract with a third-party open source commercial support vendor. The commercial open source vendors are the primary reason for the significant growth in the number of libraries choosing to use open source ILS systems.

Usually three or more fast servers are employed: one for Apache (the core web server software), one for MySQL (to store the library records), and one for the application software.

The services commercial open source vendors provide are as follows:

- **System installation**—Aside from configuring the multiple servers, installing the ILS software also entails installing and integrating a number of software components. Some of these components include the operating system, a database system, and other components.

- **Migration assistance**—The knowledge needed to map the data structure from an existing system to a new system is considerable. Once mapped, the data in each system needs to be migrated (tested and then moved), and this process can be time-consuming and problematic. This data migration assistance is perhaps the most important activity that a commercial vendor provides to a library that is embracing open source for the first time.

- **Software support**—Using free software does not mean having to forgo commercial support. The open source ILS vendors provide a demonstrated ability to provide email and telephone support to "customers" who choose free software. This means that the library customer knows what the annual support costs will be and that any software bugs will be fixed (hopefully quickly).

- **Software development**—Some libraries are willing to pay an open source vendor to develop a specific feature, component, or module (enhancements) that they feel are important and thus are willing to pay to get the work done. These enhancements are then shared with other libraries in the next general release of the software. These sponsored development activities contribute to the creation of a much more robust product that will appeal to an even greater number of libraries.

- **Training**—Knowledgeable vendor staff members can provide new library customer training on how to use the new open source ILS system. Training can be provided remotely using internet tools, or the vendor staff member can visit the library for face-to-face training (the more expensive option).

- **System hosting**—Rather than placing the server in the library or a city/county IT department, the server may be located in a "server farm" located in the cloud provided by a commercial vendor. The vendor is responsible for system backups, installation of software upgrades, and resolving any hardware problems that may arise. This hosting of servers in remote locations has come to be called software as a service, or SaaS. Typically the servers are located in a third-party commercial hosting company with hundreds of other servers.

> **Tip!** If you have a moment, check out the entertaining "Open Source ILS Song" on YouTube (available at http://www.youtube.com/watch?v=BSHBzd9ftDE).

Those involved in the open source software movement have recognized that for-profit firms need to be involved, especially if the open source product is to reach a broader market. A lot of businesses and organizations want to know that they can count on a firm to provide support, training, and other implementation assistance rather than attempting to hire and retain knowledgeable programmers themselves. In reality, the open source industry is a crucial alliance between developers, for-profit firms and the users. And as more users adopt the use of Linux, then a need for complementary products increases fueling the continuing development of the core product as well as the complementary ones.

Interestingly enough, the for-profit firm must be able to attract and retain knowledgeable programmers who at one level want to participate in continuing to enhance and improve on the open source software while also agreeing to work for a for-profit firm. Historically there has been considerable tension between for-profit firms and programmers who participate in open source software projects.

Reasons to Open Source

There are several reasons why open source software might be attractive to those involved with its development. Among these are the following:

- **Stretching a budget**—Those involved in the development of Apache, a web server, were programmers primarily from small independent internet service providers (ISPs). By banding together and working to develop an open source product, they were able to avoid paying operating system license fees. Starting with software originally developed at the National Center Supercomputing Applications, additional patches were added (thus, it was called *a patchy server*, or Apache). Some industry analysts suggest that the Apache web server is used by more than 50 percent of all websites in the world.

- **Loss leader/market dominance**—A company might be interested in distributing open source software for free in order to capture a dominant share of the market. For example, this is the strategy that both Netscape and Microsoft employed to distribute their respective web browsers.

- **Supporter/distributor**—A company such as Red Hat would invest in creating a brand name and a website with open source information and software resources so that they would be able to create a market for future add-on products and services. The lost software license revenue is made up with support and other service revenues.

- **Branding**—Establishing a brand name will provide to the business community and other organizations the perception that they can rely on the for-profit firm to provide services for open source software.

- **Frosting**—The company does not sell the software but does sell hardware. The open source software thus becomes an attractive lure, the "frosting on the cake," to increase the market size.

- **Content**—A company might give away the software in an attempt to sign people up for a subscription to its content. Content publishers and content aggregators use this approach with some effectiveness.

Size of Open Source Marketplace

At the server level, Linux (an open source variant of Unix) is predominantly used for single-use application servers in the internet infrastructure market. In addition to the internet infrastructure, Linux is seeing significant growth in the areas of server farms, embedded systems, and thin client applications. For example, Google uses several thousand Linux machine clusters, rather than a mainframe computer environment, to respond to the billions of search requests that it receives each month. Most organizations running Linux servers are using it to provide internet infrastructure database, email, file/print sharing, system management, and network management.

Linux has made inroads as a desktop operating system (especially as different distributions of desktop Linux become more user friendly) but is still not widely deployed in libraries, where Microsoft Windows remains the dominant platform. One of the authors has seen desktop Linux distributions gaining some footholds in public libraries using older, repurposed desktop computers and laptops, where Linux operating system and applications run robustly on older hardware.

Rather than taking market share from Microsoft, Linux is continually pushing into the Unix market share of the major computer hardware manufacturers—Compaq Unix, Hewlett Packard (HP-UX), IBM (AIX), SCO (UnixWare), and Sun's Solaris. It is also used at the basis for "firmware"—embedded operating systems often used for technology devices.

The for-profit firms, established to provide support and service to those organizations that wish to use Linux but do not have the in-house expertise to provide for its support, continue to grow and flourish. Among the more prominent of these firms are Red Hat Networks, Cobalt Networks, Andover .net, and VA Linux Systems.

Interestingly, several automated library system vendors whose systems run on Unix have announced their support of Linux as one of many variants of Unix that their system will operate with.

Open Source Library Systems

One of the earliest efforts to provide access to open source software within the library community was when several software developers, working on the Z39.50 protocol, made their software available for others to use without restrictions. Z39.50 is a communications protocol that retrieves bibliographic information from one automated system and then uses the MARC record at the local system (e.g., imports the record for cataloging purposes and displays the record at an online catalog).

Tip! There are several open source software projects within the library community. Some of these projects flourish, and some wither on the vine. If interested in these and other related open source projects, visit http://www.foss4lib.org for the latest information.

TABLE 6.2. Total Open Source ILS Installations

Product	Company	Installations
Evergreen	Equinox	896
Koha	ByWater Solutions	949
	PTFS Europe	78
	Equinox	34
Totals		1,957

* As of January 2019.
Source: Based on data found at Library Technology Guides,
Product Sales (https://librarytechnology.org/guides/ils-annual-sales-report.pl). Copyright © Marshall Breeding.

Some of the more visible projects developing an ILS are Evergreen and Koha, and the total number of open source systems is shown in Table 6.2.

Koha—Koha, which means "gift" in Maori, was the first open source and web-based ILS. The system was developed in New Zealand by the Horowhenua Library Trust and Katipo Communications as an ILS with cataloging, circulation, acquisitions, and online catalog modules. The system runs on Linux, uses the MySQL database, is written in Perl, and uses Apache for the web interface. The system uses PLACK to increase the speed of circulation-related transactions. Koha also has a fully responsive online catalog using Bootstrap. The Koha software code is identical for each of the twenty-three translated language versions (the text appearing in a different language is stored in a separate translation file), including right-hand justification for Arabic. There are more than 15,000 implementations of Koha worldwide.

The Koha software is fragmented into two camps, or "forks:" the Koha community and LibLime, a product owned by PTFS, a Washington, DC–based company. The majority of international development groups (libraries and more than fifty vendors worldwide supporting libraries using Koha) deposit their code in www.koha-community.org.

The LibLime code is deposited into www.koha.org (however, only PTFS makes deposits, and others are excluded from doing so). In the United States, Koha is supported by ByWater Solutions and Equinox, and the fork of Koha, now marketed as Bibliomation, is supported by PTFS LibLime.

Tip! For more information about Koha, visit www.koha -community.org.

Evergreen—Evergreen was developed by the Georgia Public Library Service as a single system to be shared by the approximately 270 public libraries in the state (and came to be known as the Public Information Network for Electronic Services, or the PINES Consortium). At the start of 2019, more than 2,000 libraries around the world were using Evergreen, including the King County Library System (Washington) and consortiums in Georgia, Connecticut, Ohio, Missouri, Michigan, and Indiana, among others. An active community of librarians and developers is involved to ensure that the software continues to evolve and mature.

Evergreen uses the Linux operating system and the applications are programmed in Perl and C++. MARC records can be imported and exported from the Evergreen system. Data are stored using the PostgreSQL database management system. Data are stored using the Unicode standard, which allows an automated system to handle Roman and non-Roman scripts—Chinese, Arabic, and so forth.

One of the strengths of the Evergreen software is that it can be organized in a treelike hierarchy where policies and parameters can be defined (and limited) to specific locations, departments, branches, and systems that are particularly useful in a consortium environment. Although a majority of Evergreen installations are for public libraries, the software is being used in academic, school, and special and corporate libraries. Release 3.3 went live in March 2019 and in the United States, Evergreen is supported by Equinox. In early 2017, Equinox Software became the Equinox Open Library Initiative, a nonprofit corporation, allowing Equinox to seek other sources of funding, including grants, to support the ongoing development of Evergreen.

> **Tip!** For more information about Evergreen, visit https://evergreen-ils.org. This site provides access to user documentation that includes release notes for each release, the database schema, an administrator's guide, and a roadmap for future development.

Kuali Open Library Environment Project

Starting in 2008 and ending in 2016, the Kuali Open Library Environment (OLE) Project was a partnership among a number of large academic libraries (Duke, Indiana University, University of Michigan, University of Pennsylvania, and the University of Chicago, among others) to develop a next-generation, open source, comprehensive library management system. Over the course of the eight years, the project was supported by over $5.6 million from the Andrew W. Mellon Foundation, and the totality of the Kuali codebase will not be used in any project going forward. And the $5.6 million does not include the in-kind contributions from the participating academic libraries—a number of librarians and software developers contributed their time to develop analysis of workflows and practices as well as developing some software.

OLE was committed to these goals:

- Developing an open source library management system that would be directed by a community of active participants

- Building a library management system that would integrate with university enterprise and external vendor systems

- Developing new workflows that reflected the changing nature of library materials

By any measure, the Kuali/OLE project failed to deliver on its goals, and as Carl Grant has noted in several of his blogs, the outcome was fairly predictable.[12] Among the lessons that might be learned are these:

- The development of any software project carries risk—the larger the project, the more the risk.

- Risks can be mitigated by involving bright, talented people at the right times in the development process.

- The Kuali foundational architecture did not look ahead.

- A great deal of time and resources were spent on meetings.

The Future of Libraries Is Open (FOLIO)

The Future of Libraries Is Open (FOLIO) is a project, announced in April 2016, to develop a next-generation library services platform. FOLIO is hosted by the Open Library Foundation, a not-for-profit organization. Interestingly, FOLIO is being financially supported by EBSCO, who will also lend its expertise in software development, business process workflows, responsive user interface design, and project management. Other commercial firms, notably Index Data, will be involved in defining the architecture as well as developing software for FOLIO.

The goal for FOLIO is to create an open source, library services platform that will manage library content in all media formats, support a variety of metadata standards used in current ILSs, and support BIBFRAME's linked data structures. The plan for the underlying system architecture is to create a web-native, multitenant platform hosted in a cloud environment, as shown in Figure 6.1. The virtues of a multitenant architecture were discussed in greater detail in Chapter 1.

The *system layer* at the bottom of the diagram focuses on providing access to all types of data. Transactional data will be stored in a Structured Query Language (SQL) database (MySQL is one example), and the bibliographic data will reside in MongoDB (an open source, non-SQL document-oriented database program with replica sets, to improve both system performance and reliability).

The *message bus* manages the communications between the applications and the System Layer, using the Hypertext Transfer Protocol (HTTP) protocol. An Okapi Framework is used to exchange data, using a variety of application programming interfaces (APIs).

The *application layer* allows libraries and vendors to develop and enhance both standard ILS modules (acquisitions, circulation, metadata control, etc.) as well as extending the library into new areas such as research administration, campus enterprise resource planning (ERP), and so forth.

The *user interface toolkit* provides a standard, default user interface as well as a set of tools that can used to create a new user interface.

As an open source project, the FOLIO software could be deployed by a single library, a consortia, and others. EBSCO plans to offer FOLIO as a cloud-based service that will be closely coupled with its EBSCO Discovery Service.[13]

An alpha version of the FOLIO software was delivered in early 2018 to three libraries. A beta version was delivered in early 2019 to the three "testing" libraries, and an additional eleven libraries are planning on implementing and testing the FOLIO software during 2019. The source code can be downloaded from the Github website.

Tip! For more information about FOLIO, visit http://www.folio.org.

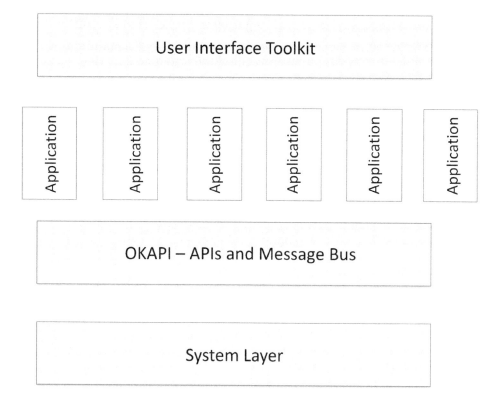

FIGURE 6.1. FOLIO Platform
Source: Adapted from FOLIO Platform found at https://www.folio.org/wp-content /uploads/2018/08/PDF-2016_08_FOLIO-Platform-Visualization.pdf.

No Free Lunch

Open source means free—free to download, free to install, and free to use. Just as there is no such thing as a free lunch, there clearly are costs that will be incurred by a library attempting to implement an open source software system. Among these costs are those listed here:

- An appropriately sized server or multiple servers to support the operating system required by the open source application software

- Support for the hardware and operating system

- Support for the database software

- Support for the open source application software, if desired by the library and provided by an outside firm or coordinating organization

- Consulting assistance to load the software, import bibliographic records, and provide other installation assistance

- One or more programmers on staff to implement the system and make changes to the software (based on library needs or to correct a software bug). Note, most libraries pay an outside support organization for this service.

- Time and computer resources for staff to train on the new system; providing a variety of training learning styles is important[14]

- Library staff member to assume responsibility for maintaining the automated system, including all of the organizations that will provide support.

Although a library may ask a vendor to assume a majority of these responsibilities by choosing a cloud-based solution, it must be remembered that ultimately the library is responsible to ensure that the system(s) delivery the quality of service needed for library staff members and customers alike.

Comparing Proprietary and Open Source ILS

One analysis found that open source ILS systems (Koha and Evergreen) compared favorably with two commercial options (Symphony and Voyager). The analysis considered functionality, usability, adoption and technical support, and economics, and concluded that any library should consider all options, including open source ILS systems.[15] Tristan Muller has suggested using a three-step process to evaluate open source ILS system:[16]

1. Only evaluate truly open source software products.

2. Evaluate the community behind the open source project, using a set of forty criteria, and

3. Compare the remaining products using a list of 800 functions and features.

Open Source Devotees

One of the realities in the marketplace is that many librarians have "embraced the vision" and become open source devotees or evangelists. A devotee believes that any open source option is *the* option to choose, regardless of the needs of the library and their users. As noted above, software, kittens, and puppies are never truly "free." In reality, the needs of the library and its customers must be the dominant motivating factor in the evaluation of any software solution being considered.

Summary

What most independent software vendors recognized long ago is that most people are users rather than builders, hackers (in the positive sense of the word), or tinkerers. People are interested in learning how to use a software product and knowing what it will do for them (i.e., make them more productive, provide a form of entertainment [game software], etc.). Thus, it is likely that, for the foreseeable future, there will be a combination of copyright protected and open source software.

Ultimately, it will be up to each library to decide whether they have personnel with the appropriate skills, interest, and time to participate in maintaining an open source product or if the library will reply on a contractual relationship with a commercial firm to provide software for the library.

Open Source Challenge

If you answer yes to one or more of the following issues, then your library may be a candidate for implementing open source software:

- Does your library have talented software programmers (or the budget to hire or contract)?
- Do the programmers have sufficient time to enhance open source software?
- Is the management of software programmers a core competency for your organization—or are you willing to adopt it as a core competency?
- Will the customization of the software significantly improve operations?
- Is the speed of implementing new enhancements critical to the operation of the library?
- Are there sufficient budgetary resources for IT?
- Can your library attract and retain talented IT staff?

Questions to Consider

- Can you articulate the difference between freeware and shareware?
- What are some of the characteristics of open source software?
- What are the seven Creative Commons license options?
- Define the term *LAMP*.
- What services are typically provided by open source vendors?
- Have you viewed the "Open Source ILS Song" on YouTube?
- What are some of the benefits of using open source software?
- Describe the differences between the two popular ILSs Koha and Evergreen?
- Can you summarize the differences that you see between proprietary and open source ILS solutions?

Suggested Web Resources

Evergreen
https://evergreen-ils.org
https://wiki.evergreen-ils.org/doku.php?id=evergreen_libraries

Folio
https://www.folio.org/

Free/Open Source Software for Libraries
http://www.foss4lib.org

Koha
http://www.koha.org

The Open Source Initiative
http://www.opensource.org

Notes

1. Richard Stallman, quoted in Jonathan Corbet and Greg Kroah-Hartman, *Linux Kernel Development: How Fast It Is Going, Who is Doing It, What They Are Doing and Who Is Sponsoring the Work*, 25th Anniversary Edition (San Francisco: The Linux Foundation, 2016), 78, http://go.linuxfoundation.org/linux-kernel-development-report-2016?utm_source=press-release&utm_medium=pr&utm_campaign=2016-linux-kernel-report.

2. Linus Torvalds Quotes, *Brainy Quotes* (n.d.), https://www.brainyquote.com/quotes/linus_torvalds_587384.

3. Michael Larabel, "Linux 5.1 Should Be Released Today with IO_uring, Faster zRAM, More Icelake," *Linux Kernal*, May 5, 2019, https://www.phoronix.com/scan.php?page=news_item&px=Linux-5.1-Today.

4. Kathleen Conner and Richard Rumelt, "Software Piracy: An Analysis of Protection Strategies," *Management Science* 37, no. 2, (1991): 125–139.

5. Harvard Business School Press, *The Browser Wars, 1994–1998*, Case Number 9-798-094 (Boston: Harvard Business School Press, 1999).

6. Eric S. Raymond, *The Magic Cauldron*, http://www.catb.org/esr/writings/magic-cauldron/.

7. Jonathan Corbet and Greg Korah Hartman, 2017 Linux Kernal Development Report, https://www.linuxfoundation.org/2017-linux-kernel-report-landing-page/.

8. Marshall Breeding, "Open Source Library System: The Current State of the Art," *Library Technology Reports* (August/September 2017).

9. Melissa LaPlante, *The Consideration of an Open-Source Integrated Library System for the Portland Public Library* (Boston: Simmons College, December 14, 2008).

10. Stephen Abram, *The Information Tornado: Toto I Don't Think We're in Kansas Anymore!,* presentation at the Northwest ILL Conference, September 15, 2005, Portland, Oregon, https://slideplayer.com/slide/1728183/.

11. Eric Maynard, *Evergreen/Horizon: A Functional Comparison*, Holmes County District Public Library, August 30, 2009.

12. Carl Grant, "The OLE Merry-Go-Round spins on . . ." *Thoughts from Carl Grant* (blog), April 27, 2016. http://thoughts.care-affiliates.com/2016/04/the-ole-merry-go-round-spins-on.html.

13. Marshall Breeding, "EBSCO Supports New Open Source Project: Software for Academic Libraries Will Be Developed Collaboratively," *American Libraries*, April 22, 2016, https://americanlibrariesmagazine.org/2016/04/22/ebsco-kuali-open-source-project.

14. Vandana Singh, "Experiences of Migrating to an Open-Source Integrated Library System," *Information Technology and Libraries* (March 2013): 36–53.

15. Joseph Pruett and Namjoo Choi, "A Comparison Between Select Open Source and Proprietary Integrated Library Systems," *Library Hi Tech* 31, no. 3 (2013): 435–54.

16. Tristan Müller, "How to Choose a Free and Open Source Integrated Library System," *OCLC Systems & Services: International digital library perspectives* 27, no. 1 (2011): 57–78.

7
Other Silos

The most technologically efficient machine
that man has ever invented is the book.

—Northrop Frye[1]

In addition to the library's integrated library system (ILS) or a newer library management platform, many libraries must also provide access to and maintain several other stand-alone systems (sometimes called silos), as shown in Figure 7.1. These may include the following:

- Electronic resource management system
- Institutional repository
- Authentication
- Link verification
- Discovery system
- eBook platform

Electronic Resource Management System

Providing access to electronic resources (journals, databases, and eBooks) is an everyday service offered by almost every library. As eResources were being introduced into libraries, staff immediately became aware that managing eResources was much more complex than traditional print resources. Responding to the reality of more complexity, library software vendors added functionality to their existing ILS systems (or developing completely new systems). These new systems or added functionality was called an *electronic resource management system*, or ERMS. ERMS options include both solutions from the commercial vendors as well as multiple open source options.

An ERMS is of value to a library for both its added functionality as well as the convenience of new library workflow processes. In general terms, an

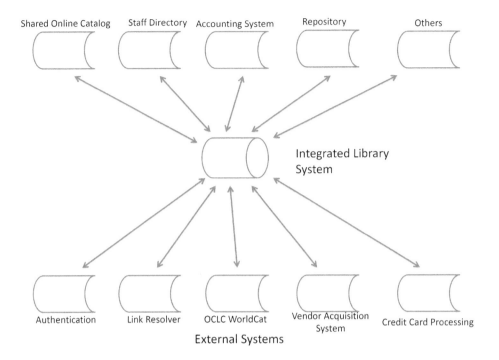

FIGURE 7.1. Connecting to Other Automated Systems

ERMS is most successful when it assists the library in tracking and communicating with a variety of vendors and eResource providers by eliminating or reducing tedious manual tasks and activities, as shown in Figure 7.2.

The physicality of print materials (and other physical types of materials such as DVDs, CDs, etc.) makes the management of the various processes much easier—an item is on order, is being cataloged and processed, is placed on the shelf, has been borrowed, is overdue, and so forth.

Electronic resources, on the other hand, have "no simple life cycle and the workflow is often iterative" and not always straightforward.[2] The library needs to communicate with a variety of organizations and individuals—vendors, other staff members, stakeholders, and customers—using a variety of communication protocols (electronic messages using standard formats, email messages, etc.). In addition, the information to manage electronic resources is complicated, as the library is often licensing multiple titles as a "package" rather than ordering one title at a time. Central to an ERMS was the development of an eResources knowledge base that would identify every eJournal title included within each aggregate content product including the specific years and issues available. It should be noted that these content products are constantly changing as titles are added and dropped. In addition, the knowledge base must identify each content product the library subscribes to.[3]

The result is a complex and rich information environment where any number of scenarios must be accommodated. The information may be needed in any number of systems, such as the ERMS itself, an A to Z list of titles

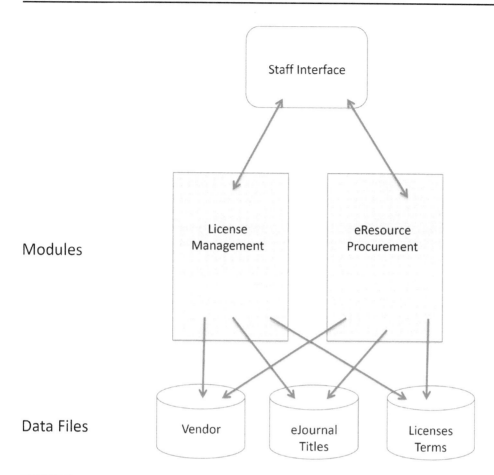

FIGURE 7.2. ERMS System Architecture
Source: Adapted from Marshall Breeding, "Current Trends in Library
Management Systems," *Slideshare*, February 24, 2011, https://www.slideshare.net
/mortenbn/current-trends-in-library-management-systems (slide 35/86).

that may be accessed using the library, the link resolver, an accounting system, and so forth.

Standards Pertaining to Electronic Resources

Almost from day one, it became clear to librarians and vendors alike that a number of standards would be needed in order to facilitate all of the communication that would be required to make an ERMS work smoothly for all concerned. The goal was to make each ERMS truly capable in interoperating with other automated systems—able to communicate data in both directions in an automatic and error-free manner.

Four standards are particularly noteworthy.

OpenURL, a National Information Standards Organization (NISO)–based standard, provides a resilient link between citation and full text, with the result that patrons are linked to directly to the licensed full text (rather than to login or payment pages). This OpenURL standard is the foundation on which link resolvers such as *SFX* from Ex Libris or *360 Link* from Serials Solutions rely. Clearly OpenURL is dependent on the link-resolver knowledge base created by each content provider so that the link remains good (incorrect or incomplete metadata about the subscriptions for each library customer leads to broken OpenURL links and great frustration on the part of the end user).[4] Link resolvers are rarely purchased as stand-alone products, as ILS and library services platforms provide their functionality as a matter of course.

The **Knowledge Bases and Related Tools** (KBART) is a NISO-recommended practice that identifies sixteen data fields that content providers should provide that improve the quality of the content metadata (which is a part of the link resolver knowledge base). The goal of KBART was to minimize the number of broken links (most often OpenURL links) to content.[5]

Improving OpenURL Through Analytics (IOTA) is a NISO working group that measures OpenURL quality from specific content providers (and then works with the provider to improve its overall quality).[6]

And fourth, **Presentation & Identification of E-Journals**, or PIE-J, is another NISO working group that works to provide standardization and consistent presentation of title changes on provider websites—changes to international standard serial numbers (ISSNs) and journal titles result in patrons receiving broken OpenURL link messages.

Electronic Resource Management Systems

Not surprisingly, ERMS are available from two sources—commercial vendors and open source projects. The commercial vendors followed two approaches in developing their ERMS: First, some vendors added functionality to their existing ILS (e.g., Innovative Interfaces followed this path with their Millennium system), and second, the vendor created a new system that combines ERMS functionality with an A to Z list, link resolver, and Counting Online Usage of Networked Electronic Resources (COUNTER) statistics (this approach was followed by the Online Computer Library Center [OCLC], EBSCO, and Serials Solutions).

Three of the more important ERMS open source projects, typically initiated by a library, are listed here:[7]

- CORAL—University of Notre Dame Library, continues to have a high level of ongoing development
- CUFTS—Simon Fraser University Library
- ERMes—University of Wisconsin—La Crosse Library.

It should be noted that there will be no more software updates for the latter two products as the libraries have migrated to a library management platform.

Functionality

It is possible to identify five broad components of an ERMS system: administration, budget, knowledge base, licensing, and reports.

Administration—A wide variety of detailed information is required to track for each journal, publisher, subscription agent, and library holdings, including contract specific content, usernames and passwords (that can frequently change), vendor contact information, IP addresses, invoices and payment information, and other related data.

Budget—Given the variety of accounting systems that libraries must contend with, tracking the library's budget for eResources is an important requirement. Libraries need to know their budget broken down into various categories, what is directly purchased and indirectly purchased through consortial agreements, and what funds are still available, along with receiving invoices and generating (physical or virtual) checks.

Knowledge base—For the purposes of an ERMS, a knowledge base contains information about journal titles contained within a subscription package or database, the specific issues for each title that is included in the package, links to the eResource package, journal titles available for licensing or purchase from a publisher or aggregator, price, and license terms for the library-licensed content. Given the rapid rate for change to journal titles, available issues for each title, links to content, usernames and passwords, vendor-curated knowledge bases are very popular—a change made once can be reflected in multiple ERMS systems immediately.

Licensing—Rather than purchasing electronic resources, a library most often must pay for a license to gain access to the eResource. A license agreement identifies the rights and responsibilities of both the supplier and the library. Given that these agreements are often written in difficult-to-understand legalese, it becomes incumbent to ensure that the ERMS is able to handle all of the complexities that will be encountered in several dozen to hundreds of these license agreements. Issues include who may access the electronic content, the number of simultaneous users, interlibrary loan restrictions (if any), start and end dates, perpetual access to the content, and many other related issues.

Some libraries are insisting that all of their license agreements be public documents to be shared with other interested libraries.

Reports—A wide variety of reports are needed by a library in order to ensure that value is received for all of the electronic content that is licensed by the library. These reports include the typical budget and serials check-in reports as well as usage statistics reports. Many libraries rely on a cost-per-download report that tracks this information for each title (package, publisher, etc.).

The accuracy of these reports is improved if the vendor is able to generate data that is compliant with COUNTER. COUNTER relies on vendors submitting voluntarily to verification that the statistics they produce adhere to COUNTER (a NISO standard). The COUNTER standard defines specific terms and insists on a specific format for each report.

A companion NISO standard, SUSHI (Standardized Usage Statistics Harvesting Initiative), allows libraries to automatically download usage statistics from a vendor SUSHI server without the need to log in each time data is required by a library. Although COUNTER data are quite helpful (and libraries obviously need to combine data from multiple publishers and aggregators in order to get the big picture), for a library to begin to understand how its licensed electronic resources are being used, COUNTER data are but one of many pieces that need to be considered.[8]

> **Tip!** Model licenses and specific suggested language for a number of licensing topics may be found at http://liblicense.crl .edu/licensing-information.

ERMS Benefits

An ERMS provides the following set of benefits:

- Saves staff time (especially if work flows are modified and streamlined)
- Reduces customer confusion and frustration
- Helps with the complexities associated with eResource management
- Provides a set of reports that helps manage the eResource budget

Institutional Repository

Institutional repositories (IRs) have been around for more than a decade and really began in earnest with the launch of *DSpace* and the *Digital Commons* platforms in 2002. *DSpace*, developed in collaboration between Hewlett Packard and MIT, provides an attractive solution because of the flexibility of its open source software, and *Digital Commons*, created by The Berkeley Electronic Press (bepress), with the University of California as its first customer, indicated the belief that a real market existed for this type of product. Flexible Extensible Digital Object Repository, or *Fedora*, another popular open source solution, merged with *DSpace*, and the combined product is now called *Duraspace*. Two other popular open source software platforms are *EPrints* (developed at the University of Southampton in England) and *irplus* (developed by the University of Rochester).

From these humble beginnings, the adoption rate of IRs has been fairly rapid. As of September 2019, the *Directory of Open Access Repositories* (Open-DOAR) includes 4,286 repository organizations around the world (the top four IR countries are the United States, Japan, Germany, and the United Kingdom). Other popular commercial and open source IR software products include CON-TENTdm (which is also a digital asset management systems [DAMS] tool used for digitized cultural heritage collections), Islandora, WEKO, OPUS, HAL, and dLibra.

The content types most frequently found in an IR include journal articles, theses, and dissertations, followed by books, chapters, reports, and conference presentations.

Institutional repositories seem to fulfill several functions for an organization:

- IRs facilitate access to scholarly information.
- IRs illuminate the depth and breadth of an organization's intellectual capital (often providing access to content that remained on an individual's workstation, such as conference and workshop presentations).
- IRs may host a new generation of scholarly eJournals (often open access journals).
- IRs may help mitigate the scholarly communications crisis—the escalating costs of scholarly materials.
- IRs provide authors with a low-cost option for disseminating their work.

- Some institutions of higher education require their faculty and staff members to contribute content to an institutional repository, whereas others make it optional. Yet even when contributing content is mandatory, the level of compliance is surprisingly low. Organizational units responsible for the IR, often the library, have tried a variety of marketing approaches to reach a number of market segments in an effort to attract content to the IR. General promotional messages seem to be effective in raising the awareness of IR as a concept and of the potential benefits for the faculty member. Specific messages often address such topics as copyright, enhanced discovery, preservation, open access, collaboration to generate new knowledge, and so forth.

> **Tip!** Directory of Open Access Journals, www.doaj.org, provides a directory of free, full-text, peer-reviewed scientific and scholarly journals—covering all subjects and languages. This searchable database is a great resource!

Attempting to assess the value and impact of an institutional repository is a real challenge. Kim and Kim suggest that looking at an IR as a whole, rather than at one or more individual factors, is more important, and the authors thus suggested an IR evaluation framework like that shown in Table 7.1.[9]

Interestingly, providing access to the total contents of search engines so as to improve the discovery process is not a part of the IR evaluation framework (but should be in the view of the authors of this book).

Ellen Duranceau and Sue Kriegsman suggest that a number of common practices have emerged that, if followed, will increase the level of participation and the number of documents contributed to an IR:[10]

- **Follow the faculty**—Faculty have a common commitment to contribute their work to the greater good.

- **Build trust through outreach**—An active, strong, and sustained outreach program is an important key to success for the IR.

- **Repurpose existing staff**—Most institutions have two to three people involved in marketing and maintaining the IR.

- **Make it easy**—Keeping the process easy to contribute content to the IR will ensure its long-term success.

- **Buy or build an infrastructure**—It is important to create a workflow match between the institution (faculty) and the infrastructure of the IR.

- **Add value**—The quality of the metadata is important. Some libraries are using the Open Researcher & Contributor ID (ORCID) project that aims to disambiguate author names in scholarly communication by utilizing a central registry. The library may also want to ensure that the university adopts an open access licensing policy such as under a Creative Common Attribution (CC-BY) that allows full reuse.

- **Engage with publishers**—Having a university open access policy allows the university to work on behalf of faculty members so that when publishers attempt to use confusing or highly ambiguous

TABLE 7.1. IR Evaluation Framework

Category	Factors	Variables
Content	Quality Diversity Currency	Number of peer-reviewed journal articles Number of other articles Number of documents published less than 3 years old Accuracy of table of contents Number of theses/dissertations Number of metadata elements Number of required metadata elements Metadata uniformity Adherence to metadata standards
Management and policy	Commitment Regulation Resource allocation Archiving	Number of archiving methods IR budget Number of marketing methods Mandatory submission of documents IR management policies University IR committee IR librarians
System and Network	System performance Multifunctionality	Retrieval speed Access to full text Existence of FAQ service Integration of OPAC and IR systems Utility of Q&A services
Use	Use performed User assistance	Number of documents downloaded Number of submitter services Number of IR training options Number of IR training options for submitters

Source: Adapted from Hyun Hee Kim and Yong Ho Kim An Evaluation Model for the National Consortium of Institutional Repositories of Korean Universities ASIS Conference 2006. Available at https://www.asis.org/Conferences/AM06/proceedings/papers/76/76_paper.html

language to negate open access policies, faculty members have a skilled advocate working on their behalf.

- **Share information and keep learning**—Raising awareness of open access policies and learning from colleagues in other institutions helps ensure the success of the IR. The Coalition of Open Access Policy Institutions (COAPI) was created in 2011 with the goal to collaborate and share implementation strategies.

One of the real challenges that continues to confront institutional repositories is that although faculty (and the university itself) wish to share their content and want to disseminate research widely, publishers are increasingly attempting to place restrictions on their published content in the form of moratoriums and other pricing mechanisms.

Tip! The Institutional Repository Software Comparison is an excellent guide to the issues surrounding the selection and implementation of an IR system.[11]

A survey of universities with institutional repositories found that organizations that mediate submissions rather than allowing self-archiving into the IR incur fewer costs (which seems a bit counterintuitive). Further, although open source IR software has lower implementation costs, annual operating costs are similar to those that rely on proprietary software solutions.[12]

Tip! The aim of the **Ranking Web of Repositories** is to promote open access initiatives and encourage global access to academic knowledge. In addition, the actual ranking of available repositories is quite popular among university administrators. *Source:* http://repositories.webometrics.info.

The composite index or rankings are based on several factors:

- *Size*—Number of web pages extracted from Google

- *Visibility*—Total number of external links or backlinks

- *Rich files*—Files provided in formats such as .pdf (Adobe Acrobat), .doc or .docx (MS Word), .ppt or .pptx (MS PowerPoint), and .ps or .eps (PostScript)

- *Scholar*—Normalized number of papers over the last five years found in Google Scholar

Authentication

Within the field of information technology, authentication is a process to ensure only authorized users are given access to a system or database, based on user credentials that imply authenticity. Users typically must provide a user name and a password, or a personal identification number (PIN), or answer one or more security questions as a means of ensuring their authenticity. Once "authorized," the user is able to use third-party electronic resources.

Link Resolvers

OpenURL, a NISO standard, is a binding agent for the infrastructure of library systems, enabling the linking of citations to full text. When links become broken for any number of reasons, the task of troubleshooting is complex and time-consuming.

The University of Michigan library tracked the amount of linkage failure using the two link resolver tools over several years and identified what they have done to reduce the number of broken links.[13]

Link Verification

Link verification, sometimes called a link resolver, is based on the OpenURL standard and facilitates linking from a citation (wherever the citation may be found, e.g., Google Scholar, an abstracting and indexing database) to the library subscribing to the full text of an article.

The link resolver relies on a knowledge base that is usually maintained by a supplier. This knowledge base maintains the necessary information about publishers, journal titles, subscriptions, and journal holdings for the library, along with links to the full text database. A knowledge base that does not contain an accurate and up-to-date database will lead to broken links; clicking on a link results in not being connected to the required full text of a journal article (even though the library has licensed access to the full text of the journal.

Discovery System

A web-scale discovery system harvests the content from multiple sources into a single searchable database. Four of the better-known discovery systems include the *EBSCO Discovery System*, Ex Libris *Primo*, OCLC's *WorldCat Discovery Service*, and ProQuest's *Summon*. A discovery system combines the library's own online catalog with citation metadata (and in some cases full text) of electronic and database content from publishers and aggregators.[14] A web-scale discovery system promises the ease and speed of Google with a relevancy-ranking algorithm to bring the most relevant resources to the forefront. Once the user enters a search request using a single search box, the display features a faceted display to give users the ability to narrow their search by author, type of material, year published, and so forth.

Marshall Breeding identified several categories of resource discovery products including the following:

- **Connected discovery**—This approach combines the discovery interface, a link resolver, the local library's OPAC and access to remote eResources using API's. Examples of this approach include Ex Libris Primo, SirsiDynix Enterprise, BiblioCommons BiblioCore, Innovative Interfaces Encore, and open system options Blacklight, VuFind, and eXtensible Catalog.

- **Central index discovery services**—A central index of eResources (principally eJournal articles) is created, combined with a discovery interface. Examples include EBSCO Discovery Service, ProQuest Summon, and OCLC's WorldShare Discovery Service.

- **Local and central index discovery services**—The contents of the local library's catalog are combined with article-level scholarly content from publishers and aggregators.

- **Non-library discovery services**—These include Google Scholar and Microsoft's Academic Search.

- **Discovery services for public libraries**—A public library discovery system should search local physical materials plus licensed eBook and eResource collections. Examples include BiblioCommons (typically installed in large and medium size libraries), ProPAC from Polaris, Encore from Innovative interfaces, AquaBrowser, and LS2 PAC from the Library Corporation.

Discovery System Indexes

All discovery system indexes are *not* created equal. Some (if not most) publishers and abstracting and indexing firms, sometimes called aggregators, are quite protective of their intellectual content. Some of these firms will only share article-level metadata (and perhaps an abstract), whereas other organizations may share the metadata plus the full text with a discovery service vendor. The end result is a really large database containing 1 to 2 billion items (a majority of which will be full-text items), as shown in Figure 7.3.

Each publisher and/or aggregator provides metadata (and perhaps the full text) in digital format that then gets ingested into the discovery service index (regular updates are also provided to keep the discovery service index current). As a new customer library of the discovery service is added, the eJournals and other eResources that the library subscribes to are added to a library filter so that users of that library only see the eResources that have been subscribed to by the library. In addition, the library shares the contents of its entire online catalog (and in some cases, the contents of the institutional repository) so that this very specific local digital content is included in the discovery service indexes.

Obviously the more text that can be indexed, the more responsive the index will be in response to user queries. Some discovery services (e.g., ProQuest Summon) maintain a single record for each unique resource by merging records for the same resource. Other Discovery Services (such as EBSCO Discovery Service) maintain separate records for each source (and merge the results when needed in response to a user query).

The end-user interface should provide a single search box for user queries, along with the option for advanced queries, and presents the search

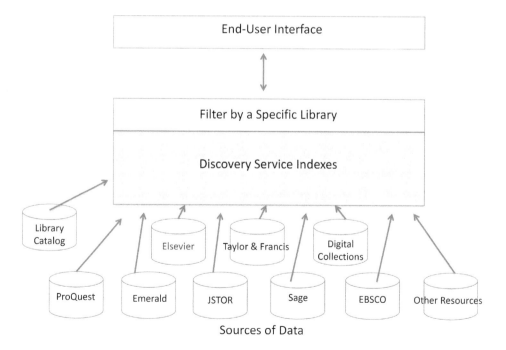

FIGURE 7.3. Discovery System Architecture

results in summary and full-record displays. In addition, the discovery service must provide the ability to interoperate with a link resolver and to communicate with the library's ILS or LSP using an application programming interface (API) to determine an item's current status, request a hold or recall an item, update the patron's account, and so forth.

A majority of the literature pertaining to discovery systems focuses on features,[15] the process of selecting a discovery service,[16] challenges of implementation,[17] an evaluation of the discovery service after implementation,[18] and an assessment of discovery systems on online journal usage.[19] In an interesting blog posting, Matthew Reidsma explores the topic of algorithmic bias in library discovery systems.[20]

Discovery service commercial options include the following:

- Ex Libris Primo
- BiblioCommons
- EBSCO Discovery Services
- ProQuest Summon
- OCLC WorldShare Discovery Service.

A vendor might provide a discovery interface to its own discovery service. Other commercial discovery interface options include those listed here:

- **ProQuest AquaBrowser**—provides a cloud of search of search terms plus faceted navigation for the end user. The data are extracted from the library's ILS, and the library maintains the index locally.
- **SirsiDynix Enterprise**—delivers an OPAC featuring a relevancy-ranking retrieval system and faceted navigation.
- **Innovative Interface Encore**—provides a single search box, relevancy ranking, and faceted navigation, but interacts with the EBSCO Discovery Services. Note: Libraries must subscribe to both the III and EBSCO products.

Open source discovery interface products include those presented here:

- **Blacklight**—A University of Virginia development project, provides a flexible toolkit that relies of Apache SOLR for indexing and search and retrieval.
- **Vufind**—developed at Villanova University using Hypertext Preprocessor (PHP) programming and the Apache SOLAR indexing engine

Non-Library Discovery Service

There is substantial evidence that, as Lorcan Dempsey has observed, "discovery happens elsewhere." The OCLC Perceptions reports found that in almost all cases, people start their search for information using Google Scholar or another search engine rather than using the library's online catalog.[21] For many members of the academic community, Google Scholar or Microsoft Academic Search is a preferred starting point, as well as the many disciplinary repositories, indexes, and other services that are available, such as MEDLINE or arXiv for physics.

Google Scholar provides a fairly comprehensive index for scholarly materials (content that it has found on various websites, content that is provided by publishers and aggregators, as well as content uploaded by numerous individuals). Google Scholar primarily relies on its own tailored harvesting robots that search for scholarly materials; however, the regular Google harvesting bots also provide content for indexing. Many estimate that Google Scholar indexes more than 200 million articles.

Roger Schonfeld has suggested that Google Scholar provides researchers with more links to relevant content than the library-provided discovery services.[22] This should not be surprising, as a user of a library discovery service is only seeing a small subset of all of the available resources available using Google Scholar. Aaron Tay has compared Google Scholar to the available discovery services with some surprising observations.[23]

> **Tip!** Libraries can improve access to their eResources by providing Google with IP addresses and the base URL of its link resolver. Using other traditional search optimization techniques will also improve discoverability.

Discovery System Challenges

A discovery system is not a panacea for problems users confront when attempting to use the traditional online catalog. Here are some of the challenges discovery systems have not solved as noted by several authors:[24]

- Inability of a user to browse a specific index
- Lack of an integrated request and delivery service
- Providing tools for deep research by expert and more experienced users
- A user interface that can be complicated to navigate

Perhaps the biggest challenge for any library with a discovery system is the reality that users simply do not use it. In short, the discovery system has become a search tool of last resort for many library users. As noted in the OCLC Perceptions report, "Not a single US respondent in 2010, including college students, began in information search on a library Web site."[25] The University of Utrecht decided not to implement a discovery system, concluding that library data should be delivered to other web-scale services (such as search engines), portals, and websites in which users are using APIs and web services. So the focus for the University of Utrecht is now on delivery rather than discovery.[26]

> The catalog itself is being reconfigured in ways that result in its disappearance as individually identifiable component of library service.
>
> —Lorcan Dempsey[27]

eBook Platform

Libraries have a lot of options when it comes to providing access to eBooks. They may choose to host their own eBook platform or provide access to one or more eBook platforms located in the cloud. The library can choose to purchase content directly from the publisher, an aggregator (provides access to the content from multiple publishers), or a distributor (provides eBooks from publishers and aggregators).

Local eBook Platform

The Douglas County (Colorado) Libraries developed their own eBook platform, which is often referred to as the "buy, own, and loan as you like" eBook model. The end result from the perspective of patrons is that they have access to eBooks that are owned by the library and shared for a specific period of time—just as for printed books. The eBook platform is hosted on an Adobe content server (which, among other things, regulates the allowable number of simultaneous "check-outs" of eBooks in the collection). Bibliographic records for the eBooks are added to the library's online catalog, and the patron selects one of more eBooks (as long as the desired eBook is not already checked out) to download. This local eBook platform has been replicated in hundreds of other public libraries.

In this model, the library essentially takes on the role of a publisher or distributor—which includes finding and selecting worthy content, securing the rights from content creators to share the eBooks, and hosting the full technology infrastructure to load the digital materials to patrons. The labor, materials, and technology required to host an eBook platform are significant— but for some organizations, it is well worth it to have greater control over the digital content offered to patrons.

Mirela Roncevic, in a Library Technology Report, suggests that there are a number of considerations that a library should address during the selection of an eBook platform,[28] among which are the following:

- **Content**—primary focus of the platform, number of titles, number of publishers, subject covered, inclusion of multimedia, and so forth

- **Technical specifications**—what download file formats are available (pdf, ePub, XHTML, others), which browsers are supported, availability of an app, integration with the local library's ILS, and so forth

- **Functionality**—the availability of MARC records for each eBook, the availability of usage information (COUNTER reports), searching options, citation tools, ability to annotate, print on demand, and more

- **Business models**—subscription option, one user/one book option, short-term loans, purchase-to-own model, patron-driven acquisitions option, pay-per-view, annual subscription fee, digital rights management (DRM) policies, and so forth

Among the more notable eBook platforms are these:

- **Academic libraries**—University press eBook platforms (Books at JSTOR; Cambridge University Press University Publishing Online [UPO]; Oxford University Press's University Press Scholarship Online [UPSO]; and University Press Content Consortium [UPCC] plus a host of publisher, aggregator, and distributor options (Books@ Ovid, eBooks on EBSCOhost, Gale Virtual Reference Library, SpringerLink, and more).

- **Public libraries**—OverDrive and Bibliotheca (who purchased the 3M cloudLibrary solution) are the dominant players in this marketplace. Biblioheca's cloudLibrary interfaces with the library's ILS to authenticate the patron, and titles can be downloaded to any digital device. No patron use data are captured by the cloudLibrary system.

- **School libraries**—The primary aggregators in this marketplace are Follett (provides a broad selection of titles) and Macklin.

Open Access eBook Platforms

There are several open access eBook Platforms that might be of interest to a library:

- Directory of Open Access Books (DOAB)
- Open Access Publishing in European Networks (OAPEN)
- Scientific Electronic Library Online (SciELO)
- Unglue.it

In addition, there are several public domain eBook Platforms for which some libraries provide links, including Internet Archive, Big Universe, Children's Books Online, Project Gutenberg, World Public Library, and the HathiTrust.

eLending Licenses

There are eight types of licenses that control the type of lending the library is able to provide to its patrons who wish to use an eBook:[29]

1. Nonconcurrent user license
2. Concurrent user license
3. Limited loan license
4. Limited term license
5. Unlimited term license
6. Perpetual license
7. Subscription license
8. Pay-per-use license

The eBook Challenges

Although more than 90 percent of public libraries provide access to one or more eBook platforms, only about two-thirds of Americans are aware they can "borrow" an eBook from their local library.[30] Within any state, there is unequal and inconsistent access to eBook resources. Thus, some states, such as Massachusetts, have adopted a consortia model and have created the Massachusetts eBook Collections to ensure equal access to eBook content for every library.[31] And some publishers continue to place restrictions and charge high prices to license rather than purchase eBook content.

Late in 2018, Canadian public libraries started a campaign to alert the public about the challenges libraries face when attempting to license eBooks and audiobooks. Some of the larger publishers will charge $100 per eBook (often with additional restrictions), and Audible, a company that owns the rights to a large number of digital audiobooks, refuses to license its content to public libraries.

A report showed that Canadian public libraries typically purchase Canadian titles in one format only, most often favoring print over the eBook format. Less than 7 percent of Canadian titles were found in both formats in public libraries across Canada.[32]

Summary

This chapter has explored a number of automation silos that many libraries are operating today. Being able to link systems in order to move data, as and when needed, makes for a much more efficient operation, but there are real challenges to accomplish this goal.

Questions to Consider

- What are the benefits from using an Electronic Resources Management System (ERMS) in your library?

- If you work in a small or medium-size library, does your library really need an ERMS?

- What do you consider the top three standards that are related to eResources? Why?

- What ERMS functionality is most important to your library?

- What challenges do you face in encouraging faculty and staff to deposit content into your organization's institutional repository?

- How does your institutional repository fare in the Ranking Web of Repositories? What can your library do to improve its ranking?

- Does you library have a program and a set of tools that it uses to minimize "link rot" on the library's website? On its institutional repository?

- What ongoing challenges do you face with the discovery service implemented in your library?

- Given that "discovery happens elsewhere," does your library need an online catalog?

- Has your library considered implementing an eBook platform? If not, why not?

Notes

1. Northrop Frye, *Anatomy of Criticism: Four Essays* (Princeton, NJ: Princeton University Press, 2000), 94.

2. Elsa K. Anderson, "Electronic Resource Management Systems: A Workflow Approach," *Library Technology Reports* 50, no. 3 (April 2014).

3. Marshall Breeding, "What Is ERM? Electronic Resource Management Strategies in Academic Libraries," *Systems Librarian* 38, no. 3 (April 2018).

4. The OpenURL standard is maintained by the National Information Standards Organization and is known as the NISO Z39.88 standard. See also, Rafal Kasprowski, "Best Practice & Standardization Initiatives for Managing Electronic Resources," *Bulletin of the American Society for Information Science and Technology* 35, no. 1 (October/November 2008): 13.

5. Sarah Glazer, "Broken Links and Failed Access: How KBART, IOTA, and PIE-J Can Help," *Library Resources & Technical Services* 56, no. 1 (January 2012): 18–19.

6. Rafal Kasprowski, "NISO's IOTA Initiative: Measuring the Quality of OpenURL Links," *Serials Librarian* 62, no. 1–4 (2012): 95–102.

7. Elsa Anderson, "Electronic Resource Management Systems: A Work-flow Approach," *Library Technology Reports* 50, no. 3 (April 2014).

8. Oliver Pesch, "Standards that Impact the Gathering and Analysis of Usage," *Serials Librarian* 61, no. 1 (2011): 23–32. See also, Shona Koehn and Suliman Hawamdeh, "The Acquisition and Management of Electronic Resources: Can Use Justify Cost?," *Library Quarterly* 80, no. 2 (April 2010): 161–74.

9. Hong Yo Kim and Hyun Hee Kim, "Development and Validation of Evaluation Indicators for a Consortium of Institutional Repositories: A Case Study of Collection," *Journal of the American Society for Information Science and Technology* 59, no. 8 (2008): 1282–94.

10. Ellen Finnie Duranceau and Sue Kriegsman, "Implementing Open Access Policies Using Institutional Repositories," in *The Institutional Repository: Benefits and Challenges*, ed. Pamela Bush and Cindy Hepfer (Chicago: Association for Library Collections & Technical Services, The American Library Association, 2013), 81–105.

11. Jean Gabriel Bankier and Kenneth Gleason, *Institutional Repository Software Comparison* (Paris: UNESCO, 2014).

12. Sean Burns, Amy Lana, and John Budd, "Institutional Repositories: Exploration of Costs and Value," *D-Lib Magazine* 19, no. 1–2 (January–February 2013), http://www.dlib.org/dlib/january13/burns/01burns.html.

13. Kenyon Stuart, Ken Varum, and Judith Ahronheim, "Measuring Journal Linking Success from a Discovery Service," *Information Technology and Libraries* 34, no. 1 (March 2015): 52–76.

14. Marshall Breeding, "Library Resource Discovery Products: Context, Library Perspectives, and Vendor Positions," *Library Technology Reports* 50, no. 1 (January 2014).

15. Andrew Asher, Lynda Duke, and Suzanne Wilson, "Paths of Discovery: Comparing the Search Effectiveness of EBSCO Discovery Service, Summon, Google Scholar, and Conventional Library Resources," *College & Research Libraries* 74, no. 5 (2013): 464–88. See also, William Chickering and Sharon Yang, "Evaluation and Comparison of Discovery Tools: An Update," *Information Technology and Libraries* 33, no. 2 (June 2014): 5–30; and Karen Ciccone and John Vickery, "Summon, EBSCO Discovery Service, and Google Scholar: A Comparison of Search Performance Using User Queries," *Evidence Based Library and Information Practice* 10, no. 1 (2015): 34–49.

16. Karen Stevenson, Sarah Elsegood, David Seaman, Cyndy Pawlek, and Michael Poltorak Nielsen, "Next-Generation Library Catalogues: Reviews of Encore, Primo, Summon and Summa," *Serials* 22, no. 1 (2009): 68–78. See also, Joseph Deodato, "Evaluating Web-Scale Discovery: A Step-by-Step Guide," *Information Technology and Libraries* 34, no. 2 (June 2015): 19–75.

17. Jeremy Darrington, "A Hybrid Approach to Discover Services: Reflection on Implementing both Primo and Summon," *Reference & User Services Quarterly* 53, no. 4 (Summer 2014): 291–5.

18. Kelsey Brett, Ashley Lierman, and Cherie Turner, "Lessons Learned: A Primo Usability Study," *Information Technology and Libraries* 35, no. 1 (March 2016): 7–25.

19. Michael Levine-Clark, Jason Price, and John McDonald, "Discovery or Displacement? A Large-Scale Longitudinal Study of the Effect of Discovery Systems on Online Journal Usage. 2013," Proceedings of the Charleston Library Conference, November 2013, http://dx.doi.org/10.5703/1288284315331.

20. Matthew Reidsma, "Algorithmic Bias in Library Discovery Systems," March 11, 2016, *MatthewRiedsma*, https://matthew.reidsrow.com/articles/173.

21. Online Computer Library Center (OCLC), *Perceptions of Libraries and Information Resources. A Report to the OCLC Membership* (Dublin, OH: OCLC, 2005).

22. Roger Schonfeld, *Does Discovery Still Happen in the Library? Roles and Strategies for a Shifting Reality* (New York: Ithaka S+R, 2014).

23. Aaron Tay, "8 Surprising Things I Learnt About Google Scholar," *Musing About Librarianship* (blog) (June 2014), http://musingsaboutlibrarianship.blogspot .com/2014/06/8-surprising-things-i-learnt-about.html. See also, Aaron Tay, "How Are Discovery Systems Similar to Google? How Are They Different?," *Musing About Librarianship* (blog) (April 2013), http://musingsaboutlibrarianship.blogspot.com /2013/04/how-are-discovery-systems-similar-to.html.

24. Melissa A. Hofmann and Sharon Yang, "'Discovering' What's Changed: A Revisit of the OPACs of 260 Academic Libraries," *Library Hi Tech* 30, no. 2 (2012): 253–74. See also Mark Dehmlow, "Editorial Board Thoughts: Services and User Context in the Era of Webscale Discovery," *Information Technology and Libraries* 32, no. 2 (2013): 1–3.

25. Online Computer Library Center (OCLC), *Perceptions of Libraries, 2010: Context and Community* (Dublin, OH: OCLC, 2010), http://www.oclc.org/content/dam /oclc/reports/2010perceptions/2010perceptions_all.pdf.

26. Simone Kortekaas and Bianca Kramer, "Thinking the Unthinkable: A Library Without a Catalogue—Reconsidering the Future of Discovery Tools for Utrecht University Library," *Insights* 27, no. 3 (November 2014), insights.uksg.org /article/download/2048-7754.174/188/.

27. Lorcan Dempsey, "Thirteen Ways of Looking at Libraries, Discovery, and the Catalog: Scale, Workflow, Attention," *Educause*, December 10, 2012, http://www .educause.edu/ero/article/thirteen-ways-looking-libraries-discovery-and-catalog -scale-workflow-attention.

28. Mirela Roncevic, "E-book Platforms for Libraries," *Library Technology Reports* 49, no. 3 (April 2013): 1–43.

29. Javier Celaya, "Free Guide to Ebook Licensing for Public Libraries and Publishers," *Publishing Perspectives*, November 24, 2015, http://publishingperspectives .com/2015/11/guide-ebook-licensing-for-public-libraries/#.VumYxI7F9EI.

30. Lee Raine, *Libraries and Learning* (New York: Pew Research, 2016), https:// www.pewresearch.org/wp-content/uploads/sites/9/2016/04/PI_2016.04.07 _Libraries-and-Learning_FINAL.pdf.

31. Jenny Arch, "How Massachusetts Libraries Are Disrupting the Ebook System," *Information Today* 33, no. 5 (June 2016).

32. Laura Dunlop, Gabrielle Narsted, and Jesse Finkelstein, *Canadian eBooks in Public Libraries: A Gap Analysis Report on Trends and Issues in eBook Collection Practices* (Toronto: eBOUND Canada, January 2018).

8
Electronic Resource Management

The real danger is not that computers will begin to think like men,
but that men will begin to think like computers.

—Sydney Harris[1]

Today, electronic resources, be they journal articles, eBooks or other content, are available from a multitude of sources, including publishers, aggregators (who combine content from several sources into a single package), and abstracting and indexing services. From the user's perspective, being able to access content from a particular academic field, such as physical sciences, social sciences, or humanities, simplifies the process of attempting to stay current in a field, as well as the process of conducting a literature review as part of a research project. The appeal for users is that they have access to these electronic resources anytime, anywhere, without the need to visit the library itself.

Today, large academic research libraries spend hundreds of thousands of dollars, and smaller academic and public libraries spend tens of thousands of dollars *licensing* electronic content. The key word in the prior sentence is *licensing* rather than purchasing. Libraries used to purchase print copies of journals and other materials that today are only available to be licensed from a vendor (publisher, aggregator, or other supplier). And because the library owned the journal, they could share this journal with their customers (within some broadly defined limits), of course.

In 2002, the Digital Library Federation (DLF) created the Electronic Resource Management Initiative (ERMI) that would allow libraries and vendors to develop a shared vision for what an electronic resource management system (ERMS) might entail. The resulting DLF final report provided a "Problem Definition and Road Map, a Workflow Diagram, Functional Specifications, Entity Relationship Diagram, Data Elements and Definitions, and an XML Schema."[2]

The NISO ERM Data Standards and Best Practices Project, a beneficiary of the Digital Library Federation efforts, created a report on the electronic resource management (ERM) standards landscape and came to these conclusions:[3]

- **Link Resolvers and Knowledge Bases**—KBART (Knowledge Bases and Related Tools) is helpful, whereas IOTA (Improving OpenURL Through Analytics) needs additional work.

- **The work, manifestations, and access points**—The following standards and best practices should be used: MARC 21, the ONIX for Serials formats (**On**line **I**nformation E**x**change, or ONIX), a set of XML formats for exchanging information about serial products and subscriptions); and Project TRANSFER (the Transfer Code of Practice), which provides recommended guidelines to assist publishers in ensuring that journal content remains easily accessible when there is a transfer from one publisher to another because of one or more journal titles being sold.

- **Cost and usage-related data**—The building blocks in this area include NISO CORE (cost of resource exchange), Recommended Practice (transferring cost, invoice, and related financial information from an ILS to an ERMS), Counting Online Usage of Networked Electronic Resources (COUNTER), and the continued refinement of Standardized Usage Statistics Harvesting Initiative (SUSHI).

- **License terms**—NISO is encouraged to develop a scalable "third way" to overcome the limitations of ONIX-PL (ONIX for publications licenses) and continue the Electronic Resource Management Initiative (ERMI).

- **Data exchange using institutional identifiers**—Continued work on the NISO I (institutional identifiers) and the WorldCat registry of the Online Computer Library Center (OCLC) should continue; and vCard (virtual business card—an electronic representation of a business card) offers real potential.

However, today the library must license access to the electronic content on an annual basis, year after year. Given the significant costs to license this electronic content, libraries are increasingly concerned about assessing the costs and benefits of providing access. The shift from print to electronic resources is quite dramatic and is illustrated in Figure 8.1. The chart shows the percent change in electronic resources compared to total collection expenditures in academic libraries over a ten-year period.

It should be noted that the use of a separate ERMS module is declining in libraries as the ERMS functionality has become a part of next-generation library management platforms that have been introduced and implemented in hundreds of libraries since 2017.

Evaluation

Several challenges are associated with the evaluation and assessment of electronic resources. To date, five types of evaluation of electronic resources have been developed:

- **Transaction-based measures** focus on counts of search sessions, type of searches performed, number of records retrieved, and so forth.

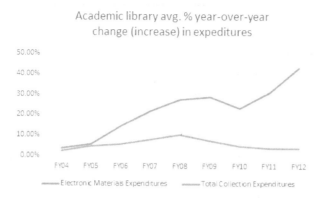

FIGURE 8.1. Academic Library eResource Expenditures Compared to Total Collection Expenditures
Source: Reprinted with permission.

- **Time-based measures** explore such topics as the length of each search session, time spent browsing versus downloading content, identifying peak periods of use, and related measures.

- **Cost-based measures** concern determining the cost to provide access to a specific journal or a group of journals (from one publisher), calculating the cost per use or cost per download, and so forth.

- **Use-based measures** identify the number of unique users, the number of journal titles and journal articles viewed online, number of journal articles downloaded, number of citations (and abstracts) downloaded, and so forth.

- **Value-based measures** attempt to determine the value to the library's customers of having access to all of this electronic content. In some cases, libraries conduct user satisfaction surveys as a surrogate measure for value. Many libraries assert that because it is important to satisfy users' needs, it is imperative to determine to what degree information resources that are provided are used, as use is considered a surrogate measure for value (if users' did not find value in searching and downloading eResources, then they would not do it).

Collecting Data

One of the significant challenges facing any library that has licensed electronic resources is gathering a variety of data pertaining to these resources. What does a download mean, and how is it consistently measured? Should libraries rely on data that they collect, or should they focus on vendor-provided data? Because vendors report statistics to their customers, how can libraries be sure that they are measuring apples and apples (not apples and oranges) from each vendor? Obviously a standard was needed to ensure the data were defined in the same way and then reported in the same way to each library. Thus, Project COUNTER was born. COUNTER is an international initiative to improve the reliability of online usage statistics from vendors. Project COUNTER has published a Code of Practice that specifies the content, format, delivery mechanisms, definitions, and rules for a set of core usage reports.

January 2019 is the effective date for compliance with the COUNTER Code of Practice Release 5 and provides four Master Reports:[4]

1.   Platform Master Report

2.   Database Master Report

3.   Title Master Report

4.   Item Master Report

Publishers, aggregators and other vendors can go through an auditing process to become COUNTER compliant and, once certified, are listed on the Project COUNTER website. To be COUNTER compliant, an organization must comply with the current version of the Code of Practice as verified by an independent auditor using a set of test scripts developed by COUNTER (www.projectcounter.org/code_practice.html).

Not too long after libraries started using COUNTER reports, it became apparent that attempting to correlate and consolidate the COUNTER reports from various vendors (visiting each vendor's website, logging in, and then retrieving the COUNTER reports) was a time-consuming and frustrating experience. This frustration led to the development by NISO of SUSHI. In slightly technical terms, the SUSHI protocol is a SOAP (Simple Object Access Protocol) request/response web services "wrapper" for the XML version of COUNTER reports.

The library's client service (initiated by a library management platform, an ERMS or other automated library system) connects to the vendor's SUSHI server service, identifies itself to the vendor, and then downloads the appropriate COUNTER report to the library. Typically, the library sets up its client service so that the entire process is repeated monthly for each vendor that it does business with and that is capable of providing COUNTER-compliant reports. Clearly SUSHI automates a very tedious and time-consuming process and will thus save the library a considerable amount of money. In the United Kingdom, a Journal Usage Statistics Portal (JUSP) has been created that consolidates COUNTER reports from a large number of publishers, allowing participating member libraries to connect to JUSP only once a month.[5]

Other initiatives that resulted from the development of the DLF ERM document include these:

- **ESPReSSO** (Establishing Suggested Practices Regarding Single Sign On) provides a set of best practices so that a user can sign on once and yet gain access to numerous online eResources at different points in the searching and retrieval process—no need to sign on to each new database during a search session.

- **PIE-J** (Presentation & Identification of e-Journals) provides guidance in the areas of title presentation and history, appropriate use of the international standard serial number (ISSN), and citation practice to enable discovery, identification, and access for publications.

Licensing

The challenges associated with the negotiating of a license for an electronic resource are considerable and require knowledge and a fair amount of time (especially for the larger libraries, who must deal with a large number of vendors). An alternative to a license agreement is the use of a Shared Electronic Resource Understanding (SERU), a best practice developed by NISO.

SERU, updated in 2012, expresses a shared agreement of content providers, the library, and authorized users; the nature of the content; use and limits on the use of the content; confidentiality and privacy issues; service expectations; archiving of content; and perpetual access. Both the vendor and the subscribing institution realize substantial benefits by removing the overhead associated with the license negotiation process when they use SERU.

Usability

One of the more discouraging aspects of electronic resources, especially those resources that provide access to journal articles, is the plethora of user interfaces that users must learn and navigate as they search for and subsequently download journal articles. Simply consider the various interfaces users encounter when they visit some of the more popular eResource sites such as EBSCOHost, Gale Virtual Reference Library, ScienceDirect, JSTOR, Project Muse, ProQuest, Emerald, PubMed, Sage, Scopus, and Web of Science, among many others.

A discovery service solves this problem of having to deal with multiple interfaces. There does not appear to be a solution to this challenge on the horizon as the vendors are not likely going to agree to use the same user interface to provide access to their licensed content (after all—from the perspective of the vendors—they each feel their user interface (UI) is quite good and that it cost a lot of money to develop and maintain).

Electronic Reference Materials

Users have been voting with their feet, indicating that they prefer convenience to quality, especially quality print reference collections. Academic libraries are reporting that only a small proportion of their print reference collections are being used each year, and thus libraries are shrinking these collections as well as purchasing/licensing electronic versions of this content.[6] Texas A&M University found that moving its reference collection primarily to eBooks resulted in a dramatic increase in use of this content.[7] Other libraries have surveyed their users, who indicated their preference for online content was due to convenience and currency.[8]

Other Options

The diversity of sources for obtaining digital resources has meant that libraries have a number of options for obtaining access to this content:

- *Interlibrary loan*—Libraries can rely on borrowing digital content from other libraries. Increasingly libraries are able to obtain copies of electronic resources in a day or two (and in some cases, in just a few hours).

- *Document delivery service*—Libraries can use a document delivery service to obtain resources that are difficult to locate.

- *Purchase one or more copies from a supplier*—Rather than licensing the digital content from a publisher or supplier, the library may simply purchase a copy of the desired resources on a case-by-case basis (sometimes referred to as by-the-drink or a pay-per-view approach).

All of this is happening in the broader context of libraries, in particular academic libraries, moving from a just-in-case collection model to a "just-in-time" approach to delivering content to patrons in order to meet their needs.

Clearly, the increasing reliance on electronic resources has elicited more organizational change and innovation in libraries than any other factor over the last fifteen years. It is possible to identify three periods of change:[9]

The first wave—Accommodating electronic resources in a print-centric structure. Library staff members usually absorbed portions of the various responsibilities associated with electronic resources, and over time a staff member might be reassigned or a new staff member was recruited to handle the increasing complexities of eResources.

The second wave—Reorganizing to support the growth of electronic resources. A majority of libraries find themselves in this wave in which electronic resources are the dominant format and represent a substantial portion of the acquisitions budget. Libraries may have created a separate unit to handle electronic resources, yet recognize that this is still a transitional stage.

The third wave—Holistic electronic resource management. An emerging unit will handle not only electronic resources but also responsibilities that have expanded to include collection development and, in some cases, access services.

The need for change was clearly articulated in the University of California Libraries Bibliographic Services Task Force, who noted the realities of duplicated work being done in several libraries and the inability to share records across multiple databases, stating, "The time and energy required to do Library business is unsustainable."[10]

Summary

Providing access to a plethora of eResources is a challenging and time-consuming task for any size library. Libraries must become more aware of the options available for managing eResources so that they can collaborate with other libraries in order to reduce the costs while improving the quality of services associated with the management of eResources.

Questions to Consider

- Has your library modified its workflow so that it is more in line with the NISO ERM Data Standards and Best Practices?

- What strategies is your library considering given the increasing costs of licensing eResources each year?

- Is your library using COUNTER/SUSHI on a regular basis to gather usage data of eResources?

- Has your library used the University of California Libraries Bibliographic Services Task Force report as the basis for a discussion on the continuing sustainability of the library?

- Have you considered joining a consortium in order to lower the costs for licensing eResources?

Notes

1. Sydney Harris, quoted in Shawn Kennedy, *Funny Cyptograms* (New York: Sterling, 2003), 84.

2. *Electronic Resource Management: Report of the DLF ERM Initiative* (Washington, DC: Council on Library and Information Resources, 2002). See also, Marilyn Geller, "ERM: Staffing, Services, and Systems," *Library Technology Reports* 42, no. 2 (March–April 2006).

3. NISO ERM Data Standards and Best Practices Review Steering Committee, *Making Good on the Promise of ERM: A Standards and Best Practices Discussion Paper* (Baltimore, MD: NISO, 2012).

4. COUNTER, *COUNTER Code of Practice Release 5* (Winchester, UK: COUNTER, July 2017), https://www.projectcounter.org/wp-content/uploads/2017/10/Release5_20171013-1.pdf.

5. Paul Meehan, Paul Needham, and Ross MacIntyre. "SUSHI: Delivering Major Benefits to JUSP," *Ariadne*, November 30, 2012, http://www.ariadne.ac.uk/issue70/meehan-et-al.

6. Heather Terrell, "Reference Is Dead, Long Live Reference: Electronic Collections in the Digital Age," *Information Technology and Libraries* 34, no. 4 (December 2015): 55–62.

7. Dennis Dillon. "E-books: The University of Texas Experience, Part 1," *Library Hi Tech* 19, no. 2 (2001): 113–25.

8. Paul Hellyer, "Reference 2.0: The Future of Shrinking Print Reference Collections Seems Destined for the Web," *AALL Spectrum* 13 (March 2009): 24–27.

9. Anne Elguindi and Kari Schmidt, "Emerging Technical Services Models In the Context of the Past," in *Electronic Resource Management: Practical Perspectives In A New Technical Services Model*, Anne Elguindi and Kari Schmidt, eds. (London: Chandros, 2012), 1–38.

10. The University of California Libraries Bibliographic Services Task Force, *Rethinking How We Provide Bibliographic Services for the University of California*, Final Report (Berkeley, CA: The University of California, December 2005), 9.

Part III

Management Issues

Rothenberg's Law
Digital data lasts forever, or five years,
whichever comes first.

—Jeff Rothenberg[1]

Managing information technology is a critical and very important responsibility for the management team of any library, and the next six chapters run the gamut from planning to system selection and implementation, to usability of systems.

Chapter 9 discusses the strategic planning process for information technology and the impacts of technology on staff members. Chapter 10 focuses on the ways information technology can affect us as individuals and our work.

Chapter 11 presents an overview of the system selection process. Chapter 12 focuses on the issues surrounding system migration and related implementation issues. Chapter 13 addresses the issues associated with the management of information technology.

Chapter 14 focuses on usability issues. This section closes with a chapter addressing management issues and identifying qualities associated with a systems or technology manager. Chapter 15 offers commonsense axioms that include guidelines for decision-makers.

Note

1. Jeff Rothenberg, "Ensuring the Longevity of Digital Documents," *Scientific American* 272, no. 1 (January 1955), 42–47.

9
Planning for Information Technology

If we continue to develop our technology without wisdom or prudence, our servant may prove to be our executioner.

—Omar Bradley[1]

Information technology is permeating all aspects of our lives, including where we work and play. The implications of this pervasive force are that we all are constantly learning new technology-related coping skills. Technology has also impacted our social structure as we increasingly use email, online chat rooms, instant messaging, social media sites such as Facebook; search Google; watch YouTube videos; share photos using Instagram; and use a variety of other apps to communicate with our family, friends, and coworkers. Technology impacts the way we work: information and productivity software collaboration tools are now accessible to all staff members—regardless of where they are located. Technology is also infiltrating the marketplace as we increasing turn to online, internet-based, eCommerce options to purchasing products for work and home.

Strategic Planning

Knowledge has been shackled to the physical.
Now that the digitizing of information
is allowing us to go beyond the physical
…the shape of our knowledge is changing.

—David Weinberger

Regardless of the size and type of library, planning for information technology should, in the best of all possible cases, occur as a part of a broader strategic planning process. Developing a technology plan that is not in concert with the goals and mission of the parent organization is simply an exercise in frustration. Although the technology plan may be good from a technical point of view, its utility for the library and its parent organization may be negligible if it is not "in synch" with the goals of the larger organization. The purpose of any strategic plan is to set a clear direction that integrates goals, policies, and actions into a cohesive whole.[2]

A library's strategic plan (assuming there is one) works best when the parent organization's mission statement is reflected in the plan. Assessing the suitability of a library plan requires answers to a wide-ranging series of questions. Does the library's vision statement, goals, and objectives assist the parent organization in achieving its goals? Does the strategic plan identify the library's core competencies? Is it clear what the library does that adds value in the life of the customer? What library services do patrons actually use and, by inference, find to be of value? And what services are used with and without library staff assistance? What is the library's role in providing distance services—selecting, acquiring, organizing, and providing access to internet-based resources? How does the library support remote online users? If the library's online catalog, discovery system, or website is accessible 24/7, are there additional services (such as an app) remote users can use regardless of the time?

Libraries without a technology plan experience a much more chaotic life and require ad hoc purchases of computer equipment and software when something no longer works. Staff generally feel uncomfortable with and perhaps are a bit fearful of information technology because they have received little or no training.

Until the 1990s, the preeminent role of most library services was to provide access to information—regardless of its actual location. David Lankes suggests in his wonderful and insightful book *The Atlas of New Librarianship*, "The mission of librarians is to improve society through facilitating knowledge creation in their communities."[3]

The library's mission is to support the goals and objectives of the institution or the interests of the population being served. The preparation of the library's strategic plan is to consider the unthinkable, to explore options that are outside the box. Too often librarians continue to make assumptions about how library services should be deliverable without exploring alternatives that might deliver more value to the customer. Libraries should be asking themselves questions such as these:

- Does the physical collection need to be as large as it currently is?

- Does all of the collection need to be housed in a single building (or could some portion of the collection be moved to a remote location or moved to an automatic storage and retrieval system?)

- Do we need to organize the collection in Dewey or Library of Congress (LC) call number sequence, or should we consider options?

Well, you get the idea.

Michael Hammer and James Champy, in their classic management book *Rengineering the Corporation*, stated that reengineering is "a fundamental rethinking and radical redesign of business (library) processes to achieve dramatic improvements in critical measurements of performance, such as cost, quality, service and speed."[4]

There are four key phrases contained within this definition: They are:

- **Fundamental rethinking**—After it is determined *what* an organization will do, the focus then shifts to *how* best to do it. The concentration is on what could be or should be—not what is.

- **Radical redesign**—A radical redesign disregards existing procedures and processes and looks for new ways to accomplish things. Boundaries need to be broken and departments may require restructuring or destruction.

- **Processes**—A set of activities that takes inputs and creates an output that is of value to a customer. The focus is not on departments or other organization units. Note that information technology can act as an essential enabler during a reengineering project.

- **Dramatic improvements**—The focus of reengineering is to aim for improvements that are an order of magnitude greater than existing processes—improvements on the order of 100 percent, 200 percent, or more, rather than small incremental improvements.

At the start of the strategic planning process, it is not uncommon for the planning team to engage in a process to identify strengths, weaknesses, opportunities, and threats (sometimes referred to as a SWOT) analysis:

- Strengths (what the library currently does well)

- Weaknesses (what are the problems currently [or what are they likely to be] facing the library)

- Opportunities (forecast future possibilities, in terms of services—not technology—that will benefit the library's users)

- Threats (what external pressures could change the competitive landscape)

A knowledgeable staff member (or consultant) can prepare a SWOT analysis, or the decision-makers and key stakeholders might engage in a brainstorming session to prepare such an analysis. Regardless of the approach, a SWOT planning document (or similar assessment) should become a part of the technology plan and thus document the participants' perceptions.

An effective strategic planning process assists the library in creating its own future and is characterized by the following:

- **A good assessment**—Before plotting your future direction, it's a good idea to know where you're starting from. In some cases, an in-depth and thorough assessment is required. For some, though, a "mini-assessment" can be enough—in the form of answering a few key questions:

  - Mini-inventory: Whom do you serve? Who are your stakeholders (including patrons, other users, and staff)? *Take care to list specific groups; for example, public libraries endeavor to serve all, but likely have a focus on specific groups such as children/early literacy, adult computer/technology users, adult learners, and many others. Academic libraries often have a focus on specific needs for students and for faculty.*

- Mini-inventory: How are they served? *For this question, it's helpful to list primary services by user groups and check for things that overlap and things that are unique to each group served.*

- Mini-inventory: What equipment do you have to meet technology needs? *Is the equipment in good condition with more useful life— or are replacements and/or upgrades needed?*

- Mini-inventory: What technology tools do staff need to do their jobs, and how well do the tools currently perform? *Gathering this information should be easy because this is generally "front of mind" for all library workers.*

- Mini-inventory: What else? *What have we missed?*

- **A customer focus**—How effective is the library in meeting the needs of its customers? Effectiveness answers the question "Are we doing the *right* things?" Could or should the library be serving more of its potential customers? How can the library attract those with library cards who have not used the library in more than a year to return? What is the appropriate balance between high-tech and high-touch? Peter Hernon and Joseph Matthews explore the structured and unstructured, solicited and unsolicited ways a library can learn more about its customers.[5]

  Another important method to better understand why people may or may not be using library services is to examine the jobs to be done (JTBD) by an individual. In reality, the customer has a job to be done and is seeking to find (in some cases "hire") the best product or service to do the job. Understanding the "jobs" your customers want done provides insights and can assist libraries design or acquire new products or services. This JTBD analysis can also highlight how existing offerings are not meeting the important needs. Customers might participate in a focus group or one-on-one interviews, or staff may observe individuals to learn more about JTBD. It is imperative that the library learn more about what current solutions are customers considering.

- **Improving relevant services**—It is important to recognize that libraries exist in a competitive environment (for instance, there are many other information providers) and that libraries must refresh its service offerings in order to stay relevant in the lives of its users. Perhaps the principal key to remaining relevant is convenience. Clearly the convenience of the Web compared to the physical inconvenience of finding and using information in a library setting must be addressed.

- **Examining efficiency**—Explore the internal procedures of the library to determine how efficient its processes and procedures are. Efficiency answers the question "Are we doing things *right*?" This may involve benchmarking your library to a set of peer libraries so that you can determine in what areas you may need to make some changes. Could the library outsource some tasks or activities? Should the library join a consortium or use a shared system?

- **Focus on outcomes**—How does the library impact its users? Impact the community? Impact the students, faculty, and staff on and off campus? The library should be able to answer the question "Of what value is the library to _____ (e.g., a specific market segment or group of individuals, the larger parent organization or community).

- **Providing access to content**—Almost every library today provides access to a range of eResources (electronic journals and databases), yet many users are unaware of this service (as they use other internet-based resources). The library should also be working hard to ensure that it is providing access to digitized content found in its special and historical collections (and that these resources are discoverable by search engines).

- **Serving as a crossroads to the community served**—Whether the library serves an academic or public community, one of the most powerful roles it can serve is to bring together people, thoughts, ideas, and knowledge from different domains. The results of these efforts can result in powerful collaborations in research, community building, instruction, and knowledge creation. Collaborative learning commons, maker spaces, and digital scholarship laboratories are all examples of these efforts.

- **Identifying ways to add value**—Increasingly, it is important to understand the ways in which your library can add value by providing tools and opportunities for people to add context to library content as a way to encourage collaboration and build community.[6]

Today, information technology allows a library to change in ways that could not be imagined twenty years ago. Moreover, insistent library customers will, in the end, force libraries to change (or they will vote with their feet and go somewhere else). The speed with which the Web is continuing to change and evolve is a constant fact of life that libraries must reckon with. The internet is dramatically lowering the transaction costs of doing business anywhere on the planet. Thus the value of the local collection is being diminished as people have a plethora of options that did not exist one or more decades ago. As Lorcan Dempsey of the Online Computer Library Center (OCLC) has observed, our users are operating at the network level while almost all libraries continue to operate at the organizational level. Lorcan further asserts that discovery happens elsewhere (e.g., Google or Google Scholar) rather than a user starting with the library's catalog.[7]

Yet the mere fact that technology continues to change at a rapid pace is not sufficient grounds to change the services provided by a library. Rather, the library should be focusing on where it can clearly provide differentiating value as the primary motivating factor in any strategic planning process. Users can utilize many technologies without them being delivered in a library setting. However, many technologies are actually an extension of current knowledge creation processes or can be significantly enhanced through the application of existing knowledge and thus are better utilized, and understood, as a result. Librarians should closely examine these technologies for utilization in the library.

The question of strategy then comes down to being able to identify the "sweet spot" that exists when three fundamental topics are overlaid: (1) What are the network-based competitive offerings being used by people? (2) What

The Strategic Sweet Spot

FIGURE 9.1. The Library Strategic Sweet Spot
Source: Reprinted with permission from Ken Chad, July 3, 2015, Connect,
Debate, Innovate: Library Service Innovation in a Competitive World: Focus on
the User. Available online at https://www.slideshare.net/kenchad/innovation-jtbd
-cilipconfjune2015.

are the needs of customers? (3) What are the capabilities that the library
has to offer, as shown in Figure 9.1?

Library staff members and decision-makers involved in the strategic
planning process must question all present practices and assumptions about
what the library is and the value it provides to its users. For example, many
libraries have decided that a single library solution is no longer providing
value to their customers, so they are joining with other libraries, typically
using a consortium, to implement shared automated systems. The user is
able to located more relevant materials using the shared system, and each
participating library typically lowers its costs. Consider, for example, the following large scale shared systems:

- BIBSYS—the National Library of Norway plus some 105 academic
  and research libraries in Norway

- California State College and Universities—twenty-three campuses

- Florida Academic Library Services Cooperative—all Florida community college and public universities

- JULAC—nine public universities of Hong Kong

- Orbis—thirty-seven colleges and universities in the US Pacific Northwest

- Wales Higher Education Libraries Forum—the National Library plus the major academic libraries of Wales

Technology Plan

Once the library's strategic plan is in place, developing a supporting technology plan is often a prudent decision. Here are the goals of a good technology plan, according to March Osten:

> Strategic technology planning is a dynamic and reflective process that organizations engage in to seize the potential of advanced technologies. Strategic technology plans are grounded in your mission and fully integrated into your overall strategic plan. The strategic technology planning process ensures that you will clarify technology goals and establish priorities, organize relevant stakeholders and create evaluation systems—all before making hardware, software or Internet presence decisions.[8]

There are a number of reasons for preparing a technology plan, including these:

- Make evident to everyone—staff, key stakeholders, and customers—what the library is doing and planning to do. In short, the library is cognizant of the need to manage technology just as it manages its other resources.

- Manage the budget process and expenditures to reduce the risks of needing to acquire equipment and software in a short period of time.

- Concentrate on ways in which technology can assist the library in achieving its vision.

- Identify the strengths and weaknesses concerning the current implementation of technologies. This will identify the gaps that currently exist.

- Rank-order the enhancements and new technology needed to assist the library in achieving its goals.

- Demonstrate that the library is effectively using technology to deliver products and services to its customers.

- Ensure that staff is aware of and trained in the use of new technologies and migrating to new versions of hardware and software.

- Create a fundraising plan if the financial resources are not available, through the normal budgetary process, to implement the needed technology. The plan should drive the budget rather than the reverse.

- Keep an eye on the leading edge of technology.

A technology plan documents the vision and direction of the library and creates a framework to set goals and identify specific deliverables. Once the plan is in place, it can help library decision-makers measure the costs and success in achieving the plan's goals. Although the plan is a document, it is much more important to recognize that it is also a process to provide staff with a road map. The technology plan connects to the library's overall strategic plan and should demonstrate how technology is assisting in meeting the library's ultimate goals and objectives. Not only should the technology plan identify ways to improve the delivery of services, programs, and operations with technology, but it should also include specific output measures that can be used to assess the plan's impact in the future.

Prior to starting the planning process, there are several issues that should be addressed. Among these are the ones listed here:

- What is the involvement of various staff members in developing and reviewing the plan? The best plans come from a variety of people who are able to offer diversified opinions.

- What about the involvement of knowledgeable individuals outside the library (chief information officer, chief technology officer, IT manager, and others from a parent organization or companies located within the community)?

- To what extent will users be involved in planning and reviewing plans? Will there be user surveys or focus groups with different types of users?

- Is the library planning to hire a consultant? What is the consultant's appropriate role—facilitator, full team-member, overall responsibility for delivering a technology plan?

Once the goals for developing a technology plan have been established, it is important to have a clear understanding of the current situation. To that end, it is helpful to create a technology inventory.

Technology Inventory

The library should update (or create) an inventory of the existing technology that is being used by the library. Note that this inventory should include technology "stuff" that is located in the library, may be located elsewhere on campus (or in a city/county facility), or is located in the "cloud." The library's technology inventory should include these considerations:

Network Infrastructure (LAN and WAN)

- Type of cabling
- Location or routes of cabling
- Routers/switches
- Bandwidth capabilities
- Internet connection and speed
- Wireless service (WiFi)

Computer Hardware (Desktop and Network Level)

- Computer manufacturer/model with amount of memory and operating system (number and location)
- Level of standardization among hardware components
- Licenses for all workstation and server software
- Licenses for all relevant cloud services

Application Software

- Desktop software (office, productivity, library-specific, other) including release version
- Licenses are in place for all software
- Degree of standardization

Technology Support

- End-user support—who provide and hours of support
- Network support
- Data backup and virus protection

Staff Skills

- Adequacy of skills among staff (will likely vary depending on the software application)
- Skills that need improving or acquiring

The elements of a good technology plan should not be overlooked:

- **Specific**—The technology plan should provide an action plan to completed over the coming two to three years. The plan should have specific phased or time-delimited deadlines and identify who is responsible for achieving each task within the plan.

- **Concise**—Anyone should be able to read and understand the plan without being a librarian or a computer nerd, so the use of any kind of jargon should be minimized. The plan itself should not be lengthy (the use of appendices is a great "holding place" for information that is important but is infrequently referenced). A good technology plan can be used to facilitate a discussion with decision-makers and with staff members.

- **Foreseeable**—Plan for two to three years ahead. Anything further and the confidence level about future technology developments will decline markedly. The plan should be considered as a "living document," and though reviewed annually, the library should embrace opportunities when they arise. Ensuring that decision-makers see the big picture is much more important than constructing a plan for each department within the library.

- **Flexible**—Long-term goals are achieved by taking a series of steps rather than attempting to cross the goal line in the first series of downs on the football field. Every plan should establish a set of realistic goals and objectives while at the same time requiring the library to stretch a bit. Although it is not always possible to achieve each goal in the planned sequence or time frame it is important to move in the desired direction by remaining agile and flexible. Technology changes rapidly, and the library's technology plan needs the flexibility to respond quickly when opportunities arise.

- **Integrated**—The technology plan should have several components:

  - *Infrastructure*—What are the immediate and future needs of the library's data network? Do users within library facilities currently experience slow response times? What are the current and future bandwidth requirements to meet the needs of staff and those users within each facility? What is the current speed of the internet connection and how will bandwidth requirements change in the coming three years? Does the library have a network diagram and an inventory of network-related equipment, such as routers, switches, cabling, and other network components?

  - *Hosted applications*—Check to determine when hosting licenses need to be renewed. Note performance of existing applications to determine whether additional computing and/or storage will be required in the near future, so this can be budgeted for ahead of need. Check that user counts planned for in the future are still within current licensing. Determine user satisfaction with the application to determine whether you might need to go to market and look at competitive offerings.

  - *Central site equipment*—Do any of the existing servers need to be upgraded or replaced? Do additional servers or disk drives need to be ordered? Is there an inventory of central site equipment?

  - *Central site software requirements*—Do the server and other equipment operating system software need to be upgraded? Are there major upgrades for the library's application software that needs to be installed? Is there an inventory of central site software?

  - *Desktop equipment and software*—What portion of the desktop workstations will be replaced each year (with what speed CPU processor, memory, and disk space)? Does the desktop operating software need to be upgraded? Is there an inventory of desktop equipment and software? The plan should assume old devices have no value and that there is a phased equipment replacement program that is a part of the plan. The plan may also specify the way in which old equipment will be recycled to minimize the impact on the environment.

  - *Standards*—What standards are being used as a planning foundation for the library? Standards might include minimum desktop workstation configurations, a specific release of an operating system, web browser, server manufacturer, database management system, communications protocol, virus scanning software, firewall software, and so forth.

- *Website*—What software will be used to develop and maintain the library's Web site? Will a content management system be used as a foundation for the website? Staff skills needed to maintain and improve the Web site?

- *Other equipment*—The library may need to acknowledge that it is responsible for additional equipment that will interact with one or more library systems. For example, the library may have installed RFID tags in each item and uses RFID for self-checkout stations, a return sorting system and a security control system near the exit(s). This equipment interacts with an automated system using an application programming interface, or API.

- *Library systems*—What major functional systems is the library currently operating—an integrated library system (ILS), an electronic resource management system (ERMS), an authentication system, an institutional repository, more than one website, and so forth? Are there upcoming software releases for each system that must be installed? Will the software release require staff training? Will the new software require an enhanced server?

- *Special projects*—Will the library be engaging in any special projects, such as digitizing photographs, technical reports, and other resources? Is the library planning a major exhibition and will need a website to provide online to the same content? The resources and staffing needed to complete these projects should be identified.

- *Staffing needs*—Are any new positions needed? What are the training needs of the existing technology staff so that they can maintain and improve their skills? Is recruiting and retaining knowledgeable staff members of concern? Are job descriptions going to change dramatically?

- *Disaster response*—What will the library do if a technology disaster occurs? A section of the technology plan should identify the library's contingency and recovery plan if a major disaster occurs and cripples technology. A disaster might include a fire, major break in a water main that floods the computer room, tornado, and so forth. A part of a disaster recovery plan includes communications with staff, key stakeholders, vendors, and customers.[9]

- *Financial aspects*—An effective plan should drive the budget rather than allow the budget to drive the plan. Identify the financial aspects, typically on a quarter-by-quarter basis, over the life of the plan.

Rather than being a high-tech wish list, a sound technology plan maps the growth of the computer and communications networks that will be needed to support the library's goals. It is vital to recognize that information technology is simply a tool to help the library provide quality service to its customers. An effective plan is one that demonstrates how effectively using information technology will improve the value of the services provided by the library to its users.[10]

Outline of a Technology Plan

Executive summary

Description of the library

Assessment of challenges facing the library

The current technology environment

Assessment of the current technology environment

Assessment of the library's website

Plan of action including timelines and budgets

Plan for revisions

Appendices (as needed)

Digital Strategic Plan

Enabled by technological change,
we are beginning to see a series of economic, social and cultural
   adaptations
that make possible a **radical transformation** of
how we make the information environment . . .

—Yochai Benkler[11]

Some libraries, especially really large libraries will create a digital strategic plan that is separate from the technology plan. The goal of this plan is to ensure that the library's digitized content is able to support teaching and research, and to connect and engage library users with their communities and history.

Typically a digital strategic plan addresses a number of important topics such as these:

Digital Content

- What content should be digitized (and in what order)? Possible criteria for prioritizing the digitization of content include: public interest, historical significance, condition, strategic alignment, grant funding opportunities, and so forth.
- Will a digital asset management system (DAMS) be used?
- Where will the digital content be stored and preserved?
- What born-digital content will be included (why?) and preserved?

Access to Digital Content

- What standards will be used to describe this digital content?
- How will users find this digital content? How detailed and what type of metadata record and/or finding guide will be created for each digital asset?

- Will search engine optimization techniques be used to increase findability?

- In what ways can a user view the digital content (does it include a page turning device, 3D viewer, and/or virtual reality)?

- Will online exhibits be created (and maintained for how long)?

- How to engage patrons in physical exhibits with digital content?

- Provide access to digital content for the HathiTrust and the Digital Public Library of America?

- Provide access to digital content to regional and state archives and historical associations?

Collaboration with Users

- What tools will be used to encourage users to add mapping components to digital content?

- What tools will be used to encourage users to transcribe digital content (e.g., letters and diaries)?

- What tools will be used to encourage users to add notes and comments to digital content?

The Charlotte Mecklenburg Library created five teams to research various topics in order to create the Library's first Digital Strategic Plan, including these five topics:

1. **Infrastructure**—Topics addressed include software development environment, how to test new software, production servers, content servers, staffing (development and support), customer interactions, and IT infrastructure.

2. **Content**—This team considered access issues, evaluation/usage of current offerings, vision for a variety of content, identification of priorities, who should create content, and considering how user- or staff-generated content fits into the library's vision.

3. **Digitization**—This team explored what digitization resources were needed; metadata standards; innovative ways to connect the past to the present, utilizing the community's unique content; and evaluating the user experience in gaining access to current content.

4. **User experience**—The team considered navigation, the search interface, website challenges, mobile compatibility, and the communications between staff and the customer.

5. **Community**—This team focused on digital programming (adult, teen, children), online communities, social media, and book clubs.

The resulting digital strategic plan was created using several guiding principles:

- Having a unified digital platform: one login, one interface, one platform
- Using a single search box
- Removing barriers: access to everything, anywhere, anytime
- Creating a platform that will be responsive and mobile friendly, supporting browsers on multiple devices and operating systems
- Making digital content accessible for all customers, including those with disabilities
- Minimizing language barriers
- Providing multiple interactive features to engage community members
- Fostering an interactive digital community by providing channels for public comments and feedback, content creation and sharing
- Empowering the individual by customizing the experience
- Reaching further with digital programming—live or archived performances, lectures, interviews, Storytimes
- Preserving our past by showcasing items of unique and historical value
- Ensuring that all digital content is discoverable
- Equipping staff for the 21st century

Staying Current

When a profession has been created as a result of some scarcity,
as with librarians or television programmers,
the professionals are often the last ones to
see it when that scarcity goes away.
It is easier to understand that you face competition than obsolescence.
                                                                —Clay Shirky[12]

   Library staff members must participate in a process of keeping current with technological developments and the possible impacts or implications for service delivery within the library. This can be done in a variety of ways, including attending conferences; taking training seminars (in person or virtually); conducting webinars; having brown-bag discussions; and/or reading books, journals, blogs, and or listservs. Oh so many possibilities and so little reading time! One sound strategy is not to expect any one staff member to be an expert in everything (which is impossible), but instead to encourage each to pursue special areas of interest—and then gather together periodically to share information. Simply scanning a number of resources will provide a general overview of what is happening in the computer and communications technology arenas. The trick is not to get immersed in the details, but rather to focus on the horizon in order to see the big picture. When reviewing an article (or a book/blog about emerging technologies):[13]

- Consider the ways in which a technology could improve service to the library's customers or its staff members.

- Clearly identify those areas of a technology you can control, as well as those technology components that are outside your control.

- Recognize that some industry players, by their immense size, will have a disproportionate impact on the marketplace. Some of the vendors that fall into this category are Microsoft, Google, Apple, Cisco, and Facebook. Be cautious in betting against these firms.

At conferences, online discussion groups, blogs, social media, and other forums, make sure you chat with your peers about the direction they are moving in and what new technologies they are currently implementing (and why).

Some new technologies that may have an impact on your library in the next few years include augmented reality, big data analysis, open hardware, beacons, the Internet of Things, and wearable technologies.

Impact of IT on Staff

Information technology (IT) is unmistakably having a major impact on staff members at all levels within the library, whether professional, para-professional, or clerical. There are six major implications concerning the use of information technology for staff members:

- **Jobs are technology dependent**—With all staff members having access to and expected to use a variety of computer-based technologies and applications, staff need to be comfortable entering data and interacting with a variety of application software or surfing the internet.

- **Skills need to be upgraded**—When confronted with a plethora of new software releases or new application software, staff are faced with the need to upgrade their skills so they can effectively use the available information technology. We have all been bombarded with technology-related jargon that has become second nature to us in libraries (well, at least some of the jargon is understood by us). Consider, *pdf, BIBFRAME,* and oh so many more acronyms that have invaded our libraries.

- **The mix of staff is changing**—Although some libraries have been able to cope with a doubling or tripling of workloads without increasing staff (especially during this last recession that started in 2008) by more effectively using the tools provided by information technology, the reality is that libraries today require an increasingly diverse set of skills that is resulting in hiring of professionals that are not librarians but are necessary in order to deliver the services being demanded by our customers today. In addition, the mix of staff is changing due to the "drift-down principles:"

  - Nothing should be done by a professional that can be done by a technician (paraprofessional).

  - Nothing should be done by a technician that can be done by a clerk.

  - Nothing should be done by a clerk that can be done by a machine.[14]

- **The workload is increasing**—Although access to computer-based resources throughout the organization improves the staff's overall productivity, this accessibility is also a double-edged sword: the workload is also increasing. Staff are confronted with pressures to respond to emails, texts, tweets, and other content that they request or is pushed to them, as well as to post content to social media sites.

- **Some skills/knowledge must be forgotten**—It is also important for staff to "let go" of some of the skills and habits that worked in the past. For example, trying to stay current by participating (or lurking) with several professional discussion groups (and the associated flood of emails) is no longer attainable.

Lean Thinking

Lean thinking is the application of lean manufacturing, a concept originally developed by Toyota, to nonmanufacturing organizations. One of the driving concepts of lean thinking is to eliminate all possible waste. Possible wastes include the following:

- *Delays*—experienced by customers waiting for service and experienced by other staff members.

- *Duplication*—Having to copy data to multiple forms and/or reports, having to reenter data, and so forth.

- *Service quality errors*—lack of quality in service processes.

- *Unnecessary movement*—having to move about in order to complete a task, poor ergonomics, trips to a printer.

- *Unclear communication*—confusion over work activities, policies, or procedures.

- *Inventory challenges*—not having the right products at the right place at the right time, for example, materials delivered to the wrong branch.

- *Overproduction*—doing work that is not needed or creating unneeded reports.

Lean thinking typically has several characteristics:

- Adopts a customer service perspective that focuses on ways to deliver value to each customer

- Involves staff members (and, at times, customers) in continual improvement activities

- Adopts a rapid continuous improvement framework that emphasizes implementation over planning.

Some of the more common lean methods include these:

- **Value stream mapping**—a map of a process that is used to deliver a service, which is then refined and revised by team members to remove non-value-adding activities.

- **Kaizen**—a rapid process improvement event that brings together a team for three to five days to review and revise the process to improve productivity and increase customer value.

- **5Ss**—a way to organize process improvements: Sort, Set in order, Shine, Standardize, and Sustain.

Summary

The importance of developing and using a technology plan for the library cannot be overemphasized. The library's technology plan must be aligned with the library's overall strategic plan, which in turn hopefully is aligned with the parent organization (or the needs of the local community). As any military commander will tell you, a plan seldom lasts longer than the firing of the first round, but the process of planning is what pays the dividends.

Questions to Consider

- Can you think of three technology-related activities that you did not do a year ago?

- Does you library have a technology plan? If not, why not?

- Is your library's technology plan aligned with the library's own strategic plan?

- Has your library engaged in "radical rethinking" of its use of technology in the areas of technical services and public services?

- What are the characteristics of an effective planning process?

- Does you library have a budget category for the periodic refreshing and replacement of existing technology?

- Does your library monitor on a monthly basis the utilization of various networks, including the backbone connection to the internet? At what point should your library be upgrading its internet connectivity?

- Has you library considered joining a consortium in order to share technology?

- Has your library considered installing a fiber-optic broadband connection to the internet?

- What are you doing to stay current with emerging technology trends?

Suggested Web Resources

NPower—Technology planning for nonprofits: http://www.npower.org
TechSoup—Technology planning for nonprofits: http://techsoup.org
WebJunction—Assists library professionals build the skills, knowledge, and support to create connected, vibrant libraries: http://www.webjunction .org
Educause—A far-reaching site where technology and higher education come together: http://www.educause.edu

Notes

1. Omar Bradley, quoted in Mary-Kate Leahy, "Keeping Up with the Drones: Is Just War Theory Obsolete?," in *Information as Power*, ed. Jeffery L. Caton, John H. Greenmyer, Jeffery L. Groh, and William O. Waddell, vol. 5 (Carlisle, PA: US Army War College, 2011), 139.

2. Joseph Matthews, *Strategic Planning and Management for Library Managers* (Westport, CT: Libraries Unlimited, 2005).

3. David Lankes, *The Atlas of New Librarianship* (Cambridge, MA: MIT Press, 2011), 13.

4. Michael Hammer and James Champy, *Re-Engineering the Corporation: A Manifesto for Business Revolution* (New York: HarperBusiness, 2006), 24.

5. Peter Hernon and Joseph R. Matthews, *Listening to the Customer* (Santa Barbara, CA: Libraries Unlimited, 2011).

6. Joseph R. Matthews, *Adding Value to Libraries, Archives and Museums* (Santa Barbara, CA: Libraries Unlimited, 2016).

7. Lorcan Dempsey, "Discovery Happens Elsewhere," *Lorcan Dempsey's Weblog* (blog), September 16, 2017, http://orweblog.oclc.org/discovery-happens-elsewhere/.

8. March Osten, *Strategic Technology Planning: What Is It?*, January 4, 2001.

9. Mary Mallery, ed., *Technology Disaster Response and Recovery Planning. A LITA Guide* (Chicago: American Library Association, 2015).

10. Jan Baltzer, "Consider the Four-Legged Stool as You Plan for Information Technology," *Computers in Libraries* 20, no. 4 (April 2000): 42–45.

11. Yochai Benkler, *The Penguin and the Leviathan: The Triumph of Cooperation over Self-Interest* (New York: Crown Books, 2011), 149.

12. Clay Shirky, *Cognitive Surplus: Creativity and Generosity in a Connected World* (New York: Penguin Press, 2010), 214.

13. See, for example, Jennifer Koerber and Michael Sauers, *Emerging Technologies: A Primer for Librarians* (New York: Roman & Littlefield, 2015). As well as Kenneth Varnum, ed., *The Top Technologies Every Librarian Needs to Know. A LITA Guide* (Chicago: American Library Association, 2014).

14. Michael Gorman, "The Organization of Academic Libraries in the Light of Automation," *Advances in Library Automation and Networking* 1 (1987): 152.

10
The Impact of Technology on Library Services

There will always be unintended effects of new technologies.
Some of these unintended effects will be fortuitous and some
less so.

—Bonnie Nardi and Vicki O'Day[1]

Information technology has a clear and persuasive impact in almost every area of the library, be it a discovery system used by a library customer or by a staff member in technical services. This chapter explores the effects that communications technology and computer-based systems have had in each of these functional areas.

Possible Benefits

Given the widespread adoption of information technology, especially handheld digital technology, in the daily lives of almost every end user, it is incumbent to recognize some of the major consequences of library information systems (LISs).

Cliff Lynch suggests that technology incorporates within it two "cultures of change": innovation, where the application of technology improves what is currently being done, and transformation, where technology changes "fundamentally what is done, or is applied to new things."[2]

There are several possible benefits that may accrue to a library as the result of using digital and information technologies. These benefits vary depending on the functional area and how well the library has revised its manual procedures and processes to complement the automated system. Among the possible benefits associated with technology are these:

- **Improved productivity**—Existing staff members are able to cope with increased workloads or take on additional responsibilities, or both, as the result of the library having installed various automated systems. Based on an initial survey (and a follow-up survey ten years later), library staff members, not surprisingly, generally feel that automation has increased their workload and responsibilities.[3]

- **Reduced staff**—In a few cases, libraries were able to reduce staff that were involved with labor-intensive, manual processes with high volumes of activity once the first automated system had been installed. However, for a majority of libraries, there has been little or no reduction in the number of overall staff as the result of automation (although for many staff members their job responsibilities have changed—often dramatically).

- **Reduced unit costs of operation**—The efficiencies that can be achieved with an automated system allow a library to reduce the costs associated with a particular activity. For example, sharing cataloging data through a bibliographic utility such as the Online Computer Library Catalog (OCLC) allowed libraries to avoid duplicating the effort associated with creating original cataloging records. This reduced the number of professional staff and resulted in delegating work to lower-skilled and lower-paid staff.[4]

- **Improved control**—An automated system accurately records the status and location of all items that are maintained in its database. Thus, rather than having silos of paper records found only in one department, the online system allows every staff member to learn about and update information associated with a particular item or record. Yet, in some cases, staff may need to log in to several systems in order to answer a particular question or solve a specific problem.

- **Reduced errors**—Using an automated system means that the number of errors that would have occurred in a manual system are significantly reduced. Because the majority of systems use barcode or radio-frequency identification (RFID) scanners to uniquely identify an item, accuracy improves.

- **Improved speed**—Using an automated system means that a variety of activities are completed in a timelier manner. For example, materials are getting on the shelves faster, and circulation-related transactions happen quicker.

- **Improved access**—Because the majority of library staff members have desktop workstations that are connected to the automated system, they each have access to the latest information about an item or record. In addition, the automated system typically provides several indexes to the library's database (e.g., keyword indexes) that are not available with manual systems.

- **Increased range and depth of service**—An automated system allows the library's customers to access the library's collection and other information resources twenty-four hours a day, seven days a week. In addition, most systems allow library patrons to view portions of their record, place holds, or be alerted when an item is available. Thus, the library patron is no longer constrained to visiting the physical library in order to receive services.

- **Facilitated cooperation**—The ability of an automated system to export standard bibliographic records allows libraries to participate in various cooperative projects (building local, regional, and state databases; lists of serials owned by participating libraries; or shared automated systems).

- **Byproducts**—An automated system allows a library to examine, using a variety of historical statistical data gathered by the automated system, the range and quality of services it provides to its customers. For example, some libraries have examined the actual usage of their collection in an effort to understand the needs of their customers better. As well, libraries have shared data with vendors (including CIVICTechnologies and CollectionHQ) to better understand who was using what services and to better manage their collections.

Next, the impacts of automated technology on the library patron using an online catalog and online databases are explored prior to examining the implications in technical services.

Impacts on Library Catalogs

With the introduction of the online public access catalog in the early 1980s, several studies were conducted to identify the problems as well as to make suggestions for improving the online catalog experience.[5] The main benefits resulting from the use of an online catalog are presented here:

- **Improved access to the collection**—The online catalog provides author, title, and subject browse indexes (left to right, character by character); it also provides keyword indexes, often with Boolean limiting capabilities. In some cases, even more sophisticated search tools, such as automatic synonym searching, were also provided to patrons. Today, some systems incorporate algorithms to recommend other materials the user might find to be of interest, as well as the ability to limit or narrow the search results using a number of factors such as type of materials, age, and so forth.

  Discovery systems provide the user with a single search box and are able to retrieve records from the library's catalog plus eResources that are owned and/or licensed.

- **Immediate access to location and status information**—Given the remote access to the library's collection and other information resources, one key benefit for patrons is being able to determine whether an item of interest can be found on the shelves or if it is checked out or missing. This allows the patron to discover the status of an item before making a trip to the library.

- **Immediate access to information resources**—Perhaps the most popular feature of 24/7 access to library eResources is that they can be immediately downloaded for use (be they journal articles, eBooks, chapters from a book, etc.) without having to visit the library.

A library catalog:
A place where bibliographic entries
get lost alphabetically.

—Anonymous

Online Catalog Problems

Christine Borgman has suggested that the online catalog user needs three layers of knowledge for successful online catalog searching:[6]

- **Conceptual knowledge** of how the online retrieval system works—how to translate an information need into a search query. Problems arise in this area because people arrive at a catalog with incomplete information for any of the indexes provided by the catalog.[7]

- **Semantic knowledge** of how to formulate a search query, that is, how and when to use different search features—For example, very few users know that they need to conduct several searches, using synonyms, for a comprehensive search.

- **Technical skills** in conducting a search query—having a basic knowledge of computing skills and any required syntax for entering a specific search query.

Conceptual Knowledge

The default search option for a majority of library catalogs is keyword searching, in part because that is what people expect based on their experience in using Google.

Searching by subject is another popular approach, yet users experience trouble conducting these searches, failing to match search requests with subject vocabulary 50% of the time.[8] Typically, users enter terms that are too broad or too narrow. It is well known that users have greater success when they are able to browse subject headings, especially when they are shown the syndetic structure of subject headings—broader headings, related headings, and narrower headings.[9]

Arranging subject terms alphabetically tends to scatter related terms and can sometimes lead the online catalog user astray (if no authority records with their associated cross-references are included in the online catalog). In general, cross-references found in authority records are limited and weak. Following cross-references often leads the user away from his or her search focus. However, using authority control provides real benefits. Recall (finding everything on a subject) is increased, and precision (excluding material on other topics) is also increased.

Semantic Knowledge

Too often users experience a dichotomy of search results—too many failed searches (no records found) or too many records are found.[10] Users of online catalogs experience a missed opportunity (e.g., a keyword search is not followed up with a hypertext subject search or call number search).[11] The lack of user perseverance—users are not inclined to try multiple indexes if their first attempt fails—means people often walk away from the catalog disappointed and often with the wrong information.

Boolean operators are not understood and are rarely used. Users often use "and" and "or" backward. To make matters worse, some systems use an implied Boolean "and" when a user enters multiple keywords, whereas other systems use an implied Boolean "or."

Most online catalogs place the burden on the user to reformulate and reenter queries until success is achieved—this is the paradox of information retrieval.

Finding something of relevance as the result of searching the online catalog is clearly challenging. In one recent study, relevance was defined as whether the user saves, prints, emails, or downloads a citation. Approximately 18 percent of all search sessions were determined to be relevant.[12]

Keyword search failures are related to linguistic problems. That is, in some cases different words have the same meanings, whereas in other cases the same word will have different meanings.[13] Also, from a pragmatic perspective, formulating a search request (e.g., "disease medication" vs. "medication side effects") will retrieve a different set of records.

The vocabulary in various domains is often jargon filled, specialized, and unique. If users have no experience in or knowledge of this specialized domain vocabulary, the search results will likely be quite poor—even if they retrieve records and feel like they have been successful.

And users have other problems associated with understanding the way information is displayed and encountering library jargon to identify data fields—an added entry means something to a librarian, but not to the end user.[14]

Technical Skills

Navigational frustrations (e.g., "Where am I? What should (can) I do now?") is a common occurrence for most users.[15] Interestingly, a review of the online catalog user log files indicates that if users make an error, they will more than likely repeat the same action (and obtain the same error message a second time—almost as if they don't believe they could make an error or they are just double-checking the machine).

Given these problems, what then can a library do to improve the user experience?

- **Improve the library's database**—If your bibliographic records have not been cleaned up, do so. Use authority control records and add cross-references on an ongoing basis. Review the frequency of subject headings in your library's catalog (a subject heading linked to a few or a very large number of bibliographic records is not likely to be of value to the library's customers). Consider adding enhanced bibliographic records to the library's database.[16]

- **Vendor improvements**—Library customers, through a Users Group, can ask for specific enhancements to the online catalog or discovery service. Among the suggestions that researchers have made for improvements are providing an option for a step-by-step approach to conducting a search or adding search assistance tools to help the user, as well as suggesting redirected searches (e.g., from a keyword search to a subject browse search).[17] David Thomas found that if subject-rich content (subject headings and summaries) were added to brief record displays, then the need to display full MARC records is reduced significantly.[18] Given this plethora of research about how to improve the online catalog, it is a bit discouraging to see that most vendors have not done much on their own to improve the end user's searching capabilities of their online catalogs.

- **Old initiatives**—Most vendors have added features to their online catalogs so the user can view the book jacket, peruse book reviews, read a summary of the book, and examine a biography of the author. Several researchers have suggested using information visualization software (e.g., when the user is browsing the thesaurus structure of subject headings).[19] Others have suggested providing some navigation assistance to help the user understand the information domain prior to actually performing a search (e.g., a front-end database or a meta database that might include dictionaries and thesauri—or perhaps a site map such as many Web pages offer).[20] Others have suggested providing access to classification information as a part of the online catalog.[21]

Amanda Spink and her colleagues found that the searching experience of online catalog users is almost identical to users searching the Web. That is, few search terms are used; queries are modified infrequently; advanced search features are rarely used; and users only look at the first few pages.[22]

The online catalog must inform users about the diversity of information resources available to them—what the library physically contains, what the library can obtain for them, and links to internet resources that users can trust.[23]

Lorcan Dempsey, in a highly cited article, explored the ways scale, attention, and workflow are affecting libraries, discovery, and the catalog.[24] Lorcan posits that rapidly changing information technology has a significant impact on libraries and the services they provide. These concerns include the following:

1. People are operating at the network level while libraries are focused on the institutional level, for example, holdings in the library catalog.

2. The library can't be a single destination, because mobile 24/7 access to services means multiple ways of connecting to people and services.

3. Community provides new content that must be embraced by libraries, for example, reviews, ratings, recommendations, discussion, and so forth on a number of platforms (Amazon, iTunes, Netflix, Flickr) and social media sites.

4. The "simple single search box" is no longer an option but has become a requirement. Providing a "bento box" style of presenting multiple streams of results allows users more control as they pick and choose.

5. Users are looking for an integrated experience so that the time they spend on the library's website adds real value in the life of users.

6. Metadata now comes from various places:

   - Produced by professional staff

   - Crowdsourced by the users themselves

   - Extracted automatically from digital content

   - Produced by data analytics of transactions and choices made by users

7. Libraries need to get in the flow in a networked environment so that they are where their customers are (in social media and using tools that their users routine engage).

8. Making library resources, especially unique digital resources, discoverable is becoming increasingly important.

9. Libraries should be moving from full "collection" discovery (as is the case if a library has implemented a web-scale discovery service) to full "library" discovery services (learning about new services, LibGuides, staff profiles, and expertise as part of the same search experience).

10. There is a growing interest in consortial (the University of California or the Orbis Cascade Alliance) or national "catalogs" such as the Digital Public Library of America, Trove in Australia, and Europeana.

11. As libraries, especially academic libraries, move portions of their collection to shared print storage facilities, such as ReCAP, as a way to both lower costs and preserve copies of their print materials, ensuring intellectual access to these "hidden" collections will become increasingly important.

12. As libraries move toward the network level, one important tool that can add value is the use of linked data.

13. Determining the scale or level at which something is done becomes important:

    • Institution-scale

    • Group or consortial-scale

    • Web scale

The OCLC *Perceptions* report[25] and the series of Ithaka S+R reports[26] demonstrate that students and faculty members rarely, if ever, start a search with the library catalog.

After analyzing the data about how users came to the online catalog, the University of Utrecht library found that a majority of their users were using web-scale services (Scopus, Google Scholar, Web of Science, PubMed) rather than starting with the library's online catalog. The library decided to eliminate its online catalog and provide an app that simplifies the discovery and authentication process so that users can have immediate access to the full-text of journal articles they discover when using web-scale discovery services such as Scopus, Google Scholar, Web of Science, or PubMed or by going directly to a publisher's/aggregator's website. Behind the scenes, the library provided its bibliographic data and SFX knowledge base to Google Scholar and Scopus and opened up its repository for harvesting by search engine bots. The results are that users are finding what they want much more quickly and with less hassle.[27]

David Weinberger, in his book *Everything Is Miscellaneous*, argues that there is no acceptable way of classifying information and that attempts to do so merely reflect the biases of the individual or group creating the classification system. Weinberger's solution is to rely on computers, specifically relevance ranking, as the way to retrieve useful information in the digital age that we find ourselves in today.[28]

We need to change the definition of the catalog from
what we (librarians) *think* it is to
what our users *wish* it were!
Our catalog should represent everything we have
and the things that we have access to elsewhere.

—Shirley Baker[29]

- **New initiatives**—Given the profession's decision to move a new cataloging standard of *Resource Description and Access (RDA)*, libraries must deal with the reality of a more complicated data structure for their catalog. RDA combines specific data elements, instructions, and guidelines for creating metadata for user-focused linked data applications.[30] The underlying conceptual models for RDA include these:

  - Functional requirements for bibliographic records

  - Functional requirements for authority data

  - Functional requirements for subject authority data

A number of tools are available for converting data from the MARC format into the new RDA format.

Linked data build on the standard web technologies such as Hypertext Transfer Protocol (HTTP), Resource Description Framework (RDF), and uniform resource identifiers (URIs).[31] Tim Berners-Lee envisions use of linked open data for building web links and metadata into a larger and more useful "semantic Web."[32]

The Bibliographic Framework, or BIBFRAME, model, the successor to the MARC data model, transitions MARC data to linked data. The BIBFRAME model is built on the entity-relationship model, developed by Peter Chen, that has three basic elements: entities, attributes, and relationships.[33] BIBFRAME allows library bibliographic data to be interoperable with a far wider range of data to be found on the internet. BIBFRAME also opens a wide door that encourages us to rethink the design and arrangement of bibliographic data in our catalogs.

As libraries become part of this larger web of data, by leveraging the use of stable identifiers to reference clearly differentiated entities, focus will shift from capturing and recording descriptive details about library resources to identifying and establishing more relationships between and among resources. This includes related resources found on the web, and especially those beyond the traditional bounds of the library universe. These relationships—these links—drive the web, transforming the information space from many independent silos to a network graph that branches out in every direction. Relationships help search engines and other services to improve search relevancy and, most importantly, help users find the information they are looking for.[34]

BIBFRAME has the potential to free library metadata from the silos where it has been stored and to link library metadata into the wider world of linked open data in the Web.[35]

One evaluation compared BIBFRAME with RDA/RDF found that:[36]

- RDA/RDF was stronger in series, notes, and inverse properties.
- BIBFRAME was stronger in identifiers, subject headings, administrative metadata, holdings information, and uniform resource identifiers (URIs).

This evaluation converted 300,000 MARC records for eBooks to BIBFRAME.

Graph Search is a semantic search engine developed by Facebook in 2013 that gives answers to a natural language search request rather than providing a list of links. The name refers to the social graph nature of Facebook, which maps the relationships among users.[37] Users find it helpful when searching for personal information about an individuals, locations an individual has visited, type of buildings visited (cafés, bookstores, gyms, hotels, etc.).

Storing data in the cloud and providing access to it is becoming the norm for most libraries. For example, Harvard University developed *LibraryCloud*, and this service aggregates bibliographic metadata from the various library silos across the campus and allows users to access these data via application programming interfaces (APIs). *LibraryCloud* consists of four sets of services: ingest, normalize, enrich, and discover.

The library data can be combined with other data from on and off campus to fuel apps and feed websites. The source code for *LibraryCloud* is offered under an open license.

All of these old and new suggestions have the potential for really improving the user experience of the online catalog.

> The convenience of the public is always to be
> set before the ease of the cataloger.
>
> —Charles Ammi Cutter[38]

Discovery Systems

A discovery service (sometimes called a web-scale discovery service, discovery system or a resource discovery service) provides a set of tools and user interface that gives patrons the ability to search (and browse) library collections, including electronic resources that have been licensed by the library. From the perspective of the user, a discovery service replaces the library's online catalog search interface.

The library's ILS database is provided to a discovery service provider and is housed on a remote server (located in the cloud). The discovery service provider also maintains a database of electronic resources that the library subscribes to. The user of the discovery service is able to enter a search in a single search box (similar to a Google search) and retrieve both journal articles, physical resources owned by the library and other electronic resources. Discovery products also typically provide relevancy-ranked results, faceted navigation, recommendations, and enriched records.

It is possible to organize discovery service literature into five categories:[39]

1. Comparison of products with one another and with Google Scholar
2. Reports on a discovery service implementation at a particular library

3. The impact a discovery service has on other library systems and resources

4. The usability and design of the discovery service

5. Student's and librarians' perceptions of a discovery service

In a systematic review of eighty articles pertaining to discovery services, Jenny Bossaller and Heather Moulaison Sandy suggest that the move to improved user experiences when confronting the library's online catalog has meant a move to embrace the single search box so that patrons can find the different kind of materials housed in various places in the library.[40] The reality imposed by a single search box was revealed when one study analyzed more than 1 million search transactions and found that

- almost one-fourth of search requests were for resources outside the library; and

- a small number of popular search queries account for a disproportionate share of the total queries (such queries may reveal latent demand for resources).[41]

A literature review focusing on the evaluation and assessment of discovery services explored the criteria used by libraries in choosing a particular discovery service.[42] Recommendations for a discovery service selection suggested that the process should be goal oriented, data driven, user centered, inclusive, and transparent.[43] Many studies compare the discovery system to federate search tools, and the results suggest that discovery systems have greater ease of use and are easier to navigate.[44] In addition, discovery systems deliver higher-quality resources, offer a variety of materials types with a single user interface, and have better relevancy-ranking capabilities.[45]

One study asked a group of individuals to perform typical search tasks, and the quality (defined as a resource from a scholarly source) of search results were judged; the results indicated that the EBSCO discovery service produced the "highest quality" results—compared to Summon and Google Scholar.[46] Yet another study found no significant differences between various discovery service products.[47] A study found no significant differences between Summon, EDS, and Google Scholar for known-item searches, although Google Scholar did better for topical searches. Another study found that Google Scholar was the least successful resource in terms of precision when compared to Summon and two publishers' discovery platforms—Emerald and Sage. The authors concluded that although subject-specific databases are more effective than search engines, the complexities involved with accessing the invisible Web are hindering their use.[48]

One study found general overall satisfaction with the ease of use and the utility of the resource revealed when the discovery service is used.[49] Marshall Breeding provides a thorough review of the various discovery service options in the marketplace in an issue of *Library Technology Reports*.[50]

Kristin Calvert found that after implementing a discovery service, use of the library's eResources experienced strong growth while use of the physical collection declined sharply.[51] Circulation of print resources increased for a majority of libraries that have implemented a discovery system, although after a few years, circulation of books tails off—especially in academic libraries.[52] One study examined the Summon discover service and found that interlibrary loan requests dropped 27 percent, and requests by undergraduates dropped even more (57 percent), suggesting that a user of a discovery service finds more of value licensed or housed in the library.[53] The perception of increased usage of library resources following the implementation of a discovery service is borne out by usage data in other settings.[54]

Auburn University library concluded that the "resources and staff required to implement a discovery system were unacceptably high when measured against perceived benefits to users." They also noted that the discovery services were deficient in two areas: controlled vocabularies and ontologies necessary for deeper and smarter connections to other resources and supportive structures for development of information literacy skills.[55]

Carl Grant has argued that the next step after implementing a discovery service is the development of knowledge creation platforms.[56] Despite the large number of discovery service products installed (mostly in academic libraries), the reality is that "discovery mostly happens elsewhere," as was so famously articulated by Lorcan Dempsey, vice-president of OCLC.[57]

Roger Schonfeld has noted that scholars in the academic environment gain access to relevant content using a variety of approaches:[58]

- Google and Google Scholar are the starting point for many individuals.
- The platforms of major content providers (ScienceDirect, Emerald Insight, Taylor and Francis Online, and SagePub) experience high volumes of traffic that have not been redirected from a library website.
- Various third-party discovery services such as ResearchGate and Academia.Edu are growing in importance.
- Library-provided discovery services account for a minor share of search-driven discovery.

Discovery System Problems

Some of the discovery system problems are listed here:

- The discovery systems are not created equal: some systems only index the citations to eResources; other discovery systems use the citations plus an abstract; and still other discovery systems are able to index the citations and abstract plus the full text of each journal article.
- A majority of users still rely on simple keyword searches and rarely employ the advanced search option.[59]
- Users have difficulty in distinguishing between types of materials.[60]
- Most users never move beyond the first page of results.
- Too many search results can overwhelm and frustrate the user.
- Some users have difficulty ascertaining the call number of an item or of its availability.
- Few books are selected by users of a discovery system.

Impacts on eResources

Publishers have been providing access to the full-text contents of their journals in electronic format, sometimes called eJournals, for more than two

TABLE 10.1. Net Impacts from Use of Electronic Journals

Activity	Net Impacts
Infrastructure/systems	Increased staffing and costs
Administration	Increased staffing and costs
Technical services	Mixed impact on staffing and costs
Circulation	Reduced staffing
Reserves	Reduced staffing
Document delivery	Reduced staffing and costs
Reference services	Unclear

decades. For libraries that have implemented a discovery service, this means that users now have the opportunity to do full-text searching on the contents of these journals (in some of the discovery services) rather than relying solely on citations and abstracts.

Although the subscription cost per journal title is typically less than the printed version, there are a variety of other cost impacts for a library to consider. Typically, access to a specific set of eJournals is bundled with other eJournals (sometimes called the "Big Deal"), so the library may actually increase providing access to the number of journals for their end users. The net impacts for a library would appear to be mixed—that is, staffing or costs increase or decrease depending on the area being considered. The implications for using electronic journals within a library are shown in Table 10.1.[61]

Impacts on Document Delivery

Historically, document delivery options have been evaluated based on four factors:

- **Coverage**—What types of documents are available from the document delivery service—copies of journal articles, technical reports, marketing reports, standards, and so forth?

- **Cost**—What is the cost for delivering a specific document? Does price vary based on the size of the document? Is there a discount for an increasing volume of purchases?

- **Speed**—How fast is the document delivered on average? What is the range of service delivery—shortest, longest?

- **Delivery options (document formats)**—What are the different ways in which the document can be delivered—email, fax, download via the internet, snail mail? Can the document be delivered in an electronic format (e.g., Word document, PDF format, etc.)? Will the document be delivered to the library or directly to the end user?

Documents can now be delivered in a matter of days for print materials and hours for electronic materials. Depending on the source, document delivery can be very expensive. Document delivery has become a component of the acquisitions budget for some libraries. After all, with document delivery, the library is assured that the item will be used by at least one user rather than being a "just in case" book or another item that is purchased by the library hoping it will be used by a library patron sometime in the future.

Impacts on Interlibrary Loan

Although interlibrary loans (ILLs) amount to a tiny fraction of a library's annual circulation, they still constitute an important library service, especially for academic and special libraries. Libraries in North America and Europe loan millions of items annually to other libraries. Almost every library encourages its customer to fill out an online form that is submitted to an automated ILL system, and this approach provides better service and lowers costs.

When evaluating interlibrary loan services, four factors are usually considered:

- What types of requests are being made (by subject area)?
- What is the fill rate (what proportion of requests are actually filled)?
- What is the service level (time from request being made to the library receiving the item)?
- What does the service cost?

Interlibrary loan costs are not inexpensive. When borrowing an item, a library can expect to incur average costs of $18.62, and lending an item will cost the library $10.93.[62] Some libraries have used ILL data to calculate the cost of providing access to articles from cancelled journals and identifying journals for reinstatement.[63]

Clearly, services such as OCLC's interlibrary loan module, as well as state and regional interlibrary loan systems run by cooperatives (which usually bypass the OCLC system), have done much to reduce the costs associated with providing an interlibrary loan service. The requesting library's ability to identify a lending library, confirm the loan of a book, and, in some states, use a fairly fast delivery service means that the patron receives the desired item much faster than even ten years ago.

The lending library can scan an article and deliver it directly to the patron or library, using email, an ILL system, or snail mail. The net impact for the patron is that he or she receives the journal article in a matter of days (sometimes hours) rather than weeks.

Other options are also available. Among these are direct consortial borrowing, peer-to-peer services, BorrowDirect, and purchase rather than borrow.

All of the libraries participating in a consortium typically allow a user in one library to see the resources located in another participating library (this is often called **direct consortia borrowing**). The patron can request an item and place a hold on the item (rather than initiating an interlibrary loan request). The item is pulled from the loaning library, transported, and the patron can pick up the item a few days later (the speed of the service is typically dictated by the speed of the delivery service among consortia library members).

A **peer-to-peer borrowing system** facilitates the borrowing and lending of resources from one automated system to another. The request may be sent to one or more library systems (or consortiums), and once filled by a library, the request is cancelled at all of the other libraries.

DirectBorrow is an unmediated library resource sharing partnership among thirteen large academic libraries. In 2017, students and faculty members in these thirteen libraries borrowed about 275,000 items.[64]

Purchase-on-demand items that have been requested by a patron, rather than borrowing them from another library using interlibrary loan. In some cases, the purchased item is sent directly from the supplier to the patron (and only later returned to the library). These are some of the issues associated with purchase-on-demand:

- Budget—establishing a ceiling on the amount of money to be spent on the program

- Criteria—determining the maximum price of an item, no older than "X" copyright date, material type, and suitability for a library's collection

- Cataloging—determining whether the item will be cataloged before being loaned to the patron

Impacts on Acquisitions

Automation has had several important impacts on acquisitions:

- The automated system can help eliminate duplicate orders by checking an on-order file and the library's catalog

- Able to download bibliographic records at time of order, which reduces costs and occurrence of error

- Access to easy-to-use currency conversion tables

- Management reports to monitor vendor performance

- Tools to track the spending of the library's entire materials acquisitions budget

- Limited access to online reviews, although this is improving each year

- Handles different business models involved in eBook acquisitions such as eBook Central (for academic libraries) and public libraries engaging with OverDrive

An LIS is designed to provide a single set of files that the library maintains. If the system does not provide an interface to a book or serials vendor, then the library must decide whether to maintain two sets of records (one in the LIS and one at the vendor) or rely on the vendor-provided system. In most cases, the vendor-provided system is designed to lock in the library. Thus, with these vendor-provided systems, there are generally no opportunities to compare prices between vendors.

Libraries have been shifting their focus from ownership to access with the result that the monograph budgets for most libraries have declined markedly. Online access to electronic resources—journals, newspapers, and other information resources—has opened up a library's limited physical collection to an almost limitless set of possibilities. In many cases, libraries are turning to consortiums to help negotiate licenses to access online content and save money at the same time.[65]

More recent changes in acquisitions have been the result of evolving technologies (eBooks, e.g.) as well as involving patrons in the acquisitions process. OverDrive is the dominant provider of eBooks for public libraries (the eBooks a library has subscribed to are visible in the library's catalog), and it maintains a central eBook lending platform. Academic libraries typically provide access to a variety of eBook titles in their online catalog. However, the library does not "pay" for the eBook until a patron requests and downloads the eBook the first time.

Increasingly, academic libraries encourage their patrons to suggest titles for the library to purchase (often called demand-driven acquisitions). Once suggested, the library uses a variety of means to quickly acquire the title from a vendor.

Data about library collections and their use can be shared by a library with a commercial vendor to provide advice about what to buy (and not buy). Companies such as Gale, with their Analytics on Demand, and Baker and Taylor, with their CollectionHQ products, have collections that are fine-tuned, and the acquisitions budget is stretched to its maximum value.

Impacts on Serials

Managing serials is an important task that can consume significant staff resources as libraries moved from a hybrid approach with subscriptions for both print journals and eJournals to an almost total eJournal world. The workflows associated with eResources are significantly different and require a different set of tools in order to maximize staff productivity. Typically libraries, especially academic libraries, are moving from an electronic resource management system (ERMS) to a library services platform as a way to gain access to a set of tools that improve workflows as well as eliminate two or more automated library silos.

Given budget constraints, some libraries are experimenting with cancelling subscriptions to "Big Deals" (a subscription to a majority or all of the publisher's journals) and moving to purchasing a copy of a journal article when requested by a patron or licensing a limited set of journal titles.

Impacts on Cataloging

Automating cataloging was the first step to create a library's machine-readable database around which other modules and services could be built. Acquisitions, circulation control, resource sharing, serials control, and collection development are all dependent on the availability of the core-cataloging database.

The availability of bibliographic records and linking computer workstations using telecommunications has allowed catalogers to share cataloging records. OCLC's union catalog (now called WorldCat) grew fairly rapidly because, as more records were added to its database, more libraries were drawn to participate.

Other options for obtaining bibliographic records, especially for new materials being added to the collection, is to get them from the supplying vendor or from another library using the Z39.50 protocol.

Among the other impacts of automation on cataloging are those listed here:

- Lower costs incurred by substituting paraprofessionals for librarians. Average cost of copy cataloging is $16.25 per hour.

- More use of copy cataloging, which helps to lower costs. Copy cataloging, while requiring some training, experience, and common sense, does not require a master's in library science (MLS) degree. As the use of paraprofessionals increased, fewer professionals chose to pursue a cataloging career, which has resulted in a shortage of cataloging librarians.

- Change in workflow has a big impact on productivity. Minimizing the number of times an item is handled helps reduce costs.

- The cost of a cataloging record varies depending on the source.

- The Z39.50 standard returns a bibliographic record to the requesting library. Some libraries are using this fact to add bibliographic records to their database instead of using the more traditional sources of cataloging records.

Besides cataloging print and other materials found in its collection, the library is faced with deciding whether to catalog information resources that may be found in other locations (i.e., on the Web). For some libraries, the catalog has exceeded its traditional role. Rather than being an inventory of what the library owns, the catalog facilitates access to a wide variety of materials, regardless of their location.[66] Libraries are also confronted with the decision of whether to use a MARC bibliographic record or a metadata standard such as the Dublin Core. Some have found it difficult to accurately and completely describe an internet resource, using a bibliographic record. This difficulty is further compounded by the fact that web resources vary greatly, which makes the descriptive process even more problematic. Most librarians see classification as the only valid subject approach for all the materials in the library's collection—no surprise there, given their training and education.

Impacts on Circulation

Vendor-provided automated circulation systems support a wide range of circulation-related activities. Using a barcode or RFID scanners at the circulation desk speeds up the checkout and check-in processes. The net effect of an automated circulation system is improved control over the library's collection, as well as increased staff productivity.

Increasingly libraries are installing patron self-checkout machines (barcodes or RFID are supported) to reduce library operating costs. In addition to borrowing materials, patrons can pay their fines or fees, see a list of what is currently checked out, and so forth. And public libraries are also installing material handling machines that automatically check in returned materials and then sort the materials into a variety of bins (typically by adult and children fiction/nonfiction, DVD/CDs, items belonging at another location, etc.). Some libraries provide windows so children (and interested adults) can see the machines in action.

Presented here are some of the benefits noted by several libraries with automated circulation systems:

- No staffing increases are required to cope with increased circulation levels. The improved productivity means that libraries have not had to increase staff even in the face of increased demand for services (in cases where annual circulation statistics are increasing). Many libraries also reduce staff by installing self-checkout machines and sorting machines to automatically check in returned materials.

- Generating timely overdue notices means faster return of overdue items. In some cases, libraries found they had a higher postage cost because overdue notices went out on time rather than being dribbled out using a manual process. Postage costs are reduced with email delivery of overdue and other types of notices.

- Fine revenues go up. There is less discussion about library fines because the computer tracks the checkout, renewal, and return dates.

- Items lost through the circulation system are reduced (i.e., an item checked out but never returned by the patron). Generally, with an automated system, the number of items borrowed but not returned is less than half of 1 percent of annual circulation.

- Patrons are usually able to view their own patron record, determine the status of a hold request, place a hold, and perform other activities remotely by using the library's website linked to or integrated with the circulation module.

- Some libraries have installed self-checkout machines to provide additional service points at the circulation desk. This can reduce staffing requirements at the circulation desk or allow staff to focus on other patron services. The use of automated systems to handle materials reduces the amount of repetitive stress injuries experienced by staff.

Summary

Clearly the impact of automated systems in libraries has been pervasive and significant. The benefits that have resulted from automation depend, in part, on the efficiency of the library before it was automated, how well the automated system has been integrated into the library's work flows, and which functional area within the library is being considered.

Perhaps more importantly, the cumulative impact of reviewing all of these various systems in libraries is that the design of any online system, and in particular the user interface, is absolute crucial in terms of acceptance and use of a system. As Peter Morville has observed,

> Calvin Mooers reminds us that design of a useful information system requires deep understanding of users and their social context. We cannot assume people will want our information, even if we know they need our information. Behind most failed web sites, intranets, and interactive products lie misguided models of users and their information-seeking behaviors. Users are complex. Users are social. And so is information.[67]

More important than focusing on information and digital technology and how a library benefits and stumbles from the use of technology, we still need to focus on what difference technology-enabled library services make in the lives of our customers. What are the outcomes from using library services and collections in terms of teaching, learning, and research?

Questions to Consider

- What is the biggest change that information technology has brought to your library?

- What are the primary benefits that have occurred as the result of implementing technology in your library?

- Do you monitor the ways in which your users search the library discovery system or online catalog to determine how you can make changes in order to improve the overall search or discovery experience?

- In what ways do scale, attention, and workflow affect the way in which users are using the library's search or discovery tools?

- In what ways are library cataloging or metadata standards changing so that they can benefit from the internet-based world in which we live?

- What impacts from information technology do you see in your library's interlibrary loan or document delivery units?

Notes

1. Bonnie Nardi and Vicki O'Day, *Information Ecologies: Using Technology with Heart* (Cambridge, MA: MIT Press, 2000), 169.

2. Clifford Lynch, "Serials in the Networked Environment," *Serials Librarian* 28, no. 1–2 (1996): 119.

3. Dorothy E. Jones, "Ten Years Later: Support Staff Perceptions and Opinions on Technology in the Workplace," *Library Trends* 47, no. 4 (Spring 1999): 711–45.

4. Michael Buckland, *Redesigning Library Services: A Manifesto* (Chicago: American Library Association, 1992); Michael Gorman, "The Organization of Academic Libraries in the Light of Automation," *Advances in Library Automation and Networking* 1 (1987): 151–69; and Karen L. Horney, "Fifteen Years of Automation: Evolution of Technical Services Staffing," *Library Resources and Technical Services* 31 (Winter 1987): 6–76.

5. The largest survey of OPAC users and non-users was sponsored by the Council on Library Resources during the early 1980s. See Joseph R. Matthews, Gary S. Lawrence, and Douglas K. Ferguson, *Using Online Catalogs: A Nationwide Survey* (New York: Neal-Schuman, 1983); and Joseph R. Matthews, ed., *The Impact of Online Catalogs* (New York: Neal-Schuman, 1986).

6. Christine L. Borgman, "Why Are Online Catalogs Still Hard to Use?" *Journal of the American Society for Information Science* 47, no. 7 (1996): 493–503; and Christine L. Borgman, "Why Are Online Catalogs Hard to Use? Lessons Learned from Information Retrieval Studies," *Journal of the American Society for Information Science* 37, no. 6 (1986): 387–400.

7. Christine L. Borgman and S. L. Siegfried, "Getty's Synonym and Its Cousins: A Survey of Applications of Personal Name Matching Algorithms," *Journal of the American Society for Information Science* 43 (1992): 459–76; H. Chen and V. Dhar, "User Misconceptions of Information Retrieval Systems," *International Journal of Man-Machine Studies* 32 (1990): 673–92; and Arlene G. Taylor, "Authority Files in Online Catalogs: An Investigation of Their Value," *Cataloging & Classification Quarterly* 4, no. 3 (1984): 1–17.

8. Bryce Allen, "Individual Differences, Values and Catalogs," *Technicalities* 11, no. 7 (1991): 6–10; and Rosemary Thorne and Jo Bell Whitlatch, "Patron Online Catalog Success," *College & Research Libraries* (November 1994): 479–97.

9. Carol A. Mandel and Judith Herschman, "Online Subject Access—Enhancing the Library Catalog," *Journal of Academic Librarianship* 9, no. 3 (1983): 148–55.

10. Allyson Carlyle, "Matching LCSH and User Vocabulary in the Library Catalog," *Subject Control in Online Catalogs* (1989): 37–63; Karen M. Drabenstott and Marjorie S. Weller, "Failure Analysis of Subject Searches in a Test of a New Design for Subject Access to Online Catalogs," *Journal of the American Society for Information Science* 47, no. 7 (1996): 519–37; Charles R. Hildreth, "The Use and Understanding of Keyword Searching in a University Online Catalog," *Information Technology and Libraries* 16, no. 2 (June 1997): 52–62; Rhonda A. Hunter, "Successes and Failures of Patrons Searching the Online Catalog at a Large Academic Library: A Transaction Log Analysis," *RQ* Spring 33, no. 1 (1991): 395–402; Ray R. Larson, "The Decline of Subject Searching: Long-Term Trends and Patterns of Index Use in an Online Catalog," *Journal of the American Society for Information Science* 42, no. 3 (1991): 197–215; Ray R. Larson. "Classification Clustering, Probabilistic Information Retrieval and the Online Catalog," *Library Quarterly* 61 (1991b): 133–73; Ray R. Larson, "Between Scylla and Charybdis: Subject Searching in the Online Catalog," *Advances in Librarianship* 15 (1991c): 175–236; Karen Markey, *Subject Searching in Library Catalogs: Before and After the Introduction of Online Catalogs*. OCLC Library, Information, and Computer Science Series (Dublin, OH: Online Computer Library Center, 1984); Karen Markey, "Users and the Online Catalog: Subject Access Problems," in *The Impact of Online Catalogs*, ed. Joseph R. Matthews (New York: Neal-Schuman, 1986): 35–69; Karen Markey, *Dewey Decimal Classification Online Project: Evaluation of a Library Schedule and Index Integrated into the Subject Searching Capabilities of an Online Catalog: Final Report to the Council on Library Resources*, OCLC Research Report No. OCLC/OPR/RR-86/1 (Dublin, OH: Online Computer Library Center, 1986b); Ann O'Brien, "Online Catalogs: Enhancements and Developments," *Annual Review of Information Science and Technology*, 29 (1994): 219–42; Thomas A. Peters, "When Smart People Fail: An Analysis of the Transaction Log of an Online Catalog," *Journal of Academic Librarianship* 15, no. 5 (1989): 267–73; and Thomas A. Peters. "The History and Development of Transaction Log Analysis," *Library HiTech* 11, no. 2 (1993): 41–66.

11. John Tolle, "Transaction Log Analysis: Online Catalogs. Research and Development in Information Retrieval," *Sixth Annual International ACM SIGIR Conference* 17, no. 4 (1983): 147–60; and Stephen E. Wiberley Jr., Robert Allen Daugherty, and James A Danowski, "User Persistence in Scanning Postings of a Computer-driven Information System: LCS," *Library and Information Science Research* 12, no. 4 (1990): 341–53.

12. Michael D. Cooper and Hui-Min Chen, "Predicting the Relevance of a Library Catalog Search," *Journal of the American Society for Information Science and Technology* 52, no. 10 (August 2001): 813–27.

13. C. B. Lowry, "Preparing for the Technological Future: A Journey of Discovery," *Library HiTech* 13, no. 3 1(995): 39–54.

14. Virginia Ortiz-Repiso and Purificacion Moscoso, "Web-Based OPACs: Between Tradition and Innovation," *Information Technology and Libraries* 18, no. 2 (June 1999): 68–77.

15. Larry Millsap and Terry Ellen Ferl, "Search Patterns of Remote Users: An Analysis of OPAC Transaction Logs," *Information Technology and Libraries* 12, no. 3 (1993): 321–43.

16. Pauline Atherton, *Books Are for Use: Final Report of the Subject Access Project to the Council on Library Resources* (Washington, DC: Council on Library Resources, 1978).

17. Karen Markey, "Alphabetical Searching in an Online Catalog," *Journal of Academic Librarianship* 14, no. 6 (1989): 353–60; and Tamas E. Doszkocs, "CITE NLM: Natural-Language Searching in an Online Catalog," *Information Technology and Libraries* 2, no. 4 (1983): 364–80.

18. David H. Thomas, "The Effect of Interface Design on Item Selection in an Online Catalog," *LRTS* 45, no. 1 (2001): 20–46.

19. Check issues of the *IEEE Transactions on Visualization & Computer Graphics* and the annual proceedings of the *International Conference on Information Visualization* for examples of how visualization software could be adapted for an OPAC.

20. Marcia Bates, "Rethinking Subject Cataloging in the Online Environment," *LRTS* 33, no. 4 (1989): 400–12; Marcia Bates, "Subject Access in Online Catalogs: A Design Model," *Journal of the American Society for Information Science* 37 (1986): 357–76; Karen M. Drabenstott, "Enhancing a New Design for Subject Access to Online Catalogs," *Library HiTech* 14, no. 1 (1996): 87–109; Karen M. Drabenstott and Marjorie S. Weller, "Testing a New Design for Subject Searching in Online Catalogs," *Library HiTech* 12, no. 1 (1994): 67–76; Charles Hildreth, "Pursuing the Ideal: Generations of Online Catalogs," *Online Catalogs, Online Reference: Converging Trends*, Proceedings of a Library and Information Technology Association Preconference Institute, June 23–24, 1983; Brian Aveney and Brett Butler, eds., *Subject Access in Online Catalogs* (Chicago: American Library Association, 1984), 31–56; Charles Hildreth, *An Evaluation of Structured Navigation for Subject Searching in Online Catalogs*, unpublished doctoral dissertation, Department of Information Science, City University, London, UK, 1993; Efthimis N. Efthimiadis, "User Choices: A New Yardstick for the Evaluation of Ranking Algorithms for Interactive Query Expansion," *Information Processing and Management* 31, no. 4 (1995): 237–47; Stephen E. Robertson and Micheline M. Hancock-Beaulieu, "On the Evaluation of IR Systems," *Information Processing and Management* 28, no. 4 (1992): 457–66; and Stephen Walker and Micheline M. Hancock-Beaulieu, *OKAPI at City: An Evaluation Facility for Interactive IR*, British Library Research Report No. 6056 (London: British Library, 1991).

21. Elaine Servenious, "Use of Classification in Online Retrieval," *Library Resources & Technical Services* 27, no. 1 (1983): 76–80.

22. Amanda Spink, Dietmar Wolfram, Major B. J. Jansen, and Tefko Saracevic, "Searching the Web: The Public and Their Queries," *Journal of the American Society for Information Science* 52, no. 3 (February 1, 2001): 226–34.

23. Jane E. Hughes, "Access, Access, Access! The New OPAC Mantra," *American Libraries* (May 2001): 62–64.

24. Lorcan Dempsey, "Thirteen Ways of Looking at Libraries, Discovery, and the Catalog: Scale, Workflow, Attention," *EDUCAUSE Review*, December 10, 2012, http://er.educause.edu/articles/2012/12/thirteen-ways-of-looking-at-libraries-discovery-and-the-catalog-scale-workflow-attention.

25. Online Computer Library Center (OCLC), *Perceptions of Libraries and Information Resources: A Report to the OCLC Membership* (Dublin, OH: OCLC, 2005). See also, OCLC. *Perceptions of Libraries, 2010: Context and Community*. Dublin, OH: OCLC, 2010.

26. Christine Wolff-Eisenberg, "Ithaka S+R U.S. Library Survey 2016," *Ithaka S+R*, April 3, 2017, https://doi.org/10.18665/sr.303066. See also Roger Schonfeld and Matthew Long, "Ithaka S+R U.S. Library Survey 2013," *Ithaka S+R*, March 11, 2014, https://doi.org/10.18665/sr.22787; and Roger Schonfeld and Matthew Long, "Ithaka S+R U.S. Library Survey 2010," *Ithaka S+R*, April 11, 2011, https://doi.org/10.18665/sr.22360.

27. Bianca Kramer, "University Library: The Utrecht Approach," A presentation to the JIBS User Group, July 2014, *SlideShare*, July 22, 2014, https://www.slideshare.net/bmkramer/the-utrecht-approach-jibs-user-group-july-22-2014.

28. David Weinberger, *Everything Is Miscellaneous: The Power of the New Digital Disorder* (New York: Holt Publishing, 2008).

29. Shirley Baker, quoted in Jenny Emanuel, "Next Generation Catalogs: What Do They Do and Why Should We Care," *Reference & User Services Quarterly* 49, no. 2 (2009): 120.

30. Philip Hider, *Information Resource Description: Creating and Managing Metadata* (Chicago: American Library Association, 2013).

31. Seth van Hooland and Ruber Verborgh, *Linked Data for Libraries, Archives and Museums: How to Clean, Link and Publish Your Metadata* (Chicago: Neal-Schuman, 2014).

32. Tim Berners-Lee, James Hendler, and Ora Lassila, "The Semantic Web," *Scientific American*, May 17, 2001.

33. Peter Pin-Shan Chen, "The Entity-Relationship Model: Toward a Unified View of Data," *ACM Transactions on Database Systems* 1, no. 1 (1976): 2.

34. *Bibliographic Framework as a Web of Data: Linked Data Model and Supporting Services* (Washington, DC: Library of Congress, 2012), 43.

35. Qiang Jin, Jim Hahn, and Gretchen Croll, "BIBFRAME: Transformation for Enhanced Discovery," *Library Resources & Technical Services* 60, no. 4 (2016): 223–35.

36. Joseph Kiegel, *BIBFRAME Projects at the University of Washington*, Paper presented at the annual meeting for the American Library Association, San Francisco, California, June 25–30, 2015.

37. Steven Levy, "Facebook's Bold, Compelling and Scary Engine of Discovery: The Inside Story of Graph Search," *Wired*, January 15, 2013, https://www.wired.com/2013/01/the-inside-story-of-graph-search-facebooks-weapon-to-challenge-google/.

38. Charles Ammi Cutter, W. P. Cutter, Worthington Chauncey Ford, Philip Lee Phillips, and Oscar George Theodore Sonneck, *Rules for a Dictionary Catalog* (Washington, D.C.: Government Printing Office, 1904), p. 12.

39. Doug Way, "The Impact of Web-Scale Discovery on the Use of a Library Collection," *Serials Review* 36, no. 4 (2010): 214–20.

40. Jenny Bossaller and Heather Moulaison Sandy, "Documenting the Conversation: A System Review of Library Discovery Layers," *College & Research Libraries* 78, no. 6 (September 1, 2017), https://crl.acrl.org/index.php/crl/article/view/16714.

41. Cory Lown, Tito Sierra, and Josh Boyer, "How Users Search the Library from a Single Search Box," *College & Research Libraries* 75, no. 5 (May 2013): 227–41.

42. Nadine Ellero, "An Unexpected Discovery: One Library's Experience With Web-Scale Discovery Service (WSDS) Evaluation And Assessment," *Journal of Library Administration* 53, no. 5–6 (2013): 323–43.

43. Joseph Deodato, "Evaluating Web-Scale Discovery: A Step-by-Step Guide," *Information Technology and Libraries* 34, no. 2 (June 2015): 19–75.

44. Sarah C. Williams and Anita K. Foster, "Promise Fulfilled? An EBSCO Discovery Service Usability Study," *Journal of Web Librarianship* 5, no. 3 (2011): 179–98.

45. Andrew D. Asher, Lynda M. Duke, and Suzanne Wilson, "Paths of Discovery: Comparing the Search Effectiveness of EBSCO Discovery Service, Summon, Google Scholar, and Conventional Library Resources," *College & Research Libraries* 74, no. 5 (2013): 464–88.

46. Andrew Asher, Lynda Duke, and Suzanne Wilson, "Paths Of Discovery."

47. Jonathan Rochkind, "A Comparison of Article Search APIs Via Blinded Experiment and Developer Review," *Code4Lib Journal* 19 (2013): 1–15.

48. Helen Timpson and Gemma Sansom, "A Student Perspective on e-Resource Discovery: Has the Google Factor Changed Publisher Platform Searching Forever?," *Serials Librarian* 61 (2011): 253–66.

49. Courtney Lundgrigan, Kevin Manuel, and May Yan, "'Pretty Rad': Explorations in User Satisfaction with a Discovery Layer at Ryerson University," *College & Research Libraries* 77, no. 1 (January 2016): 43–62.

50. Marshall Breeding, "Library Resource Discovery Products: Library Perspectives, and Vendor Positions," *Library Technology Reports* (January 2014): 1–45.

51. Kristin Calvert, "Maximizing Academic Library Collections: Measuring Changes in Use Patterns Owing to EBSCO Discovery Service," *College & Research Libraries* 77, no. 1 (January 2015): 81–99.

52. Calvert, "Maximizing Academic Library Collections."

53. Linda Musser and Barbara Coopey, "Impact of a Discovery Service on Interlibrary Loan," *College & Research Libraries* 77, no. 6 (September 2016).

54. Valerie Spezi, Claire Creaser, Ann O'Brien, and Angelea Conyers, *Impact of Library Discovery Technologies: A Report for UKSG* (Lougborough, UK: Lougborough University, November 2013).

55. Nadine Ellero, "An Unexpected Discovery: One Library's Experience with Web-Scale Discovery Service (WSDS) Evaluation and Assessment," *Journal of Library Administration* 53 (2013): 323–43.

56. Carl Grant, "Knowledge Creation Platforms: The Next-Step After Web-Scale Discovery," *027.7* 2 (2013): 67–73.

57. Lorcan Dempsey, "Thirteen Ways of Looking at Libraries."

58. Roger Schonfeld, *Does Discovery Still Happen in the Library Roles and Strategies for a Shifting Reality* (New York: Ithaka S+R, 2014).

59. Kelly Meadow and James Meadow, "Search Query Quality and Web-Scale Discovery: A Qualitative and Quantitative Analysis," *College & Undergraduate Libraries* 19, no. 2–4 (2012): 163–75; Asher, Duke, and Wilson, "Paths Of Discovery."

60. David J. Comeaux, "Usability Testing of a Web-Scale Discovery System at an Academic Library," *College & Undergraduate Libraries* 19, no. 2–4 (2012): 189–206; Jody Condit Fagan et al., "Usability Test Results for a Discovery Tool in an Academic Library," *Information Technology & Libraries* 31, no. 1 (2012): 83–112; and Sue Fahey, Shannon Gordon, and Crystal Rose, "Seeing Double at Memorial University: Two WorldCat Local Usability Studies," *Partnership: The Canadian Journal of Library & Information Practice & Research* 6, no. 2 (2011): 1–14.

61. Carol Hansen Montgomery and JoAnne L. Sparks, "Framework for Assessing the Impact of an Electronic Journal Collection on Library Costs and Staffing Patterns," Paper presented at the PEAK 2000: Economics and Usage of Digital Library Collections conference, Ann Arbor, Michigan.

62. Mary E. Jackson, *Measuring the Performance of Interlibrary Loan and Document Delivery Services* (Washington, DC: Association of Research Libraries, 1998).

63. Mary Dabney Wilson and Whitney Alexander, "Automated Interlibrary Loan/Document Delivery Data Application for Serials Collection Development," *Serials Review* 25, no. 4 (1999): 11–19.

64. For more information, visit BorrowDirect, http://www.borrowdirect.org/.

65. Catherine Moffat, *The Future of Library Acquisitions. The Australian Library Journal* 45, no. 3 (1996): 209–14; Glenda A. Thornton, "Impact of Electronic Resources on Collection Development, the Role of Librarians and Library Consortia," *Library Trends* 48, no. 4 (2000): 842–51.

66. Mary Beth Weber, "Factors to be Considered in the Selection and Cataloging of Internet Resources," *Library HiTech* 17, no. 3 (1999): 298–303.

67. Peter Morville, *Ambient Findability* (Sebastopol, CA: O'Reilly Media, 2005), 45.

11
System Selection

Technology is anything that wasn't
around when you were born.

—Alan Kay[1]

This chapter presents an overview of the system selection process and implementation issues associated with installing an automated library system. The system options available to libraries are reviewed, and then a variety of issues associated with selecting and installing a library information system (LIS) are discussed.

Processes and Services

The processes and services provided by libraries and librarians can be viewed as being a part of technical services, public services, or administrative planning and decision-making. Arguably, some processes or services cross one or more of these artificial boundaries, but that is not the point here. For the moment, consider these divisions for the purposes of examining technology applications to library-related processes and services.

Technical Services Functions

Technical services include those backroom tasks conducted by librarians and other staff members that often go unnoticed by patrons and others unfamiliar with library procedures. In fact, many of these tasks include the most important decisions to be made by the professional librarian! Having made a decision to purchase a particular item, whether it is a monograph, audiovisual, or other material type, the task of managing the acquisition of that object becomes paramount. This task might be considered somewhat repetitive in nature, making it a good candidate for using technology (criteria for automation: tasks that are detailed, form driven, and repetitive). In addition, the library will need to manage the eResources that it licenses and provides access to for its patrons. Acquisition systems are important components within the overall automated library system.

In the 1960s, the Library of Congress undertook a massive bibliographic project that resulted not only in the international standardization of the bibliographic record known as MARC (ANSI/NISO Z39.2-1994, the Information Interchange Format—now MARC 21) but also spawned the development of large centralized bibliographic databases such as the Online Computer Library Catalog (OCLC). These bibliographic utilities provided a centralized means for sharing cataloging records across thousands of library institutions.

Cataloging is an important task that places the acquired object within the context of the physical collection owned and held by that library system as well as eResources owned or licensed by the library. Cataloging is now primarily a shared or collaborative process, with authoritative standardized bibliographic records being readily available (in most instances) for particular resources.

The cataloging software must be robust enough to support several ways of entering, modifying, and viewing bibliographic data. Resource Description and Access (RDA) is the standard for descriptive cataloging and is the successor to the Anglo-American Cataloging Rules, 2nd edition (AACR2). The underlying conceptual model for RDA is the Functional Requirements for Bibliographic Records (FRBR) that is applied to linked data applications. Rather than a focus on bibliographic records with associated fields of data, RDA embraces bibliographic objects or elements called RDA Vocabularies. The use of RDA linked data has a number of benefits, including these.[2]

- Linked bibliographic data can be "connected" with resources out on the Web.

- Linked data are being used to make sense of the resources on the Web.

- The linked data can pull together multiple manifestations of a work, as well as identify subsequent translations.

- Linked data provide for an expanded visibility for a library on the Web.

The Library of Congress established the Bibliographic Framework, or BIBFRAME, initiative as a foundation for the future of bibliographic description, both on the Web and in the broader linked networked world. BIBFRAME is a data model designed to replace MARC standards and to use linked data principles to make bibliographic data more accessible and useful. BIBFRAME is expressed using the Resource Description Framework (RDF) and is based on three categories of abstraction (work, instance, and item).[3] It is hoped that the BIBFRAME initiative will

- differentiate between conceptual content and its physical/digital manifestation(s);

- leverage and expose relationships among and between entities; and

- unambiguously identify information entities.

Tip! The Library of Congress maintains a website that provides a wealth of BIBFRAME resources and tools. Visit https://www.loc.gov/bibframe/.

Libraries may acquire cataloging records from a variety of sources including OCLC, SkyRiver, other libraries using Z39.50, vendors that supply physical and electronic resources, and outsourcing vendors. An environmental scan explores the issues associated with obtaining cataloging records in greater detail.[4] Some of the concerns that ultimately determine the quality of each alternative follow:

- **Breadth of the database**—The larger and more diverse the database in terms of language and type of formats, the better (especially for academic libraries).

- **Quality of the database**—Adherence to content and classification standards and authority control improves the quality of the metadata.

- **Ease of use**—The ease of use of searching, viewing, selecting and using a bibliographic record is important.

- **Costs of use of the database**—What is the cost of downloading and using one or more records?

Nearly all libraries circulate their materials, thereby necessitating a need to control their inventory of books, periodicals, and other media. Circulation control, once done by hand, then later by using punched card technologies, is now primarily done using software applications capable of handling millions of transactions and correctly identifying those materials checked out by patrons that might be overdue. In fact, circulation systems solutions comprised the first application leading to the development of the library systems marketplace in the 1970s.

The circulation module has to deal with more complex situations, including the option of controlling *floating* collections for libraries with multiple branches. Rather than returning items to their "home library" location, the collection is allowed to stay at the library where it was returned (e.g., float). However, there is still a need to ensure that if too many materials are returned to a location, these materials are flagged so that they can be moved to a location where the demand is higher and the library has shelf space to store the materials—this process is sometimes called load balancing.

In addition, today's automated systems must be able to provide interoperability between an eBook lending platform and the integrated library system (ILS).

Additional processes within technical services include serials control, materials booking (holds and reserves), and interlibrary loan, all of them sharing with circulation the same properties that make them ideal candidates for technology solutions.

As more libraries join consortiums, the opportunity arises for the participating libraries to share and consolidate technical services activities as a way to improve consistency and quality of processes while reducing costs. Shared systems also afford the opportunity for libraries to streamline and simplify the loan checkout options.

Public Services

Public service functions within the library include those services provided by both the collection and by library professionals to the end user. Technology applications in the 1980s modernized the former card catalog into what is called the online catalog. New developments have pushed that envelope even further, transforming the online catalog into a one-stop service that can access not only the collection of materials held by the local library but can also provide access to the collections in other libraries as well as to materials located on the internet. Initially intended to provide access to union catalogs across libraries within an institutional library system, online catalogs now extend to provide access to collections around the world, in some cases extending reciprocal borrowing privileges to end users seeking to borrow materials from other library systems.

Now libraries face the challenge of tying these and other information services together into a neatly designed set of public service offerings. The Web is an access and delivery tool. As the Web has grown, not just in popularity and use but also in content, librarians in their quest to meet the needs of users have found it necessary to provide access to new resources. Often the end user is quite unaware that the various information services offered by libraries involve sources from distinctly different origins. In a sense, that is the beauty of the Web, that link pages can be designed to mask the distinctions between various resources—some owned, some licensed, and some freely available.

One problem associated with providing links to licensed information is that not all sources are full text, and only excerpts of the information are provided. In the instances where the user identifies a resource—say a particular issue of a journal or an article within that issue—the library must attempt to provide that information object to the end user in some convenient fashion. And the problem is further compounded because the vast majority of people do not use the library catalog to discover information resources, but rather rely on Google, Google Scholar, Google Books, or other search engines.

One troublesome problem in providing robust access to web-based resources is the ongoing problem of linking. The Web, despite its utility and ubiquity, is nonetheless quite simple when it comes to linking. Generally, links are static (point to one hard-coded location) and singular (unable to point to multiple destinations). OpenURL, a NISO standard, provides links for bibliographic resources that enable richer linking services. It is designed to solve the problem of sending the user to the content licensed by the library (the "appropriate copy" problem) rather than sending the user to a nonlicensed copy. OpenURL also provides opportunities for providing links to other services (such as links to articles by the same author). Given today's complex electronic publishing environment, URLs that change are a real challenge for article reference linking purposes.

One solution to this problem is that publishers have adopted digital object identifiers (DOIs) as unique article identifiers that do not change. *CrossRef* was created so that DOIs could be used for retrieval purposes based on metadata, such as author name. SFX, a proprietary product that uses OpenURL, allows libraries to establish rules that allow SFX to create links regardless of who hosts them—the library or external information providers. The user is directed to the eResources the library has licensed.

Administrative Planning and Decision-Making

To do a great job of planning and making decisions, it's important to frame the perspectives of library staff, library patrons, and library management. To many librarians, technical services are the most important set of professional tasks. To end users, public services are the most visible part of the library. Both groups might forget that library administration is also an important consideration in the context of LISs!

Management is responsible for drafting strategic priorities for the library. These priorities typically include such topics as providing excellent customer service, providing access to relevant information, improving the skills of staff members, and providing access to contemporary technology. The library's management team needs to ensure that technology products and services are meeting the strategic priorities of the library and its parent organization. In particular, the library must anticipate the needs of the library for the next five to ten years.

System Selection

Historically, the process recommended to librarians is that they employ a request for proposal process to select an LIS. Because the ILS often carries high costs, an RFP process is often an institutional requirement. An overview of the selection and implementation process suggests that five steps should be employed:

1. Identify a library's needs.
2. Document the library's needs.
3. Evaluate alternatives.
4. Prepare written agreements.
5. Begin the implementation process.

Identify a Library's Needs

Almost all libraries in North America, Europe, Australia, New Zealand, China, and the Far East are already automated. So, these libraries will not be assessing their needs in terms of moving from a manual-based system to an automated system. Rather, these libraries will be focusing on the issues surrounding the process of migrating from one automated system to another.

The reasons libraries wish to migrate from one system to another vary, but, as shown in Figure 11.1, two-thirds of the libraries responding to a 2007 survey indicated that the primary reason is the need for increased functionality.[5] About half of the libraries need to move to another hardware platform or are concerned about scalability issues. Problems with support and lack of confidence in the existing vendor are also frequently cited. Surprisingly, cost issues were the least frequently cited reason for wanting to make a change.

Another survey conducted in 2009 found these were the reasons for migrating to a new automated system:[6]

- Enhanced functionality in the new system
- Support for the old system on the decline or ending
- Joining a consortium (that used a different system)
- Lack of functionality in old system
- Aging system hardware (reliability and cost issues)

More recently, libraries (especially academic libraries) have moved to library services platforms as a way to reduce multiple system silos and to

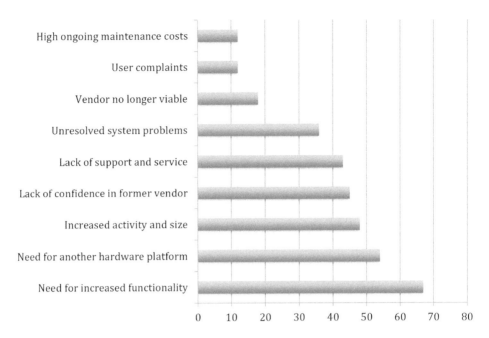

FIGURE 11.1. Reasons Libraries Choose to Migrate

have access to tools that provide improved system functionality for dealing with eResources—journals and eBooks.

However, the process of identifying a library's needs is virtually identical in either situation. When a library's current operations are analyzed to improve efficiencies, five general areas should be considered: costs, control, service, time, and communications. An analysis of current operations should identify for each broad functional area, answering these questions:

- How much staff time is devoted to it (in smaller libraries, staff can estimate the time they spend in various activities)?

- What does it cost to provide a particular function, activity, or service?

- Are the records in a system being adequately controlled in terms of quality and security?

- Is there a duplication of effort? Are materials or records handled multiple times and could the workflow be simplified?

- Are the existing LIS set-up parameters—types of patrons, types of materials, location (location codes), statistics, and circulation options—still appropriate?

- Is it possible to involve patrons in maintaining their own patron record and providing self-service that has not been considered previously? For example, can the patron view the list of items on hold or overdue, renew items, or send an email request for service to the librarian?

- How does an activity relate to other areas?

- What activities are frequently occurring? What is the volume of transactions?

- What are the existing levels of service for each functional area, activity, or service? For example, are there backlogs in cataloging, receiving serials, or placing orders?

Tip! For an activity that is done frequently (e.g., checking out materials at a public library, it is important to consider implementing self-checkout machines and automated sorting systems for materials being returned.

Those involved in the analysis process might employ a variety of techniques (e.g., flow-charting an activity or activity-based costing). However, it is important to exert a level of effort for the analysis that is proportional to the size of the financial decision. Thus, a library that is able to spend $20,000 would spend considerably less time than a very large library whose investment in a new system might exceed $1 million. In short, the library should not engage in a "paralysis of analysis."

A beneficial activity that a library might want to consider is to identify what systems are installed at peer libraries. More importantly, one or two staff members might visit multiple libraries to learn what each did well, what they wish they could do over, and what lessons were learned the hard way (those the visiting librarians should avoid at all costs). The idea is to learn how the library "stretched" the automated library system or, as a result of automation, was able to introduce new levels of service.

The result of this analysis might be a report describing the results of the analysis, but typically the library will produce a document that lists its needs for a new automated library system. The document need not be very long, but it should clearly identify the most important features and functions that the library needs.

Document the Library's Needs

The list of needs should be organized into similar functional areas, but the document should not attempt to develop an exhaustive list of functions and features that the ideal system should possess. Rather, the library should focus on identifying those ten or fifteen functions or features that will really make a positive productive impact on staff activities as well as significantly improve the level of service offered to the library's users in that particular library. The reality is that there is a significant difference between features that will have a major impact on a library (and should be considered essential) and the system features and functions that are desirable.

Once the list of functions and features has been prepared, some libraries will then assign weights to each specification to indicate its relative importance. Usually, an arbitrary scale is chosen, for example, 1–10, with 10 being most important. When assigning weights, make sure that a function with a weight of eight is actually four times as important as a feature with a weight of two.

One approach that libraries frequently use is to review the literature for a list of features and functions that might be considered. Libraries have also been known to collect requests for proposals that have been issued by other libraries. When these two techniques are employed, it is not unusual for a fairly lengthy and exhaustive document to emerge. Joan Frye Williams calls these extensive lists of functions and features the equivalent of "recombinant DNA" that take on a life of their own and never seem to die. For hopefully obvious reasons, this approach is not recommended.

Rather than employing the checklist approach, many libraries create a brief list of the most important modules and functionality that they would like in a future system. They then invite vendors to demonstrate their system, and a team of librarians uses this brief list of priorities as a basis for evaluating each vendor's offering. In the long run, ease of use and flexibility in how the system can be configured is much more important than the availability of a specific feature.

Evaluate Alternatives

Once a library clearly understands its needs, it should consider several alternatives for meeting those needs. Three broad categories are available:

- Stand-alone, in-house system
- Shared system—consortium
- Cloud-based service

In-House System

A stand-alone, in-house system means that the library purchases a system from its preferred vendor. After installation and training, the library assumes responsibility for operating the system, involving the vendor when necessary to troubleshoot problems that will come up from time to time. In broad terms, this approach means that the library will

- select the best system to meet the needs of the library;
- be able to exercise absolute control about the decisions governing the operation of the system (i.e., setup parameters);
- need to have the necessary budget, as up-front capital costs are involved; and
- have trained staff to support and maintain the automated systems (including making backups).

Tip! Very few libraries continue to operate in-house systems, but rather have migrated to a system located in the cloud.

Shared System

The shared-system option means that the library shares an LIS(s) with one or more libraries. The shared system is typically governed by a decision-making board, and it may involve a consortium or cooperative that already exists or a new consortium could be created.

These are the principal reasons for joining a consortium:[7]

- Improving access to resources
- Sharing resources
- Working to fulfill a particular need
- Reducing costs

Among the types of shared systems are the following:

- A multibranch or regional library system such as SWAN (system wide automated network) in Illinois
- A multicampus shared system, for example, the twenty-three campuses of the California State University system
- A shared infrastructure system, for example, Orbis-Cascade for the academic libraries located in the states of Washington and Oregon or Georgia PINES (Public Information Network for Electronic Services) which is available to all public libraries in the state.

Obviously, it is much easier for a library to join an existing shared system than it is to organize a new cooperative. Sharing an automated system with other libraries means that

- the selected system will likely meet most but not all of the needs of a specific library;
- the choice of system parameters will be a compromise for all libraries;
- data conversion and other up-front costs may be incurred;
- typically, a formula of some kind is used to determine a library's share of costs;
- meetings may mean higher administrative costs; and
- a shared system usually requires lower costs for each participating library compared to an in-house system;

One of the most important issues arising from a shared system is how to equitably allocate a share of the costs to each participating library. Although the approaches taken by a number of consortiums are numerous and creative (as they must be; finding common ground among libraries with diverse needs is a mighty endeavor), they all basically boil down to the use of a formula. The question to be answered is "What measures or factors do we include in the formula?" Table 11.1 illustrates one formula used by a consortium composed of different types of libraries. This group of libraries selected three factors as the basis for a cost allocation formula. The formula is updated each year. The factors include the number of volumes in a library's collection, the number of patrons, and the number of workstations. The

TABLE 11.1. Sample Factors Used in a Consortium Cost Allocation Formula

	Number of Volumes	%	Number of Patrons	%	Number of Workstations	%	Average Percent
Public A	250,000	30	100,000	51	250	48	42%
Public B	125,000	16	60,000	31	75	15	21%
Academic A	150,000	18	12,000	6	40	8	11%
Academic B	300,000	36	24,000	12	150	29	26%
Totals	825,000	100%	196,000	100%	515	100%	100%

library's percent of the total is calculated for each factor, and then the percentages are averaged to determine the library's share of the costs.

Cloud-Based Service

Under the cloud-based alternative, a library rents access to a service (sometimes called software-as-a-service, or SaaS); in this case, access to an LIS. With this option,

- a library transfers the *total responsibility of ownership* to a vendor, which is dedicated to designing, implementing, and hosting services for its clients;
- the total cost of ownership is reduced—often significantly;
- the time to migrate from an old system to a cloud-based service happens in days (and not months);
- the need to recruit, train, and retain "technology-smart" staff members to support host servers, software, and data storage is eliminated;
- the library does not need to perform routine system maintenance, data backups, and installation of new software releases;
- the vendor is responsible for installing, maintaining, and upgrading the operating system, database, and application software;
- initial capital expenditures for the system may be eliminated; and
- the library retains ownership of its own data.

It is also important to note that when a vendor is hosting the system for the customer library, they may provide up to four systems:

1. A production or "live" system that the library is using

2. A replication of the "live" system to improve redundancy and thus improve system reliability

3. A test system, sometimes called a "sandbox," for the library to use for training and the testing of a new release of the software

4. A backup system used to back up the library's data

A vendor may host a legacy system using the cloud for some of its customer libraries. However, it is important to note that the cloud must be used if a library wishes to implement a multitenant platform as more and more libraries are choosing to use.

Service-level agreement—A service-level agreement identifies and discusses the rights and responsibilities of two parties (the customer and the supplier) pertaining to an automated system. A service-level agreement can be used between the consortium and its member libraries to define the quality of services to be provided. Issues that should be typically addressed by a service-level agreement may be found in an exhibit at the end of this chapter.

Evaluating Alternatives

To evaluate each of these options fairly, it is necessary to prepare a cost analysis that compares apples to apples (and not apples to oranges). To that end, all of the likely cost components for each of the alternatives should be identified. It is important to identify the initial out-of-pocket costs (purchase price) as well as the annual maintenance charges. Determining the total five-year costs is important. The total five-year costs are calculated by adding the first-year costs plus the ongoing costs over the remaining five years. This is done to clarify actual costs, because some vendors have low initial pricing but high ongoing maintenance charges.

Usually a library prepares a report documenting the results of this analysis to share with funding decision-makers and library boards, among others. A summary of the costs for each of the three broad alternatives is shown in Table 11.2. Note that these costs are not based in reality, but are meant to illustrate the analysis.

To RFP or . . .

A request for quotation (RFQ) or request for bid (RFB) is used when the specifications for a particular product can be clearly identified (e.g., paper towels), and several competing suppliers are willing to bid for the business. Using the RFQ process, cost quotes or bids are receiving by the purchasing department, and the selection of the vendor is based *solely* on price. A request

TABLE 11.2. Summary of Alternative Library Information System Costs

	In-House	*Shared*	*Cloud-Based*
Public Library*:			
Hardware	$25,000	$15,000	—
Software	200,000	120,000	—
Maintenance	90,000	54,000	—
Staff	300,000	180,000	—
Telecom	—	75,000	—
ASP service	—	—	51,500/yr.
Total 5-year cost	$885,000	$660,000	$257,500
Average cost/year	$117,000	$132,000	$51,500
Academic Library**:			
Hardware	19,000	17,500	—
Software	105,000	100,000	—
Maintenance	189,000	177,000	—
Staff	150,000	70,000	—
Telecom	40,000	70,000	40,000
ASP service	—	—	234,000
Total 5-year cost	$518,500	$422,000	$234,000
Average cost/year	$103,700	$84,400	$46,800

* Public library has a database with 250,000 titles, 190,000 patrons, and 115 workstations.
** Academic library has 115,000 titles, 10,000 students, and 100 workstations.

for proposals (RFP), on the other hand, uses several criteria to make a selection decision; and price is only one and not the *sole* selection criteria.

The intent of the RFP, RFI, or other procurement process is to select the best possible system for its needs. An RFP process may be mandated by local purchasing rules and regulations.[8]

Should a RFP be used, the library will want to ensure that the document addresses the following topics:

- Overview of the project
- Required deliverables
- Proposal format
- References
- Submission deadline
- Specifications within a RFP should address several dimensions or concerns:
  - *The functional dimension*—the robustness of the features and functionality of the ILS system as well as its usability
  - *The architectural dimension*—the system architecture (hardware and software), likely longevity, supportability, and scalability
  - *The community dimension*—the level of involvement among library customers of each product, number of installed systems, software licensing approach, existence of service options, and the roadmap for development
  - *The code dimension*—The code design, level of code reuse, proprietary versus open source code
  - *The schema dimension*—the database schema and the availability of database documentation.
  - *The interoperability dimension*—the ability for the library to use APIs to provide access to the library's data and extend the systems capabilities as well as connect with other systems.
  - *Other concerns* that must be addressed include cost, reliability, security, and system flexibility.
- Evaluation process to be followed by the library
- Vendor presentations

In some cases, the RFP process does not seem to be objective. Rather, the RFP process can be used to justify a decision that has been made prior to the RFP document actually being issued. It needs to be recognized that a vendor invests considerable time and money responding to a RFP. All of the questions must be answered (often in a very prescribed format); a detailed cost proposal must be prepared; and multiple copies of the proposal must be submitted. And these costs are in fact passed on to all customers in the marketplace.

Recognizing the potential unfairness in the RFP process, many vendors will refuse to respond to an RFP if one of the vendor's salespeople has neither visited the library nor had several candid telephone conversations with one or more library staff members. Contributing to the corruption of the process, most vendors are more than willing to share a copy of their preferred, draft RFP document in word processing format. This preferred RFP document contains specifications that emphasize their product's strong points and most flatter the vendor. If a library uses such a preferred RFP, all vendors are, not surprisingly, able to recognize the source of the RFP document and thus the identity of the preferred vendor of choice. Consequently, it should not be surprising that most vendors fail to respond to a "less than open" RFP process.

Evaluating Proposals

Should a library decide not to use the RFP process, what are its options? Some libraries have used the list of their requirements or needs and issued a brief request for information (RFI) to determine what vendors are most likely to meet their needs. The library then asks the selected vendors to schedule a visit to the library so that library staff members can see how the vendor accomplishes the most important tasks and activities that the library has previously identified.

Any vendor sales representatives worth their salt will want as much time as possible to demonstrate all of their system's features. Although understandable, all the features found within a system are not equally important, so a full system demonstration should be avoided. Rather, the library should control the demonstration by very clearly asking the vendor to perform a particular task or activity—and then asking the vendor representative to keep quiet while the staff members think about what they have just seen and how it might relate to their library. This approach allows the library staff to understand how a system performs the functions that are most important to the library. Developing a list of questions allows the staff to control the sequence of questions asked and prevents a "carefully scripted" approach to the demonstration.

After the library staff clearly understand the strengths and weaknesses of each vendor's system, they should ask the vendors for a cost proposal. Waiting until after the functional evaluation of a vendor system means that the costs for a system are not clouding the judgment of library staff members during the evaluation process.

Although it is true that most automated systems provide an equivalent level of functionality, these same vendors offer systems that differ in how a task or activity is accomplished. What will be a one- or two-step process with one vendor's product may require four or more steps in another vendor's offering. A system that minimizes those tasks and activities that are performed most frequently is one that will, over time, allow staff to be the most productive.

To evaluate an automated system, library staff might consider any number of factors. Historically, these factors have, in some cases, included the following:

- Software functionality

- Software ease of use

- Adaptability/flexibility—system sets up parameters so the software will follow the library's policies

- Documentation—typically includes user manuals for each module

- Hardware manufacturer—the reputation of the company

- Scalability—ability of the system to easily expand
- System reliability—are there system availability (uptime) statistics to demonstrate the server's reliability?
- System response times—what are the response times experienced by other customers? Does the vendor provide any benchmarking data?
- Training services—time spent training staff on-site
- Vendor support services—can a customer visit a website to report a problem or track the status of a previously reported problem? How often are new releases of the software distributed to customers?
- Purchase/maintenance agreement guarantees
- Vendor's past performance
- Vendor's financial stability/profitability
- Overall suitability of the system.
- Cost—includes both the purchase price as well as ongoing maintenance charges as part of a five-year total cost calculation
- Other

A survey compared how libraries rated the above evaluation factors before and after a library had implemented an automated library system.[9] After installation, librarians were much less focused on cost and software functionality and were more concerned about system reliability and hardware support. Were this same survey to be conducted today, system reliability would be much less of an issue.

Another survey identified the top ten reasons for choosing a library information system:[10]

- Ease of use by patrons
- Availability of application modules and subsystems
- Completeness of modules and subsystems
- Cost of system
- Cost of hardware
- Need for local programming staff
- Service reputation of vendor
- Ease of use by staff
- Comparable installed site
- Previous experience with vendor

Tip! What Vendors Want to Know

Is there funding?

What is the evaluation process?

Who are the decision-makers?

What is the time frame?

Are there any data conversion needs?

Are there any hardware or software constraints?

A library has access to several other information sources about the vendors in the marketplace and their products. Reviewing the literature often provides systematic product reviews that will prove to be of value. *Library Journal* and *American Libraries* provide an annual automated systems marketplace article that discusses each of the vendors and provides statistics about their total revenues, number of new customers, and other relevant information.

Visiting other libraries that have a system installed can be quite revealing. It is best if you have a list of questions to ask to ensure that you are collecting the same information at each site. If two or three staff members visit their counterparts in the nearby library, make sure that they get together afterward to resolve any inconsistencies that may have arisen. It is not unusual for the visiting staff members to feel like they are the "six blind men describing their encounter with an elephant"—or, in other words, "Are you sure we visited the same library?" In some ways, this is analogous to assembling pieces of a puzzle.

> **Tip!** The same process of identifying and documenting needs and then evaluating and comparing options can be used to select other software products. For example, in an excellent article Graham Sherriff documents the process used at his library to select an interactive tutorial platform.[11]

Using Consultants

Consultants can add real value to the process of selecting a new LIS. Their experiences in helping libraries allows the consultant to make sure that a library is not overlooking some information or placing too much emphasis on a particular factor. However, it must be remembered that the library will have to live with the results of the selected LIS, so the library should control what the consultant does.

It is also true that any consultant will bring a bias, both positive and negative, about each of the vendors in the marketplace. Determining what systems the consultant's clients have selected over the last year or two will reveal any bias that may exist. Some consultants will explain this bias by stating that they want to ensure that their clients only choose vendors that have a proven track record. Forearmed with this knowledge, a library can then use the consultant more effectively—choosing to use or ignore portions of the advice that is offered.[12]

Consultants are typically compensated on a time and materials basis, or a project will be completed for a fixed price. If the consultant is being involved to help select and implement a new LIS, then it is probably better to use the time and materials approach. The library can manage the costs by controlling the amount of time the consultant is working on the library's project. If there is a specific deliverable, then a fixed price approach is usually followed.

Written Agreements

Once a vendor has been selected, the library enters the next phase of the selection process. For systems that cost less than $25,000, vendors typically will not enter into a negotiation about the terms and conditions surrounding the purchase of the product. Rather, there is either a "shrink-wrap agreement" or a "click-through agreement" that details the terms under which the library can use the software. In systems that cost more than $25,000, most vendors are willing to negotiate a purchase agreement and a maintenance agreement, although most vendors want to use their standard agreements as a starting point. As the cost of the system increases, the more willing most vendors will be to make accommodations to their standard-form agreements. Remember that any negotiations are a series of compromises, and the objective is to make sure that the interests of both parties are protected and that neither party has an unfair advantage.

It is really helpful if the library has a clear understanding of what it wants from a system in terms of reliability, response times, scalability, and software functionality. The agreements will spell out the responsibilities for each of the parties as well as the remedies when the system fails to perform as specified. The agreements must also provide a framework that will be followed should any future conflicts, misunderstandings, or disagreements occur.

Listed here are the more important topics that should be addressed in the system purchase agreement and system maintenance agreements:

Deliverables—Exactly what is being delivered to the library is specified. A description of the software modules, hardware (if part of the agreement), training, and so on.

Pricing—The purchase price for each deliverable is specified in the System Purchase Agreement. The ongoing maintenance charges are also detailed.

Payment schedule—Although any number of progress payments can be made, normally there are three such payments at contract signing, installation of the system, and acceptance of the system. Obviously, the vendor will want as much of the money as soon as possible (vendors incur the majority of their costs in the first few months of a contract), whereas the library will try to delay a large payment until final acceptance. This is a topic that clearly will involve some negotiation.

Delivery and installation—The delivery schedule for various components of the system is specified. Note that whenever there are delays to the schedule, in a majority of cases the library is the cause.

Training and documentation—The amount of training to be provided by the vendor is specified along with any limits on class size. In addition, the provision of training or user manuals is addressed. Most vendors provide such documentation in machine-readable form, so a library can modify the users manual as it sees fit.

Warranties—Most vendors provide a warranty period during which the library does not pay for support. Warranty periods can be as short as ninety days and as long as a year. An important issue that needs to be resolved during negotiations is exactly when the warranty period begins (At the time of installation? When the system is accepted by the library? What are system acceptance criteria?).

Termination—This section details the conditions under which the library can cancel the system purchase agreement with the vendor. Such conditions might include failure to deliver software as scheduled or failure to deliver software that meets minimum acceptable performance levels (may be defined as importing and indexing the library's database within certain time limits, etc.).

Typically, a separate system maintenance agreement is signed at the same time the system purchase agreement is signed. Once the library has accepted the system, the terms and conditions of the system maintenance agreement then become operative. Important topics that need to be addressed in this agreement include the following:

Support—What are the hours of support and what are the ways in which a library can contact the vendor (toll-free telephone, fax, email, the Web)? Are reports of software bugs categorized and the more serious problems worked on first? What is the maximum time period that will elapse between the time a bug is reported and when it is fixed (does this vary by the seriousness of the bug)?

Enhancements—How frequently are new releases of the software distributed to customers? What influence do customers have in determining what enhancements are included in future releases of the software?

Exhibit - Service-Level Agreement

A service-level agreement (SLA) identifies the duties and responsibilities of both parties entering into the agreement. A good service-level agreement between a library coopera-tive and a vendor should address the following topics:

Purpose and scope— Details what services are included in the agreement, specifi-cally the operation and support of an ILS.

Use of the system—What modules or functionality is included in the ILS? What reports are available for each participating library on a daily, weekly, monthly, quarterly, and annual basis?

Data communications network—Acknowledging that the operation of the ILS requires a high speed and reliable data communications network. The responsibility for maintaining the data communications network within the library belongs to the library. The responsibility for the operation of the network between the library and the server must be specified.

System reliability—The level of expected system reliability should be stated, for example, 99.9% or better. How is reliability measured (at the server or at the library)? System reliability can be improved by providing redundancy of servers and disk drives.

What remedies (financial or otherwise) will be used when the reliability standard is not achieved for a specific period of time?

System response times—How will response times be measured for various types of transactions? What transactions will be measured? During some periods of the month, significant demands may be placed on the system—for example, running monthly or ad hoc reports. However, such demands should not impact the overall performance of the system. What remedies (financial or otherwise) will be used when the system response time standards are not achieved for a specific period of time?

Communication—What communication methods will be used to alert participating libraries when the server is experiencing downtimes (email, telephone, texting, etc.)?

Confidentiality of data—Acknowledging that each library's data are owned by the library and may not be used for any other purpose unless authorized by the library. Data include bibliographic records, authority records, item records, patron records, and associated transaction records; also, acknowledging that the confidentiality of the patron data is very sensitive and deserving of extra security measures. What procedures should be followed to notify the library (and the patrons themselves) if the library's patron database is breached in any manner?

Copy of data—Acknowledging that the organization hosting and managing the system will provide a machine-readable copy of the library's data within ninety days of a written request. The costs of providing such a service should be specified up front. All bibliographic, item, authority, patron, vendor, and transaction records and other files should be provided in an industry standard format.

Hosting responsibilities—Acknowledging that the organization hosting and managing the system will back up all system data on a nightly and weekly basis and that some system backups will need to be stored off-site. Testing and installation of new software releases shall be completed by the hosting organization. Other responsibilities are also identified.

Customer responsibilities—The responsibilities that the library cooperative has are identified.

Internetworking of devices—Acknowledging that the ILS will need to interface with a variety of devices (self-checkout machines, telephone notice systems etc.) using some industry standard protocols or an application programming interface (API). Some specific standards should be identified, for example, Standard Interchange Protocol (SIP2), Z39.50, Z39.83; downloading MARC records; and so forth.

Training—The amount and type of training (on-site or via the Web) should be specified.

Help desk—Procedures to be followed by a library to report a problem to a help desk should be specified. The hours when the help desk is staffed by people and the procedures to follow for after-hours service should be specified. How are problems escalated, and how is progress in problem resolution reported? Problems should be grouped into one of three categories: urgent, important, or minor. Each problem category needs to be defined, and the anticipated time frame in which each problem category will be resolved should be stated.

Problem resolution—The maximum time needed to respond to and resolve a previously reported problem (problems may be sorted by how serious they are). What remedies (financial or otherwise) will be used when the time to resolve a problem within the required time frame is not achieved?

New software releases—Who is responsible for testing and installing new software releases should be specified. If the server is being hosted by a vendor, then it should be the vendor's responsibility to test and load new software releases.

Costs—All costs that must be paid by the customer should be clearly and explicitly stated.

Cost increases—Limiting cost increases to the lesser of (1) a maximum percent increase, for example, 4% per year; or (2) a regional cost indicator, for example, the Consumer Price Index (CPI).

Payment—How payments will be made. The number of payments per year should be specified. Does the invoice reflect services already performed?

Term of the agreement—The beginning and ending dates of the agreement are specified.

Extension—The method for extending the agreement is specified.

Amendments—Amendments must be in writing and agreed to by both parties.

Termination—The time period needed to give notice of the Inland Library System's decision to terminate the agreement should be specified.

Dispute resolution—How are disputes resolved—by arbitration or the filing of a lawsuit? If a lawsuit will be used, what court will be used to file the lawsuit? If arbitration, what arbitration service will be used?

Other language—Each party may wish to add additional language to cover the standard terms and conditions in a contract between a municipal library and another agency. Such language might include governing law, notices, entire agreement, and so forth.

Summary

Selecting and implementing a system has a logical order and progression of tasks, but that doesn't mean the process itself will be simple or without complications.

To avoid the problems associated with GIGO (garbage in, garbage out), it's a winning strategy to start with your library's approach to bibliographic standards and processes, to ensure that your system supports key technical services objectives and workflows.

Next, the system's circulation module must support the library's day-to-day needs, whether they consist of offering materials form a single site or involve a large library system or consortium that must share items between locations.

As important as the back-end functionality of the system is, remember that functions used most by people (both library patrons and staff) must be intuitive and effective, whether they entail working with the library's physical collections or all manner of digital collections.

When procuring a system, don't forget to gather all the relevant stakeholders to identify the requirements of the system (including performance and features) before launching a procurement process. Procurement approaches vary, but with the cost of an ILS system, a request for proposal (RFP) is a common approach. The process should include these steps:

1. Identifying a library's needs

2. Documenting the library's needs

3. Evaluating alternatives

4. Preparing written agreements

5. Beginning the implementation process

The RFP process is not without its complications, but it also covers many bases and helps create confidence in one of the most important decisions a library makes.

Questions to Consider

- Four concerns were identified for the consideration of cataloging alternatives. Are there another one or two considerations that are important to your library?

- In selecting systems, does your library use a request for proposal process? If yes, have you considered other options for the system selection process?

- What reason(s) would cause the library to migrate from its existing automated system to a new system?

- Has your library compared its mix of installed technology with that of other peer libraries?

- What options other than a stand-alone, in-house system has your library considered for its automated systems?

- Has your library considered the use of a service-level agreement?

- Have you calculated the total five-year costs for all alternatives?

- Can you articulate the differences between a request for quotation (RFQ), a request for information (RFI), and a request for proposals (RFP)?

- Do you understand the need to separate the costs from all other aspects of evaluating alternatives?

- What characteristics should be included for the evaluation of a new automated library system for your library?

- When should your library consider using a consultant?

Suggested Readings

Corrado, Edward, and Heather Lea Moulaison. *Getting Started with Cloud Computing. A LITA Guide.* New York: Neal Schuman, 2011.

Ippoliti, Cinthya. *The Savvy Academic Librarian's Guide to Technological Innovation: Moving Beyond the WOW Factor.* Chicago: American Library Association, 2018.

Jost, Richard. *Selecting and Implementing an Integrated Library System: The Most Important Decision You Will Ever Make.* London: Chandos, 2016.

Knox, Karen. *Implementing Technology Solutions in Libraries: Techniques, Tools, and Tips From the Trenches.* Medford, NJ: Information Today, 2011.

Miller, Joseph B. *Internet Technologies and Information Services*. 2nd ed. Santa Barbara, CA: Libraries Unlimited, 2014.

Taylor, Nick D. *Raising the Tech Bar at Your Library: Improving Services to Meet User Needs*. Santa Barbara, CA: Libraries Unlimited, 2017.

Webber, Desiree, and Andrew Peters. *Integrated Library Systems: Planning, Selecting, and Implementing*. Santa Barbara, CA: Libraries Unlimited, 2010.

Wilkinson, Frances C., and Sever Bordeianu, eds. *The Complete Guide to RFPs for Librarians*. Santa Barbara, CA: Libraries Unlimited, 2018.

Notes

1. David Greelish, "An Interview with Computing Pioneer Alan Kay," *Time*, April 2, 2013.

2. Online Computer Library Center (OCLC), *OCLC and Linked Data* (Columbus, OH: OCLC, n.d.). See also Carol Jean Godby and Ray Denenberg, *Common Ground: Exploring Compatibilities Between the Linked Data Models of the Library of Congress and OCLC* (Dublin, OH: Library of Congress and OCLC Research, 2015).

3. Kenning Arlitsch, "Being Irrelevant: How Library Data Interchange Standards Have Kept Us Off the Internet," *Journal of Library Administration* 54, no. 7 (2014): 609–19; and Tom Heath and Christian Bizer, "Linked Data: Evolving the Web into a Global Data Space," *Synthesis Lectures on the Semantic Web: Theory and Technology* 1, no. 1 (2011): 1–136.

4. Joseph R. Matthews, "An Environmental Scan of OCLC Alternatives: A Management Perspective," *Public Library Quarterly* 35, no. 3 (2016): 175–87.

5. Frank Cervone, "ILS Migration in the 21st Century: Some New Things to Think About This Time Around," *Computers in Libraries* 27 (July–August 2007): 6–14.

6. Zhonghong Wang, "Integrated Library System (ILS) Challenges and Opportunities: A Survey of U.S. Academic Libraries with Migration Projects," *Journal of Academic Librarianship* 35, no. 3 (May 2009): 207–20.

7. James J. Kopp, "Library Consortia and Information Technology: The Past, the Present, the Promise," *Library Consortia and Information Technology* 17, no. 1 (March 1998): 7–12.

8. Joan Frye Williams, "The RFI, RFP, and the Contract Process," in *Integrated Online Library Catalogs*, Jennifer Cargill, ed. (Westport, CT: Meckler, 1991), 1–15; Joseph R. Matthews, Stephen R. Salmon, and Joan Frye Williams, "The RFP—Request for Punishment: or A Tool for Selecting an Automated Library System," *Library HiTech* 5 (Spring 1987): 15–21; and M. Stowe, "To RFP or Not to RFP: That is the Question," *Journal of Library Administration* 26, no. 3–4 (1999): 53–74.

9. Russell T. Clement, "Cost Is Not Everything: How Experience Changed Some Librarians' Views of the Important Factors in Selecting Automated Systems," *Library Journal* 110, no. 16 (October 1, 1985): 52–55.

10. Peggy Johnson, *Automation and Organizational Change in Libraries* (Boston: G. K. Hall, 1991), 113.

11. Graham Sherriff, "Interactive Tutorials—The Platform Matters," *C&RL News* 78, no. 4 (April 2017): 212–16.

12. Joseph R. Matthews, "The Effective Use of Consultants in Libraries," *Library Technology Reports* 30, no. 5 (November–December 1994): 745–814.

12
System Migration and Implementation

There can be any number of reasons why a library might be interested in migrating from one automated system to another. Among these reasons might be financial (the new system might have lower annual system support costs or the library is faced with the need to purchase a new server or other expensive equipment), strategic (a group of libraries have decided to share a system as a foundation for a larger set of shared services), philosophical (the library wants to embrace open source systems), practical (moving from local hosting to a system in the cloud), or technological (the vendor is refusing to keep pace with current technology or the need to connect to various third-party vendors is not supported with the current system).

In a survey of libraries that have migrated to a new system, Wang found that these were the top five reasons for making the switch:[2]

1. Better system/functionality with the new system
2. Diminishing support for the old system
3. Consortium requirement
4. Insufficient old system features or functionality
5. Aging system or hardware.

Wang also found some of the aspects of the old system that were disliked included lack of integration, slowing support and development, nonrelational database management system, limits on expandability, and "clunky" workflows.

However, unless there is sufficient planning and forethought given to the process of migrating from one system to another, the experience is likely to be more frustrating, more time-consuming, and perhaps more expensive than was originally planned. So what then are the secrets to success of migrating systems? The purpose of this chapter is to identify and discuss the more important issues that should be addressed in order to have a smoother transition to a new system.

The multiplicity of issues surrounding the selection of a new automated system was discussed in the prior chapter. At this point, the assumption is made that the library has signed a contract with the vendor of choice, and the library is now moving forward with the migration from the old to the new system.

Among the more important system migration topics are the following:

- Migration team
- Premigration decisions
- What data to migrate
- How to clean up data
- Whether the data should be enhanced
- How much testing should be done
- How to best phase in a migration
- How to train staff
- Why communication is vital
- Security issues

Migration Team

The key to a smooth and successful transition from one system to another is to create a migration team that will assume responsibility for the project. Aside from involving the library's system manager (perhaps this individual should head up the team?), it is important to have knowledgeable and experienced team members from several areas in the library (circulation, acquisitions, cataloging, etc.). It is important to choose individuals who have a positive outlook on life and are energetic and welcome a challenge. After all, this team will be responsible for introducing a new system that will cause serious change within the organization.

As the transition from one system to another is going to take a fair amount of time, it is also important for the project manager heading this team to be aware of any constraints in terms of the availability of staff (vacations, training sessions, conference attendance, etc.).

If the IT department is a separate department, as is often the case on campus and in municipal organizations, then it is incumbent for the project manager to develop a relationship with the key IT staff members, as well as inviting their participation as a member of the migration team. The IT department must understand the importance of library software vendors gaining access to the server (wherever it is located) in a timely manner so that they can provide necessary support when needed. For example, the New York University Health Sciences Library was forced to migrate to a new system when a change in the campus network topology removed the secure connection method Innovative Interfaces had been using, and the virtual private network (VPN) chosen by the campus IT department could not be supported by Innovative.[3]

Relationships with other departments and groups within the larger organization, for example, the campus registrar's office, the accounting department, and others may need to be developed so that they are aware of the coming changes and their likely involvement in terms of providing information and testing of new systems.

The migration team and its leader must be empowered to keep the project on schedule. One of the challenges to a migration project for many libraries, especially in a consortia setting, is the need to involve every library, with the result that the project timetable suffers a significant delay as a result of "death by committee" deliberations.

Larger libraries or a consortium of libraries may wish to create several working groups that report to the overall migration team. Possible teams might include acquisitions, cataloging, circulation, online catalog/discovery system, and publicity/communications.

The first priority for a migration team is to develop a carefully considered plan, as a number of balls must be juggled to complete a project successfully. Although it is true that whales and birds can complete a migration by instinct (one of the wonders of our world), migrating a new system by instinct is a certain recipe for disaster.

Premigration Decisions

Every automated system has a set of parameters or options that control what the system will do and how data are going to be displayed. The library (or libraries in a shared system environment) must become very knowledgeable about what parameters control what aspects of the system. These parameters control such things as patron type categories, item categories, location codes, tables that combine patron types and material types in order to control circulation checkout periods, and so forth.

The library should also identify what standards and how consistent various codes will be used for statistical purposes or what abbreviations will (and will not) be used to improve the quality of the data in the system.

A new system also provides the library with the opportunity to reexamine all of its various policies and practices (overdue notices timing, amount of fines and fees, at what point a patron become delinquent, etc.). The system also allows the library to explore changing its work processes (or even dropping some processes that no longer add value to the customer) to take advantage of the new system's strengths. For example, the library may have new opportunities for collaborating and establishing working relationships with other departments on campus such as the registrar, financial services, and so forth.

More importantly, any new system will have a different user interface and will have new functionality (and will also likely be missing some functionality found in the old system), which will require staff to adapt and adjust when they learn the new system.

What Data to Migrate?

Libraries invest a considerable amount of time, energy, and money in creating and maintaining data in any number of data files, so it is not surprising that a great deal of attention is paid to the migration of various data files from the old to the new system. It is not unusual for a library to need to convert several different file types. Among the data files that might be migrated are the following:

Bibliographic	Authority
Item	Patron
Circulation transactions	Holds
Acquisitions vendor	Financial—Fund accounts
Open orders	Order payment
Serials holdings	Statistical
Electronic resources	Other

Some libraries are surprised to discover that it may not be possible to export one or more files because of restrictions in the agreement between the vendor and the library or because of system design limitations. The library may need to consider paying the vendor to write a custom program so that one or more data files can be exported (whether the library should pay for such a project will depend on costs to export a specific data file and the number of records in the file compared to the likely costs to recreate the data file in the new system, starting from scratch).

> **Tip!** It is critical that any agreement between a library and a vendor clearly address the issue of data ownership—all of the data in any automated system belong to the library (whether the data are located on a server located at the library, on campus, or up in the cloud). And any costs associated with the export of the library's data should be identified as a part of the written agreement and not left to be negotiated at some future date (when a crisis or dispute has arisen). Ideally, the data format to be exported should be identified for each type of data.

Data Cleanup

Once the various data files have been exported, the library may wish to have some portion of the data made more consistent (this is often referred to as data cleanup). The cleanup process can convert various abbreviations (St, st, ave, Ave, Ln—with and without punctuation) to a standard abbreviation or a full word (Street, Avenue, Lane). In some cases, the new vendor may provide this data cleanup service for little or no charge, or the library may need to turn to another vendor (such as Backstage Library Works, or MARCIVE) for such a service. Cost is typically charged on a per record basis, based on the amount of data cleanup to be performed.

A number of data cleanup activities are typically done for bibliographic records, including correcting filing indicators, making subject heading consistent, checking the genre or form heading, checking name authority records, and so forth. In addition to validating content in the bibliographic record, the vendor may also provide deduplication checking (identifying duplicate records and moving all holdings information to one record). The vendor may also provide to the library an authority record for each unique name, subject headings, and uniform titles.

Some of the cataloging problems that have come to light as libraries move from the traditional online catalog to a discovery service are listed here:[4]

- Inconsistently coded fixed fields in the bibliographic record
- Inconsistent maintenance of name and subject authority headings
- eResources often not being classified
- Challenges associated with the integration of multiple controlled vocabularies
- Integrating machine-readable cataloging (MARC) and non-MARC bibliographic data

Adding or editing bibliographic records provided by eBook vendors can be a challenging proposition for any library. Often the records provided by the supplier do not conform to the MARC 21 format, and they are often incomplete and sometimes inaccurate. The library should determine the maximum amount of work it is willing to invest to upgrade these records in order to make them visible in the library's online catalog.

> **Tip!** *MarcEdit* is a popular software suite that provides metadata editing and support tools for a wide range of library and non-library metadata formats for users all around the world.[5] The *MarcEdit* tools allow a user to

- perform character set conversions;
- validate, extract, join and split records and record sets;
- merge and deduplicate data sets;
- edit metadata record by record or across a data set;
- work directly to harvest non-MARC data; and
- perform advanced metadata manipulation.

Should Data Be Enhanced?

It is possible to add additional content to an existing bibliographic record so that it becomes an enhanced record—the additional content, such as table of contents, index terms and/or an abstract or summary, creates additional index entries. These enhanced records can be purchased from several sources, but few libraries will find that the benefits of enhanced records rarely exceed the costs (given that a majority of discovery is happening with an internet search engine—and they index the full contents of a book rather than a surrogate record of the contents of the book).

Libraries can also run their bibliographic records through an authority control processing service that will return an authority control record for every author, subject heading, and uniform title contained in the bibliographic records. These authority control records significantly improve the quality and consistency of the bibliographic data (eliminate variant spelling of an author's name, e.g.). These authority control records will also be of value as the library moves from MARC-based records to the new and evolving data structure being developed by the Library of Congress—BIBFRAME.

Thus, one of the questions a library needs to answer is whether it wants its bibliographic records to be discovered by internet search engines. If the answer is yes, then the data contained within the library's catalog need to be structured using BIBFRAME.

How Much Testing Should Be Done?

Libraries should recognize that training on the new system will be required for all staff members. Remember that the new system will not be the same as the old system and that every system has strengths and weaknesses. Provide group classes as well as the opportunity for staff to drop in and practice on their own

Testing of atypical cases is usually more informative (for what it reveals about the system and its possible limitations) than testing the routine. Although the use of scripts for routine processes is important, make sure to develop scripts for situations that currently are a challenge. Being able to use a "test instance" of the system is preferable to testing on the actual system that will be used to go live, as any changes to the testing system can be done without worrying about affecting the "real" system.[6]

In general, it is not possible to do too much testing, but at the same time there is continuing pressure to get the new system to go live. All testing should carefully examine that each data file has been accurately moved to the new system by ensuring that

- the number of records in the new file match the number of records in the old file;
- each field in the record contains the expected data (data from an adjacent field has not found its way into another field);
- a consistency check is performed for each field of data if possible (the data in the field is all numeric, or all text, or whatever it should contain); and
- a check is made for outliers (if all the values in a field of data are likely to fall within a certain range, check for data outside that range).

How to Best Phase in a Migration

Deciding when to "turn the switch" for the new system can have important repercussions, so the decision must be made carefully. Some libraries make the switch at the end of a fiscal year (so less data need to be transferred, and the resulting reports between the old and new system are cleaner); others make the switch at the end of a semester (when the library has less activity).

Some libraries, especially larger libraries with multiple branch locations or consortiums, make the transition in phases, whereas others prefer to do it in a short period of time (weeks or a month or two).[7] Some "turn on" a system module by module (e.g., cataloging, acquisitions, etc.), whereas others "turn on" a system by location.[8]

Implementation

Implementing an integrated library system (ILS) is an activity that will benefit from thorough planning. The library can take advantage of the experiences of its vendor of choice, who has been involved in the implementation process involving a number of libraries. But ultimately, it is important to remember that it is the library staff that will have to live through the experience of implementation on a daily basis, so good planning will pay significant dividends.

Library Policies

Ensuring that library policies are reflected in the ILS software is the responsibility of the library's system manager. The system manager controls the software's operation by using the setup parameters. These parameters allow the system manager to directly control what data elements are used to build each index, to specify what indexes are made available to the public, to decide what types of patron categories will be created and maintained, and whether fines will be charged for overdue materials, and so forth. The available parameters within the software are typically documented within a setup manual or a series of checklists. Most vendors provide a system overview class that introduces the library to the various setup parameters and options that control the software's operation.

Types of Barcodes

Within the library community, two types of barcodes are typically used. The industry standard, originally established by CLSI, uses a 14-digit Codabar barcode label (all numbers). The first digit identifies the type of label (patron or item). The next four digits can be used as a unique library ID number. The next eight digits represent the unique item ID number (leading zeros are used as fill characters). The last digit is a check digit. The second type of barcode label is called the Code 3 of 9, or Code 39. This barcode allows alphanumeric characters (both letters and numbers) in the barcode. Typically these Code 39 labels have eight characters and no check digit.

RFID

Radio-frequency identification (RFID) technology is used in patron self-checkout machines, returned material sorting systems, and larger material handling systems. Collectively, all of these machines are normally referred to as automated materials handling (AMH) systems. The National Information Standards Organization (NISO) has developed a Recommended Practice (NISO RP-6-2012) that ensures interoperability between vendor systems. And although twenty-six fields of data can be written to an RFID tag, normally libraries only use one to three fields:

- Unique identifier (barcode number)
- Owner institution
- Set information (e.g., one of three).

A majority of RFID tags are 2×2 inches square; however, a somewhat larger 2×3 inch tag will provide a better signal. The NISO Recommended

Practice established ISO 18000-3, Mode 1 tags as the standard RFID tag for US libraries.

A library must, of course, add a RFID tag to each item in the collection and link that unique tag to the library's automated system (staff typically have higher accuracy rates when installing the RFID tags than do volunteers). Libraries that have implemented RFID have found that use of the technology

- saves staff time and money;

- better secures the collection; and

- enables staff to conduct regular inventories (soon robots will handle inventories when the library is closed).

The Library Communication Framework (LCF) is a joint effort between libraries and various ILS and AMH vendors to develop a set of interoperability communication formats in order to standardize a set of principles, variables, and data values. Although LCF was developed in the United Kingdom, all of the AMH and library automation vendors support LCF. Libraries should be asking their vendors to be compliant with LCF as this helps prevent vendor lock-in. A number of LCF-related documents can be downloaded by visiting http://www.bic.org.uk/114/lcf.

> **Tip!** For additional information about RFID and automated material handling systems, visit the Galecia Group online www.galecia.com.

Data Migration

If your library is migrating from one automated system to another, then the new vendor will work with your library to ensure that all of your data are accurately and completely moved from the old system to the new system. Examples of fixed data include bibliographic, authority, patron, vendor, fund, and order payment records. In some cases, the vendor of choice can assist in migrating transaction-based files (e.g., items on hold, overdue items, items checked out, etc.), although a majority of libraries migrating do not attempt moving this type of data.

Libraries make a substantial investment when they create data files for their existing automated library system. These records will likely include bibliographic, authority, patron, fund accounts, serial prediction patterns, and vendor files). The implementation team for the vendor will assist a library to develop a set of mapping tables to ensure that data from the old system are preserved and moved to the correct place within the new system. Frequently, coded data in the old system can be updated or converted to a word or phrase. It is important to obtain a relatively large sample of records to be migrated so the new vendor will have an opportunity to test its conversion programs and identify any data elements that are surprises. An example of such a surprise might be the type of patron codes that have been entered creatively (all uppercase, upper and lower, various abbreviations, etc.). The more opportunity there is for testing and refining the data mapping, the happier the library will be with the resulting database.

Another important factor in the migration of bibliographic/authority records is the need to provide time to adequately test the bibliographic and authority records that are output from the old system and need to be imported into the new system. A related issue involves how copy and item records are linked to the bibliographic record itself during the export process. *Caveat emptor!* Testing, testing, and more testing is required.[9]

> **Tip!** Some libraries send their bibliographic/authority records to a firm that provides authority record processing to have their records "cleaned up" and enhanced. Several vendors provide this service for a reasonable fee.

Nonbibliographic data, such as patron and vendor records, are complicated by the fact that there is no standard structure to assist in migrating these data. And while the library or vendor might export the data in a "comma delimited format" the data will still need to be manipulated to create an import file that is compatible with the new vendor's system.

Converting transactional data files is more complicated because the transaction files are often stored in a proprietary coded format. However, most vendors will work with the library to determine whether migrating this type of data is possible and cost effective.

Training

The training provided by a vendor is designed to train the library's trainers. Usually there is a limit on the class size, for example, six to eight people per module. Thus, different staff members will participate in different sessions, depending on the module being covered. The library staff members being trained become the experts for that particular module and should be carefully selected for their ability to learn quickly and train other staff members. Vendors provide both live and recorded training webinars (rather than traveling from one library to another). Recorded webinars can be viewed again and again by staff so that they can improve their skills.

Each staff member attending the vendor-provided training must have his or her own workstation and sufficient desktop space for taking notes. Vendor experience suggests that training will be more effective if the library can place the students in a room that is separate from the rest of the library. This will ensure minimal disruption of normal day-to-day events so those attending training can derive maximum benefits.

The vendors make the assumption that the staff members attending the application training are experienced and knowledgeable about information technology. If staff members attempt to participate in a vendor-provided class without this background, they will find they are either not learning much or they are holding back the rest of the class.

> **Tip!** Have every staff member create a list of things he or she doesn't like about the existing system, and then save these lists. When people become frustrated with the new system, the lists can be shared to help people find the right perspective.

Although the training provided by a vendor is important, ultimately the quality of the training program that is administered to all other library staff members will have the biggest impact on improving the skills and confidence that staff need to perform their work efficiently.[10] Several things can be done to improve the effectiveness of the training provided to staff members:

- Keep staff informed about the automation project from the outset. Explain why change is necessary so people can begin the process of making adjustments. Let people know that changes to the implementation and training schedules mean problems will inevitably arise.

- Start each training session with a review of the big picture.

- The focus on the library-provided training must be on the practical day-to-day activities that staff will actually perform (e.g., checkout, check-in, adding bibliographic and item records, etc.). Providing step-by-step instructions has proven to be very helpful in many libraries.

- Schedule training close to the "go live" date, and train again if there are implementation delays.

- Each training session should be no longer than two or three hours. Otherwise, people will start to have information overload problems. Allow staff the opportunity to practice what they have learned before moving on to the next scheduled class. Schedule optional review sessions.

- The key for an effective trainer, aside from being knowledgeable about the system, is to be enthusiastic!

- Make sure that you provide cross-training opportunities to minimize the impact if a key employee leaves.

One of the biggest challenges facing a library and a vendor when the library is moving from one automated system to another is confronting expectations. The old system, despite all of its known flaws, will be familiar to staff. In spite of clear and consistent statements by the library system's staff and the vendor's trainer that the new system will not operate exactly like the old one, it should not be surprising that some staff members will be resistant to change or have longer-than-average learning curves.

> The hardest lesson to learn is learning is a continual process.
> —David Gerrold[11]

Despite the abundance of evidence to the contrary—that change is almost an everyday event in our lives—some people seem to work hard at resisting change. As Spencer Johnson suggests:[12]

- Change happens.
- Anticipate change.
- Monitor change.
- Adapt to change quickly.
- Acknowledge thee importance of change.
- Enjoy change!
- Be ready to change quickly.

In today's world, why would anyone trust a librarian,
whose profession is about information and knowledge,
who hasn't mastered a computer?

—Eric Lease Morgan[13]

Adapting Procedures, Forms, and Workflow

After the new application software has been installed for a few months, staff members should carefully examine their existing procedures, forms, and workflow. Designing forms so they look like the data-input templates found within the application software greatly improves the efficiency of the data-entry process. The library should consider eliminating some of its existing forms, as the data is readily available to all staff members online via a workstation.

The library's workflow, especially in technical services and at the circulation desk, should also be carefully examined. One objective of examining procedures is to determine how many of them can be eliminated or streamlined. Minimizing the number of times an item is handled before it is placed on a shelf for the patrons should be another objective. Studies have shown that organizations that modify their procedures, forms, and workflow to complement the capabilities of their automated information management system will reap significant benefits. In fact, in most cases, streamlining workflows and reengineering the various tasks will produce more benefits than automating an activity.[14]

> **Tip!** John Huber, an experienced productivity consultant, has written a wonderful book, *Lean Library Management*, that should be thoroughly read and his strategies implemented while the new system is being put into service.[15]

Typical Implementation Schedule

The following project plan illustrates the sequence of activities typically associated with implementing the new automated library system (see Table 12.1).

Successful Systems

Despite all of the planning that libraries typically complete in anticipation of installing a new or replacement system, some systems are just not successful. Here are some mistakes librarians are likely to make:

- Failing to evaluate a vendor's financial viability or calculate the total five-year cost

- Holding unrealistic expectations or implementation schedules

- Not meeting responsibilities of the library

- Refusing to plan adequately

- Ignoring retrospective conversion or data migration issues

- Not defining decision-making responsibilities clearly

TABLE 12.1. Typical System Installation Schedule

Activity	Date	Responsible Party
Agreement signed. Help Desk services for the application software and installation services begin.	0	Vendor/library
Vendor project manager and library system manager develop a series of data mapping tables to migrate all of the existing files to the new application software (if applicable).	+2–4 weeks	Vendor/library
Loading and indexing library's existing database into the new LIS system.	+6 weeks	Vendor
Training for setup, cataloging, OPAC, and circulation modules occurs.	+7 weeks	Vendor/library
Use of cataloging, OPAC, and circulation modules begins.	+9–10 weeks	Library
Training for acquisitions and serials control modules occurs.	+12–14 weeks	Vendor/library
Use of acquisitions and serials control modules begins.	+16 weeks	Library

Vendors are not immune from making mistakes either, the most notable of which include these:

- Lack of communication at many levels
- Failing to meet promised delivery dates
- Providing inadequate or underpowered systems
- Providing only marginal system support during implementation and after acceptance of the system

Communication Is Vital

Communications, especially in larger libraries and consortiums, is vital to the success of a migration project. The migration team needs to communicate with all library staff members, key stakeholders, and representatives from other organizations, including both the old and new system vendors.

Tools such as conference calls, shared drives, Google docs, Wikis, and discussion lists can assist in ensuring everyone has access to the latest information. These tools further assist in encouraging staff in learning about the new system.

A communications plan should be created so that the most effective communication tool is used to reach each group of people that will be affected by the new system. Tools range from newsletters (printed or delivered via email), blogs, presentations, written reports, posters, flyers, Facebook postings, and so forth.

Summary

This chapter has discussed a number of significant issues that must be confronted and planned for when migrating from one automated library system to another.

Questions to Consider

- Could you merge acquisitions and cataloging departments?
- Could the use of electronic data interchange (EDI) be used more effectively to reduce acquisition costs?
- Can you reduce or eliminate the number of tasks performed in each department?
- Could you implement shelf-ready for print materials?
- Can you define "acceptable" or "good enough" bibliographic records?
- Have you considered implementing patron-driven acquisitions?
- Can you rely on vendor-provided bibliographic and authority records?
- Can you make the library's bibliographic and authority records more discoverable?
- Have you thought about reformatting your bibliographic and authority records, using the linked data model?

Notes

1. Douglas Adams, *The Hitchhiker's Guide to the Galaxy* (New York: Del Ray, 2017), 149.

2. Zhonghong Wang, "Integrated Library System (ILS) Challenges and Opportunities: A Survey of U.S. Academic Libraries with Migration Projects," *Journal of Academic Librarianship* 35, no. 3 (May 2009): 207–20.

3. Ian Walls, "Migrating from Innovative Interfaces' Millennium to Koha," *OCLC Systems & Services: International Digital Library Perspectives* 27, no. 1 (2011): 51–56.

4. Susan C. Wynne and Martha J. Hanscom, "The Effect of Next-Generation Catalogs on Catalogers and Cataloging Functions in Academic Libraries," *Cataloging & Classification Quarterly* 49 (2011): 179–207.

5. Terry Reese, "Working with MARC Data," in *Migrating Library Data: A Practical Manual*, Kyle Banerjee and Bonnie Parks, eds. (Chicago: Neal-Schuman, 2017), 49–108.

6. Kyle Banerjee and Bonnie Parks, *Migrating Library Data: A Practical Manual* (Chicago: American Library Association, 2017).

7. Emily Morton-Owens, Karen Hanson, and Ian Walls, "Implementing Open Source Software for Three Core Library Functions: A Stage-by-Stage Comparison," _Journal of Electronic Resources in Medical Libraries* 8, no. 1 (2011): 1–14.

8. Janet Balas, "How They Did It: ILS Migration Case Studies," *Computers in Libraries* 31, no. 8 (2011): 34–41; Karen Kohn and Eric McCloy, "Phased Migration to Koha: Our Library's Experience," *Journal of Web Librarianship* 4, no. 4 (2010): 427–34.

9. Kyle Banerjee and Bonnie Parks, *Migrating Library Data: A Practical Manual* (Chicago: American Library Association, 2017).

10. Marshall Breeding, "The Systems Librarian: Systems Migration: Opportunities Revamp Automation Strategies," *Computers in Libraries* 38, no. 2 (March 2018).

11. David Gerrold, Quoted in Theodor H. Nelson. *Computer Lib: You Can and Must Understand Computers Now* (San Francisco, CA: Nelson, 1974), 79.

12. Spencer Johnson, *Who Moved My Cheese? An Amazing Way to Deal With Change in Your Work And In Your Life* (New York: G. P. Putnam's Sons, 1998).

13. Paul A. Strassmann, *The Squandered Computer: Evaluating the Business Alignment of Information Technologies* (New Canaan, CT: The Information Economics Press, 1997).

14. John Huber, *Lean Library Management: Eleven Strategies for Reducing Costs and Improving Customer Service* (New York: Neal-Schuman, 2011).

15. Eric Lease Morgan, "Computer Literacy for Librarians," *Computers in Libraries* 18, no. 1 (January 1998): 39–40.

13
Managing Library Information Systems

The real danger is not that computers
will begin to think like men, but that men
will begin to think like computers.

—Sydney Harris[1]

Clearly, the integrated library system (ILS) has a major impact on the functioning of a library. Not only does staff use it on a daily basis, but the automated system is the library's public face as users visit the building and use the online catalog. In addition, the library has another public face with its website/library portal and the Web-based online catalog providing library services remotely. Thus, managing all of these information technology–based services assumes a much more important role within the library than in years past.

Information technology does not exist in a vacuum. Implementing and managing technology is at least as important as the technology itself. Planning for new technology is vital because technology must be implemented in order to support organizational goals, organizational culture, and social mores. Libraries must provide the necessary infrastructure of communication networks, application software, access to external information resources, and knowledgeable employees to manage the technology located in the library.

Managing an ILS is an important responsibility. A smooth-functioning system is one that remains invisible until there is a problem with the software or the total system ceases to work because of a hardware failure. Then the telephone calls; help desk tickets; texts; instant messages; social media pings; and terse, urgent messages from any number of communication channels come! The personality and technical skills of the systems librarian and the computer support staff are crucial in determining how quickly the problem is identified and solved.

System Manager Characteristics

Although it is difficult to generalize about people who are system managers, libraries generally are able to attract talented but inexperienced people, or they are willing to train an in-house "tech savvy" individual. Yet, because of the substantial shortage of trained IT people at all levels, some libraries have found that they are proving to be a training ground. After acquiring a year or two of experience (especially in non-library-specific technology skills), it is not surprising that systems personnel will move on to higher paying jobs in the private sector.

A successful system manager and computer-related support staff will exhibit the following characteristics:

- **Excellent communicator**—The system manager needs to be able to communicate in nontechnical terms, with a wide variety of people, including vendors, library staff members, library managers, and library decision-makers. The system manager must be equally comfortable dealing with the jargon-rich terminology of the computer hardware and software industries.

- **Thorough and detail-oriented**—Computer systems and networks require retaining a tremendous amount of technical information and understanding how all the hardware and software pieces work together. Installing new software releases and anti-virus updates and troubleshooting the interaction of software are part of the daily routine. Sometimes the installation is automated and will guide the system manager through the process in a step-by-step manner, but other times it will be necessary to follow a detailed set of instructions. Being adventurous and attempting to take shortcuts is a surefire way to cause system downtime and damage.

- **Patient**—There are times in the life of a systems manager that would try the patience of a saint. Even after following all of the appropriate directions, checking and double-checking the cabling, equipment, and software, something continues to be "not quite right," and so an application doesn't work; a computer workstation can't be connected to the LAN; the blue screen of death keeps popping up (the operating system crashes)—well, you get the picture. At times like these, it's often necessary to take a break and start the troubleshooting process again to identify and solve the problem. All of this takes patience—lots of patience.

- **Appreciates puzzles**—Time after time, tracking down the root cause of a problem is very much like solving a puzzle or finding your way out of a maze. For some reason, what has worked in the past is not working now. Software that worked fine yesterday will not work today (a new release of another software product may or may not have been installed). A really good systems person will enjoy the thrill of the hunt and have the persistence of a homicide detective.

- **Organized**—The system manager will know the value of being organized. This individual will ensure that the library management team participates in setting priorities for the communications infrastructure and the ILS. Having a clearly defined set of priorities means that the systems office staff is able to proactively handle the inevitable problems and challenges that will arise. Without the proactive approach, staff will simply be in a reactive mode, often rushing to solve the problem for the person who is the loudest "squeaky wheel."[2] While establishing the priorities, the library management team should likely consider financial benefits, business objectives, intangible benefits, and technical importance.

- **Flexible**—Given the broad range of responsibilities, a system manager needs to remain flexible about a wide variety of things including schedules, changing priorities, and being able to keep multiple balls in the air.

- **Establishes balance**—A good system manager recognizes that things only get accomplished through the collective efforts of many different organizations and individuals. Yet maintaining an appropriate sense of firmness will ensure that people recognize that there are limits and boundaries that must be adhered to.

- **Has a positive outlook on life**—Typically, the only time a library staff member calls the system manager is to report a network problem or some other system-related problem that needs attention. Over the course of time, this constant bombardment of problems can lead to a negative view of the world—or at least a negative view of the ILS. It's not too often that someone will call the system manager and compliment him or her on the fact that the LAN has not suffered any downtime in the last six months!

- **Conservative**—A good system manager is cautious and conservative. Rather than trusting a vendor, system managers become adopted sons and daughters of the great state of Missouri whose nickname is "The Show Me State." A system manager will test and retest new software releases, using a demo database prior to move the software into a production environment. Unfortunately, this conservative side has been developed as the result of too many bad experiences.

- **Creative**—Perhaps most importantly, a good systems manager is creative and recognizes the need to embrace change as technology is constantly changing. However, the changing technology must always be implemented with the library's customer in mind—how will this new technology directly benefit the customer? How will this technology assist the library is achieving one of its objectives?

Specific Job Skills

The job skills for an effective system manager and his or her staff are quite wide ranging, including these:[3]

- **Library skills**—For example, knowledge of the cataloging and other metadata record structures, library services, administrative structure, organization and classification issues, and information retrieval.

- **Library systems skills**—Aside from a good understanding of the typical functions that are automated in most systems, the system manager should be aware of the vendors and products in the marketplace, know hardware and software capabilities, and have a basic understanding of contracts.

- **Computing skills**—The system manager must be aware of desktop operating environments, server operating systems, software programming fundamentals, database design, system design, and troubleshooting skills.

- **Database management skills**—A system manager often needs to learn about a specific database management system to help a vendor expand tables, restore corrupted tables, and produce ad hoc custom reports using a report generation tool.

- **Networking skills**—Understand network design, network services, protocols, network applications, network management, and internet technologies. Some portion of a system manager's time will be spent on issues such as validating and authenticating users so they can access a wide range of information resources.

- **Management skills**—A good system manager will have basic management skills, be able to manage resources and technology, deal with security, and assess risk. Most important, the system manager and his or her team must ensure that they have the necessary people skills to maintain and nurture the relationships that will inevitably exist with outside partners.

Because system managers will likely deal with a veritable potpourri of information technologies, the system manager and his or her coworkers will seem like they are consummate jugglers. The technologies and tasks being handled by the systems librarian are shown in Table 13.1.[4] Note that if the library moves the ILS (and other systems) to the cloud, it can free up as much as 25 percent of the system librarian's time—see the responsibilities near the bottom of Table 13.1.

Managing in the Cloud

As almost every application becomes Web enabled, the need for local hosting is significantly reduced (if not eliminated). So many of the traditional responsibilities of the system manager—installation of new software releases, ensuring backups are completed on schedule, confirming the backup of data in a secure off-site location, and so forth—are eliminated. The focus is no longer on the hardware and the need for on-site programming to make the various systems work well. However, the system manager must now address other important concerns when the library's important applications are in the cloud. Among these responsibilities are the following:

- Ensuring the *interoperability* of the various systems—This typically requires the testing of two systems to ensure they work well together, that messages move between the systems (using APIs or other communication protocols) as expected, and that there are not surprises before the systems are "released" to the users.

- Understanding the *user interface* of each system and how users interact with each system—It may be necessary to examine the logs of each system, consider the data made available when Google Analytics or another data collection or visualization platform is used, and possibly involve a small set of users in a user experience assessment of the system.

TABLE 13.1. System Librarian Responsibilities

Responsibilities	Workload Percentage
Managing ILS applications	10%
Managing other automated silos—discovery systems, ERMS, link resolver, etc.	10%
Day-to-day operations—supervision, troubleshooting, user support	10%
Customization and integrations	5%
Produce statistical and management reports	5%
Primary representative to library system vendors	5%
Maintain current awareness of information technology and tools	5%
Professional and scholarly activities	10%
Serving on teams and committees	5%
Providing training to staff	10%
Options:	
Server and database maintenance and backups	10%
Equipment configurations	5%
Upgrades and enhancements	5%
Install patches or other fixes	5%
Totals	100%

Source: Created from Ping Fu and Moira Fitzgerald, "A Comparative Analysis of the Effect of the Integrated Library System on Staffing Models in Academic Libraries," *Information Technology and Libraries*, September 2013, 47–58.

- *Connecting with users where they are* (which in many cases is not in the physical or virtual library)—Achieving this latter objective means that the library and systems manager must adopt a user-centric view of the services the library provides, rather than a library-centric view of the world (we've got good stuff here, so come and visit us!).

Systems Integration

One of the latest challenges for a system manager is dealing with the possibility of automatically moving data from one application to another. The data movement is accomplished using application programming interfaces, or APIs. An API is an agreed-upon communication format that will facilitate moving data or providing inquiry access to another system. An example of an API in the library community is the Z39.50 standard.

The first set of APIs was developed using the MARC format as a model. The Book Industry Standards Advisory Committee (BISAC) and the Serials Industry Standards Advisory Committee (SISAC) developed two of the more popular fixed-length records, MARC-based APIs. A few library automation vendors and only a couple of book and serial vendors actually implemented these API standards (each implementation was actually unique rather than complying with the proposed standard).

The next attempt to develop a set of useful APIs was based on electronic data interchange (EDI) technology. Again, both BISAC and SISAC committees worked to develop useful message sets so a library could place an order, receive an acknowledgment of the order, receive an update on the status of an order, and so forth. An EDI-based message provides a fair amount of flexibility, yet it is limited primarily to using codes. The intent of the proposed standards was to mask the complexity of the codes from the user with a helpful and informative front-end interface. In most cases, EDI-based transactions had to be moved from one location to another using a value-added network (VAN). Yet, just as these EDI standards were about ready to be adopted, work stopped as XML appeared on the scene. XML is a markup specification language, and XML files are just data. The data file will simply sit there until a program is run that can display the data (like a web browser), does some work with the data (imports and verifies the data as a part of an application), or modifies the data (using an editor).

XML transactions have two appealing characteristics. First, it is relatively easy to identify each data element and the value of each data element that is included in a message. Second, the messages, particularly RESTful APIs, can be quickly and easily moved from one location to another, using the internet.

Integration with other important technology-based equipment and systems include automated material handling (AMH) systems (patron self-checkout machines and check-in sorting systems), automatic storage and retrieval systems, materials dispensing machines, regional or statewide catalogs, shared ILS systems, shared authentication systems, virtual reality, and maker spaces technology, among others.

Patron self-checkout machines allow the patron to borrow materials without the assistance of staff—see Figure 13.1, check on the status of holds, and pay fines and fees.

Automated material handling systems, specifically a check-in or return sorting system (see Figure 13.2), improve the productivity of staff and reduce the number of errors associated with the check-in process. These systems allow a library to continue to use the barcodes or radio-frequency identification (RFID) tags that already identify an item. RFID tags are particular effective if the library wishes to install a return sorting system. The benefits of AMH systems are that they can create

FIGURE 13.1. Self-Checkout Machine
Source: Reprinted with permission from Bibliotheca.

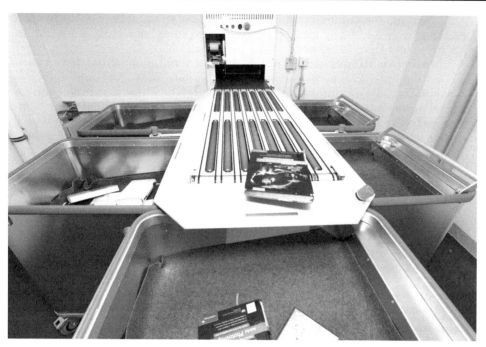

FIGURE 13.2. Return Sorting Machine
Source: Reprinted with permission from Bibliotheca.

efficiencies that may reduce the need for staff and reduce the potential for repetitive stress injuries (for staff handling the movement of materials at check-in and moving items to be reshelved). RFID also allows for greater efficiencies for both staff and patrons at checkout—whether through staff assisted or self-check options.

Automatic storage and retrieval systems (AS/RSs) are comprised of a computer-controlled system for placing, retrieving, and maintaining control over items in a defined storage area. The benefits of an AS/RS system include reduced costs for storage, space savings, and more accurate tracking of the items. The first AS/RS to be installed in a library occurred in 1991 at the California State University, Northridge campus at a cost of $2,000,000.[5] The life cycle of an AS/RS is about twenty years, and then a major hardware and software upgrade will likely be needed. Items are typically placed in bins according to size rather than in call number sequence (this results in greater storage density).

A patron uses the online catalog to perform a search, and if the desired item is stored in the AS/RS, the system automatically forwards a request to the AS/RS system, which then retrieves the appropriate bin. A staff member locates the item and provides it to the patron a few minutes later. Most AS/RS systems support the SIP2 protocol to interface the ILS with the AS/RS system. About 24,000 bins for storing books and journals (1,200 shelf racks for storing archival boxes and elephant folios) are stacked into racks 50 feet tall, with the overall capacity of storing some 3.5 million books and other materials. When a patron makes a request for an item from the online catalog, one of five robotic cranes moves along the track and retrieves the appropriate bin. A staff member then locates the item, scans it, and makes it available to the requesting patron in a matter of five to ten minutes.[6]

The annual estimated costs of storage and maintenance of books in open stacks is over $4.00 per volume per year; the same materials stored in an AS/RS is less than $1.00 per volume per year.

Materials dispensing machines (or a vending machine, if you will) are available from several vendors, and the machines store and dispense books, CDs, DVDs, laptops, tablets, and so forth. These machines can be placed at various locations around the community. For example, the Contra Costa County Library has a "Library a-Go-Go" machine on a BART station platform, so commuters have ready access to library materials—and two other machines are located at another BART station and a shopping center. The Spokane Public Library has a large unit installed at the entrance to a Community Center. The machines communicate with the library's ILS using the SIP2 protocol. Other libraries have placed a materials dispensing machine in the library itself to control access to foreign language DVDs.

Some libraries use "vend" machines to dispense laptops and tablets to their customers. Several hundred laptop/table dispensing machines have been installed in both academic and public libraries (some libraries loan the laptops for free and others charge by the hour to borrow the devices). The dispensing machines use the SIP2 protocol to link to the ILS system. Some of the benefits and challenges of providing tablets and/or laptops are explored in an issue of *Library Technology Reports*.[7]

eBook patron kiosks provide a visual interface for a patron to browse and/or to search for eBooks that they can then download to their personal device.

Makerspace technology includes more than the 3D printer itself. Although any library space where people gather to make physical things together—including low-tech approaches such as sewing circles—are also considered makerspaces, technology-based maker areas that often require special spaces and environments. Users need to be able to access one or more 3D design software packages that interface with the library's 3D printer. Tools and other components that might be found in a technology-forward makerspace include those listed here:

- Workspace
- Woodworking tools
- Metalworking tools
- General tools
- Electronic tools and components
- Textiles
- Computers and associated software for planning, design, and fabrication
- Laser cutting machine (desirable but expensive)
- Safety equipment
- Consumables, parts, and materials

Digital display screens (which can be very large by combining multiple screens) can function as message bulletin boards announcing upcoming events, provide a rotating display of images and videos about the library and its community, serve to display visual art, and so forth. The display screens typically use a data cable in order to update the content that is displayed on the screen.

Interactive public kiosks can provide a variety of information but typically are used to provide a map of a library (especially if there are multiple floors). An individual touches the screen to interact with the content.

Interactive table displays (sometimes called a touch table) come in a variety of sizes (from multiple manufacturers) that users interact with by touching the surface of the table. These table displays can be used for interactive maps, video or virtual reality games, or as a way to engage users with content from the library's special collection.

Exhibits with various technologies—for example, large-screen displays, an area dedicated to virtual reality, and so forth—may be used by a library to improve the user experience.

Beacon technology is a small Bluetooth radio signal broadcaster that can be attached to a location or object and whose signals are received by a smartphone app. The physical proximity to the beacon allows a business or library to push timely and contextual notifications to customers, based on their actual location. Major league baseball uses beacons to reach out to fans in stadiums during a game. You can find them in public spaces, where they act as guides, maps, or links to more information.

The Somerset County Library System in New Jersey provides an app that directs patrons to special displays, alerts them to programs happening that day, suggests areas of the collection that might interest them, and tracks foot traffic in the building. After patrons have loaded the app on their smartphone, they still have the choice to opt in each time they visit the library.

Geographic information systems (GISs) typically operate as a standalone application using data from a variety of sources. Some libraries have imported patron registration files into a GIS in order to produce a set of maps showing the physical distribution of patrons around each library facility.

A more sophisticated GIS system combines census data along with consumer lifestyle data (spending patterns vary by different market segments—traditional family of four [two adults and two children], dual income and no children, etc.). Companies such as CIVICTechnologies, Gale, and Orange Boy provide solutions that assist libraries in better understanding the various market segments they reach with their current library services and collections.

In a survey of ARL libraries, Ann Holstein found that the Esri ArcGIS is the most frequently used software, and most libraries also provide access to Google Maps and Google Earth.[8] About a third of the libraries provide access to GIS where their paper maps are located, whereas another 20 percent have a separate GIS data center. On average, two professionals and three student assistants staff the GIS unit, primarily serving users who are students.

Collaboration tools enable and encourage users to contribute ratings, reviews, comments, and so forth. Some tools that might be employed include transcription of digital content and creating alternative ways of navigating content,

Mash-ups automatically push content of various types of content from both internal and external sources (often including social media sites

(Facebook, Flickr, Snapchat, Twitter, etc.). Mash-ups are made possible via APIs.

Technology Planning

Perhaps the most important responsibility for a systems manager is to develop and then periodically refresh a technology plan for the library. Although the plan itself is very important, the process to create the plan provides much more value—assuming the planning process involves all of the key stakeholders.[9]

Among the reasons for technology planning are the following:

- Aligning technology with library and other broader institutional priorities
- Identifying the likely budgetary impacts of implementing/refreshing hardware, software, infrastructure, and technical support
- Addressing existing technology-related problem areas
- Creating alliances and partnerships with decision-makers (inside and outside the library).

In the author's view, even a cursory review of most library technology plans reveals the failure to identify the way in which technology will be used by the library to assist in helping the larger organization achieve its goals and objectives.

Management of Infrastructure

Given the reality that a majority of libraries have automated systems in the cloud, the traditional responsibilities of a systems manager are changing.

Upgrades

ILS vendors periodically release new versions of their application software (the frequency of new releases varies from quarterly to once every eighteen months). This new release has to be installed when it will have minimal impact on the library's operation. In general, it is important that the library keep pace with its vendor as new releases of the ILS software become available. Installing the new releases will fix software bugs that the library may be experiencing, as well as provide access to new features that will improve the library's productivity. From a contractual standpoint, the library may need to keep up with the releases to ensure ready access to the vendor's support infrastructure.

Given the use of multitenant platforms, vendors are able to keep all their customers on the most current software release.

Once installed, the software needs to be tested to verify that it has not corrupted any files and that it's working in a normal manner. The system manager needs to determine, prior to installing the new release, whether the minimum hardware requirements have changed. A new function or feature in the software may require additional RAM memory on desktop workstations.

The key to installing new software releases is a systematic approach, and part of this approach is ensuring that backups are in place should they be needed.

Backups

The importance of performing backups on all of the library systems on a regular basis cannot be overemphasized. The information contained in a variety of databases found within the library is probably its most important asset. Fortunately, system backups can be scheduled to run unattended (without a computer operator standing by) in the early hours of the day, when backup operations will not impact the use of the computer systems.

In the cloud environment, backups are a vendor responsibility, and most vendors employ the use of a continuous backup system.

However, it is crucial for the library system's staff to periodically verify that not only have the backups been made but also that the data contained in the backups can be restored (used again). Given the busy schedules in some libraries, it is not surprising that some will skip the verification of the restore option. Once this step is skipped, Murphy's law ("Anything that could go wrong will go wrong") will rear its ugly head when the library discovers that it is unable to read and restore the data from a backup. This may mean that the library will lose a day's, a week's, or several weeks' worth of data. Imagine losing your library's circulation data, cataloging records added to the library, or material orders placed for several days or weeks—not a pretty picture. Thus, the final word regarding backups—have a schedule to check and double-check your ability to restore the data from a partial or full backup.

The other component of backups is that some copies of the backups should be stored off-site at a relatively secure location. These off-site backups should be done on a regularly scheduled basis.

Staff members should be encouraged to back up the work files that exist on their desktop workstations to a network drive so their data is protected and available for use should they experience a hardware failure or have their disk drives become infected with a virus. In many cases, backups of staff data are managed by the systems department.

Both desktop backups and virus control can be managed at the system level for some software systems, with system-wide scans and periodic backups of all workstations.

The Rule of Three (or 3-2-1)

To prevent the loss of important data, many follow the "rule of three"—also called the rule of 3-2-1—when managing backups. The rule is simple:

- Always have **three digital copies** of anything you really care about
- Use at least **two types of backup media**
- **At least one copy** should be stored off-site

The rule of three is one of the best hedges against Murphy's law. If you have three copies of your data, you're covered if copies 1 and 2 fail; using two types of media protects against read errors in a particular physical format; and storing one copy off-site is a hedge against physical disasters, including fire, theft, and more.

As you might imagine, lots of permutations can be used in following this guideline. For one example, let's use a personal PC that has an important oral history recording stored on it (see Table 13.2).

TABLE 13.2. Are Your Backups Following the Rule of Three?

File/Directory or Collection	Copy 1	Copy 2	Copy 3
Example: Library founder's oral history interview recording— original 1978 cassette tape has been digitized and stored on CD-R	**Location:** *Digital file on director's laptop*	**Location:** *Digital file on director's laptop; laptop is backed up to USB drive in office*	**Location:** *Digital file on director's laptop; laptop is automatically backed up to crashplan*
	Media Type:	**Media Type:**	**Media Type:**
	[✓] Local [_] Network	[_] Local [_] Network	[_] Local [_] Network
	[_] Cloud	[_] Cloud	[✓] Cloud
	[_] USB drive (big)	[_] USB drive (big)	[_] USB drive (big)
	[_] USB drive (small)	[✓] USB drive (small)	[_] USB drive (small)
	[_] Tape	[_] Tape	[_] Tape
	DO NOT rely on CD-R or DVD-R	***DO NOT rely on CD-R or DVD-R***	***DO NOT rely on CD-R or DVD-R***
	Local or Remote?	**Local or Remote?**	**Local or Remote?**
	[✓] On-site Location(s): <u>laptop</u>	[✓] On-site Location(s): <u>Thumb drive</u>	[_] On-site Location(s): _____
	[_] Off-site Location: _____	[_] Off-site Location: _____	[✓] Off-site Location: <u>Crashplan</u>

Managing Applications and Licenses

The system manager may also manage several software licenses. Depending on the ILS that is installed at the library, the library may have to purchase licenses for different types of software. Among the software licenses that the library may need to maintain are ILS application software, other application software, search engine software, database management system software (e.g., Oracle, MS SQL Server), utilities, and operating system software. These software licenses are needed for all the servers connected to the library's LAN and all of the desktop workstations.

Besides purchasing the initial license to use the software, the library must also budget and pay for the annual software maintenance licenses. Unfortunately, there is a bewildering variety of ways to license software, and in some cases the library needs to count the total number of desktop workstations, the number of simultaneous users, the size of the database, and so on. Some applications can only have designated or named users. Other applications restrict the number of simultaneous users that can access the software. Usually, the LAN software (or the application software itself) provides a set of tools for setting and monitoring an application's use.

Any software vendor can request the opportunity to visit the library and verify that the library is paying for the requisite number of licenses—this is often given the unpleasant term *audit*. Should the library not have the required number of licenses, it can not only look

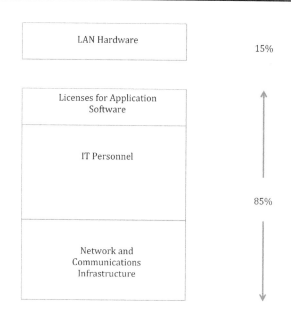

FIGURE 13.3. Annual IT Operating Costs per User

forward to paying for the additional licenses required, but it can also expect to pay a fine (and the size of the fine is often significant). The annual estimated costs of storage and maintenance of books in open stacks is over $4.00 per volume per year; the same materials stored in an AS/RS are less than $1.00 per volume per year (Courant and Nielsen, 2010; see Figure 13.3.[10]

Emergency/Recovery Support

A disaster recovery plan anticipates the consequences of being without some or all of a library's information systems and determining what can be done to mitigate the disaster. The cause of the disaster might arise from several sources:

- **Power brownout or blackout**—If the library has installed battery backup capabilities, then staff will have the time for an orderly shutdown of some or all of the applications.

- **Physical disaster**—This includes fires, floods, and earthquakes, among other things. If the equipment or software is seriously damaged, then the library should have an action plan for quickly replacing the necessary components so it can become operational again.

- **Security disaster**—This occurs when the library's computers that are connected to a LAN or ILS have been infected with a computer virus or hacked, and the various databases have become corrupted. This portion of the emergency disaster plan may well be identical to a computer security plan.

The disaster recovery plan should provide a step-by-step blueprint of the actions to be taken and the people to be notified in the event of a major emergency. Besides notifying library staff members, it may be necessary to inform personnel from the parent organization (e.g., IT staff members), as well as contacting selected vendors about the emergency and actions that might be required by them.

Depending on the seriousness of the situation, it may be necessary to order—on an emergency basis—replacement equipment and software so the library can become operational as soon as possible.

Security

Security issues are a serious concern for any organization, including a library. Because of the proliferation of security incidents, including viruses and denial-of-service attacks, any computer system that is accessible via the internet must have the appropriate security hardware and software in place to protect the library and its valuable databases. A security breach is a silent venom that can infect and seriously damage the library's ability to provide service. For example, in early 2017, the St. Louis Public Library was hacked by ransomware that rendered every computer inoperable—staff and public—meaning that there was no internet access, and the ILS was unable to operate for more than a week.

Threats to a computer system's security fall into three possible categories: natural (e.g., fire, lightning strikes, electrical surges, flood, earthquakes), unintentional (carelessness, poor training, and bad habits [e.g., leaving passwords and login commands on visible sheets near a desktop workstation]), and intentional. Obviously, the most dangerous threat comes from a disgruntled employee who wants revenge against a supervisor or the institution.

Vulnerability in a computer system is a weakness that could be exploited. The vulnerability might be physical (providing easy access to the computer equipment), hardware related, or software related. A countermeasure is an action, device, or procedure that reduces the vulnerability of an information system.

Libraries, similar to any other organization connected to the internet, have experienced hacking of their computer systems and hacking of library websites, as well as receiving countless email viruses. In addition, libraries that provide public access to the internet must also be aware that one or more of their users may be downloading pirated software, visiting pornographic websites, obtaining dangerous information (about bombs or drugs), or engaging in illegal activities. For example, a patron of the Brooklyn Public Library, using the internet from the library, was able to discover personal information about a number of wealthy individuals and then was able to transfer funds to his own account by impersonating these individuals.

The Computer Security Institute, in conjunction with of the Federal Bureau of Investigation, has conducted an annual "Computer Crime and Security Survey."[11] Survey respondents to the 2010–2011 survey (the last of fifteen annual surveys) are primarily large companies and federal government agencies, and they indicated the following:

- About half of these detected computer security breaches within the last year.

- 67 percent indicated that malware was the most commonly encountered problem.

- The primary loss was the result of the theft of proprietary information.

- Few organizations reported that security problems are attributable to malicious insiders.

The National Computer Security Act of 1987 requires federal government agencies to develop a security plan and provide periodic security-related training. There are a host of publications devoted to the topic of computer security and security planning that would be of assistance should a library wish to create a computer security plan.[12] In all probability, a majority of libraries that are responsible for maintaining their own ILS and IT infrastructure have not developed a security plan. Unfortunately, the need for such a plan will not become obvious until the library experiences a major disaster from an unauthorized user. Security requires constant monitoring and is a continual process rather than a one-time event such as installing firewall software.

Those within the library or IT department responsible for computer system security must constantly monitor and audit all security points for threats. A recent survey suggests that organizations learn about security threats in a variety of ways, such as these:

- Analyzing server and firewall logs
- Being alerted by colleagues
- Using an intrusion detection system
- Noticing damaged data
- Receiving a heads-up from a supplier or partner[13]

An intrusion detection system attempts to identify suspicious patterns from someone trying to compromise or hack into a system by examining all network activity. An intrusion detection system could use one of three methods:

- **Passive system versus reactive system**—A passive system identifies and logs the potential security breach and issues an alert. Even though an alert has been issued by a passive detection system, the intruder is still active within the computer system and may do serious damage. A reactive system, however, will detect the security breach and either log off the user or reprogram the firewall to block network traffic from the suspected hacker. A reactive system is sometimes called an intrusion prevention system.

- **Misuse detection versus anomaly detection**—A misuse detection system will analyze the suspected threat and compare it to a large database of known attack signatures and characteristics. This approach is particularly effective when a specific attack has already been recognized, for example, an email virus. An anomaly intrusion detection system monitors the network, looking for irregularities.

- **Network-based versus host-based systems**—A network-based detection system looks for packets that may have been overlooked by the firewall and builds a database based on all the analysis of the many systems linked to the detection system. A host-based intrusion detection system only examines the activity on each individual computer or server, looking for problems.

Once a threat has been identified and a patch has been developed to fill the security hole that exists within the operating system or other software, it is incumbent on the system manager to download the patch and then install the patch on the appropriate machines. This would be a relatively simple task if there were only one or two software products to track regarding security alerts. Typically, though, the number of software products that need to be tracked can be quite large.

Furthermore, applying a patch is not necessarily a trivial task. Applying a patch to one product may well cause a problem, even a serious problem, in another software product. It gets worse when a software vendor warns a customer that if one or more patches are applied to another software product, then the vendor will cease supporting its own product.

There are security standards that the library may wish to explore as it reviews the current status of its security measures.[14]

Security of any computer-based system is important, as hackers and others are obviously very creative and determined to unleash their destructive talents on any system that lacks adequate safeguards. The threats and malware sent out each day by hackers to organizations large and small is simply staggering.[15] These threats take many forms:

- **Viruses**—A virus contains executable code that, once in a computer, will either infect files of all types or the computer start-up (boot) files.

- **Worms**—A worm turns a computer into a malicious machine by sending out copies of itself or participating in denial-of-service attacks.

- **Trojan horse programs**—These programs pretend to be something good but in reality are malicious. A Trojan horse program requires that the user run the program, and then it can inflict great damage.

- **Ransomware**—A type of Trojan horse program that takes control of a computer and then promises to return control to the user for the payment of a "nominal" ransom.

- **Rootkits**—A rootkit is a variation of a Trojan horse program that can control the computer or hijack programs; examples include spambots and keyloggers.

- **Spam**—Spam or junk email is unwanted email messages sent to thousands or millions of users daily. Many experts estimate that as much as 80 percent of emails are spam.

- **Phishing**—A type of email that attempts to trick individuals to reveal personal information by posing as a legitimate organization such as a credit card company, email provider, and so forth.

- **Fake sites**—A website that attempts to mimic or replicate the appearance of a legitimate organization in order to capture personal information.

An entire industry works round-the-clock to develop and enhance tools that are designed to prevent hackers from breaching the security of a system. When IT responsibilities are placed within the library, then those responsible must take adequate measures to safeguard the library's data and systems from unauthorized access.

Ideally, the library will have developed a written plan to cope with a security breach, should one occur, rather than reacting to an emergency situation. The plan should identify the members of the incident response team as well as the vendors (hardware and software) that may have to be contacted to cope with the situation. The plan should outline the escalation of procedures that will be followed should the attack turn out to be protracted or especially damaging. At some point, it may be appropriate to contact the suitable government agencies to get them involved in providing technical assistance as well as gathering information for possible prosecution.[16]

Among the responses to a security threat that can assist the library in minimizing the security challenges are the following:

- **Antivirus/Antimalware programs**—An up-to-date antivirus/ antimalware program is an effective line of defense, although by its very nature it is always reactive to new attacks. The antivirus/antimalware program will automatically scan each email or file being downloaded, in an effort to detect a security threat. Among the more frequently used antivirus programs are McAfee, Symantec, Malwarebytes, and AVG.

- **Firewalls, routers, proxy servers, and VPN**—Firewalls are designed to keep unwanted (e.g., spam) and unauthorized traffic from an unprotected network out of a LAN, yet still allow users to access network services. The firewall, which is similar to a security gate for a gated community, provides security to those components inside the gate and controls who can get in and go out.[17] The firewall can be a separate device, or it can be integrated into a router.

- **Software application updates**—Keeping the operating system and all application software, especially email and office products, current is an effective way to minimize security threats, as groups and organizations that develop this software are constantly adding patches to fix identified security "holes" in their software.

- **Password security**—The use of user IDs and passwords is fundamental to the protection of any automated system from unauthorized outside threats. The best practices for passwords are that they should be unique for each system or device and should be changed regularly. Unfortunately, most people and organizations ignore these best practices. Some of the most popular passwords include the very predictable "123456," "qwerty," "admin," "password," "111111," "123123," and "letmein."[18]

Good security requires ongoing staff training and expenditure of capital to ensure that the appropriate set of tools are in place. Because of the complexity of security technology, this is an area that the library might wish to consider outsourcing to a security service provider.

Assistive Technology

Computer technology is available to assist individuals who have a variety of disabilities. Public and academic libraries will, in general, provide computer hardware and software that is primarily intended for vision-impaired or blind users and people with physical handicaps that restrict typing. Libraries that provide assistive technology are using the technology as part of the library's response to ensure compliance with the Americans with Disabilities Act. There is a wide variety of computer hardware and software that will assist individuals who

- are blind or visually impaired;
- are deaf or hard of hearing;
- have learning disabilities;
- have cognitive disabilities;
- require mouse alternatives;
- require keyboard alternatives;
- require text-to-speech converters; or
- can benefit from speech recognition software.

The systems librarian is usually responsible for ensuring that this assistive technology can be used in conjunction with the internet and the library's local information system as well as in a stand-alone mode. For additional information about assistive technology, see "Suggested Web Resources" at the end of this chapter.

Should a library decide to provide assistive technologies, then it will need the obvious: space to place the equipment (typically a separate room to contain voices coming from machines) and staff to manage and provide assistance and training in how to use the equipment. Usually, the systems manager does not need to be concerned about the communication protocols required by the assistive technologies because these devices are designed to interface and interact with most systems.

Summary

Managing an ILS is crucial because it determines what services are provided to its patrons, wherever they may be located. The personality characteristics of the systems manager determine the kind of response that will be provided when the inevitable problems arise. Effectively managing the library's network infrastructure, system backups, system upgrades, and applications and their associated licenses are all important tasks. The library should also prepare a disaster plan, acknowledge and address security issues, assess the ergonomic factors for employee work areas, and modify workflows. More recently, the fundamental issue of system integration has arisen and must be addressed by the library.

Questions to Consider

- If you are a library systems manager, would you add or emphasize a characteristic mentioned in this chapter?
- If you are a library systems manager, what specific job skills do you consider need to be strengthened or acquired?

- How has your job changed as a result of moving systems to the cloud?
- Do you use a set of APIs to connect one system to another?
- Has your library considered installing an AMH system?
- Has your library installed RFID tags? If not, does the installation of RFID tags and materials handling systems make economic sense?
- Has your library considered installing interactive public kiosks, interactive table displays, or beacon technology?
- Do you know what it costs to provide information technology infrastructure to all of your users per year?
- Does you library have all of the required licenses for the network software, database software, and all of the applications software? If not, why not?
- Does your library have an information technology disaster recovery plan?
- Has your library had a system security audit performed in the last two years to determine the level of risk and vulnerability that exists?
- Does your library require the regular changing of passwords?

Suggested Web Resources

Adaptive Technology for the Internet: Making Electronic Resources Accessible to All ala.org/Template.cfm?section=ContentManagement /ContentDisplay.cfm&ContentID=22254

Adaptive Technology Resource Center https://www.abilities.ca/techno logy/adaptive-technology-resource-centre

Alliance for Technology Access http://www.ataccess.org

Cast Bobby (a site that checks your HTML code) http://wave.webaim.org

Equal Access to Software and Information http://easi.cc/

Enablemart http://www.enablemart.com

IBM Accessibility Center https://www.ibm.com/able/

LibraryLaw Blog http://www.librarylaw.com

W3C Web Accessibility Initiative (WAI) http://www.w3c.org/WAI

WebABLE http://www.webable.tv

Notes

1. Sidney Harris, *The Best of Sydney J. Harris.* New York: Houghton Mifflin, 1976, 84.

2. Scott P. Muir, "Setting Priorities for the Library's Systems Office," *Library HiTech* 19, no. 3 (2001): 264–73.

3. Thomas C. Wilson, *The Systems Librarian: Designing Roles, Defining Skills* (Chicago: American Library Association, 1998).

4. Ping Fu and Moira Fitzgerald, "A Comparative Analysis of the Effect of the Integrated Library System on Staffing Models in Academic Libraries," *Information Technology and Libraries* 32, no. 3 (September 2013): 47–58.

5. Helen Heinrich and Eric Willis, "Automated Storage and Retrieval System: A Time-Test Innovation," *Library Management* 35, no. 5–6 (2014): 444–53.

6. Peter Murray, "Robots, Not Humans, Retrieve Your Books at $81 Million 'Library of the Future,'" *SingularityHub* (blog), May 24, 2011.

7. Rebecca Miller, Heather Moorefield-Lang, and Carolyn Meier, "Intentional Integration of Tablets and Mobile Devices into Library Services," *Library Technology Reports* 51, no. 7 (October 2015).

8. Ann Holstein, "Geographic Information and Technologies in Academic Libraries: An ARL Survey of Services and Support," *Information Technology and Libraries* 34, no. 1 (March 2015): 38–51.

9. Joseph R. Matthews, *Technology Planning: Preparing and Updating a Library Technology Plan* (Westport, CT: Libraries Unlimited, 2004).

10. Paul N. Courant and Matthew Nielsen, *On the Cost of Keeping a Book, in The Idea of Order: Transforming Research Collections for 21st Century Scholarship* (Washington, DC: Council on Library and Information Resources, 2010), 96.

11. A copy of the 15th Annual 2010/2011 Computer Crime and Security Survey is available at https://cours.etsmtl.ca/gti619/documents/divers/CSIsurvey2010 .pdf.

12. The INFOSEC Rainbow Series of publications is available from the National Computer Security Center. See also Federal Information Processing Standards (FIPS) publications at https://www.nist.gov/itl/itl-publications/federal-information -processing-standards-fips.

13. George V. Hulme, "Management Takes Notice," *Information Week* 853 (September 3, 2001): 28–34.

14. For information about ISO 17799, including the ability to download a copy of the standard itself, a directory of software that will assist in preparing an ISO 17799 audit, and other helpful resources, go to https://www.iso.org/standard/39612 .html.

15. The Center for Internet Security (CIS) develops standards for operating systems, firewalls, routers, and virtual private networks (VPNs), http://www.cisecurity .org. Common Criteria is a set of broad guidelines for evaluating IT security products (http://www.commoncriteria.org). DITSCAP (Department of Defense Information Technology Security Certification and Accreditation Process) is a process that documents, assesses, and certifies the security of computer systems (http://iase.disa .mil/ditscap). The Federal Information Technology Security Assessment Framework is a tool for assessing IT security programs and developing goals for improvement. The Federal Information Systems Controls Audit Manual (FISCAM) is available at http://www.gao.gov/policy/12_9_6.pdf. The Generally Accepted System Security Principles (GASSP) were developed by the International Information Security Foundation (http://www.auerbach-publications.com/white-papers/gassp.pdf). The Internet Engineering Task Force (IETF) Site Security Handbook is available at http://www .ietf.org/rfc/rfc2196.txt?number=2196; Information Systems Audit and Control Association (ISACA) is available at https://www.isaca.org/pages/default.aspx. The National Institute of Standards and Technology's (NIST) Generally Accepted Principles and Practices for Securing Information Technology Systems is available at https://www.nist.gov/publications/generally-accepted-principles-and-practices -securing-information-technology-systems.

OCTAVE (Operationally Critical Threat, Asset, and Vulnerability Evaluation), a process to conduct an IT security risk assessment, is available at http://www.cert .org/octave. SysTrust Principles and Criteria for Systems Reliability is available at https://resources.sei.cmu.edu/library/asset-view.cfm?assetid=13473.

16. Possible government agencies that could be contacted include the Electronic Crimes Branch of the Secret Service (www.ustreas.gov); the FBI's Internet Fraud

Complaint Center (https://www.ic3.gov/default.aspx); US Department of Justice Computer Crime and Intellectual Property Section (www.cybercrime.gov); and CERT Coordination Center (https://www.sei.cmu.edu/about/divisions/cert/).

17. William Cheswick and Steven Bellovin, *Firewalls and Internet Security: Repelling the Wily Hacker* (Reading, MA: Addison-Wesley, 1994).

18. Nina Golgowski, "The Most Common Passwords in 2016 Are Truly Terrible," *The Huffington Post*, January 18, 2017, http://www.huffingtonpost.com/entry/2016-most-common-passwords_us_587f9663e4b0c147f0bc299d.

14
Usability and User Experience

We are stuck with technology
when what we really want
is stuff that works.

—Douglas Adams[1]

User experience and usability refer to the design of a product (or service or system), and although they are often used interchangeably, there are important distinctions between them:

- **Usability** focuses on ease of use—the goal is to minimize user frustration by providing a product or service that "works well."

- **User experience** encompasses usability but also considers other meaningful dimensions, for example, joy, reflection, meaning, desire, and the value of the experience.

Peter Morville has developed the "user experience honeycomb," see Figure 14.1, so that we may better understand the components of user experience.

Products, services, or systems that have a really good user experience provide real value to the user, which is why "valuable" is at the center of the honeycomb. The other elements—useful, desirable, accessible, credible, findable, and usable—all contribute in their own way to this value.

First impressions count. Yet even a good first impression will not keep users coming back time after time. The usability of any system has always been recognized as important, but more often than not, very little attention is paid to this important issue. This is surprising because for most people, the user interface is the experience—whether it is application software, such as an integrated library system (ILS), or the Web. It's the user interface the user is immersed in, becomes a part of, and becomes frustrated with if something is not quite right. When the user interface is truly intuitive ("I can't define intuitive, but I know it when I see and interact effortlessly with it"), the user reaches a moment of epiphany and says, "Yes, I get it!"

As information technology has moved from character-based software products to a graphical user interface (GUI), to web-based products, to a "natural" user interface found on smartphones and tablets, it is quite clear that usability too often takes a back seat to other system factors (e.g., features and functions, use of graphics and animation). Too often, the realities of Moore's law, which states, "An information retrieval system will tend not to be used whenever it is more painful and troublesome for a customer to have information than for him not to have it," are ignored.[2]

FIGURE 14.1. Peter Morville's User Experience Honeycomb
Source: Reprinted with permission.

The experience IS the product and the only thing users care about.

—Peter Morville[3]

Where are people going to get their information? The Web! No surprise there. When a library's web page has not undergone any fundamental change for a week or more, it is sending a clear message to those who take the time to visit—the library does not care![4] Websites that are "sticky" are sites that provide the user with compelling reasons to return again and again. The reasons for the stickiness might have to do with current information resources and an easy-to-use site, among others.

According to one survey, people come back to a website for the following reasons:[5]

Very entertaining	56%
Grabs my attention	54%
Extremely useful content	53%
Information tailored to my needs	45%
Thought provoking	39%
Visually appealing	39%
Highly interactive	36%
Loads quickly	21%

Jared Spool, a usability author and consultant, suggests that a website's design has several characteristics that must be met so visitors will find the website compelling and return again and again.[6] After examining numerous websites and studying how users are actually exploring and using them, he found that navigation and content are inseparable. Users have no patience, so the website should be designed in such a way that the user should have a clear sense of how to accomplish a variety of tasks at the website. In addition, a website search engine is almost a mandatory requirement. Users don't want to scroll through long lists to find valuable information.

Another usability expert, Steve Krug, suggests in his book *Don't Make Me Think* that when people are visiting a website:[7]

- They don't read pages; they scan them.

- They don't make optimal choices; they are willing to accept a less than perfect solution.

- They don't figure out how things work; they muddle through.

A library's website may be in one of several evolutionary stages, such as one of these:

- **We are here**—task-oriented, traditional library message. In a similar vein, early commercial websites were often called "brochure ware" sites.

- **User-centered digital library**—Besides having access to the library's online catalog and several online databases, users were able to find information about the status of various activities and communicate with the library to place a hold, change their mailing address, and so forth.

- **Personalization**—Users are able to specify how they want "their" version of the library's website, including the online catalog, to look and feel.

- **Digital branch library**—The design of the website is optimized to provide users with a library experience truly optimized for a mobile platform.

However, before visiting some of the fundamental design concepts that should be followed when creating or redesigning a website, it is important to ask yourself (and know the answers to) the following questions:

- Why are you creating a website? What are the goals or purpose of the site? What specific groups of people are expected to use the website?

- What do you want to accomplish with this site? What should the user be able to accomplish when using the library's website?

- What do you want your users to accomplish with this site? What can library patrons accomplish directly? Can they customize the site? Can they sign up for an alert service (be informed about new programs for kids, learn about recently arrived new materials, etc.)?

- What provides the "stickiness" for your site? What keeps the user coming back time after time? What nontraditional services, such as contacting the library via email, instant messaging, or chat, are provided? What eResources can the user access on an ongoing basis?

- What will encourage a user to return? Is content updated regularly? Does the library provide free email, downloadable wallpaper designs, e-postcards, community message boards, and so forth?

The flashiest graphics will never save a poor user interface.
Sexy graphics are like lipstick on a bulldog.
Lipstick may make the bulldog look better
but you still don't want to kiss it.
                                    —Norm Cox, designer of the Xerox Star[8]

Website Design

Websites are designed to provide access to a plethora of different types of information. Some commercial websites, for example, provide a wide range of information about their products and services and will often provide an e-commerce component so visitors can complete a purchase transaction. Yet because users become frustrated with their inability to complete the purchase process, more than 30 percent abandon their shopping carts.[9] So what are some of the more important factors that determine whether library website visitors become frustrated and abandon the site, never to return again?

The whole experience of using a website is tied to a variety of factors, including how the site is organized and what navigation features, such as buttons, tabs, menus, links, graphics, site maps, and search engines, are provided. When visiting a website, users have a set of expectations; to be successful, the website must either meet or exceed those expectations.

Individuals involved with designing and maintaining a website may have a work experience background from one of three professions, as shown in Figure 14.2. This may include a librarian (with a historical focus on text), a graphics designer (with a traditional focus on design and graphics), and finally a computer coding person (whose interest is with the technology itself). If only one or two people are responsible for the website, it should not be surprising that the website reflects their backgrounds and work experiences. The ideal is to achieve a balance from all three points of view so that the

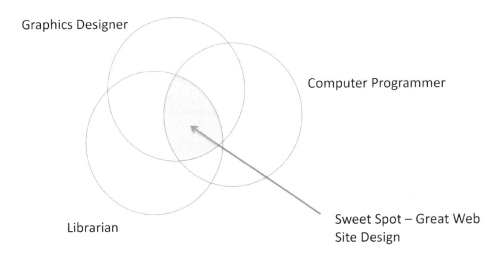

FIGURE 14.2. Perspectives on Website Design

end result is a website that really works—from the user's perspective. Further, studying how users currently navigate the library website can suggest great ideas (please see the section at the end of this chapter).

People come to the library's website for a variety of reasons, including, but not limited to, the following:

- Search the library's catalog.

- Place a hold for an item.

- Gain access to eResources.

- Learn something through the use of a "how to" guide or tutorial.

- Browse historical materials.

- Read a library blog.

- Learn about upcoming events and programs.

So the library's website must accommodate all of these various reasons for using the website by providing a variety of tools and making navigation easy. Among the best practices that distinguish a really good website from the truly mundane are browser and device neutrality, navigation, and readability; and being understandable, familiar, searchable, and accessible.

Browser and Device Neutrality

Today, it is mandatory that your library's website be device agnostic. That is, although what is displayed on the screen may vary (depending on the size of the screen), all of the content should be displayed on any device—be it a smartphone (iPhone or Android), tablet (Apple, Android, or Windows), or laptop. And please don't even consider a separate mobile-friendly library website.

Kimberly Pendell and Michael Bowman provided evidence that a fairly quick assessment of a library's website from the perspective of people using mobile devices pays real and immediate benefits (for the user!).[10]

> **Tip!** Use a template such as WordPress, Drupal, or Blogger that is already proven to work in every environment.

> **Tip!** You might want to hire an experienced library website developer for your library. A number of companies specialize in library web design, and there are even more general web designers in communities across the globe. When using either, be sure the designer understands enough about your library to reflect both the services and the "feel" of the library, to convey things properly online. Fancy websites are wonderful—but even simple ones that are designed well can get the job done. As well, websites based on content management systems (CMSs) are desired because they can be structured to allow library staff with little or no web skills to easily update key content on the website.

Navigation

People obviously will not return to your website if they can't find their way around it. People using your library's website must have a clear sense that they are making progress toward their goal (whatever that may be) or else they get frustrated and move on. This reality suggests that you eliminate horizontal scrolling, use dropdown menus, minimize the number of clicks to accomplish a task, and ensure that the user is always able to get back "home" from any other page.

Design consistency helps the user navigate the site. The library should consider developing, and then frequently updating, a style guide that clearly delineates the look and feel of the library's website.[11] Recognize that both novice and experienced individuals will use the website, and that both groups should be able to navigate smoothly.

Acknowledge that users have difficulty in searching (one library found that almost one-fourth of searches in the single search box were *not* for journal articles and books),[12] users may have unrealistic expectations of what the single search box will do for them,[13] finding and navigating to links for full-text pdf files,[14] and having more than one search box can be confusing unless carefully labeled (e.g., website search and library catalog).[15]

When users are transferred to external sites, a whole host of new challenges may be encountered, including link resolver issues, consortial catalogs, needing to authenticate multiple times, and different user interfaces at publisher or aggregator sites.[16]

Hypertext links that are no longer up to date or that point to resources that no longer exist are an obvious source of frustration for website users. Several search engines found that about 25 percent of all links more than a year old will no longer work. This condition is sometimes referred to as "link rot." Web-page developers and designers should use a software tool to check the integrity of all links on a regular basis (at least weekly) and repair any broken links as quickly as possible. One of the reasons for link rot is that some websites are constantly evolving, which means that the site is pointing to pages that change continuously.[17]

Readable

It is important to remember that people only scan web pages—they hardly ever read. Studies that track eyes of users looking a websites show time after time that an individual scans across (left to right), then down a bit on the left-hand edge before scanning partway across the page before returning to the left-hand edge and continuing down to the bottom (much like the shape of the letter "F"). If the user has not encountered something of interest, he or she clicks and then moves on to something else (usually to a new website).

This scanning, rather than reading, reality suggests that it is important to avoid visual clutter, choose a comfortable color scheme (with good contrast between the color of the font and the background), and avoid dense text. Simplify and shorten what text is displayed, and the user experience will improve substantially.

Understandable

Websites need to be presented in plain language, so it is important to avoid jargon of any kind, especially technology- or library-related jargon. Do we understand what terms such as interlibrary loan, database, and circulation mean to our users? John Kupersmith, in a review of fifty-one usability studies, found that acronyms and product brand names (EBSCOHost or Emerald), and library jargon such as E-journals, index, serials, reference, and many more terms, are frequently misunderstood or not understood at all by library users.[18] John also found that the average success for finding journal articles or journal databases was only 52 percent. Another study at the University of Houston Libraries found the use of jargon to be a major contributing factor in a user being unable to complete a task during a usability study.[19] Still another study suggested creating a glossary of "library jargon" used on the library's website.[20]

Familiar

Recent research found that almost 75 percent of users were searching for multiple pieces of information, and another 25 percent were looking for something specific.[21] Users visit a website to compare or choose something in order to make a decision, acquire a fact or a document, or gain an understanding of some topic. Thus, the site needs to be well structured and organized.

According to Jared Spool, information has a "scent" that people pick up on as they move from page to page (Peter Pirolli at Xerox PARC calls this information scent "information foraging").[22] Marcia Bates has described the approaches that people take to find valuable information, all of which can be supported in the Web environment, as "berrypicking."[23] Strive for efficiency. Make the paths to an information resource as short and productive as possible.

A consistent look and feel, consistent terminology and placement of features (e.g., the site search box and login should be in the upper right-hand corner) will improve the overall usability of the website. Help users decide where *not* to go by using clear navigation signposts. Make sure your site uses existing web conventions (e.g., use blue font for hyperlinks, no underline for normal text). Make sure the paths from one point to another are as direct as possible (eliminate unnecessary clicks). Should someone become lost, he or she is not likely to return!

Searchable

Being able to search from every web page is an absolute requirement, and the search box should indicate whether the user is searching the catalog or the website. Make sure you test to ensure that all content is searchable—including events on your calendar. In addition, make sure your website is discoverable by the Google search engine crawler. Optimizing a website so that it receives the highest possible ranking from Google or any other search engine is called search engine optimization (SEO). One study noted that being aware of the importance of and working toward making the library's website visible to search engine indexing robots was a key factor in optimization efforts.[24] Ted Fons also offers a host of practical suggestions for improving web visibility.[25]

Among the more noteworthy books on this topic are Adam Clarke's *Search Engine Optimization 2016*;[26] Jason McDonald's *SEO Fitness Workbook 2016*;[27] Eric Enge, Stephen Spencer, and Jessie Stricchiola's *The Art of SEO*;[28] and Bruce Clay's *Search Engine Optimization All-in-One for Dummies*.[29]

At some sites, almost half of all users will use the website's search engine.[30] The success of searching a specific website is not known, but the success rate in searching for a broader set of information available via the Web is truly disappointing—between 60 percent and 80 percent of people fail.[31]

Accessible

In addition to usability, the library should also be concerned about accessibility, especially for those with handicaps (more than 10% of the population).[32] The Americans with Disabilities Act, amended in 2010, seeks to ensure equal treatment for those with disabilities. In addition, Section 508 of the Rehabilitation Act of 1973 insists that those organizations that receive federal funds cannot discriminate against people with disabilities.

A library can check the accessibility of its website by using one or more validation tools (e.g., Bobby—http://www.cast.org/bobby/). Check to ensure that your library's website complies with Section 508 standards (http://section508.gov). In addition, the World Wide Web Consortium (W3C) has established Web Content Accessibility Guidelines 2.0 that should be consulted to be sure nothing is missed.

Usability Guidelines

Although several authors, perhaps a majority of authors, who are considered to be usability experts have developed usability guidelines, these seem to be based on observations and personal recommendations rather than the results of careful research.[33] The majority of these guidelines could be placed into three broad groups: navigational characteristics, practical considerations, and visual characteristics.

D'Angelo and Little, after thoroughly reviewing the literature, developed a list of ten factors that could be used to evaluate websites.[34] The pair then evaluated twenty websites, using these evaluation criteria, by asking their subjects to perform a series of tasks. They found that, on average, the websites incorporated about six and a half of these evaluation factors. Sites that included more of these factors were more successful, and users spent more time at the website.[35] The ten evaluation factors are listed here:

Visual Considerations

1. Use of all capital letters is a no-no.
2. Make links visible in text fields.
3. Organize content with headings and subtopics
4. Use just one font.
5. Use white space effectively.

Practical Characteristics

1. Limit images to three per page.
2. Make sure colors do not clash
3. Provide good contrast between the background and text.
4. Background options include light blue, gray, or white
5. Limit colors to four per screen.

It doesn't matter how many times I have to click,
as long as each click is a mindless, unambiguous choice.
—Krug's First Law of Usability[36]

Roger Black suggests that good websites come from the principles that have informed quality print design for hundreds of years.[37] His ten rules of good design include:

1. Put content on every page. And make it easy to read since people skim and surf a web page.

2. The first color should be white.

3. The second color should be black.

4. The third color could be red or . . .

5. Never add spacing for lowercase text.

6. Avoid using all caps.

7. A cover should be a poster.

8. Use only one or two typefaces.

9. Make everything as big as possible. Use fonts with larger point sizes.

10. Get lumpy! Break up the consistent look and feel occasionally.

Design shouldn't be mere decoration; it must convey information.
A reader should never have to plow through
forests of buttons to get simple news.
—Roger Black[38]

As library websites have grown in size and complexity, attempting to maintain an HTML-only site will display the limitations of this primitive tool. A design approach that uses an application server with a database of information resources will allow the library's website to scale (this is often called a content management system or CMS). While HTML is great for displaying data, a database is a good way to manage data about information resources. A database-driven website will combine the best of both worlds and reduce the personnel costs associated with maintaining a website.[39]

Libraries should embed keyword attributes in an HTML meta tag in their websites and HTML documents because this significantly improves accessibility when a search engine is used.[40]

First released in 2014, the fifth version of HTML—not surprisingly called HTML5—is the most powerful and flexible version of the Web markup language yet. Considered a "software solution stack" (which includes a number of programming components that work together to offer a complete platform), HTML5 offers a number of capabilities for websites and web page content, including using powerful application programming interfaces (APIs); supporting consistency for cross-platform access (via web browsers); and natively supporting scalable graphics, multimedia, geolocation, and other services.

Usability Testing

A team of librarians has worked long and hard to design and build the library's website. A celebration is called for! But then what? Well, some libraries adopt the *Field of Dreams* approach to website availability: "If you build it, they will come." But do they? And more important, when people do come to the library website, are they likely to return again and again?

Sometimes the pride of authorship hides the reality of actual use of the website. In fact, some website design team members will need to go through a process of grieving to let go and then move forward to a better design.[41] Team members may experience:

- **Denial**—"But this feature is important. Users just don't know how important it is, and we should keep things as is."

- **Anger**—"Really, how stupid can users be."

- **Depression**—Some team members may become silent and simply withdraw. "I invested so much in this project and this stinks."

- **Acceptance**—"Well, maybe if we moved . . ." This is where good design begins.

Fortunately, redesigning a website does not have to be expensive and time-consuming. Table 14.1 shows a range of methods available to assess the usability of a website.

It is possible to develop paper mock-ups of the proposed changes and then ask users to assess the changes by giving them several tasks to perform and observing and recording what they would do using the mock-ups. Getting the reactions to the proposed changes from five to eight users should be a sufficiently large sample size.[42] Testing typically takes from one to two hours (asking a user to perform several tasks); in some cases, two users are asked to perform the tasks in collaboration with each other. The cost involved in usability testing is normally quite low, while the value of information collected from the test participants is very high.

Rather than a one-time project, a library's website should be considered an ongoing, iterative process. This iterative design process means that a new prototype is created, tested, redesigned, released, and then reevaluated. Relentless adjustment is crucial. A criticism of Microsoft, for example, is that it hardly ever creates new, great technology. But it does constantly and relentlessly adjust its products so that, over time, they become useful and usable products and in some cases become the "usability standard."

Barbara Buttenfield suggests that evaluation may occur at different stages in the development of an online system: During system design, during system development, and during system deployment.[43] The library may wish to administer a questionnaire to obtain a more formal reaction to their web pages. The system usability scale (SUS) is a ten-question survey that uses a Likert scale. SUS scores range from 0 to 100.[44] A longer, fifty-statement questionnaire, known as the Software Usability Measurement Inventory (SUMI), assesses the usability of a system from five perspectives: efficiency, effect or the emotional reaction, helpfulness, control, and learnability.[45]

As noted above, a library can solicit feedback using a variety of methods, including email links, posting a web form, conducting surveys, and so on. However, using prototypes is highly recommended by many authors and consultants in the field. Although it is possible to use HTML coding or a

TABLE 14.1. Usability Test Methods

Method	Advantages
Automated data collection—Software that tracks how users perform a specific task. Can be used anytime.	Automates the data collection process.
Card sort—An index card is created for each web page. Users are asked to sort cards logically into categories. Typically used early in the design process.	Shows how users organize and name categories of information.
Category expectation—Tests the understanding of each category, including what users think should be in a category and what the category should be named.	Identifies any use of jargon and identifies users' expectations.
Cognitive walkthrough—Designers try to mimic actual users by performing various tasks themselves.	No need to recruit users for testing.
Field study—Observe users as they carry out normal tasks.	See what users are actually doing and how they navigate around a website.
Focus groups—A small group of users are asked to discuss their reactions and use of the website.	This method leads to more qualitative feedback.
Formal testing—Asks a sample of users to perform specific tasks and to "think out loud" about their thoughts, feelings, and reactions.	Probably the most thorough method, especially if user reactions are taped, transcribed, and then analyzed. Can be a time-consuming process.
Interview—Provides a semi-structured conversation about the Website.	Allows an individual to provide extensive feedback about the site.
Opinion poll—Intended to obtain feedback on a specific topic.	A relatively quick method to gather data, but difficult to interpret the data.
Paper mock-ups—Users are asked to react to the proposed web pages on paper.	Can be prepared quickly.
Questionnaire—Designed to collect opinions and feedback from a larger sample of users.	Relatively easy to conduct, but wording questionnaires is an art.
Site usage logs—The data will reveal how users move about the website.	Requires careful analysis.

software package to develop prototypes, these tools should only be used if the total development time can be measured in hours rather than days or weeks. Remember, the purpose of the prototype is to elicit feedback about possible changes, and thus the software coding used for the prototype will be abandoned.

Judy Jeng summarized the research on the usability of academic library websites and suggested that libraries should be evaluating the learnability, efficiency, effectiveness, and satisfaction from the user's perspective.[46]

The library should also make extensive use of web statistics. Software programs are available that track which web pages are visited (called "hits"), as well as the paths traveled by people who visit the site. Using this information can provide a clearer picture of what portions of a library's website are being used, as well as what navigation paths are actually being used. In addition, web developers and administrators can identify where users originate, what connection speeds are in use, and what sort of technologies are being used by the end user (e.g., type of desktop computer, operating system, brand of browser, etc.).

There have been several published reports comparing task performance efficiency before and after a redesign. On average, the gain in efficiency was 50 percent.[47] Many libraries have gone through the iterative redesign process, and they all report a significant increase in the amount of traffic to the library's website after their sites had been revised.[48] For example, the University of Nevada Las Vegas experienced a nearly 100 percent increase in the number of hits at its website after its website redesign.

Content Management System

A content management system, sometimes called a web content management system, manages and delivers content for a website. A database holds the contents while a scripting language, such as Hypertext Preprocessor (PHP), in conjunction with style sheets is used to generate the necessary web pages. The strength of a content management system (CMS) is that any number of people can contribute content while the CMS automatically updates and formats the content for any device.

Popular content management systems include open source options such as Drupal, WordPress, and Joomla, or hosted options such as Weebly.com, and Wix.com.

You can think of a specialized CMS for building subject guides such as Springshare's LibGuides.

Intranets

Librarians are increasingly being asked to participate as team members in developing and maintaining an intranet for their parent organization, be it a city, county, or federal government agency; corporation; or other information agency. An intranet is a website that is behind a firewall and visible only to employees and select outsiders through login privileges. Besides content from within the organization, many intranets also provide electronic content from external suppliers. This external content might be news feeds, stock quote information, general business news, or content solely focused on the needs of a particular organization. For example, a hospital might provide access to medical information and related resources to end users.

Even an intranet with a great look and feel does not address the fundamental underlying reasons for an intranet. An effective intranet should address the issues of information overload, effective information access and retrieval, organization of intellectual assets, and the potential for providing a sense of communities built around common interests and practice rather than departmental boundaries.

Yet given the "invisible" nature of an intranet, there is usually little incentive to make improvements. Thus, it is not surprising that many usability experts have noted common design mistakes with intranets.

Google Analytics—A Two-Edged Sword

There are several software tools available that will analyze the log files for your website (Google Analytics being the most popular—oh yes, its free; perhaps that's why it's so popular). Google Analytics is used by about half of the top 1 million websites, by lots of libraries and well over 30 million websites. The benefits of using such a tool are several:

- **Provide information about who uses your website**—The number of unique users can be identified along with where the visitors are coming from and how long they stay. You can find out if they arrived by using a search engine, typing in your specific web address, or through the use of a link you provided on a social media site

- **Determine what is important**—Knowing what pages are most frequently accessed means they can be moved about your website. This usage information could also mean that there is some unmet need, and perhaps additional complimentary information is needed.

- **Determine what is not being used**—Analyzing what is not being used may mean repositioning the pages, embedding metadata tags to improve the indexing, and so forth. It might also point out the need to improve any navigational tools that might be connected to the site.

- **Determining the paths followed by users**—Navigation bottlenecks can be identified, as well as pages that may need to be repositioned should they require a large number of clicks to get to that web page.

Tabatha Farney provides a number of useful tips on implementing Google Analytics in a issue of *Library Technology Reports*.[49] Google Analytics provides a snippet of JavaScript code that the website administrator ads to every page on the website. The tracking code collects data using cookies for each visitor and then sends the data to a Google data collection center (not surprisingly, Google uses this information to improve its profile for each individual visiting the website). The website administrator can run a report whenever needed.

What that means is that Google is aware of who is visiting what websites, which raises privacy concerns in the minds of many people (and lots of librarians). Although individual users (and libraries) can set "Do not track" variables in their browsers, almost no one does this. For libraries using Google Analytics, it should be aware that its public access computers might be capturing personal identifiable information (PII) such as when an individual uses an online form to submit information to another website. In some cases, an individual will think that a site search is a login box and enter their username and password.

Some Google Analytics options that gather visitor information and the data never leave the site include the ones here:

- Open source analytics—Analog, Fathom, Matomo, Piwik, Simple Analytics, W3Perl, and Wealizer

- Proprietary analytics—Angelfish, Mint, and Urchin

- Hosted analytics software—Bango Mobile Web Analytics, ClickTale, and Quantcast

Increasingly, librarians will have the opportunity to offer their users tools that allow them to customize their online catalog as well as the library's website. These personalization tools provide people, especially knowledgeable and frequent visitors to the library's website, with the ability to customize their experience so they are more productive. It will be interesting to observe whether libraries that offer personalization options will also need to develop and recommend style guides or templates so users—even those with the best of intentions—don't produce customized versions of a library website/online catalog that renders it virtually unusable.

Summary

This chapter highlighted the importance of good design for library websites, automated library systems, and the need to focus on the total user experience. A synopsis of the recommendations of numerous knowledgeable individuals suggests these nine guidelines:

1. **Establish clear goals**—Create a one- or two-sentence statement of the goals of each technology or system (online catalog, website, discovery service, etc.). Make sure the goals are aligned with the library's mission.

2. **Provide easy access to search**—A single search box in a prominent position near the top of the web page is critical, as most people coming to the website want to search.

3. **Simplify navigation**—Common high-level navigation topics include Search, My Account, Services, Research, About Us, and Help.

4. **The user is not like any staff member**—We can't expect our users to become skilled mini-librarians, so we must simplify.

5. **The home page is a gateway**—Simplify the number of options available on the home page (the home page is just the first step on a journey elsewhere).

6. **Eliminate jargon**—Library jargon (librarian-ese) is a significant barrier to understanding and ease of use.

7. **Ensure accessibility**—Inaccessible websites, for whatever reason, lead to a sense of helplessness and frustration.

8. **Conduct usability testing**—Usability testing should be an ongoing activity that will lead to continuously improving the system or website.

9. **The quality of your website requires effort and resources**. A great website requires good design, useful content that is engaging, well-written text, quality images, plus navigation that is intuitive and never requires your to think. Your high-quality website will thus require a fair amount of effort (on the part of several staff members) plus other resources. The library's website cannot be an afterthought. It is as important (perhaps more so) than any physical location that delivers library services. Remember that your library's website is never finished.

The goal for any library is to ensure that every customer has an awesome user experience and wants to return to the physical and/or virtual library again and again.

Questions to Consider

- Do you think there are other components that Peter Morville has not identified in his "user experience honeycomb"?
- What reasons do people have to come back to your library's website?
- Do you use Google Analytics or another analysis product to monitor the use of your library's website?
- What are the goals for your library's website?
- Is your library's website device agnostic? Mobile device agnostic?
- Does your library use a content management system for its website?
- Do you use periodic testing with real users to determine the ease of navigation of your library's website?
- Is the library catalog search box in a prominent location? Do you provide the option to search the library's website?
- What are the pros and cons of using Google Analytics?
- Does you library provide sufficient resources to keep your library's website constantly refreshed and usable?

Suggested Web Resources

Human Computer Interaction Bibliography http://www.hcibib.org
IBM's Ease of Use Website http://www.ibm.com/easy
Information and Design http://www.infodesign.com.au/usability/webcheck
   .pdf
Jakob Nielsen's Heuristic Evaluation http://www.useit.com
Really Bad Websites http://www.webpagesthatsuck.com
Usability First http://www.usabilityfirst.com
Usability Methods Toolbox http://www.best.com/~jthom/usability/usa
   home.htm
Usability Professionals Associations Resources http://www.upassoc
   .org/html/resources.html
Usability Testing at Washington State University http://www.vancouver
   .wsu.edu/fac/diller/usability/website.htm
Useable Web http://www.useableweb.com
User Interface Engineering http://www.world.std.com/~
Web Accessibility Initiative http://www.w3.org/wai
Web Design/Usability http://www.webreference.com/design/usability.html
Web Review: Usability Matters Design Studio http://webreview.com/97
   /04/25/usability/index.html

Suggested Readings

Campbell, Nicole. *Usability Assessment of Library-Related Web Sites: Methods and Case Studies*. LITA Guide No. 7. Chicago: American Library Association, 2001.

Donnelly, Vanessa. *Designing Easy-to-Use Websites*. London: Addison-Wesley, 2001.

King, David Lee. *Face2face: Using Facebook, Twitter, and Other Social Media Tools to Create Great Customer Connections*. Medford, NJ: Information Today, 2012.

King, David Lee. *Designing the Digital Experience: How to Use Experience Design Tools & Techniques to Build Better Websites Customers Love*. Medford, NJ: Information Today, 2008.

Krug, Steve. *Don't Make Me Think: A Common Sense Approach to Web Usability*. Indianapolis, IN: New Riders, 2000.

Lynch, Patrick, and Sarah Horton. *Web Style Guide*. New Haven, CT: Yale University Press, 1999.

Nielsen, Jakob. *Designing Web Usability: The Practice of Simplicity*. Indianapolis, IN: New Riders, 2000.

Reiss, Eric L. *Practical Information Architecture*. London: Addison-Wesley, 2000.

Rosenfeld, Louis, and Peter Morville. *Information Architecture for the World Wide Web*. Sebastopol, CA: O'Reilly, 1998.

Schmidt, Aaron, and Amanda Etches. *Useful, Usable, Desirable: Applying User Experience Design to Your Library*. Chicago: American Library Association, 2014.

Spool, Aaron, Tara Scanlon, Will Schroeder, Carolyn Snyder, and Terri DeAngelo. *Web Site Usability: A Designer's Guide*. San Francisco: Morgan Kaufman, 1999.

Veen, Jeffrey. *The Art & Science of Web Design*. Indianapolis, IN: New Riders, 2001.

Wittmann, Stacy Ann, and Julianne T. Stam. *Redesign Your Library Website*. Santa Barbara, CA: Libraries Unlimited, 2016.

Notes

1. Douglas Adams, *The Salmon of Doubt: Hitchhiking the Galaxy One Last Time* (New York: Crown, 2002), 74.

2. C. N. Mooers, "Mooers's Law: Or Why Some Retrieval Systems Are Used and Others Are Not," *American Documentation* 11, no. 3 (1990): 1.

3. Peter Morville, *Ambient Findability: What We Find Changes Who We Become* (Sebastopol, CA: O'Reilly Media, 2005), 164.

4. Helge Clausen, "Evaluation of Library Web Sites: The Danish Case," *The Electronic Library* 17, no. 2 (April 1999): 83–87; L. A. Clyde, "The Library As Information Provider: The Home Page," *The Electronic Library* 14, no. 6 (1996): 549–58; Randy Rice, *Randy Rice's Software Testing Site: Web Usability Validation*, https://www.riceconsulting.com/home/index.php/Web-Testing/web-usability-validation.html; and E. B. Lily and C. Van Fleet, "Measuring the Accessibility of Public Library Home Pages," *Reference and User Services Quarterly* 40, no. 2 (Winter 2000): 176–80.

5. IntelliQuest Web Evaluation Services.

6. Jared Spool, "Real Implications from Usability Testing," *Webreview* (September 23, 1998).

7. Steve Krug, *Don't Make Me Think: A Common Sense Approach to Web Usability* (Indianapolis, IN: New Riders, 2000).

8. Norm Cox, quoted in J. W. S. Maxwell, ed., *Applications of Information Technolgoy Construction* (London: Thomas Telford, 1991), 149.

9. Alice Hill, "Top 5 Reasons Your Customers Abandon Their Shopping Carts," *Smart Business* 14, no. 3 (2001): 80–84.

10. Kimberly Pendell and Michael Bowman, "Usability Study of a Library's Mobile Website: An Example from Portland State University," *Information Technology & Libraries* 31, no. 2 (June 2012): 45–62.

11. Patrick J. Lynch and Sarah Horton, *Web Style Guide: Basic Design Principles for Creating Web Sites* (New Haven, CT: Yale University Press, 1999). Also, examples of Web style guides can be found at Tomas Laurinavicius, "How to Create a Web Design Style Guide," *designmodo* (March 9, 2017), https://designmodo.com/create-style-guides/.

12. Cory Lown, Tito Sierra, and Josh Boyer, "How Users Search the Library from a Single Search Box," *College & Research Libraries* 74, no. 3 (2013): 227–41.

13. Patrick Newell, Henry Delcore, Amanda Dinscore, Allison Cowgill, and Jason McClung, "Collaborating for Change: Leveraging Campus Partnerships to Create a User-Centered Library Website," *Internet Reference Services Quarterly* 18, no. 3–4 (2013): 227–46.

14. Erin Cassidy, Glenda Jones, Lynn McMain, Lisa Shen, and Scott Vieira, "Student Searching with EBSCO Discovery: A Usability Study," *Journal of Electronic Resources Librarianship* 26, no. 1 (2014): 17–35. See also Jody DeRidder and Kathryn Matheny, "What Do Researchers Need? Feedback on Use of Online Primary Source Materials," *D-Lib Magazine* 20, no. 7–8 (July 2014): 54–70.

15. Jeanne Brown and Michael Yunki, "Tracking Changes: One Library's Homepage over Time—Findings from Usability Testing and Reflections on Staffing," *Journal of Web Librarianship* 8, no. 1 (2014): 23–47.

16. Bonnie Imler and Michelle Eichelberger, "Commercial Database Design vs. Library Terminology Comprehension: Why Do Students Print Abstracts instead of Full-Text Articles?," *College & Research Libraries* 75, no. 3 (2014): 284–97.

17. Link-checking programs include WWW Link Checker (for Unix systems); LVRFY: A HTML Link Verifier, https://www.crowcastle.net/preston/lvrfy.html; and MOMspider (multi-owner maintenance spider), http://www.ics.uci.edu/WebSoft/MOMspider/WWW94/paper.html.

18. John Kupersmith, "Library Terms That Users Understand," *eScholarship*, February 29, 2012, http://escholarship.org/uc/item/3qq499w7.

19. Kelsey Brett, Ashley Lierman, and Cherie Turner, "Lessons Learned: A Primo Usability Study," *Information Technology and Libraries* 35, no. 1 (March 2016): 7–24.

20. Roger Gillis, "Watch Your Language: Word Choice in Library Website Usability," *Partnership: The Canadian Journal of Library and Information Practice and Research* 12, no. 1 (2017), https://doi.org/10.21083/partnership.v12i1.3918.

21. Jakob Nielsen, "The 3Cs of Critical Web Use: Collect, Compare, Choose," *Nielsen Norman Group*, April 14, 2001, https://www.nngroup.com/articles/the-3cs-of-critical-web-use-collect-compare-choose/.

22. Richard Koman, "The Scent of Information," *Webreview*, May 15, 1998, http://www.webreview.com/1998/05_15/strategists/05_15_98_1.shtml.

23. Marcia J. Bates, "The Design of Browsing and Berrypicking Techniques for the Online Search Interface," *Online Review* 13, no. 5 (October 1989): 409–24.

24. Zoe Dickinson and Michael Smit, "Canadian Public Libraries and Search Engines: Barriers to Visibility," *Aslib Journal of Information Management* 68, no. 5 (2016): 589–606.

25. Ted Fons, "Improving Web Visibility: Into the Hands of Readers," *Library Technology Reports* 52, no. 5 (July 2016), https://doi.org/10.5860/ltr.52n5.

26. Adam Clarke, *Search Engine Optimization 2016: Learn SEO with Smart Internet Marketing Strategies* (New York: CreateSpace, 2015).

27. Jason McDonald, *SEO Fitness Workbook 2016: The Seven Steps to Search Engine Optimization Success on Google* (New York: CreateSpace Independent Publishing Platform, 2015).

28. Eric Enge, Stephen Spencer, and Jessie Stricchiola, *The Art of SEO: Mastering Search Engine Optimization* (Sebastopol, CA: O'Reilly Media, 2015).

29. Bruce Clay, *Search Engine Optimization All-in-One for Dummies* (New York: For Dummies, 2015).

30. Jared M. Spool, Tara Scanlon, Will Schroeder, Carolyn Snyder, and Terri DeAngelo, *Web Site Usability: A Designer's Guide* (San Francisco: Morgan Kaufman, 1999).

31. Richard Saul Wurman, "Redesign the Data," *Business2.com* (November 28, 2000): 210–22.

32. Terry Brainerd Chadwick, "Web Site Accessibility: What, Why and How," in *Internet Librarian 2001 Collected Presentations* (Medford, NJ: Information Today, 2001), 36–41.

33. Jackob Nielsen, "10 Usability Heuristics for User Interface Design," *NN/g Nielsen Norman Group*, April 24, 1994, http://www.useit.com/papers/heuristic/heuristic_list.html.

34. John D'Angelo and Sherry K. Little, "Successful Web Pages: What Are They and Do They Exist?," *Information Technology and Libraries* 17, no. 2 (June 1998): 71–81.

35. John D'Angelo and Joanne Twining, "Comprehension by Clicks: D'Angelo Standards for Web Page Design, and Time, Comprehension, and Preference," *Information Technology and Libraries* 19, no. 3 (September 2000): 125–35.

36. Steve Krug, *Don't Make Me Think: A Common Sense Approach to Web Usability* (Berkeley, CA: New Riders, 2006), 104.

37. Roger Black, *Web Sites That Work* (San Jose, CA: Adobe Press, 1997).

38. Roger Black, *Web Sites That Work*, 123.

39. Kristin Antelman, "Getting Out of the HTML Business: The Database-Driven Web Site Solution," *Information Technology and Libraries* 18, no. 4 (December 1999): 176–81.

40. Thomas P. Truner and Lise Brackbill, "Rising to the Top: Evaluating the Use of the HTML META Tag to Improve Retrieval of World Wide Web Documents Through Internet Search Engines," *LRTS* 42, no. 4 (October 1998): 258–71.

41. Kelley Schmidt, "Good Grief! The Highs and Lows of Usability Testing," *Web Review* (December 15, 2000), https://people.apache.org/~jim/NewArchitect/webrevu//2000/12_15/strategists/index01.html.

42. Christine Perfetti, "Eight is Not Enough," *User Interface Engineering*, https://articles.uie.com/eight_is_not_enough/.

43. Barbara Buttenfield, "Usability Evaluation of Digital Libraries," *Science & Technology Libraries* 17, no. 3–4 (1999): 39–59.

44. John Brooke, "SUS: A 'Quick and Dirty' Usability Scale," *Usability Evaluation in Industry*, Patrick W. Jordan, Bruce Thomas, Bernard A. Weerdmeester, and Ian L. McClelland, eds. (London: Taylor and Francis, 1996), 189–94.

45. Jurek Kirakowski, "The Software Usability Measurement Inventory: Background and Usage," *Usability Evaluation in Industry*, Patrick W. Jordan, Bruce Thomas, Bernard A. Weerdmeester, and Ian L. McClelland, eds. (London: Taylor and Francis, 1996), 169–77.

46. Judy Jeng, "Usability Assessment of Academic Digital Libraries: Effectiveness, Efficiency, Satisfaction, and Learnability," *Libri* 55 (2005): 96–121.

47. Thomas K. Landauer, *The Trouble with Computers: Usefulness, Usability and Productivity* (Cambridge, MA: MIT Press, 1995).

48. Jason Vaughan, "Three Iterations of an Academic Library Web Site," *Information Technology and Libraries* 20, no. 2 (June 2001): 81–92; Kate McCready, "Designing and Redesigning: Marquette Libraries' Web Site," *Library HiTech* 15, no. 3–4 (1997): 83–89; Bruce Harley, "Electronic One-Stop Shopping: The Good, the Bad, the Ugly," *Information Technology and Libraries* 18, no. 4 (December 1999): 200–9; David King, "Library Home Page Design: A Comparison of Page Layout for Front-Ends to ARL Library Web Sites," *College & Research Libraries* 59, no. 5 (September 1998): 458–66; Ruth Dickstein and Vicki Mills, "Usability Testing at the University of Arizona Library: How to Let the Users in on the Design," *Information Technology and Libraries* 19, no. 3 (September 2000): 144–51; David King, "Redesigning the Information Playground: A Usability Study of kclibrary.org," *Internet Librarian 2001 Collected Presentations* (Medford, NJ: Information Today, 2001): 93–102; and Anne M. Platoff and Jennifer M. Duvernay, "User Testing Made Easy," *Internet Librarian 2001 Collected Presentations* (Medford, NJ: Information Today, 2001): 155–64.

49. Tabatha Farney, "Google Analytics and Google Tag Manager," *Library Technology Reports* 52, no. 7 (October 2016): 1–42. See also Tabatha Farney and Nina McHale, "Introducing Google Analytics for Libraries," *Library Technology Reports* 49, no. 4 (June 2013): 1–42.

15
Basic Technology Axioms

A meeting is an event at which the minutes are kept
and the hours are lost.

—Joseph Stilwell[1]

This chapter presents several axioms that appear to have a high degree of relevance or "truism." You might think of them as guiding principles (i.e., these axioms are frequently found in most situations where library professionals cross paths with information and communications technologies).

The dictionary specifies an axiom to be "(1) A self-evident or universally recognized truth; (2) An established rule, principle or law." In mathematics, an axiom is a truth. Such truths rarely exist in the world of library information systems (LISs), but there is a world of experience, both positive and negative, in libraries and in other organizations, that allows us to formulate the axioms discussed in this chapter.

These principles, or axioms, deal with these issues:

- Standards
- Information databases
- Hardware platforms
- Applications software
- Decision-making
- Management

They do not necessarily deal with the functional or performance issues associated with information technology applications in libraries. After their initial presentation, most of these axioms will, hopefully, seem "self-evident." They become important when considering various strategies for implementing technology applications in libraries and related information agencies.

Axiom 1: Standards Are Critical; Recommended Practices Are Vital

Standards are important when applying technology to library processes and supporting the provision of services. Recommended practices can often suggest an exceptional model or proven practice. Chapter 3 discussed the role of information standards and the associations that administrate formal standards. In this chapter, we only consider the concept of standards as a critical component in identifying, selecting, and implementing an LIS.

Picture the situation where a professional librarian begins to define those fields that might be incorporated into a database design used to represent bibliographic objects. The individual must specify such attributes as field name, length of field (number of characters), type of characters allowed in each field, the order of the occurrence of each field, and related details. Clearly, if left to design such a structure in a vacuum, each professional would come up with a unique design that emphasizes one or more attributes, orders fields differently, excludes certain fields, or assigns different characteristics to various fields identified for use in each specific instance.

Now imagine if all libraries had their own proprietary design for a bibliographic record. Quite possibly one might have a slight advantage over the next, but none of the institutions would be capable of communicating with another: their record structures would be incompatible. They would be unable to identify works held in common or resources held uniquely (for purposes of reciprocal borrowing). In addition, they would not be able to share cataloging records or online catalog access, or conduct bibliographic verification and many other technical and public service tasks commonly associated with cooperating libraries. In essence, they would be operating as independent agencies in the information world.

The agreement among various libraries to adhere to and comply with various standards allows the development and refinement of cooperative services to occur; an even more critical need as budgets flat line or reduce and the need to innovate continues to grow. Cooperating and collaborating becomes a pathway forward under these conditions. There are many standards in the areas of libraries, information services, and the database industry, but the most important ones relating to technology are standards that address communications structures and interoperability issues.

The primary standards for communications include those identifying the MARC 21 bibliographic record, along with the patron, transaction, and holdings file record structures. Z39.50, the standard that addresses interoperability of diverse computing platforms, is the predominant development standard of interest to systems designers attempting to connect formerly disparate systems. Adherence to standards is a most important axiom, worthy of serious professional consideration.

Axiom 2: The Converted Data Are an Important Asset—If You Make Them Work Hard

Many professionals who become involved in selecting an integrated library system (ILS) focus a significant amount of their decision-making energies on the hardware and software choices associated with a given system.

Decision-making groups need to recognize that the hardware base and its accompanying applications programs—traditional acquisitions and demand-driven acquisitions (DDAs), circulation, reserves, ILL, and so on for the management of print materials; licensing, tracking, of eResources; Institutional Repository (sometimes called digital asset management) functions; cataloging and collaborative metadata management; and providing link resolution (support of the OpenURL standard)—will be continually upgraded and eventually replaced after some period of time. This is not to say that system functionality is not an important issue. Many library institutions maintain a specific vendor's system for up to ten years, and it is important to have a reliable and fully functional system in place. However, it is the data stored within these systems that will be carried over to whatever hardware or software system is chosen to upgrade or replace the current system.

After the irreversibility and the standards axioms, the focus shifts to data stored as records. Collectively, these records form a set of data representing various objects of interest to librarians in support of technical, public, and administrative services. These records represent things like metadata, community data, holdings information, and transaction data. The creation and ongoing maintenance of these various data files is extremely time-consuming and fraught with detail.

For these reasons, the portability of data stored as records becomes a very important consideration. Portability is enabled by two important attributes: ownership and adherence to standards. First, the library must retain ownership of its own records; second, adhering to standards specifying nationally recognized data and record structures ensures that those owned records can be migrated to newer systems should that be necessary. Failure to follow standards results in the need to reconvert or reenter records, which is a costly and time-consuming (and not terribly exciting) process. Data that adhere to national and international standards are important considerations in your decision-making process.

Axiom 3: Conversion, Maintenance, and Training Are Always Underestimated

Historically, hardware and software costs overshadow the costs associated with other considerations that are part of the entire ILS. In the 1990s, hardware was the most expensive component among all cost categories; in some cases, as much as three out of every four dollars spent were associated with hardware. Cloud computing and the mass production and distribution of small but powerful distributed computing systems has shifted the dominance of costs toward the development of sophisticated software that provides the functionality of any successful implementation. More than 75 percent of the revenues of library system vendors originate from that applications software base. So it is not unexpected for decision-making groups to place a greater emphasis on the software and less on the hardware that runs those applications.

So much emphasis and planning surrounds these critical decisions resulting in functional systems that other, very important considerations can go either unnoticed or unplanned. Converting data, maintaining systems (including hosting costs and/or hardware and software), and training staff are examples of such overlooked consideration or preparation in planning.

As mentioned earlier, conversion is an important consideration that is often difficult to plan and estimate. It also is not an exciting task from an administrative perspective. Converting records in accordance with standards represents a large commitment and often does not attract much of the technology spotlight. In some cases, decision-making groups have actually failed to recognize or budget for the costs to migrate existing records from either print or existing digital representations.

The hosting or maintenance associated with hardware and software (depending on the type solution selected) is a negotiated point between the library and the selected vendor. Maintenance can range from 8–15+ percent of the cost of the system per year. Over a ten-year life span, the cost to host or maintain a system can exceed the cost to purchase that system.

Maintenance includes both replacement and upgrade of initial hardware and software. As many professionals have experience with personal computing systems and forego services associated with hardware maintenance, this experience often translates into a less than full interest in providing such services for their ILS solutions. When one considers the impact of such a decision on the public user base, the results can be disastrous. Replacement is also a consideration that needs to be planned for. At some point new solutions are needed, and whether the current vendor is the source or whether a new procurement is called for, these replacement costs are often left unplanned.

A perfectly configured system with excellent functionality and quality-controlled databases is only as good as those who seek to use that system. Library professionals, paraprofessionals, clerical staff members, and the end user need to be trained in properly using the new system. Corporate America spends a significant portion of its revenues on developing and training its employee base. In many libraries, such training is often done by injection, osmosis, or—worse—not done at all. Injection training occurs at one time, when the system is first installed. This may be successful for those present at the training but doesn't help those who were not invited or not on staff at the time. Osmosis training occurs when learning is absorbed from others over time. It can be an effective approach if properly planned and coordinated. Vendors "train the trainers," who then pass their knowledge on to their colleagues. Some vendors are now offering new, multimodal training options, including video training or cohort training. These should be investigated, as they are a cost-effective option to traditional training methods. Canned video training sessions suffer in that they aren't customized for a particular library's workflows, but offer advantages in that they can be taken repeatedly until the material is learned, and they can be taken in segments that fits the trainee's schedule. Cohort training involves engaging users who've been through the training and are using the system, in training new users. Because the cohort trainers tend to have practical rather than theoretical experience with the system, this kind of training can be very effective.

What must be avoided is a lack of training. It is inexcusable in today's environment (particularly given some of the new training options available) but does occur in some instances. Costs or time can exceed allocated amounts, and training is often the first commodity to be sacrificed. It is a bad mistake to make. Imagine the reaction of the patron who finds that the reference librarian doesn't know every trick and nuance in searching the online catalog. Why would he or she bother to ask for help in subsequent situations? What is the net effect of such an event on the relationship between the librarian and the patron?

Another option that is strongly recommended is to plan on retraining staff approximately six months after the initial training. Again, this can be a very low-cost option with the new video-based training and can pay major benefits. Here's why: when staff is trying to learn a new system, the focus is on "How do I do my job, using this new system?" This is an entirely rational and understandable point of view. So most people learn a pathway through the system that allows them to keep the work they are assigned moving forward. But their understanding of the system at this point is limited, just as a result of lack of experience. The purpose of the retraining is to realize that after six months of day-to-day use in a production environment, users will understand how the system works and alternative ways to do things, and will feel secure that they can do their jobs, using the system. This is the time to reexpose them to the full functionality of the system and let them explore the alternative and potentially faster pathways that could be utilized. Some libraries put an element of challenge and reward in this process, soliciting recommendations on improvements that can be made to workflows after redoing the training, and awarding some kind of recognition or prize for the best suggestions that are implemented. It can prove to be a very cost-effective approach.

 ## Axiom 4: Use of Technology Will Grow to Fill the Available Capacity

The classic line uttered by the police chief in the original 1973 *Jaws* movie occurred when the chief saw the shark up close for the first time. Just after slinging some chum over the side, the shark burst out of the water, surprising the chief into proclaiming to the captain, "You're going to need a bigger boat."

The experts knew a lot about the shark: his type, his bite size, his feeding habits, and so forth, but they hadn't seen the creature up close and personal as the chief had. This can be the case with information technologies as well. Most of us are familiar with desktop devices, networked workstations, and the like arranged in rather small settings with limited numbers of concurrent users.

Library information systems provide remote, distributed, concurrent access to sizeable amounts of bibliographic and full-text information to a significant number of users. The success of introducing a new LIS, whether new or a replacement, often leads to an increase in the use of that service or system. Any system implemented should be capable of expansion without having to replace the initial central computing resources.

The key is to be able to reconfigure the initial system to accommodate increased demand, should that be the case. The experience in most libraries is that their disk storage space fills faster than expected; there is an almost constant pressure to add workstations for the library's customers to use. The newer cloud computing–based systems make this task easy in terms of effort, although it can still be costly. With these systems, additional capacity is usually added with a simple phone call to the vendor and/or by logging into the system account and requesting the capacity needed. But in either case, the shark looks larger than life!

Axiom 5: Information Technology Is the Central Nervous System of Strategy

Information technology has become a core function within the library. The library needs to have an ILS technology that provides all of the functional richness to help staff complete their jobs in a productive manner and to support users in their quest for information. At the same time, the standards-based library services platform (LSP) needs to be flexible enough so that it can quickly incorporate new technologies, as well as communicate with a diverse set of other systems—both within the parent organization and also with other libraries and organizations outside the library.

The time is long past for a LSP to act like a stand-alone system, or "silo," and ignore the need to communicate with other libraries and other systems.

Axiom 6: You Need Sociable Network Bandwidth

The most significant development in information technology over the last decade or so is data networking. Everyone is part of a network, and now almost all networks are connected. What this means is exponential connection and the power that connectivity brings. The network is global; the internet is global; and the Internet of Things (IoT) is a frequent part of today's discussions. And your neighborhood is the network. Thus, your network needs to be able to support not only the anticipated volume of transactions based on your existing types of applications, but it must be able to grow to support the multitude of devices that will be connected to it, while also supporting larger image files, audio, and video streaming applications as well as interactive events. Just as information technology is the heart of the system, so is networking bandwidth the key to connecting lifelines across great distances. Simply put, regardless of your current network speed, plan on needing more in the future. The path to more is through network components and connections that have the ability to scale to meet growing demands.

Axiom 7: Support Costs for Technology Sources and Services Are a Significant Part of a Library's Budget, Whether This Is Recognized or Not

The cost to acquire technology is often given prime consideration when planning for technology innovations within the library. In some cases, initial cost becomes a key decision point for both administrators and members of the decision-making team. What is often neglected or underemphasized is the fact that after a new system or service is first installed, much remains to be done in terms of supporting the continued successful use of that existing technology base.

Just as the initial purchase of a vehicle or a house does not signal the end of expenditures of time, effort, and monies, so too is the attention needed to support the installed ILS solution. Axiom 4 stated, "Use of technology will grow to fill the available capacity." This means that somewhere along the line, new resources will have to be committed to sustaining and growing the network infrastructure and the services behind that technology. This includes developing and training staff to maintain the new system, training staff to teach others how to maximize the capabilities of the system, and paying continued attention to upgrading components contained with the new system.

There are costs associated with all of these new ventures, and funds must be established and set aside for future needs, such as providing mobile devices (laptops and tablets), upgrading network connections to higher speeds, and upgrading servers to support increased demand for services. You might expect to keep your car for up to 10 years, but you will be changing your fluids and filters, adjusting mechanical components, replacing brake parts, and doing tune-ups all along the way. A good long-term plan identifies likely commitments and injections of funds to support such maintenance requirements. Be prepared to respond to demands for support and for new services that were not originally thought of during the initial planning stages of the project.

 ## Axiom 8: APIs Are Playing an Increasingly Important Role as Libraries Move to Embrace Web-Based Services

Everything and everyone is increasingly being connected using application programming interfaces (APIs). APIs are central to every cloud, social, and mobile computing strategy. This explosion in connected devices—in its many types, forms, and configurations (often called the Internet of Things)—permits the integration and sharing of information and Web-based services in new and interesting services.

This "API-ificaiton" is the result of mobile, social, and cloud computing and is changing the information landscape while we are watching from the sidelines. And the use of APIs allows libraries to make more of their collections and resources discoverable and visible in a variety of search engines. Libraries will increasingly be connecting with other network-based resources using APIs.

Axiom 9: We Live in a Network-Centric World

Library customers are operating at the network level (spending time online using a variety of devices and interacting with their peers, colleagues, fellow students, etc.) while libraries are primarily focused on the library itself (an institutional-centric perspective). Libraries need to understand much more about how their customers and potential customers are spending their time and what network-level tools they are using on a routine basis. The ready availability of information leads to a poverty of attention. Libraries must learn to be where their "customers" are.

 ## Axiom 10: A Library's Information Technology Budget Should Be Sizable

The costs associated with the care and feeding of the information technology within a library are significant if the library is going to provide high-quality services to those who use the virtual library. Many and perhaps a sizable majority of libraries live with really bad websites (often with the rationale that the library does not have the staff or the skills to maintain or improve the website). And the lack of trained and knowledgeable staff is a reflection of the library's budget process that fails to introduce line-item budget items either to train existing staff or to recruit talented staff to do the job. Alternatively, the library could engage a firm to maintain the library's website. In either case, tools such as analytical analysis tools should be used on a regular basis to improve the library's website.

Summary

This short list of essential axioms will hopefully prepare you and your institution to tackle the difficult challenges associated with implementing technology solutions within the context of your specific library or consortia. Your own experiences will allow you to add your personal reflections to this beginning list of axioms.

Questions to Consider

- Do you have any axioms related to library technology beyond the ten identified in this chapter?
- Are your library data visible to the Google spiders that crawl your website? Is the library catalog visible? Is your library catalog data formatted so that it is compatible with the linked data formats?
- Does your library provide sufficient budget resources so that all staff members have their technology skills upgraded each year?
- Does your library have sufficient bandwidth so that everyone's system response times are quick? Even WiFi users?
- Have you considered installing a fiber-optic connection to the internet?
- What is your library doing to be visible to your users at the network level?

Notes

1. Joseph Stilwell, *AZ Quotes*, https://www.azquotes.com/quote/836953.

The Axiom logos are reprinted using Creative Commons CCBY. Axiom 1: Best practices by Bold Yellow from the Noun Project; Axiom 2: Data transformation by Becris from the Noun Project; Axiom 3: Training by Musmellow from the Noun Project; Axiom 4: Efficiency by priyanka from the Noun Project; Axiom 5: Strategy by GD Creativ from the Noun Project; Axiom 6: Scale by Ben Davis from the Noun Project; Axiom 7: Budget by Chameleon Design from the Noun Project; Axiom 8: API by mikicon from the Noun Project; Axiom 9: Globe by Amanda from the Noun Project; Axiom 10: Pricing by Gregor Cresnar from the Noun Project.

Part IV

Future Considerations

Part IV begins with Chapter16, which explores the implications of a rapidly evolving information technology environment. Chapter 17 considers how mobile devices are impacting libraries and the services they provide.

Chapter 18 considers how digital content from libraries will become an important piece of the puzzle of future library services that are relevant in the lives of library customers.

16
Evolving Technology Trends

For more than 150 years, modern complex democracies
have depended in large measure on an industrial information economy...
In the past decade and a half we have begun to see a radical change
in the organisation of information production.
Enabled by technological change,
we are beginning to see a series of economic, social and
cultural adaptations that make possible
a radical transformation of how
we make the information environment...

—Yochai Benkler[1]

One of the undeniable facts associated with computer and communications technologies, often referred to as the information technology (IT) marketplace, is that emerging technologies are being adopted with increasing speed by the marketplace; thus, the need for librarians to be aware of some of the more significant technologies trends likely to impact libraries in both the near term and the longer range future. These technologies will challenge libraries to address issues such as service delivery, how a library can add value for its patrons, and how to support new ways to deliver information to the library customer, wherever that customer is located. As current emerging technologies are adopted, they will be replaced by even newer emerging technologies. Therefore, any list of technology trends will be constantly evolving and changing over time. This chapter discusses those trends that are likely to impact libraries in the next three to five years.

The internet is not included as a trend, as it is a reality, but it should also not be ignored. As a carrier of data of all sorts, the ongoing evolution of the internet is a fundamental component of many projections of the future. The internet is impacting libraries directly as more students and other individuals visit websites to find bibliographic citations and the full text of journal articles to complete projects and other homework assignments, rather than visiting a library.[2] Academic libraries report declining use of reference services, and annual circulation figures for books and these same statistics are also falling in public libraries.

Digital technology is transforming business models in almost every sector of the world for three fundamental reasons:

1. Digital signals can be transmitted without error, regardless of the distance involved, unlike analog signals.

2. Digital signals can be replicated indefinitely without any degradation.

3. Once the digital network infrastructure is in place, digital content can be communicated at almost zero incremental cost. A digital task (with such low marginal cost) will have immediate and sustaining impact compared to the costs of any traditional analog task.

It is these three fundamental properties that drive the transformation enabled by ubiquitous digital technology.

Technology Trends

For more than a decade, a series of *Horizon Reports* have identified six technology trends that industry leaders have recognized as both important and likely to impact organizations in a significant way.[3] Table 16.1 points out these six trends over the course of the last eight years. Looking back at these predictions, it is clear that the *Horizon Report* does a good job of pinpointing technology trends with a fair degree of accuracy. Thus, it would be prudent to look for future editions of the *Horizon Report* to see what new technologies are on the horizon (pun intended!). Jason Vaughn explores the topic of innovation in libraries, especially innovation with a strong technological underpinning.[4]

IFLA Trend Report

The International Federation of Library Associations and Institutions (IFLA) Trend Report has identified five high trends that are shaping the global information environment and that will have lasting impact on libraries specifically and more generally on societies around the world:[5]

1. **New technologies will both expand and limit who has access to information**—Those with digital literacy skills will do better than those who lack these skills, leading to a "digital skills gap."

2. **Online education will democratize and disrupt global education**—Traditional "classroom style" learning is being threatened by online education resources and courses sometimes referred to as massive open online courses, or MOOCs.

3. **The boundaries of privacy and data protection are being redefined**— More and more data are being routinely gathered by every website people visit, leading to concerns about privacy and trust in an online world.

4. **Hyper-connected societies will listen to and empower new voices and groups**—Opportunities abound for collective activities,

TABLE 16.1. Horizon Reports Technology Trends

2010	2011	2012	2013
Mobile computing	eBooks	Mobile apps	Massively open online courses
Open content	Mobiles	Tablet computing	Tablet computing
eBooks	Augmented reality	Game-based Learning	Games & gamification
Augmented reality	Game-based learning	Learning analytics	Learning analytics
Gesture-based computing	Gesture-based computing	Gesture-based computing	3D printing
Visual data analysis	Learning analytics	Internet of Things	Wearable technology
2014	2015	2016	2017
Flipped classroom	Bring your own device (BYOD)	Bring your own device (BYOD)	Adaptive learning technologies
Learning analytics	Flipped classroom	Learning analytics	Mobile learning
3D printing	Makerspaces	Virtual/augmented reality	Internet of Things
Games & gamification	Wearable technology	Makerspaces	Next-generation LMS
Quantified self	Adaptive learning technologies	Affective computing	Artificial intelligence
Virtual assistants	Internet of Things	Robotics	Natural user interfaces

Source: EDUCAUSE Horizon Report: 2019 Higher Education Edition. Available at https://library.educause.edu/resources/2019/2/horizon-report-preview-2019.

with the prospect for increased transparency among governments that embrace open access to public sector data.

5. **The global information economy will be transformed by new technologies**—The proliferation of mobile devices, billions of sensors (that gather and report data) connected to the network (sometimes called the Internet of Things, or IoT), and the digital infrastructure are transforming the global information economy. These connected devices will provide for[6]

- environmental monitoring—think smart appliances;
- smart clothing and smart accessories—think health monitoring;
- beacons using Bluetooth low-energy technology; and
- near field communications—allow a user to download additional information and resources about photos, paintings, videos, displays, and so forth.

Another interesting and compelling perspective is offered by Kevin Kelly, information technology industry guru and the editor of *Wired* magazine, in his book *The Inevitable*.[7] Kevin posits that the constant change that pervades our society around the world is being fueled by technology and that this change is being accelerated year after year in an exponential manner. In order to represent this relentless change, Kelly identifies twelve verbs that are shaping and accelerating actions. These important continuous and intermingling verbs include *becoming, cognifying, flowing, screening, accessing, sharing, filtering, remixing, interacting, tracking, questioning,* and *beginning.* This is a great read, and once you immerse yourself with its contents, you will begin to envision new and interesting services you could be offering your library customers.

Cognifying

Artificial intelligence is software that has the potential to learn and improve. Once the domain of science fiction books, artificial intelligence is making massive strides in delivering systems that will be the cause of significant change—consider driverless cars and trucks. The improvements in the field of artificial intelligence are the result of the availability of parallel computing, very large data sets (often called "big data"), and improved algorithms.

Industrial robots, powerful and capable machines, have always been quite expensive (a half million dollars or so) to install and maintain. Yet recently an affordable robot ($25,000), called *Baxter*, has been introduced, and this development is significant because Baxter is aware of its surroundings and can easily learn new tasks.

Singapore's Agency for Science, Technology and Research has developed the Autonomous Robotic Shelf Scanning System (AuRoSS) that scans the RFID tags in books, looking for misshelved items.[8] It generates a report of misplaced items every morning after a night crawling the stacks.

Flowing

Increasingly people are operating at the network level, using social media apps and other tools to help them find, organize, discuss, and share interesting content. As a result, copies of ideas, data, stories, photos, and audio/video files are created and shared using a variety of tools.

In the first age of computers, as Marshall McLuhan has noted, new technologies imitate the medium they replace. Thus, the first Macintosh and Windows-based computers used the "office" metaphor with its files, folders placed on the "desktop." In the second age of computing, the Web helps us organize "pages" of information with its links and relevance rankings. And as we move into the third age of computing, we are dealing with flows and streams. We watch streamed movies from Netflix and streamed videos from YouTube and are notified of Twitter messages and Facebook postings. Kelly suggests we are moving from "fixity to flows."[9]

The number of people connecting to the internet, using their smartphones, tablets, and computers, will continue to grow for the foreseeable future, and in addition, an increasing number of other things are being connected to the internet using computer chips, RFID tags, embedded sensors, beacons, and other types of devices. These devices transmit across networks (the internet in most cases), creating informational feedback loops. Kevin Kelly calls these feedback loops virtuous circles.[10] These virtuous circles feed on themselves, so prices decline and quality improves significantly over time. In computer chip technology, this phenomenon is referred to as "Moore's law."

The Death of Moore's Law?

In 2019, a number of expert resources (including *MIT Technology Review* and *ARS Technica*) have indicated that Moore's law—which was in some manner based on observations of actual component density and other factors—has run its course, with some declaring the law "dead." Still, Moore's law is a useful concept in understanding the potential for all technology to scale over time. More reading can be found here:

- Tim Simonite, "Moore's Law Is Dead. Now What?," *MIT Technology Review*, May 13, 2016, https://www.technologyreview.com/s/601441/moores-law-is-dead-now-what.

- Peter Bright, "Moore's Law Really Is Dead This Time," *Ars Technica*, February 10, 2016, https://arstechnica.com/information-technology/2016/02/moores-law-really-is-dead-this-time.

The glue that connects all of these devices to the internet is TCP/IP software. TCP/IP provides telephone services via the internet (called VOIP—Voice over Internet Protocol), desktop videoconferencing, audio and video broadcasting, and on-demand movies (streaming). The reason for all of this activity is that using TCP/IP significantly decreases the complexity and therefore the cost of providing the service. Having one network communication protocol means that *from* anything, you can communicate *to* anywhere.

Metcalfe's law, which indicates that the value of a network increases exponentially as more participants are included, results in what is sometimes called the network effect—value rises exponentially as the number of devices increases. Today, because everybody is linked, more goods and services gain their value from this widespread network effect.

One of the implications of making connections to all of these devices is that a wide range of services is now available without regard to distance. No longer is it necessary to visit a bank branch; to physically be present to attend a university; to call a broker to execute a stock transaction; or to obtain a cost quote for insurance, a product, or a service. All of this—and much, much more—is now being accomplished using the internet. Consequently, a library must consider and identify ways that it can provide some or all of its services without requiring the customer to physically visit the library. Whether it is document delivery, online 24/7 reference services, borrowing and loaning of materials, or providing access to online databases, libraries must change the way they provide services.

> In the networked age, in the digital era, power and value lies in the connections.
> It's exactly the process of thesis, antithesis, and synthesis—
> the search for new and different connections—
> where exponential power and value can be found.
> —Carly Fiorina[11]

Accessing

As more and more business is conducted over the internet, organizations face the problem of making their applications work with those of their suppliers and customers. This process of having applications communicate with one another is called integration or systems integration. There are several approaches to integration, but they can be grouped into three categories:

Custom integration—The two parties agree on a communications standard or protocol and write any needed data conversions, and the two applications are linked. The obvious problem with this approach is that, as the number of applications or partners increase, the number of possible data protocols and custom data conversion begins to increase—seemingly at an exponential rate. Clearly this is an expensive process.

Middleware product—The organization could purchase a "middleware product," which establishes a common communications standard. The organization simply writes a data conversion routine (software program) for each application it wishes to integrate. The problems with this approach are threefold: first, the middleware software is not inexpensive; second, the organization must have, or contract to an outside third party, the necessary computer programming resources to create and maintain these data conversion programs; and third, the organization must convince each of its customers or suppliers that they should adopt the same middleware software product.

Web services—Web services are applications that have been enabled to use a standard universal language to send data and instructions to one another, with no data translation or conversion required. Because the internet is being used, the connection problems are minimized or eliminated. To date, people using a browser view most data and information that is accessible via the internet; thus, the internet can be thought of as "people-centric." To be used by an application within an organization, the information must either be "scraped" from the screen or sent by the information supplier (the variety of nonstandard formats depends on the number of information suppliers).

Rather than relying on the brute-force, custom approach or using proprietary middleware software, web services rely on an open, standards-based approach that, at least in theory, obviates the disadvantages of the first two options. Some examples of a web service are listed here:

- A credit checking service using a person's social security number
- A purchasing service that automatically buys something when given an item code and a quantity
- A stock quote service for a particular ticker symbol
- Paying library fines with a credit card

Let's look at a library-based example to better understand some of the possibilities that could be achieved by effectively using web services. Consider a library that wishes to place an order for several books (or whatever). The library may enter the information into an Acquisitions module that is a part of its library information system (LIS). The LIS will then send the order electronically using an electronic data interchange (EDI) protocol to the vendor of choice. Alternatively, the library can connect to several vendor sites to discover the pricing and availability of the items they wish to order—a fairly time-consuming process.

> **Tip!** The majority of electronic data interchange (EDI) implementations between commercial-based LIS and book and serial vendors are a one-off, custom implementation using an EDI-based standard as a starting point. Thus, a minimal amount of benefits accrue to either party.

Using web services, a different approach would be taken. The LIS vendors, or the library itself if it has the programming resources to develop and maintain its own systems, could set up a price/availability, comparison-shopping option within the Acquisitions module. This optional comparison-shopping feature would then automatically check with several vendors about price and availability for the items of interest. The results would then be displayed so the library could make a decision about where to place the order.

Each book and serial vendor or other suppliers could set up a Web-based pricing and availability service. Vendors would include information about the associated application programming interface (API) so that libraries can request a service and return the desired information.

Web services are likely to be at the heart of the next generation of distributed services. Here's why:

- **The internet**—The internet links millions and millions of applications and services in increasingly new and creative ways.

- **Interoperability**—Web services interact with other web services using APIs.

- **Low barrier to entry**—Understanding web services is easy and straightforward. They offer a more flexible or loosely coupled way of linking applications. In addition, free toolkits are being provided by a host of vendors that allow software programmers the ability to quickly develop and deploy a new web service. Web services are a way to link existing applications rather than a platform for new development.

- **Ubiquity**—Web services are based on the foundational building blocks of the internet—Hypertext Transfer Protocol (HTTP) and Extensible Markup Language (XML). Any device that supports these fundamental technologies can access web services. Even WiFi-based services can be provided using Web services.

- **Industry support**—Every vendor and entrepreneur is involved with extending web services. The use of standard-based services lowers the entry cost for new web services.

The book or serial vendor would verify the accuracy of the information using authentication procedures through passwords, public keys, or some other mechanism. The vendor may extend to the library a higher than normal discount because of the amount of prior spending or the presence of a contractual agreement between the vendor and the library.

One of the interesting side effects of web services is that the range of services can be extended beyond the simple sending and receiving of

EDI-based messages. After the order has been placed, the Acquisitions module could automatically search for and download a cataloging record (MARC, XML, etc.). Once the library has received the order and invoice, the module could automatically alert the library's parent organization's accounting system that funds have been expended and that the book or serial vendor should be paid. The possibilities for new and unforeseen applications that will emerge are only limited by our imagination. Obviously, in such an environment the number of transaction messages moving about the internet will increase the amount of network traffic.

There are, however, some issues that must be addressed before web services become more popular:

- **Reliability**—To have value and to attract and retain users, web services must be available and behave in a consistent manner day after day. What happens when a web service is unavailable for some period of time?

- **Security**—Will the web service use encryption plus authentication to improve the level of security? Will the authentication process identify the required level of security for a transaction to occur?

- **Transactions**—In a closed, client-server–based system, a transaction is performed once the appropriate records have been locked so that another transaction does not alter the record or data field until the original transaction is completed. Such an approach will not work using web services because transactions may span minutes, hours, or even days.

- **Scalability**—Supporting distributed web services will require system monitoring tools to make sure the system can support the volume of transactions, recognizing that there will peaks and valleys of demand.

- **Accountability**—How are web service users charged? How long can a user use a web service for a specific charge?

- **Testing**—When a system is made up of many distributed web services (some services may be located around the World), testing becomes even more challenging. Will web services be quality assured and certified?

Sharing

The internet is a happening place. The amount of sharing, collaborating, cooperating, participating, observing, engaging, lurking, discussing, and so forth is simply amazing. For example, more than 1 billion Creative Commons permissions were granted in 2015. Look at the number of postings on Facebook and Twitter, the sharing of photos on Snapchat and Flickr, the contributions to Wikipedia, and the number of blogs and websites that people subscribe to, as an indication that people are simply using all of these technology-based tools as a way to engage with other people.

A makerspace is an informal workshop environment where people gather to create prototypes of objects in a collaborative, do-it-yourself setting. A makerspace provides a range of tools including 3D modeling software, a 3D printer, and other tools, as well as learning experiences to assist people in the creation of their ideas. As libraries increasingly reposition themselves as learning commons that promote curiosity, creativity, and discovery, many academic and public libraries are setting aside space for makerspaces.

The *MakeSchools Higher Education Alliance* provides great resources and news about projects in academic institutions, and demonstrates how makerspaces lead to active learning, creativity, and cross-disciplinary approaches in higher education.[12]

Filtering

The exponential growth and availability of data, often called "big data," has led to the recognition of three important activities: capture, curation, and analysis. Some academic libraries are becoming active participants in the overall research process in their colleges and universities by creating research data services that assist campus researchers in data curation, data curation and storage tools, archiving, developing ontologies and metadata schemes, and aggregating data from a variety of sources.

Some libraries have been exploring the use of big data with great success. Some projects have put together library transaction data with student demographic and student performance data in order to identify possible relationships between use of library collections, services, and student success. Some of these more notable library big data projects include those at Hong Kong Baptist University,[13] the Library Impact Data Project in the United Kingdom,[14] Wollongong University in Australia,[15] and the University of Minnesota.[16] Typically the analysis uses standard statistical analysis packages such as Statistical Package for Social Sciences (SPSS), but other more advanced tools are optionally available.

Yale University's *Robots Reading Vogue* project created a humanities digitized database consisting of 400,000 pages and 2,700 book covers that is used by faculty and students from several disciplines, using text mining and topic modeling software.[17] The *HathiTrust Digitized Library Big Data Project* uses text mining tools to collect, connect, and analyze both the full text as well as the accompanying metadata.[18] The *Library Data Labs Project* in the United Kingdom analyzed library data from twenty-three universities to garner insights into library-related services, using appropriate data visualizations.[19]

While using analytics to investigate the content and relationships of big data, libraries must ensure that the privacy of individuals is protected and preserved. Firms such as CIVICTechnology, Orange Boy, and others routinely receive patron registration and circulation transaction files from a customer library in order to prepare a detailed market segmentation analysis (who has a library card and where do they live? Who is using the library (borrowing materials), and who is not? What kinds of library materials is each type of market segment borrowing?).

Remixing

Digital content can be sniped, cut, or "borrowed" quite easily, whether it is text, audio, video, photos, or digitized materials. There are thousands of apps to assist the individual in borrowing and adding their own "two cents worth" and then this "new" creation is shared using social media.

Devices with natural user interfaces accept input in the form of taps, swipes, resizing, hand and arm movements, gesture recognition, and natural language. Already, about three-fourths of smartphone users use voice commands (think Siri for Apple products).

Aside from Google, Apple, Amazon, and many other companies, researchers at universities around the world are developing a wide range of natural user interfaces that will work in a wide range of situations and as training aids. This means that the amount of "borrowing" of a portion of a blog post, tweet, song, video, and other content will be shared with others as the user interface becomes more intuitive and easy to use.

Interacting

Technology is allowing us to interact with others and with digital content in new and interesting ways. As more sensors are added to devices, the amount of information continues to increase. Sensors in our smartphones provide GPS location awareness, vertical and horizontal orientation, and other services. *Fitbit* and offerings from many other companies track our bodies' temperature, heart rate, number of steps, and so forth, to allow us to more easily track our activity levels.

Augmented reality (AR) strives to blend reality with the virtual environment by including video, images, and audio into real-world spaces, allowing users to interact with both digital and physical objects. One popular augmented reality is the apps provided by various libraries, museums, and other institutions that provide a historical perspective as the person walks around town or on campus. Point your smartphone at a restaurant, and you might see a summary of the reviews and what's on the menu.

Virtual reality (VR) enables users to become immersed in a computer-simulated alternate world where sensor experiences occur. A head-mounted device such as Oculus Rift or Google Cardboard is used to deliver the experience in a dedicated simulation room or space.

The University of Oklahoma Libraries has used virtual reality in their Galileo's World Exhibition that allows participants to view the universe as Galileo thought it existed as well as a view of the universe as it exists today (using images from the National Aeronautics and Space Administration [NASA]).[20] The University of Oklahoma Libraries then expanded VR by creating the Oklahoma Virtual Academic Laboratory to show users how to use this technology in their teaching and research activities. The end result is that the use of VR within the library positions itself as the point to engage with, learn about, and experience state-of-the-art technologies.

Tracking

The amount of direct and indirect surveillance or tracking of our daily lives is simply staggering. Consider just a small sampling of the devices and systems that track our movements in a typical day: highway traffic monitoring (and the payment of tolls); air and train itineraries; closed-circuit television cameras in cities, airports, buildings; smart home sensors; home security systems; car movements; loyalty cards; our online purchases; cell phone location; utility consumption; and on and on and on.

So there is much to think about and to track over time. The technology and the ways in which technology is being integrated into new products and services is a never-ending reality. And the speed with which technology is being adopted is increasing year after year.

Emerging Technologies

Sometimes it is difficult to resist the temptation of the siren call of emerging technologies. A new technology or the latest iteration of an existing product sounds so good that some people simply cannot resist. People will line up for days or hours to be among the first to have the latest and greatest. The bragging rights are simply too important to cast a jaundiced eye and consider other alternatives.

Here are some of the more interesting emerging technologies (as of early 2019):

- Blockchain
- Internet of our bodies—self-monitoring technologies moving closer to and even inside the human body
- Digital swag—purchases of content from within a game or app
- Self-driving cars and trucks
- Artificial intelligence robots
- Drones (that deliver)
- Next-generation (5G) high-bandwidth networks
- Facial recognition to identify a person
- Immersive (virtual) reality
- Video chat messages

All or some of these technologies may sound really appealing to you, and you can hardly wait. But wait!

Rather than focusing on a specific appealing technology, you should first be focusing on the needs of your customers (those that visit the library and those that choose to use online services) and of your staff members. What specific problem will a new emerging technology potentially solve, and is that new technology the best (and most cost effective) over the long term?

Clearly it is important to recognize that new, emerging technologies may have a role to play, but any technology must be viewed as a tool to assist the library in solving problems for its customers and to provide great services (rather than being an end in itself).

Summary

Attempting to keep up with technology can be a daunting task. Although it is important to systematically review the library literature, it is equally important to spend some time reviewing the technology literature as well. Reading current awareness publications and periodically visiting some of the technology-oriented websites can assist in the process of trying to see the big picture.[21] Connect with people, whether it's participating electronically with a discussion group, personally with colleagues via email, or attending professional conferences. Observe yourself in terms of what you are personally paying attention to and how your life is changing as a result of a new technology. And never forget to challenge your assumptions. Why do you think something is or is not going to change?

The fundamental evaluation criteria for any new technology is to make sure that it is going to provide value to the library's customers (as opposed to being some really cool or "sexy" new technology). For a number of years Michael Stephens has been warning about the dangers of "technolust." Michael suggests that "technolust combines an irrational love for new technology combined with unrealistic expectations of the value" it will bring to the library.[22] Michael's recommendations for overcoming "technolust" and planning to implement technologies that will add value for customers include

- forgetting about control;
- involving users in testing software;
- maintaining transparency—a key element;
- finding and using tools that fit;
- creating opportunities to test technologies;
- providing opportunities for learning;
- trying something and then figuring out how to make it better;
- planning on planning;
- having a mission statement for everything; and
- evaluating your services.

Questions to Consider

- What emerging information technologies do you think will have an impact on libraries in the coming five years?
- In what ways has your library embraced digital technologies in the past year or two that are noticeable to your users?
- Can you foresee how the Internet of Things is likely to impact your library?
- Would you suggest an important trend or two that the IFLA did not identify in their Trend Report?
- Has your library converted to RFID tags yet? If not, what are the reasons for failing to do so?
- In what ways is your library moving to embrace web services?
- Is your library suffering from an acute case of "Technolust"?

Suggested Web Resources

World Wide Web Consortium has information about Web-based standard activities at http://www.w3c.org.

Organization for the Advancement of Structured Information Standards (OASIS) has cataloged more than 100 standard vocabulary definition projects at their website: http://www.xml.org.

Notes

1. Yochai Benkler, *The Wealth of Networks: How Social Production Transforms Markets and Freedom* (New Haven, CT: Yale University Press, 2007).

2. Philip M. Davis and Suzanne A. Cohen, "The Effect of the Web on Undergraduate Citation Behavior 1996–1999," *Journal of the American Society for Information Science and Technology* 52, no. 4 (April 2001): 309–14.

3. To download one or more of the Horizon Reports, visit https://www.nmc.org/nmc-horizon.

4. Jason Vaughn, "Technological Innovation: Perceptions and Definitions," *Library Technology Reports* 49, no. 7 (October 2013): 1–74.

5. International Federation of Library Associations and Institutions (IFLA), *Riding the Waves or Caught in the Tide? Insights from the IFLA Trend Report* (Brussels: IFLA, 2016), https://trends.ifla.org/insights-document.

6. Jim Hahn, "The Internet of Things: Mobile Technology and Location Services in Libraries," *Library Technology Reports* 53, no. 1 (January 2017): 1–28.

7. Kevin Kelly, *The Inevitable: Understanding the 12 Technological Forces That Will Shape Our Future* (New York: Viking, 2016).

8. Danny Lewis, "This Robot Librarian Locates Haphazardly Placed Books," *Smithsonian*, June 14, 2016, https://www.smithsonianmag.com/smart-news/robot-librarian-locates-haphazardly-placed-books-180959381/.

9. Kevin Kelly, *New Rules for the New Economy: 10 Radical Strategies for a Connected World* (New York: Viking, 1998).

10. Kevin Kelly, *The Inevitable*, 67.

11. Carly Fiorina, *Thesis, Antithesis, Synthesis: Policymaking in an Internet Age.* 2001 Progress & Freedom Foundation Aspen Summit, August 19, 2001, http://www.pff.org/aspensummit/aspen2001/Fiorinaspeech.htm.

12. For more information about the MakeSchools Higher Education Alliance, visit http://make.xsead.cmu.edu.

13. Shun Han Wong and T. D. Webb, "Uncovering Meaningful Correlation between Student Academic Performance and Library Material Usage," *College & Research Libraries* (July 2011): 361–70.

14. Graham Stone, "Library Impact Data Project: Looking for the Link between Library Usage and Student Attainment," *College & Research Libraries* 72, no. 4 (November 2013): 546–59.

15. Brian Cox and Margie Jantti, "Discovering the Impact of Library Use and Student Performance," *EDUCAUSE Review Online* (July 18, 2012): 1–9. See also, Brian Cox and Margi Jantti, "Capturing Business Intelligence Required for Targeted Marketing, Demonstrating Value, and Driving Process Improvement," *Library & Information Science Research* 34, no. 4 (2012): 308–16; and Margie Jantti and Jennifer Heath, "What Role for Libraries in Learning Analytics?," *Performance Measurement and Metrics* 17, no. 2 (2016): 203–10.

16. Krista Soria, Jan Fransen, and Shane Nackerud, "Library Use and Undergraduate Student Outcomes: New Evidence for Students Retention and Academic Success," *Portal: Libraries and the Academy* 13, no. 2 (2013): 147–64.

17. Daniel Dollar, Lindsay King, Peg Knight, and Peter Leonard, "Data Mining on Vendor-Digitized Collections," *2014 Charleston Conference*, November 7, 2014, https://2014charlestonconference.sched.com/event/1vfY1sC.

18. Jodi Heckel, "Project Will Help Researchers Explore Big Data in HathiTrust Digitized Library," *Illinois News New Bureau*, February 23, 2016, https://news.illinois.edu/blog/view/6367/331211.

19. Siobhan Burke, *Transforming Our Library Support Services*, Joint Information Systems Committee (JISC), October 17, 2016, https://www.jisc.ac.uk/rd/projects/transforming-library-support-services.

20. Carl Grant, "Do You See What I'm Saying? Why Libraries Should Be Embracing Virtual Reality," *Thoughts from Carl Grant* (blog), January 9, 2017, http://thoughts.care-affiliates.com/2017/01/do-you-see-what-im-saying-why-libraries.html.

21. Roy Tenant, "Technology Decision-Making: A Guide for the Perplexed," *Library Journal* (April 15, 2000): 30.

22. Michael Stephens, "Taming Technolust: Ten Steps for Planning in a 2.0 World," *Reference & User Services Quarterly* 47, no. 4 (Summer 2008): 314–17.

17
Mobile Devices

Ah, the good old days when we ignored each other
with books instead of smartphones.

—darrickmaureen[1]

The ubiquitous device of our times is clearly the smartphone. Almost every American owns a cell phone, and according to a recent Pew Research survey (2018), smartphone ownership is now 78 percent, up from 35 percent in 2013. Slightly more than 50 percent of Americans own a tablet computer, and ownership of desktop computers and eReaders remains fairly constant at 73 percent and 25 percent, respectively.[2] An annual survey conducted by the US National Center for Health Statistics indicates that almost half of American homes rely solely on cell phones and have discontinued use of their landline telephone service.[3] And low-income people typically rely on smartphones for day-to-day internet tasks, as they may lack desktops or laptops.[4]

Given the many wireless networks, it is not surprising that American rely on wireless devices to perform a wide range of activities. Eight in ten Americans surveyed indicated they access the internet daily, using their smartphones or tablets (two-thirds go online multiple times per day). These same individuals indicate that they are active on social media that allow them to stay in touch with people that are important to them.[5] To say that consumers are enthusiastic about these digital devices is a massive understatement. More than two-thirds of consumers feel it is important to have the latest and greatest device, much to the pleasure of the manufacturers (think Apple and Google Android devices) and service providers (consider AT&T, Sprint, Verizon, and others). People are spending more time online shopping; using social media to share information and to engage with other family members, friends, and online associates; searching for information; getting directions and a map for a destination; playing games; texting; and so much more. One mobile designer suggested four types of mobile interaction:[6]

- Check-in/status—"I want to stay current about something important to me, so I frequently check the status."

- Edit/create—"I need to accomplish something now that can't wait."
- Explore/play—"I am bored and want to spend some time playing."
- Look up/find—"I want to find an answer to something now."

Clearly handheld digital devices are not a flash-in-the-pan event, but rather are a sustaining and expanding reality that libraries of all types must recognize and embrace. This means that libraries must be able to deliver digital services that are compatible with mobile devices from the get-go and not considered an afterthought. Convenience and being able to provide 24/7 access to resources and services should be key motivators for libraries. There are two things a library must do to ensure it is providing responsive digital services—a website that is compatible with handheld digital devices as well as providing one or more apps that run on a smartphone. An *app*, short for "application," is software designed to run on a smartphone and other mobile devices. In many cases, a patron can accomplish the same task with a mobile-compatible website, although the app may provide a better and more intuitive experience.

Responsive Website

A responsive web design ensures the web page looks good regardless of the screen size of the device. A responsive Web design acknowledges that a web browser can (and frequently is) resized by the user, who may also change the font size, thus making the web browser a dynamic medium. If a website is not responsive, then the content will disappear (or be cropped) when the user makes the browser window smaller or larger. Designing a responsive website is significantly easier if a modern content management system (CMS) such as WordPress (used on more than a quarter of all websites), Drupal, DSpace, Fedora, or openCMS, among a host of other options, is used. A content management system separates the content from the user interface so that the content can be pushed (or pulled) in a form that is best for the device that will display the content.[7]

Note that in the next decade almost every website is going to change drastically. Today a website relies on an individual to decide to visit (typically as a result of a Google search), and thus the content is "pulled" back to the individual. The future is all about "push-based" content appearing before we even think of searching for it. This is especially true today for such "platforms" as Facebook, Pinterest, Snapchat, Flickr, and a host of others. Increasingly, we are receiving notifications about events and content from friends and colleagues that we can immediately take action on (decide to explore or ignore).

Apps

Apps, short for application software, are ubiquitous and seemingly do everything, whether the app is found on your smartphone, iPad, tablet, or laptop computer. The use of apps is having a significant impact on how people spend their time and what technology is being used while people are online and using either a wireless network or the internet. Attesting to the popularity of the app is the fact that both the Apple App Store and Google Play have over 4.4 million apps available (as of August 2019 for download and that over 500 billion apps have been downloaded from both sites.

The Basics

The two dominant mobile operating systems, iOS (from Apple) and Android (from Google), have such a large market share that it is safe to ignore the offerings from other suppliers (Windows Phone from Microsoft, Symbian from Nokia, among several other also-rans). The iOs operating system, developed by Apple, is used by devices such as the iPhone, iPod Touch, iPad, and Apple TV. The user of these devices accomplishes things by touching the screen with such gestures as tap, swipe, pinch, and expand. Android, an open-source operating system developed and enhanced by Google, runs on various brands of handheld electronic devices, smartphones, games consoles, and televisions. It allows for the same direct manipulation of the touchscreen as Apple's iOS.

Many app developers work to ensure that their app runs on both platforms in order to maximize market share (and revenues). Both Google and Apple work hard trying to convince developers to write apps only for their operating system platform.

An ecosystem is an important mobile technology concept and describes how various types of apps work simultaneously on a variety of platforms and devices. Differences exist between a native app and a web app:

- **A native app** has been designed to operate using a specific operating system and hardware, and the app is downloaded from an app store.[8]

- **A mobile web app** operates from inside a mobile web browser, using such standards as HTML5 and CSS3 (Cascading Style Sheets). In many cases, features available on a native app are not available when using the mobile web app.

Jakob Nielson and Raluca Budiu found in a usability study that users perform better with native apps than with a mobile optimized website.[9]

One of the real benefits that arises from using an app is that the same app can operate on all of your various devices, and the app will keep all of the data in synch. This means that the user's data is available anywhere, anytime, providing they have online access. Michael Levin has identified three features of the multidevice user experience that are important: (1) consistency—functionality of the app is available regardless of the device being used, (2) continuity—the synching of data across all devices means that the user is always "up to date," and (3) complementary—the user experience is agnostic in terms of the device being used.[10]

The concept of an ecosystem will expand as digital devices with communication capabilities (sometimes called the Internet of Things) continue to explode. Devices are being embedded in clothing and on wristbands (think Fitbit), scattered across farming fields (to alert farmers of the need to water or add fertilizer), and so forth. The ecosystem is built on the foundation of technologies that are built in to smartphones, tablets, and other handheld devices including cameras (still and video), microphone, accelerometer, gyroscope, compass, GPS, WiFi, and cellular connectivity, Bluetooth, and near field communication capabilities, data storage, and much more.[11] App developers are able to build on these technologies to provide some really amazing mobile computing experiences.

Popular Apps

Based on a number of recent surveys, the most popular apps include:

1. Facebook
2. YouTube
3. Facebook Messenger
4. Google Search
5. Google Play
6. Google Maps
7. Pandora Radio
8. Gmail
9. Instagram
10. iTunes Music
11. Apple Maps
12. Yahoo Stocks
13. Amazon Mobile
14. Twitter
15. Pinterest

Other app categories that will likely be of interest for library staff members and their customers include social media apps, productivity apps, communication apps, content creation apps, note-taking apps, multimedia apps, research apps, reading apps, and library-focused apps.

Social Media Apps

Aside from the very popular social media apps noted above, other social media apps include the following:

- Sharing photos—Flickr
- Writing your blog—WordPress
- Managing social media content—Social Flow

Productivity Apps

Productivity apps allow you to share resources with others while you are collaborating. Some of the more popular productivity apps are listed here:

- Managing files in the cloud—WeTransfer, Dropbox, Box, Google Drive
- Managing To-Do Lists—Todo, Paperless, Wunderlist, Clear
- Managing calendars—Fantastical 2, Calendars by Readdle
- Accessing your desktop remotely—LogMeIn

Communications Apps

Communication apps to consider:

- Audio and video calls—Skype
- One-on-one or group video chats—Google Hangout
- Instant messages—imo

- Text messaging—WhatsApp, GroupMe
- Location check-in—Foursquare

Content Creation Apps

The following content creation apps might be of value:

- Creating presentations—Keynote, SlideShark Presentation, Haiku Deck
- Create interactive books—Book Creator, iBooks Author
- Screencasting—Explain Everything, Doceri Interactive Whiteboard
- Creating 3D designs—123D Design, Makies FabLab, Thingiverse
- Curating web content—Flipboard, Scoop.it

Notes and Writing Apps

Notes and writing apps to consider:

- Taking/organizing notes—Evernote, OneNote
- Capturing citations and managing bibliographies—Papers 3, Mendeley, ZotPad
- Voice recording—iTalk, Notability
- Speech recognition—Dragon Dictation
- Document scanner—JotNot Pro
- Mind mapping—MindMeister

Multimedia Apps

Some of the more popular multimedia apps:

- Visiting museums—MoMA, Guggenheim Bilbao, Love Art (National Gallery in London)
- Viewing art—Art Envi Deluxe, Behance
- Drawing—Bamboo Paper, Adobe Ideas
- Create comic books—ComicBook, Comic Life, Strip Designer
- Creating photo collages—Diptic, Layout, FrameMagic
- Editing photos—Photoshop Express, Photogene 4, Photo Editor
- Editing movies—iMovie
- Identifying music—SoundHound, Shazam
- Streaming music—Pandora Radio, iTunes Radio, Spotify Music
- Composing music—GarageBand,
- Creating sounds—Bloom HD, NodeBeat, TonePad
- Streaming video—Air Video, AirVid

- Free educational content—iTunes U, TuneSpace, Khan Academy, Udemy
- Listening to podcasts—Podcasts, Downcast, Pocket Casts

Research Apps

Research apps of note:

- Answer questions—Wolfram Alpha, Articles (Wikipedia)
- Private search engine—DuckDuckGo
- Dictionaries—Merriam-Webster Dictionary, Languages, WordReference
- Learning a language—Duolingo, Brainscape
- Translate a language—Google Translate
- Movies—Flixster, IMDb Movies and TV
- Finding journal articles—BrowZine, arXiv, and arXiv Mobile

Reading Apps

Reading apps to consider:

- eBook readers—Kindle, Nook, Kobo, Google Play Books, iBooks, MegaReader
- Reading/annotating documents—GoodReader 4, iAnnotate
- Saving web pages—Instapaper, Pocket, Readability
- Reading community—Goodreads
- Short-form books—TED Books

Library-Focused Apps

Apps that go beyond the library catalog:

- The Orange County Library System *Shake It!* provides a suggestion for something to read, watch, or listen to. Want another suggestion? Give it a shake!
- The University of Oklahoma's *Nav App* assists users in navigating the 400,00-square-foot system.
- Barcode scanning—RedLaser, NeoReader (QR code reader).
- Digital Library Card—Capira Technologies
- Kiosks—Kiosk Pro

The typical library app allows customers to conduct a catalog search, use a map to find a library, access various eResources, see a calendar of programs and events, use a Ask-a-Librarian service, manage their account, download eBooks, use a stack map to find an item in the library's collection, and more.

A group of libraries developed an app called SimplyE that provides an easy-to-use interface that will assist the user in finding eBooks, facilitate borrowing of eBooks, and allow reading borrowed eBooks on the same device, thus simplifying a many-step process. Any library can download and provide access to the SimplyE app.[12]

Boopsie conducted a survey of libraries that found that about 15 percent of libraries spend from $2,000 to $5,000 on mobile apps; another 15 percent spend from $5,000 to $11,000 per year; and over 50 percent had no idea what they spend. Most libraries decide to provide an app for their customers for convenience reasons and a because of a desire to connect with their communities. And most libraries track usage as a means for gauging the success of providing their app(s).[13]

The usability of an app is absolutely crucial in terms of attracting new customers and retaining existing users. In one survey, more than half of the respondents indicated that a poor app experience would make them less likely to use a company's (or a library's) products or service.[14]

Keeping Up

Given the millions of apps that are available, one obvious question is how to keep up with what's hot and what's helpful. Not surprisingly, there is an app for that! Consider looking at AppAdvice, Appstart, or Best Android Apps. A majority of people rely on recommendations from their peers that they receive on social media or by conducting a search for "best app" on a particular topic or field. Nicole Hennig's book *Apps for Librarians* provides a good overview of popular apps.[15]

Development

One of the challenges facing a library is that an app designed to provide an easy-to-use and seamless experience requires that the app interact with any number of vendor products (eBooks, eResources along with the library's online catalog and more). The Queens Library in New York has published the "Queens Library API Requirements Document for e-Content Partners" as a way to encourage vendors to adopt and use a more open set of application program interfaces (APIs).[16] The National Information Standards Organization (NISO) is using the Queens document as the foundation to develop a foundational framework called a NISO Recommended Practice for E-Content in Libraries.[17] The goal is to simplify access to multiple services so the library patron experiences a service that is comparable to those found in a multitude of other apps. Apps designed from the ground up will take advantage of the swiping and resizing capabilities of a smartphone. As Mike Grasee has noted, "'Tap/tap/tap' is a lot more responsive than 'type/type/type.'"[18]

Implications

Given the popularity and increasing use of smartphones and other handheld digital devices, as well as the proliferation of people using apps on these devices, libraries should be moving toward these goals:

1. Ensure that your library's website is mobile friendly.

2. Insist that your library's catalog can operate effectively with mobile devices. An app from your ILS vendor or, alternatively, Boopsie or Library Anywhere may provide a solution.

3. Insist that the Search Box is on your website homepage and is mobile friendly.

4. Demand that *all* library account features work well on mobile devices.

5. Continue to add mobile-friendly content and resources that will be of value to your customers.[19]

Beacons

Beacons are wireless devices that use Bluetooth signals to other Bluetooth devices around them. Beacons use batteries to generate the radio waves; they are quite small and are easy to install and move if needed. A smartphone can receive messages from a beacon and thus provide information based on your location. When a smartphone receives a beacon signal, it can "wake up" one or more apps, thus providing targeted content. BluuBeam and Capira Technologies are two vendors that provide location-based apps for libraries. For example, when entering the library, a customer could be alerted to that day's programs, to holds that are waiting for pickup, or to alert the customer to new items that might be of interest. Beacons could also be used to provide supplemental information about a display or art/photographs hanging on a wall.

Summary

Recognizing the 24/7 "always on" society—people are constantly interacting with mobile devices—means that libraries must provide a range of services that will appeal to a broad range of people and what interests them using handheld devices.

Questions to Consider

- Do the residents in your community own fewer or more than the average number of smartphone users?

- Do you run or receive a monthly report indicating the periods during the day when there is peak periods of WiFi usage that is causing slow internet speeds?

- Is your library's website response to the mobile user?

- Does you library encourage its users to download one or more library apps?

- Has the library developed its own app?

- Do you understand the difference between a native app and a mobile web app?

- How many of the apps identified in this chapter are your familiar with and/or use?

- Has you library considered installing beacons?

Notes

1. darrickmaureen, *someecards* (n.d.), https://www.someecards.com.

2. Paul Hitlin, "Internet, Social Media Use and Device Ownership in U.S. have Plateaued After Years of Growth," *Pew Research*, September 28, 2018, http://www .pewresearch.org/fact-tank/2018/09/28/internet-social-media-use-and-device -ownership-in-u-s-have-plateaued-after-years-of-growth.

3. Stephen J. Blumberg and Julian V. Luke, *Wireless Substitution: Early Release of Estimates from the National Health Interview Survey, January–June 2015* (Washington, DC: National Center for Health Statistics, 2015), http://www.cdc.gov /nchs/nhis.htm.

4. Aaron Smith, "U.S. Smartphone Use in 2015," *Pew Research Center*, April 1, 2015, http://www.pewinternet.org/2015/04/01/us-smartphone-use-in-2015/.

5. FTI Consulting, *Allstate/National Journal Heartland Monitor XXIV Key Findings*, September 18, 2015, http://heartlandmonitor.com/wp-content/uploads /2015/09/FTI-Allstate-NJ-Heartland-Poll-XXIV-Findings-Memo-Sept-24-2015.pdf.

6. Luke Wroblewski, *Mobile First* (New York, NY: A Book Apart, 2011), 50.

7. For more information about a responsive web design, see Bohyun Kim, "The Library Mobile Experience: Practice and User Expectations," *Library Technology Reports*, August–September 2013.

8. Jacob Nielson and Raluca Budiu, *Mobile Usability* (Berkeley, CA: New Riders, 2012), 34.

9. Nielson and Budiu, *Mobile Usability*, 34.

10. Michael Levin, *Multi-Device Experiences: An Ecosystem Approach to Creating User Experiences Across Devices* (Sebastopol, CA: O'Reilly, 2014).

11. Nicole Hennig, "Selecting and Evaluating the Best Mobile Apps for Library Services," *Library Technology Reports*, November–December 2014.

12. James English and Leonard Richardson, "SimplyE—More People Discovering More From the Library," *D-Lib Magazine* 23, no. 5–6 (May–June 2017).

13. "Boopsie for Libraries," *Going Mobile: The New Normal for Libraries of all Types* (2016), http://www.boopsie.com/mobile-trends-libraries.

14. Oracle, *Mobile Apps are the New Face of Businesses* (London: Oracle, April 27, 2015), https://www.oracle.com/se/corporate/pressrelease/millennials-and-mobility -survey-20150427.html.

15. Nicole Hennig, *Apps for Librarians: Using the Best Mobile Technology to Educate, Create, and Engage* (Santa Barbara, CA: Libraries Unlimited, 2014).

16. Surinder Singh and Ankaj Patidar, *Queens Library API Requirements Document for e-Content Partners.* (Queens, NY: Queens Library, 2016), http:// virtuallibrary.queenslibrary.org/sites/default/files/library-api-draft/Library -Webservice-API-Specification-Draft-V1_4.pdf.

17. More information about the NISO Recommended Practice in "NISO launches New Project to Create a Flexible API Framework for e-Content in Libraries," *NISO*, August 25, 2016, http://www.niso.org/news/pr/view?item_key=e18a9742103bc94586 8a51a1e196e62b68879df6.

18. Mike Grasee is quoted in Matt Enis, "Growing Mobile," *Library Journal* 141, no. 14 (September 1, 2016): 42.

19. Bohyun Kim, "The Library Mobile Experience: Practices and User Expectations," *Library Technology Reports* 49, no. 6 (August–September 2013), 1–40.

18
Digital Libraries

The digital revolution is far more significant
than the invention of writing or even of printing.
It offers potential for humans to learn new ways
of thinking and organizing social structures.
Right now we're evolving without much vision.

—Douglas Engelbart[1]

As the internet grew and expanded during the last two and a half decades, the notion of a digital library grew and expanded in a similar manner. As digital technology became more affordable, it also at the same time became more capable. Libraries began to realize that by embracing digital in a more affirmative and effective manner, they would be able to share their unique collection and, more importantly, engage a wider audience.

Digital Asset Management System

Thus, it is not surprising that many libraries provide access to digital content using a digital asset management system (DAMS) as a foundation. A DAMS allows the library to provide access to a plethora of digital content that often includes

- digitized images from historical photograph collections;
- historical newspapers—most often local newspapers;
- audio and video recordings;
- musical scores;
- digitized maps;
- digitized historical or rare books and manuscripts; and
- digitized diaries.

In an academic setting, a digital asset management system is often called an institutional repository, as it includes digital content from the library as well as other departments on campus. This additional content might include faculty research publications, faculty presentations at conferences and other venues, photographs of art collections, and so forth. A majority of the content found in an institutional repository is typically self-archived by faculty members.

A digital asset management system is most often centrally managed, and the digital content is only added at the behest of librarians who have added metadata, ensured that the digital content meets certain minimum technical standards, and ensured that intellectual property rights have been respected and that preservation policies will be enforced.

Librarians typically bring a collections-centered approach to the implementation and maintenance of a digital asset management system, and as such, the primary focus is on preservation of and access to digital content. Preservation implies a significant, long-term commitment to providing access to the digital content for users in future generations. Detailed plans need to be in place to address such issues as backups and disaster recovery, maintenance and storage of materials that have been digitized, what digital file formats must be used for different file formats (documents, images, audio, video, etc.), refreshing files on a regular basis, and migration to new file formats as and when needed. Technology changes and improves over time, so the migration of an existing file, say a jpeg file, to the "new and improved" standard for a jpeg file will need to be done at some point.

Access to digitized content is provided by creating a database containing descriptive metadata, the full text of digitized materials (the digitized text has been converted to machine readable text, using optical character recognition [OCR] software), and an access interface that provides both search and browsing to the user. In some cases, primary source materials such as handwritten letters, diaries, and manuscripts can't be converted to text using OCR, so the library may provide a transcription tool that allows users to transcribe analog content.

The University of Iowa libraries provide a set of tools that allows people to transcribe manuscripts and other materials in their special collections. This "do-it-yourself" (DIY) approach improves the retrieval of primary source materials, but more importantly, it facilitates the engagement of people with the library on many different levels.

DAMS Options

Determining what digital asset management system is best for your library can be a challenge. The Open Archival Information System (OAIS) reference model provides a framework that can be used to assess systems, as the model provides definitions for common terms and concepts.[2] An OAIS conforming system should be able to perform the following tasks:

- *Ingest digital content*, identify file information associated with the digital object, and link the object to metadata and other descriptive content.

- *Manage data*, including controlled vocabularies, schemas, taxonomies, and other metadata. The system must update all of the indexes as content is added, and respond to search queries. In some cases, the system should load a batch file of metadata that was created elsewhere.

- *Archive materials* and provide options for the backup of the database, for disaster recovery, and for the migration of data to new storage media and file formats of the future.

- *Preserve content* by migrating data to new file formats and refresh data on a periodic and scheduled basis.

- *Provide access* to the digital content by giving a set of tools to the user that can accessed anytime, anywhere, by any browser.

- *Include administrative* features to control access and security levels, manage workflows, facilitate rights management, monitor system status, and support eCommerce activities.

The digital content has four types of information objects: content information, descriptive information, packaging information, and preservation descriptive information (provenance information and unique identifiers).[3] Three types of metadata are necessary to implement a digital asset management system: descriptive, administrative (rights management and preservation requirements), and structural metadata (the relationships between two or more files). Among the metadata standards that will typically be supported in a digital asset management system are Dublin Core, EADS (Encoded Archival Description), MARCXML, METS (Metadata Encoding and Transmission Standards), MODS (Metadata Object Description Schema), and XML.[4]

Among the commercial digital asset management systems are Asset Bank, BAM!, Collabro, CONTENTdm, Daminion, Data Dwell, Libris, and Widen Collective among a host of other options.

Available open source digital asset management systems include the following:

- **Fedora**—jointly developed by Cornell University and the University of Virginia. Fedora is being used by VTLS to develop a tool called Valet and by a number of universities to develop a variety of projects. The strength of Fedora is that is supports the use of many complex objects and media types and that it runs as a web service—all of its services can be accessed using REST and SOAP interfaces.[5] Fedora Commons - combined with Drupal and other software, forms the basis of the Islandora platform.

- **Activae**—uses the Cherokee web server and provides an advanced set of APIs to interface with other systems

- **EnterMedia**—developed using the OpenEdit content management framework

- **Gallery**—used primarily for photographs and image collections

- **NotreDAM**—uses Python and a SQLLite database

- **Phraseanet**—uses Hypertext Preprocessor (PHP) and MySQL and includes a thesaurus

- **ResourceSpace**—uses PHP and the MySQL database

- **TACTIC**—typically used when large files, such as video files, must be accommodated.

Tip! A digital asset management system vendor comparison guide is available to be downloaded from Bynder.[6]

Digital Asset Management System Challenges

Digital asset management systems are more than some hardware and software. If the digital asset management system is to be more than yet another automated silo among others, then a number of important issues must be addressed.

First, librarians and other staff members must ensure that the content being ingested into the system meets the established quality criteria, as well as making sure the software is updated as new releases become available.

Second, staff should be testing the user interface on a regular basis to determine what problems users are facing in order to make any necessary changes to the system in order to improve the overall user experience.

Third, the digital asset management system must become visible to the search engine robots so that the content of the system is discoverable when users are using a search engine such as Google.

Fourth, the digital asset management system must either (1) provide a set of tools for harvesting or transferring content to the DPLA via OAI-PMH or other protocols, or (2) adopt and use the application programming interface (API) provided by the Digital Public Library of America (DPLA) or other national digital aggregators, for example, Trove in Australia (trove.nla.gov .au) and Europe's Europeana (www.europeana.eu) so that the library's, museum's, galleries, and archive's content is visible to these increasingly important aggregated digital destinations.

Fifth, the digital asset management system must become an integral part of the complexity mixture of automated systems providing services to all library customers. As such, it must be able to interact with any number of other systems using APIs, and it ceases to be an automated silo, but rather becomes an important resource that is available for users to discovery interesting and useful digital content.

Sixth, the data in the digital asset management system must work harder so that users are receiving real value when they interact with the system. The library should be exploring the many ways it can enhance the user interface so that users start collaborating with the library staff members and other users of the system in new and creative ways. Users want to interact with content by posting ratings, reviews, and notes, and engage with other interested users.

The importance of adding value in new and creative ways is explored in depth in a recent book, *Adding Value in Libraries, Archives, and Museums: Harnessing the Force That Drives Your Organization's Future*.[7] This book encourages cultural organizations to add value now and into the future using the five "Cs"—content, context, connection, collaboration, and community, as shown in Figure 18.1.

In a report prepared for England's public libraries, BiblioCommons suggests:

> In other words, the problem is not that public library users are leaving the library as their lives move online. It's that the library is not showing up to meet them there. As a result, public libraries are failing to serve those who need them most, and losing the interest of those who have the luxury to choose to go elsewhere—for some of what they sought at the library.[8]

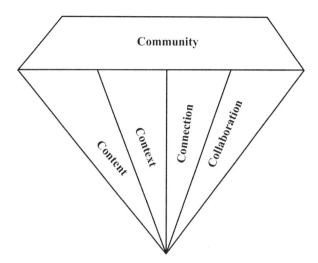

FIGURE 18.1. The Five "Cs"—The Adding Value Diamond

The reality of the digital library concept, from its humble beginnings until today, is that it is just one of many library services. As such, the digital library is simply on the edge or periphery of library services, rather than "digital" being at the core of the library.

Institutional Repositories

Making things free, perfect, and instant might seem like unreasonable
 expectations
for most products, but as more information is digitized,
more products will fall into these categories.
—Erik Brynjolfsson and Andrew McAfee[x]

An institutional repository (IR) is a digital archive for collection, preserving, and sharing copies of the intellectual output or knowledge of an organization, particularly a research university. The value of a repository is that it provides broader dissemination and enhanced professional visibility of scholarly output. In particular, the benefits that arise from an institutional repository include the following:

- *Universal access* to scholarly content (journal articles, book chapters, conference presentations, etc.) for all, greatly enhancing the public value of research. In addition to scholarly materials, IRs often contain historical and creative content.

- *Easier discovery* means that users find content of value when they use Google, Google Scholar, and other search engines.

- *More exposure* results from the contents of an institutional repository being accessible to search engines indexing robots, with the result that scholarly output is cited more frequently.

- *Persistent access* results from the repository providing a persistent URL (uniform resource locator)—no more dead links (sometimes called link rot).

- *Assured preservation* is the result of an organization committed to long-term access and preservation of the collection of materials contained in the IR.

Among the many institutional repository systems are these:[9]

- **Archimede**—developed by Laval University Library in Quebec City, Canada

- **ARNO**—developed by the Academic Research in the Netherlands Online

- **CDSware**—developed by CERN

- **Digital Commons**—developed by bePress (University of California Berkeley Press)

- **DSpace**—developed by the Massachusetts Institute of Technology and Hewlett Packard

- **EPrints**—developed by the University of Southampton

- **i-Tor**—developed by the Innovative Technology section of the Netherlands Institute for Scientific Information Services

- **MyCoRe**—developed by the MILESS Project at the University of Essen

- **OPUS**—Online publications of the University of Stuttgart

Listed here are some of the key factors to consider when implementing an institutional repository:

- *The institutional culture*—What encourages faculty members and researchers to contribute content?

- *The scope of the repository*—What kinds of materials may be deposited?

- *Access control*—Will all of the content be accessible, or will some content be restricted to specific types of individuals?

- Legal concerns—What policies are in place to ensure all legal requirements are met?

- *Digital rights management*—Will some content require a license before it can be used?

- *Standards*—Important standards that should be considered include Open Archival Information System (OAIS), Open Archives Metadata Harvesting Protocol (OAI-PMH), and Metadata Encoding and Transmission Standard (METS).

- *Sustainability*—Building a sustainable IR requires collaboration, creativity, and commitment.

- *Operational control*—What department within an organization is going to be responsible for the maintenance and operation of the institutional repository? For many organizations, it is the library.

SPARC provides an IR checklist and resource guide that may be helpful if you are actively involved in implementing an institutional repository.[10]

Digital Media Labs

For many libraries, one important community content-creation space is the digital media lab (DML), although the DML may have a variety of other names such as "The Bubbler," DesignLab, CreateSpace, YOUmedia, and many others. The digital media lab provides the equipment and resources that encourage original digital content to be created. In addition, tools may be provided that will convert analog content to a digital format.

Amanda Goodman has suggested the following criteria for a digital media lab:[11]

- The primary focus is digital content creation.

- Equipment is provided for members of the community to create audio, video, or other digital content.

- Tools are provided to convert analog materials (phonograph records, audio tapes, video tapes, 35 mm slides, photographs, etc.) to digital formats.

- Programs are provided so that community members can learn how to create digital content.

Funding to create and sustain a digital media lab might come from a Friends group, a Library Services and Technology (LSTA) grant, corporate and/or community grants, or crowdfunding. Costs to create a DML can range from a few thousand to $30,000 or so. Increasingly in public libraries, digital media labs (often under the umbrella term of "makerspaces") are funded as a library expense.

A digital media lab might be modest in its beginnings (no dedicated space) to relatively robust (perhaps more than one lab—a DML and a makerspace). Some of the topics that should be addressed in the planning of a digital media lab include these:[12]

- **The space**—This includes number of tables and desks, storage space (locked and otherwise), power outlets or strips, internet bandwidth and WiFi, air-conditioning, noise suppression, green screen (for video content), and the general layout of the room.

- **Computers**—Given that the digital content that is created will most like need to be edited, remixed, and shared, the necessary software to accomplish these tasks will be required. This editing software will generally run on Mac or Linux hardware products that are equipped with large-screen monitors.

- **Audio**—Among the types of equipment that will be needed are microphones, headphones, mixer, preamps, equalizer, and associated cabling.

- **Video**—The equipment that may be of use includes lighting equipment, camera, tripod, digital card reader, microphones, webcam, and fabric backgrounds.

- **Photography**—This equipment may include lightbox (taking a photo of a small item), tripod, camera, lighting equipment, car reader, and fabric backgrounds.

- **Analog to digital**—Some equipment that should be of value includes: VCR to DVD machine, record player, reel-to-reel player, eight-track and/or cassette audio player, and scanners (photo negative scanner, slide scanner, microfilm scanner).

- **Graphic design**—Graphic design requires powerful hardware plus associated software. Some open source software that might be of interest includes Animatron, GIMP, Inkscape, Pixir Editor, and SAI. Licensed software might include Flash, Photoshop, Illustrator, Maya, and 3D Studio Max.

- **Other equipment**—Some equipment that many libraries have installed that complements a digital media lab or makerspace includes a button maker, a laminator, a sewing machine, a vinyl cutter, a laser cutter, and other hand tools.[13] And the increased activity and attendance that results from the digital media lab may require the library to upgrade its WiFi or internet broadband connectivity capacity.

- **Virtual reality**—VR equipment may include a viewer (Oculus Rift, HC Vive, Google Cardboard, and/or a Yay3D VR Viewer for the iPad Mini), a 360-degree camera, a dedicated laptop with a high-end video card, and perhaps a dedicated space for VR activities.[14]

Some of the other important issues include staff training, programs for patrons (such as computer coding programs for teens and adults), liability (damage to equipment and the building), and policies governing the use of the digital media lab.

Social Media

Social media and the internet have become an ingrained part of everyday life for billions of people around the world. Social media is all about transforming monologue into dialog. The popularity of social media sites is attested to by the fact that a majority of adults around the world have Facebook accounts and are also active using Twitter, Instagram, Snapchat, Flickr, and Pinterest, among a host of other sites. Almost two-thirds of Facebook users visit the site daily, and many people visit multiple times during the course of the day.[15]

Lorcan Dempsey, vice-president for the Online Computer Library Center (OCLC) Research, has noted that it is important for libraries to be "in the flow."[16] The reality is that people are spending more and more time online in a networked environment (almost always using a handheld mobile device) for work and for recreation. Dempsey suggests that libraries need to organize library services around the tools and online places (including social media) that people use for their workflows, research flows, learn flows, or recreation flows.

One important way for libraries to get "in the flow" is to have an active presence in social media. Clearly it would be important to know what social media channels the library customers use on a regular basis and to know what the library is hoping to achieve by using social media. David Lee King has suggested there might be five reasons to use social media:[17]

1. **Listening**—Social media provides an easy way to learn what your community members are saying about the library, as well as what topics are of interest at a moment in time. Several tools can be used to discover what's being said about the library.

2. **Connecting**—Social media channels afford people the opportunity to connect with others and to share their thoughts and observations about things they are interested in. This allows others to chime in and to share their thoughts and ideas and become a part of an ongoing conversation.

3. **Interacting**—Asking for comments and feedback about the library and its services will often open new opportunities to learn what the community is thinking about the library. Interaction with the community is strengthened when you can show that "we listened and we acted."

4. **Real-time**—The ubiquitous nature of mobile technology means that people are constantly turning to it for any number of reasons. In short, mobile technology affords everyone with the opportunity for anywhere, anytime service.

5. **Outreach**—Perhaps three-fourths of library customers are already using social media. Engaging with the current customers of the library affords these individuals the chance to share library news, events, and suggestions with others in their social networks. This, in turn, opens up the opportunity for the library to indirectly reach nonusers of the library as socially affirmed content validates the value and importance of the library within a community.

Using social media channels allows the library to become involved in the lives of others by answering questions, engaging in conversations about books and program offerings, promoting library events, sharing tips and the "top five ideas" that were presented at a recent library program, presenting brief book reviews, and so forth.

Some of the social media channels that a library might consider using are Facebook, Twitter, YouTube, LinkedIn, Tumblr, Pinterest, Instagram, Snapchat, Vine, Google Plus, and Flickr. David Lee King goes on to suggest ten tips for the effective use of social media:[18]

1. Be relevant.

2. Consistency is important.

3. Know what segments of your community use what social media channels.

4. Share the story of the library.

5. Write like you talk.

6. Provide helpful content.

7.　Think pithy content.

8.　Use a human casual writing style.

9.　Use a visual image or video.

10.　Encourage participation.

Several authors suggest that it is important to establish goals such as increasing the number of people at events and programs or reaching a goal for the number of followers or friends on a specific site.[19] More recently, Doralyn Rossmann and Scott W. H. Young suggest five principles a library should follow for building and engaging a community. The authors provide a handy roadmap of the ways in which a library can easily implement these five principles:[20]

Principle 1—Create content that can be shared. Figure out what content resonates and is passed on.

Principle 2—Simplify sharing. Provide linking buttons for social media sites.

Principle 3—Reward engagement. Hold contests; highlight the posting of your customers; and be visible in online communities.

Principle 4—Encourage sharing and remixing.

Principle 5—Measure use. Among the measures might be activity metrics, audience metrics, engagement metrics, and referral metrics.

Librarians can make significant contributions to Wikipedia (and other similar "–pedia" sites) by adding and editing local content that would be of interest to their communities. Further, librarians can add citations to improve the accuracy of content already found on Wikipedia. Some libraries (and museums and galleries) have created a Wikipedian in Residence program to demonstrate their commitment to the Wikipedia worldwide audience. Other libraries have created edit-a-thons to involve a wider community and to make significant contributions in a short period of time.[21]

Summary

Although our legacy library systems were designed to support access to physical objects, libraries increasingly are connecting patrons to digital objects. Digital asset management systems (DAMS) are designed to manage the digital content of many types, including images (still and moving), audio, video and more as new content types emerge. DAMS help the library ingest and share digital objects. Many academic libraries use DAMS as the platform for institutional repositories.

DAMS represent a shift for libraries. In legacy systems that manage physical objects, the content was often created by others and acquired by the library to share with patrons. With DAMS, the content is most often created by the library through a process of digitization. Examples include scanning vintage newspapers and photographs, digitizing oral histories that were recorded on analog equipment, and more.

To be findable, these original digital objects must also contain metadata added by the library, including information about the content of the digital object, descriptive information, packaging information, and unique identifiers.

Digital media labs, which can offer great breadth and depth of digitization equipment, are often used to convert physical objects to digital objects for DAMS. In terms of access as well as solid metadata, many libraries get great success from leveraging social media to create awareness and increased use of their digital collections.

Questions to Consider

- Has your library installed or does it need to install a digital asset management system?

- Did you library consider installing an open source digital asset management system?

- What challenges does your library face with its installed digital asset management system?

- Has your institution installed an institutional repository?

- How well does your institutional repository rank worldwide (visit http://repositories.webometrics.info to determine your ranking)? What can you do to improve your IRs ranking?

- Has your library considered not using a discovery system? If so, does the Knowledge Creation Platform articulated by Carl Grant appeal to you?

- Has you library thought about installing a digital media lab in one of its locations?

- If your library has a digital media lab, what have you learned about community needs in this area—and the library's capacity to meet those needs?

- Is your library taking full advantage of social media? Does you library connect daily with a variety of users on social media?

- Is your library using the five principles for engaging a community suggested by Doralyn Rossmann and Scott W. H. Young?

Notes

1. Quoted in Alf Chattell, *Creating Value in the Digital Era: Achieving Success Through Insight, Imagination, and Innovation* (New York: New York University Press, 1998): 2.

2. Brian Lavole, "Meeting the Challenges of Digital Preservation: The OAIS Reference Model," *OCLC Newsletter* 243 (January/February 2000): 26–30.

3. OCLC/RLG Working Group on preservation Metadata, *Preservation Metadata and the OAIS Information Model: A Metadata Framework to Support the Preservation of Digital Objects* (Dublin, OH: Online Computer Library Center, 2002), 6.

4. Kyle Banerjee and Terry Reese Jr., *Building Digital Libraries. A How-To-Do-It Manual for Librarians*, 2nd ed. (Chicago: American Library Association, 2019).

5. More information about Fedora is available at https://fedoraproject.org/wiki/Objectives.

6. Bynder, *Vendor Comparison Guide*, Bynder white paper (n.d.), https://info .bynder.com/vendor-comparison-guide.

7. Joseph R. Matthews, *Adding Value in Libraries, Archives, and Museums: Harnessing the Force That Drives Your Organization's Future* (Santa Barbara, CA: Libraries Unlimited, 2016).

8. "Essential Digital Infrastructure for Public Libraries in England: A Plan for Moving Forward," *BiblioCommons*, November 24, 2015, https://www.libraries connected.org.uk/sites/default/files/Essential%20Digital%20Infrastructure%20 for%20Public%20Libraries%20in%20England_0.pdf.

9. Open Society Institute, *A Guide to Institutional Repository Software*, 3rd ed., 2004, https://www.budapestopenaccessinitiative.org/pdf/OSI_Guide_to_IR_Soft ware_v3.pdf.

10. SPARC, *Institutional Repository Checklist & Resource Guide* (Washington, DC: SPARC, 2002), https://sparcopen.org/wp-content/uploads/2016/01/IR_Guide_ _Checklist_v1_0.pdf.

11. Amanda Goodman, "Digital Media Labs in Libraries," *Library Technology Reports* 50, no. 6 (August/September 2014), 1–43.

12. Jeffrey P. Fischer, *Building and Operating a Digital Media Lab—Free to PLA Members!*, PLA Quick Reads Series. 03 (Chicago: Public Library Association, 2016), http://publiclibrariesonline.org/2016/09/new-quick-reads-series-building-and -operating-a-digital-media-lab.

13. Jennifer Dixon, "Making It Happen," *Library Journal* 142, no. 10 (June 1, 2017): 48–51.

14. Michael Figueroa, "In a Virtual World," American Libraries (March–April 2018): 26–33, https://americanlibrariesmagazine.org/2018/03/01/virtual-world-vir tual-reality-libraries/.

15. Aaron Smith, "6 New Facts About Facebook," *Pew Research Center*, February 3, 2014, http://www.pewresearch.org/fact-tank/2014/02/03/6-new-facts-about -facebook.

16. Lorcan Dempsey, "Reconfiguring the Library Systems Environment: Guest editorial," *Portal: Libraries and the Academy* 8, no. 2 (April 2008): 111–120.

17. David Lee King, "Managing Your Library's Social Media Channels," *Library Technology Reports* 51, no. 1 (January 2015): 1–35.

18. David Lee King, *Face2Face: Using Facebook, Twitter, and Other Social Media Tools to Create Great Customer Connections* (Medford, NJ: Information Today, 2012).

19. Laura Solomon, *The Librarian's Nitty-Gritty Guide to Social Media* (Chicago: American Library Association, 2013). See also, Scott Woodward Young and Doralyn Rossmann, "Building Library Community Through Social Media," *Information Technology and Libraries* 34, no. 1 (2015): 20–37.

20. Doralyn Rossmann and Scott W. H. Young, "Social Media Optimization: Principles for Building and Engaging Community," *Library Technology Reports* 52, no. 8 (November/December 2016): 1–53.

21. Merrilee Proffitt, ed., *Leveraging Wikipedia: Connection Communities of Knowledge* (Chicago: American Library Association, 2018).

Glossary

802.11—See *IEEE 802.11*.

abstract—A nonevaluative summary of a book, journal article, or other information resource.

acceptable use policy (AUP)—A written policy specifying how an employee should use, not abuse, network resources.

access control—The ability to selectively control who can access a software application or manipulate information in a computer-based system.

Active Server Pages—A specification developed by Microsoft for a dynamically created web page with an .ASP extension that utilizes ActiveX scripting. Active Server Pages run under Microsoft's Internet Information Server on a Microsoft web server; although referred to with the acronym ASP, they should not be confused with Application Service Provider.

ActiveX—A Microsoft component standard designed to allow interoperability between common desktop and web-based applications; ActiveX's strength lies in its ability to allow development in a wide variety of programming languages, such as Visual Basic, Java, or C++.

agent—Software applications that carry out pre-programmed functions on behalf of a user, operating within specific, tailored boundaries (e.g., an "intelligent" email filter used to eliminate spam or scan for viruses or a shopping device that can search the Web and transact a purchase under predetermined price parameters).

algorithm—A set of rules used to solve problems, especially in computer programs.

Ajax—Ajax is short for Asynchronous JavaScript and XML, which provides a method of exchanging data with a server, and updating parts of a web page, without reloading the entire page.

American National Standards Institute (ANSI)—ANSI, pronounced "antsy," is the US-based organization dedicated to developing industrywide standards for technology. ANSI is a member of the International Organization for Standardization (ISO). ANSI has assigned responsibility for library-related standards to the National Information Standards Organization (NISO).

American Standard Code for Information Interchange (ASCII)—A text code that uses seven or eight bits to represent textual or numeric data.

analog—The distinguishing feature of analog representations is that they are continuous (e.g., the human voice). In contrast, digital representations consist of values measured at discrete intervals.

android—An open source operating system developed by Google.

annotation—A resource that enhances knowledge about another resource when knowing the source of the annotation is important. This is an important part of the BIBFRAME Model.

antenna—A device that facilitates the transmission and reception of radio signals.

antivirus—Software used to detect viruses and stop them from infecting a computer or network.

Apache server—A free, open source, cross-platform software for a web server and is the dominant HTTP server.

Apache Solr—Solr (pronounced "solar") is a popular, open source search engine for websites and supports RSS and JSON formats.

API—See *application programming interface.*

app—An app is a computer program designed to run on mobile devices, for example, smartphones and tablets.

applet—A program designed to be executed from within another program. Because applets have small file sizes, are cross-platform compatible, and can't be used to gain access to a user's hard drive, they are ideal for small internet applications accessible from a browser. Applets are often embedded in web pages.

AppleTalk—A local area network architecture built into all Macintosh computers and Apple laser printers.

application—Also seen as "application program" and sometimes abbreviated to "app," an application is a software program that performs a specific task such as word processing, spreadsheets, accounting, and so forth.

application logic—The computational aspects or business rules that tell a software application how to operate.

application programming interface (API)—A set of routines, protocols, and tools for building software applications. A good API makes it easier to develop a program by providing all the building blocks and links. A programmer puts these blocks together. Most operating environments, such as Flickr, Twitter, Google, Goodreads, LibraryThing, and the Online Computer Library Catalog (OCLC), provide a set of APIs so programmers can write applications consistent with the operating environment. Although APIs are designed for programmers, they are ultimately good for users because they guarantee that all programs using a common API will have similar interfaces. This makes it easier for users to learn new programs.

application service provider (ASP)—An ASP deploys, hosts, and manages access to a packaged software application by multiple parties from a centrally managed facility typically referred to as a cloud-based application or service. The applications are delivered over networks on a subscription basis.

Ariel—Ariel software (available from the Research Libraries Group) allows a library to scan articles, photos, and other documents; transmit the electronic images to other Ariel workstations anywhere in the world, using either FTP or email; and convert them to PDF for easy patron delivery. Ariel provides superior document transmission faster and clearer than a fax, and there are no long-distance phone charges.

ASCII—See *American Standard Code for Information Interchange.*

assembler—A computer software program that translates programs from assembly language to machine language.

asymmetrical digital subscriber line (ADSL)—The most common form of DSL. "Asymmetrical" indicates that the service is faster for downloads than uploads.

asynchronous—Asynchronous communication is sometimes called "start–stop transmission" because start and stop bits are used with each message. Data can be transmitted intermittently rather than in a steady stream.

asynchronous transmission mode (ATM)—An information transfer standard for routing high-speed, high-bandwidth traffic such as real-time voice and video as well as data bits.

authentication—The process for identifying an individual, usually based on a user name and password. Authentication is distinct from authorization, which is the process of giving individuals access to system components based on their identity.

authority—A resource reflecting key authority concepts that have defined relationships in the BIBFRAME Model Work and Instance. Examples of authority resources include people, places, topics, organizations, and so on.

authority control—The process for ensuring that the headings in surrogate records are consistent with the headings established in an authority file.

authority file—A collection of authority records.

authority record—A record that contains all of the decisions made about an authority work. Typically an authority record will contain the "authorized" heading along with cross-references.

availability—The portion of time that a system can be used for productive work, expressed as a percentage. Sometimes call uptime.

backbone—A backbone is a network that only has other networks attached to it, instead of user devices like PCs and servers. This allows backbones to operate at much faster speeds than local networks.

bandwidth—The transmission speed or the number of information bits that can move through a communications medium in a given amount of time; the capacity of a telecommunications circuit/network to carry voice, data, and video information. Typically measured in Kbps, Mbps, and Gbps.

BIBFRAME—The BIBFRAME initiative is the future of bibliographic description in a networked and web-based world. The BIBFRAME initiative will

- differentiate between conceptual content and the physical/digital manifestation(s);
- unambiguously identify information entities; and
- leverage and expose relationships among and between entities.

BIBFRAME model—A conceptual/practical model that has four high-level classes or entities:

- BIBFRAME work
- BIBFRAME instance
- BIBFRAME authority
- BIBFRAME annotation

BIBFRAME is a set of tools for making library data a part of the larger web of data, where links between things is paramount.

bibliographic record—A description of a book, journal, or other materials located in the library. It may include author, title, publication information, collation, and subject headings.

bit error rate—The number of transmitted bits expected to be corrupted when two computers have been communicating for a given period of time.

bits per second (bps)—A measure of data transfer rates. Faster is better and the bigger the number, the faster the rate.

bloatware—Software programs that require large amounts of disk space and RAM (random access memory), effectively consuming valuable computer resources.

Bluetooth—A short-range wireless specification that allows for radio connections between devices within a 30-foot range of one another, including phones, laptops, speakers, keyboards, and printers.

Boolean logic—Connecting terms that enable the user to conduct a more specific search of an online catalog or database. The Boolean connector "and" narrows a search; "or" broadens a search; and "not" eliminates items from a search.

Boolean searching—The process of searching using keywords that are linked by Boolean operators (some systems require the user to select a Boolean operator, and other systems use an implied operator if none are specified).

bots—Bots (from the word *robots*) are smart software programs that run in the background of a computer, performing specific repetitive tasks. A bot can search the internet, comparison shop, clip news articles, and so forth. Hotbots, search bots, shopping bots, and spiders are among the species of bots. They are sometimes called intelligent agents.

broadband—A generic term used for various high bandwidth connection technologies.

browser—Software that is used to view various internet resources and is capable of viewing text, images, and various other file formats, as well as playing sound and showing videos.

C—A popular programming language that has been supplanted by C++ and Java.

C++—A high-level programming language that adds object-oriented functions to its predecessor language, C. C++ is a popular language for GUI-based applications that run on Windows or the Macintosh.

cache—Information saved in computer memory for later use. For example, web browsers save recently viewed pages in a cache so the exact pages are not downloaded again, should the user request them. This feature saves the internet resources and time.

call number—A combination of letters and numbers assigned to each book and other materials in a library's collection. The purpose of a call number is to group materials on the same subject together plus provide a unique shelf location or address to the item. Most academic libraries use the Library of Congress system, whereas public libraries rely on the Dewey system.

capacity—The ability of a network to provide sufficient transmitting capabilities among its available transmission media and respond to customer demand for communications transport, especially at peak times.

CAT-5 wiring—CAT is short for "category," and there are five categories of twisted-pair wiring specified by the American National Standards Institute/ Electronic Industries Association (ANSI/EIA).

catalog—A file of library materials, which describes and indexes the resources of a collection or library. A catalog may be an online catalog, a card catalog, a microform catalog, or a book catalog.

channel—A broad term referring to the pathway between two locations on a voice or data network.

channel server unit/digital server unit (CSU/DSU)—A device used to terminate telephone company equipment and prepare data for router interface.

chat—A real-time conversation, typically using text, among multiple online users. Chat rooms have discussions focused on a particular topic.

CIP2—Circulation Interchange Protocol (Version 2) is a NISO Z39.83 and the latest release, version 2.02, was approved and release in 2002. CIP2 provides for the limited exchange of messages between and among computer-based applications necessary to lend and borrow items.

circuit—A line that connects devices.

citation—The basic information needed to find specific information. Citation information might include author name, title of book or article, journal name, page numbers, and publication information.

click-stream—Information collected about where a web user has been on the Web.

client/device—Hardware that retrieves information from a server.

client-server—Client-server replaced mainframe computing as the dominant system for business information architecture in the late 1980s; clients (see *client side*) are typically less powerful, graphically enabled software platforms that request computation from a server. The server is typically a more powerful processing platform that serves requested data or tasks back to the requesting clients. Web browsers have emerged in the 1990s as a universal client able to access multiple applications, fueling the movement away from the client-server to the ASP business.

client side—The side of an application that resides on the user end of a network; the PC or terminal where the end user works would be the client side of a client-server model; the client side of an ASP application would be the browser.

cloud computing—Software and hardware as a service that is delivered to users via the Web.

clustering—Group of independent systems working together as a single system. Clustering technology allows groups of servers to access a single disk array containing applications and data.

codabar barcode label—A barcode label that uses 14 numeric-only digits.

code 39 barcode label—A barcode label that can use both alpha and numeric characters.

collaboration—A set of software applications designed to assist groups of people in communicating and sharing information in order to complete a task or activity.

collocation—The placement of one company's computer or network equipment on the premises of another company's.

comma-delimited—A data format in which each piece of data is separated by a comma. This is a popular format for transferring data from one application to another because most database systems are able to import and export comma-delimited data.

common gateway interface (CGI)—A specification for transferring information between a World Wide Web server and a CGI program. A CGI program is any program designed to accept and return data that conforms to the CGI specification. The program could be written in any programming language, including C, Perl, Java, and Visual Basic. One problem with CGI is that each time a CGI script is executed, a new process is started. For busy websites, this can slow down the server noticeably.

Common Object Request Broker Architecture (CORBA)—An architecture that enables software programs, called objects, to communicate with one another regardless of the programming language the object is written in. Two competing models are Microsoft's COM and Sun's RMI.

communications medium—The component used to connect two network devices to facilitate data transmission—normally refers to a type of data cable (twisted pair, coaxial, fiber optic) or a telecommunications line.

Component Object Model (COM)—A binary code developed by Microsoft. Both OLE (Object Linking and Embedding) and ActiveX are based on COM.

content management system (CMS)—A content management system is a software program that separates content and the presentation of content, allowing multiple users to add and edit content simultaneously.

cookie—While browsing certain web pages, small files are downloaded to your computer that hold information that can be retrieved by other web pages on that site. Cookies contain information that identifies each user: login or registration information, specified preferences, passwords, shopping cart information, and so on. When the user revisits the website, his or her computer will automatically distribute the cookie, establishing the user's identity.

Cooperative Online Resource Catalog (CORC)—An OCLC web-based system that helps libraries provide guided access to web resources, using automated tools and library cooperation.

COUNTER—Counting Online Usage of Networked Electronic Resources (sometimes called Project COUNTER) is an international organization serving libraries, publishers, and other organizations by setting standards that facilitate the recording and reporting of online usage statistics in a consistent, credible, and compatible way.

cracker—An individual who intentionally breaches the security of a computer system, usually with the intent of stealing information or disabling the system.

creative work—A resource reflecting a conceptual essence of a cataloging resource. The concept is a part of BIBFRAME.

CrossRef—CrossRef interlinks millions of items from a variety of sources, using digital object identifiers (DOIs).

cross references—Instructions, which lead to related information, listed under other subject headings or terms. A *see* reference leads to the "correct" headings, whereas a *see also* leads to a related heading.

cross talk—Interference on analog lines created by cables that are too close together. Cross talk may produce static, buzzing, or multiple conversations on one line.

customer relationship management (CRM)—An application that manages crucial customer relationships by automating customer-related services (e.g., order processing, sales, marketing, and help desk assistance).

cyber fraud—The most common crime using the internet is online credit card theft. Typically, someone will order goods over the internet, using stolen credit cards. Another form of cyber fraud is nondelivery of merchandise or software bought online.

data center—A centralized computer facility for remote access by customer end users.

database—A group of records in machine-readable form, which is accessible by computer.

database management system (DBMS)—Sophisticated software system that stores and retrieves information from a database.

datagram—A packet of information sent to the receiving computer. It is conceptually similar to a telegram in that the message can arrive any time, without notice.

data mining—An analytic process that examines large sets of information for hidden patterns and relationships.

data rate or data transfer rate—The number of bits that can be transferred across a network in one second.

data service unit (DSU)—A wide area network (WAN) device that is equivalent to a network interface card (NIC).

data warehouse—A database containing copious amounts of information, organized to help organizations make decisions. Data warehouses receive batch updates and are configured for fast online queries, to produce succinct data summaries.

dedicated line—A point-to-point, hard-wire connection between two service locations.

denial of service (DOS) attack—An attack by a hacker who generates so many messages to a website that regular users cannot get through or the site shuts down.

descriptive markup—Markup that identifies a function or style instead of specific formatting.

digital—Data are represented by 0 ("off" or "low") and 1 ("on" or "high"). Computers must use an analog modem to convert digital data into analog form for transmission over ordinary telephone lines. Alternatively, no conversion is necessary if a digital modem and digital data communications option is chosen.

digital humanities—An area of teaching and research at the intersection of computing technology and the disciplines of the humanities.

digital object identifier (DOI)—A unique and persistent string of characters used to identify a journal article, website, or other item of intellectual property.

digital subscriber line (DSL)—A technology designed for the internet that brings high-speed digital data to a home or office over ordinary copper telephone lines. It comes in various bandwidths and simplicity for installers and users. Asymmetric digital subscriber line, or ADSL, supports data rates from 1.5 to 9 Mbps when receiving data. Symmetric digital subscriber line, or SDSL, supports data rates up to 3 Mbps.

DoCoMo—DoCoMo means "anywhere" in Japanese and is the name of Japan's biggest mobile service provider. It has overtaken traditional Japanese internet service providers to become Japan's biggest internet access platform.

DOI—See *digital object identifier.*

document type definition (DTD)—Defines how the markup tags in SGML and XML documents should be interpreted by the application presenting the document.

domain name—The name of a service, website, or computer in a hierarchical system of delegated authority—the domain name system.

domain name system (or service) (DNS)—An internet service that translates domain names into IP addresses. Because domain names are alphabetic, they're easier to remember. Every time a domain name is used, a DNS service must translate the name into the corresponding IP address. For example, the domain name www.example.com might translate to 128.105.732.14.

download—To receive data from a remote computer.

downstream—The direction data flows from a remote computer to your computer.

downtime—When your computer, computer network, access to the internet, or an internet-based service provider isn't working. The opposite of uptime.

Drupal—A content management system (CMS) used by libraries that works with Apache Solr and produces RSS and JSON feeds fairly easily.

DS-1—Data communications circuit capable of transmitting data at 1.5 Mbps. Currently, DS-1 or T-1 lines are widely used by organizations for video, voice, and data applications.

DS-3—A data communications circuit capable of transmitting data at 45 Mbps. A DS-3 or T-3 line has the equivalent data capacity of 28 T-1s. Currently used only by organizations and carriers for high-end applications.

Dublin Core—A set of fifteen fields that can be filled in by the creator of an electronic document to create a metadata record for the document.

Dynamic Host Configuration Protocol (DHCP)—Allows computers using the TCP/IP protocol to be assigned an IP address automatically rather than requiring that a fixed IP address be assigned to the computer.

dynamic HTML—New HTML extensions that enable a web page to react to user input without sending requests to the web server. Both Microsoft and Netscape have submitted proposals to the W3C, which is developing a final specification.

dynamic IP address—An IP address that is assigned by a device acting as a High-Bandwidth Digital Content Protection (HDCP) server. A dynamic IP can be different each time you turn on your computer.

EAD. See *Encoded Archival Description*.

eBook—The contents of a book that may be downloaded for viewing and/or printed locally.

eJournal—A magazine or scholarly journal that is available online. The online version may stand alone, or it may be published in conjunction with a print version.

electronic data interchange (EDI)—The electronic communication of business transactions (e.g., orders, confirmations, invoices) of organizations with differing platforms. Third parties provide EDI services that enable organizations to connect with incompatible equipment.

electronic resource management system (ERMS)—An ERMS handles the selection, acquisition, licensing, access, usage, maintenance, evaluation, and deselection for electronic information resources.

Encoded Archival Description (EAD)—An XML-based description of archival materials. The EAD header consists of four sub-elements: EAD identifier, file description, profile description, and revision description.

encryption—The translation of data into a secret code. To read an encrypted file, you must have access to a secret key or password that enables you to decrypt it. Encrypted data are sometimes called cipher text.

EPUB—An open standard for eBooks and files that have the extension .epub.

enterprise resource management (ERM)—ERM is business process management software that automates and manages technology, human resources, and services.

entry—A citation or record in an index or catalog.

ePUB—ePUB is an open standard for eBooks (the eBook can be read on multiple hardware devices).

ERM—See *enterprise resource management*.

Ethernet—A local area network used to connect computers, printers, workstations, and other devices within the same building. Ethernet operates over twisted wire and coaxial cable.

Extensible Markup Language (XML)—A version of the Standardized General Markup Language (SGML) designed especially for the Web.

extranet—An intranet that is partially accessible to authorized outsiders using a username and password. Typically, suppliers and important customers are able to access an extranet.

eXtensible Markup Language—see *Extensible Markup Language (XML)*.

Fast Ethernet—A LAN transmission standard that supports data transmission rates up to 100 Mbps. Fast Ethernet is ten times faster than standard Ethernet and is sometimes called 100 Base-T.

fat client—A computer that includes an operating system, random access memory (RAM), read-only memory (ROM), a powerful processor, and a wide range of installed software applications that can execute either on the desktop or on the server to which it is connected. Fat clients can operate in a server-based computing environment or in a stand-alone fashion.

fault tolerance—A design method that incorporates redundant system elements to ensure continued systems operation in the event any individual element fails.

Fiber distributed data interface (FDDI)—A standard for transmitting data on optical-fiber cables at a rate of about 100 Mbps.

fiber optics—Fiber-optic technology—again, made possible by photonic science—uses glass, plastic, or fused silica threads to transmit data. A fiber-optic cable consists of a bundle of super-thin glass threads that are capable of transmitting data via pulses of light. Key advantages of these laser-powered cables include vastly higher-speed data transmission over longer distances and with less data loss.

field—A category of information, typically found in a record. A record is composed of several fields.

File Transfer Protocol (FTP)—The protocol used on the internet for transferring or sending files.

firewall—A system designed to prevent unauthorized access to or from a private network. All messages entering or leaving the Intranet pass through the firewall, which examines each message and blocks those that do not meet the specified security criteria.

folksonomy—A merging of folk and taxonomy that are unrestricted user-generated vocabularies describing content.

frame—The basic logical unit in which bit-oriented data is transmitted. The frame consists of the data bits surrounded by a flag at each end that indicates the beginning and end of the frame. A primary rate can be thought of as an endless sequence of frames.

frame relay—A high-speed packet-switching protocol popular in networks, including WANs, LANs, and LAN-to-LAN connections across vast distances.

frames—A feature support by most web browsers that divides the browser display area into two or more sections (frames). Although frames provide great flexibility and data can be drawn from two or more sources, many designers avoid using frames because web browsers support them unevenly.

FRBR—Acronym for Functional Requirements for Bibliographic Records.

gigabits per second (Gbps)—A measurement of data transmission speed expressed in billions of bits per second.

graphical user interface (GUI)—Pronounced "GOO-ee"; Microsoft Windows and the Macintosh are examples of computers with a GUI.

groupware—A class of software that helps groups of colleagues, sometimes called workgroups, organize their activities. Groupware supports meeting scheduling, email, preparation of documents, file distribution, and electronic newsletters.

handheld computer—This is a portable computer that is small enough to be held in a person's hand. Although extremely convenient to carry, handheld computers have not replaced notebook computers because of their small keyboards and screens. The most popular handheld computers are those that are specifically designed to provide PIM (personal information manager) functions, such as a calendar and address book. Some manufacturers are trying to solve the small keyboard problem by replacing the keyboard with an electronic pen. However, these pen-based devices rely on handwriting recognition technologies, which are still in their infancy.

handheld device markup language (HDML)—Used to format content for web- enabled mobile phones. HDML is phone.com's (formerly known as Unwired Planet) proprietary language, which can only be viewed on mobile phones that use phone.com browsers. HDML came before the wireless application protocol (WAP) standard was created.

heading—A word or phrase used to indicate some aspect of an item. For example, an author or subject.

high-bit-rate digital subscriber line (HDSL)—Also called G. S. HDSL. A DSL that delivers up to 1.544 Mbps of data symmetrically over two copper twisted-pair lines. The range of HDSL is limited to 12,000 feet; signal repeaters extend the service farther from the local telephone company office.

holdings—Materials owned by a library; frequently used to denote the number of volumes and journals owned by the library.

hop—An intermediate connection in a string of connections linking two network devices. The more hops, the longer it takes for data to go from source to destination.

host—Any computer on a network that is a repository for services available to other computers on the network.

host name—The name given to an individual computer or a server attached to a network or the internet.

hot spot—A place, such as a hotel, restaurant, museum, or library, that offers WiFi access (normally a free service).

hub—A network device that forwards packets to every other device connected to it.

hyperlink—Text that contains a word or phrase that can be clicked on to cause another document, record, or website to be retrieved and displayed.

hypertext—Documents that contain links to other documents. When a user selects a link, the second document is automatically displayed.

hypertext markup language (HTML)—The authoring language used to create documents on the World Wide Web. HTML defines the structure and layout of a web document by using a variety of tags and attributes.

Hypertext Preprocessor (PHP)—PHP is a widely used general-purpose scripting language.

Hypertext Transfer Protocol (HTTP)—The underlying protocol used by the World Wide Web. HTTP defines how messages are formatted and transmitted and what action web servers and browsers should take in response to various commands.

iBeacon—A communication protocol developed by Apple that transmits to Bluetooth enable devices such as smartphones. The technology enables devices to receive information when in close proximity to an iBeacon.

IEEE 802.11—A group of wireless specifications developed by the Institute of Electrical and Electronics Engineers (IEEE) to manage packet traffic over a network.

in-app browser—A web browser built into an app (so the user does not leave the app when following a link).

independent software vendor (ISV)—Generally, a firm that develops software applications not associated with a computer systems manufacturer.

instance—A resource reflecting an individual, material embodiment of the work. A core class of BIBFRAME.

instant messaging (IM)—Provides the ability to identify someone who is online and send and receive messages with them in near real time.

integrated services digital network (ISDN)—An information transfer standard for transmitting digital voice and data over telephone lines at speeds up to 128 Kbps.

interface—The part of the system that controls the interaction between the computer system and the user.

International Federation of Library Associations and Institutions (IFLA)—An organization that promotes library standards and the sharing of ideas and research.

internet—A global network connecting hundreds of thousands of networks, with compatible communication standards, that connect millions of computers. Each internet computer, called a host, is independent.

Internet Message Access Protocol (IMAP)—A standard format for retrieving email messages. IMAP uses simple mail transfer protocol (SMTP) for communication between the email recipient and the server.

Internet Protocol (IP)—The protocol that governs how computers send packets of data across the internet. It allows a packet to traverse multiple networks on the way to its final destination.

internet service provider (ISP)—A company that provides access for users and businesses to the internet.

internetworking—Sharing data and resources from one network to another.

Internetwork Packet Exchange (IPX)—A Novell NetWare networking protocol. IPX is used for connectionless communications.

interoperability—The ability of systems or products that adhere to standards to work together automatically. Examples of such standards include HTTP and TCP/IP.

intranet—A network belonging to an organization, accessible only by the organization's members, employees, or others with appropriate authorization.

iOS—Apple's operating system for the iPhone, iPod Touch, iPad, and Apple TV.

IP address—A numerical identifier for a device on a TCP/IP network. The IP address format is a string of four numbers, each from 0 to 255, separated by periods.

ISDN digital subscriber line (IDSL)—A form of DSL providing a symmetrical speed of 144 Kbps over the copper wire provisioned for integrated services digital network (ISDN). Repeaters enable service up to 35,000 feet from the local telephone company office.

JSON—See *JavaScript Object Notation*.

Java—A high-level programming language developed by Sun Microsystems. Java is an object-oriented language similar to C++ but simplified to eliminate language features that cause common programming errors.

Java 2 Enterprise Edition (J2EE)—A Java platform designed for mainframe-scale computing that provides an environment for developing and deploying enterprise applications. J2EE simplifies development and decreases programming by utilizing modular components and allowing the middle tier to handle much of the programming automatically.

JavaBeans—A Sun specification that defines how Java objects interact. JavaBeans are similar to Microsoft's ActiveX controls, except they can run on any platform.

JavaScript Object Notation (JSON)—JSON is an open-standard, language-independent file format using human-readable text to transmit data objects.

Jini—Based on Java, this is a Sun system for easily connecting any type of devices, including a net device, to a network.

Joint Photographic Experts Group (JPEG)—Pronounced "jay-peg", this is an image compression technique that reduces file sizes to about 5 percent of their normal size.

Journal Storage Project (JSTOR)—A not-for-profit organization that provides electronic access to scholarly journals. JSTOR began as an effort to ease the increasing problems faced by libraries seeking to provide adequate stack space for the long runs of back files of scholarly journals. The basic idea was to convert the back issues of paper journals into electronic formats to save space while simultaneously improving access to the journal content. Linking a searchable text file to the page images of the entire published record of a journal offers a level of access previously unimaginable.

kernel—The core components of an operating system.

key—In security systems, a password needed to decipher encoded data.

kilobits per second (Kbps)—A data transmission rate of 1,000 bits per second.

LAN—See *local area network*.

latency—In networking, the amount of time it takes a packet to travel from source to destination. Together, latency and bandwidth define the speed and capacity of a network.

legacy application or system—Computer systems that remain in use after more modern technology has been installed. Organizations are often reluctant to cease using legacy applications because they represent a significant investment in time and money.

Library of Congress subject heading (LCSH)—A word or phrase that indicates a book's subject; LCSHs are created and maintained by the Library of Congress.

Lightweight Directory Access Protocol (LDAP)—A set of protocols for accessing information directories. LDAP should eventually make it possible for almost any application running on virtually any network to obtain directory information, such as email addresses and public keys.

linked data—A set of best practices for the publication of structure data for the Web.

Linux—An open source, multitasking operating system written in the C programming language that is a variant of Unix; named after the developer of the kernel, Linus Torvalds of Finland.

local area network (LAN)—A network of workstations that are linked together. Each node (individual computer) in a LAN has its own central processing unit (CPU) with which it executes programs, but it is also able to access data and devices anywhere on the LAN. This means that many users can share expensive devices, such as printers, as well as data. Users can also use the LAN to communicate with one another, by sending email or engaging in chat sessions.

local loop—The wires that connect an individual subscriber's telephone or data connection to the telephone company central office or other local terminating point.

location awareness—The ability to track (and in some cases show) the location of a device such as a smartphone or tablet. For example, Google Maps can show where you are on the map.

lossy compression—A data compression technique in which some amount of data is lost.

Machine Readable Cataloging (MARC)—MARC is a standard method for encoding surrogate records so that they can be read and processed by a computer.

MARC 21—An international MARC standard agreed upon by Canada, the United States, and England, that represents the consolidation of USMARC, CAN/MARC, and UK/MARC.

markup languages—Text-based languages that use special characters to convey structural or presentational information to a computer program.

mash-up—Hybrid functionalities made possible through share APIs.

massive open online classes (MOOCs)—Online web-delivered classes that are available to anyone, with few, if any, restrictions.

megabits per second (Mbps)—A transmission rate where one megabit equals 1,024 kilobits.

metadata—An encoded description of an information package.

middleware—Software that connects two otherwise separate applications. Middleware is the "plumbing" that passes data from one application to another.

minicomputer—A minicomputer is a mid-sized computer whose size lies between mainframes and workstations; typically, it can support several hundred users simultaneously.

Moving Picture Experts Group (MPEG)—A family of digital video compression standards and file formats. MPEG (pronounced "EM-peg") generally produces higher-quality video than competing formats, such as QuickTime. MPEG files can be decoded by special hardware or by software. MPEG achieves high compression rate by storing only the changes from one frame to another, instead of each entire frame.

MS-DOS—A disk operating system developed by Microsoft for the IBM personal computer or PC.

Multimedia Internet Mail Extensions (MIME)—A protocol that defines several content types, which allows programs like web browsers to recognize different kinds of files and deal with them appropriately.

multiplexing—Combining multiple data channels onto a single transmission medium; sharing a circuit—normally dedicated to a single user—between multiple users.

multiuser—The ability for multiple concurrent users to log on and run applications from a single server.

name server—A computer that matches website names to IP addresses. Also sometimes called a DNS (domain name system) server.

National Information Standards Organization (NISO)—An organization that oversees the creation and maintenance of standards used in information processing.

net-centric software—Ready-to-use software solutions that can be downloaded or delivered via the internet rather than out of the box from a retailer (or e-tailer).

net neutrality—A policy that states that all packets are treated equally and that no packets are given priority over others.

network access point (NAP)—A location where ISPs exchange one another's traffic.

network computer (NC)—A "thin" client hardware device that executes applications locally by downloading them from the network. NCs adhere to a specification jointly developed by Sun, IBM, Oracle, Apple, and Netscape. They typically run Java applets within a Java browser, or Java applications within the Java Virtual Machine.

network computing architecture—A computing architecture in which components are dynamically downloaded from the network onto the client device for execution by the client. The Java programming language is at the core of network computing.

network file systems (NFS)—A set of protocols that allows files located on other computers to be used as if they were located locally.

network interface card—Often abbreviated NIC, a network interface card connects devices to a network.

network packets—Units into which data transmitted over a network are subdivided.

NISO Circulation Interchange Protocol (NCIP)—An interoperability standard that facilitates communication between self-service equipment and library circulation systems and between two or more circulation systems and/or interlibrary loan applications developed and maintained by different vendors.

off-site storage—A web-based service that rents computer disk space for storing documents and files to individuals and companies. Access is available twenty-four hours a day, seven days a week (24/7).

online—Direct communication between a user and a computer that allows a request to be processed and the results to be displayed immediately on the monitor.

online profiling—A profile of customers' buying and browsing habits a website creates by using cookies and personal information obtained from other sources.

Open Archival Information System (OAIS)—A specialized content management system (CMS) for managing digital content and its associated metadata for the purposes of long-term curation.

open source—Source code, or "source," is the instructions created by programmers to develop software. Most source code is proprietary for obvious reasons, for example, Microsoft's Windows. Advocates of open source projects, such as Linux and the Mozilla browser, claim that others can quickly and easily enhance a product that then can be shared by others. Opponents point to the incompatible product versions that are available.

OpenURL—A standard for encoding a description of a resource within a uniform resource locator (URL) and is defined in the ANSI/NISO Z39.88 standard.

optical character recognition (OCR)—A method for the conversion of images of text into machine-readable text.

outsourcing—The transfer of components or large segments of an organization's internal IT infrastructure, staff, processes, or applications to an external resource such as an application service provider.

packaged software application—A computer program developed for sale to consumers or businesses generally designed to appeal to more than a single customer. Although some tailoring of the program may be possible, it is not intended to be custom-designed for each user or organization.

packet—A bundle of data organized for transmission, containing control information (e.g., destination, length, origin), the data itself, and error detection and correction bits. In IP networks, packets are often called datagrams.

packet switching—A network in which messages are transmitted as packets over any available route rather than as sequential messages over switched or dedicated facilities.

PageRank—An algorithm developed by Google founders Larry Page and Sergey Brin that uses link analysis to contribute to a relevance measure.

password—A secret series of characters that enables a user to access a file, computer, or program. The password helps ensure that unauthorized individuals do not access the computer.

password authentication procedure—A procedure for validating a network connection request. The requester sends the network server a user name and password. The server can validate and acknowledge the request.

personal digital assistant (PDA)—A handheld device that combines computing, telephone, and networking features. Most PDAs use a stylus rather than a keyboard for input.

peer-to-peer (P2P)—A type of network in which each computer has equivalent capabilities and responsibilities.

performance—A major factor in determining the overall productivity of a system, performance is primarily tied to availability, throughput, and response time.

permanent virtual circuit (PVC)—A PVC connects the customer's port connections, nodes, locations, and branches to one another. All customer ports can be connected to one another, resembling a mesh, but PVCs usually run between the host and branch locations.

personal computer (PC)—A small, relatively inexpensive computer designed for individual use and often called a PC. The IBM PC was first introduced in 1981.

plain old telephone service (POTS)—Standard telephony for placing and receiving calls.

Plone—A content management system (CMS) used in some libraries.

point of presence (POP)—A dial-in location so you can connect to the internet. To the user, a POP is a local telephone number.

point-to-point protocol (PPP)—This protocol allows a computer to use the TCP/IP protocols with a standard telephone line and a high-speed modem.

point-to-point protocol over Ethernet (PPPOE)—A protocol that allows digital subscriber line (DSL) providers to meter connection time and to acquire a smaller, cheaper block of IP addresses. PPPOE changes DSL from an always-on to an on-demand service and lets providers reduce the size and cost of their internet connection infrastructures.

Portable Document Format (PDF)—A file format developed by Adobe Systems that captures formatting information to preserve the look and feel of a document viewed online or sent to a printer.

portal—A website or service that offers a broad array of resources and services.

post office protocol (POP)—A mail protocol that allows a remote mail client to read mail from a server.

POTS—See *plain old telephone service.*

practical extraction and report language (Perl)—Perl is a programming language designed for processing text.

precision—A performance measure that is based on the proportion of relevant retrievals within a set of retrieved records.

privacy—The right to freedom from unauthorized intrusion. The proliferating use of several technologies has made it easier to gather volumes of information about individuals and companies. Some concerned citizens are calling for legislative protection.

protocol—A definition of how a computer will act when talking to other computers. Standard protocols allow computers from different manufacturers to communicate.

proxy server—A server that sits between a client application, such as a web browser, and a real server. It intercepts all requests to the real server to see whether it can fulfill the request itself. If not, it forwards the request to the real server. Proxy servers are designed to improve performance and filter requests.

public-key encryption—A cryptographic system that uses two keys—a public key known to everyone and a private, or secret, key known only to the recipient of the message. Only the public key can be used to encrypt the message, and only the private key can be used to decrypt the message. What's needed is a global registry of public keys, which is one of the promises of Lightweight Directory Access Protocol (LDAP) technology.

PURL—An acronym for persistent uniform resource locator, a PURL is a permanent web address that acts as a permanent identifier in the face of a dynamic and constantly changing web infrastructure.

quality of service (QoS)—A collective measure of the level of service a provider delivers to its customers. QoS can be characterized by several basic performance criteria, including availability (low downtime), error performance, response time and throughput, lost calls or transmissions because of network congestion, and connection setup time.

radio frequency (RF)—

random access memory (RAM)—A type of computer memory that can be accessed randomly. Dynamic RAM must have its contents constantly refreshed, whereas static RAM does not need to be refreshed.

RDF—See *Resource Description Framework.*

recall—A performance measure based on the number of relevant retrievals compared to the total number of relevant records within a set of records.

redundant array of inexpensive disks (RAID)—A category of disk drives that employ two or more drives in combination for fault tolerance and improved performance.

relational database management system (RDBMS)—A system that stores data in the form of related tables. Oracle and MS SQL Server are examples of RDBMS systems.

Regional Bell Operating Company (RBOC)—Pronounced "R-bock," seven "Baby Bells" were created with the 1983 breakup of AT&T, or Ma Bell. The seven include Ameritech, Bell Atlantic, Bell South, NYEX, Pacific Bell, Southwestern Bell, and US West.

Really Simple Syndication (RSS)—A widely employed basic web service that can be used to publish updated content such as blog entries, podcasts, or news headlines.

remote access—The hookup of a remote-computing device via communications lines such as ordinary phone lines or wide area networks (WANS) to access distant network applications and information.

Remote Presentation Services Protocol—A set of rules and procedures for exchanging data between computers on a network, enabling the user interface, keystrokes, and mouse movements to be transferred between a server and client.

resource description framework (RDF)—A general framework, developed by the World Wide Web Consortium, for describing a website's metadata. For example, RDF will identify the website's map, keywords for search engines to use in indexing, and the web page's intellectual property rights.

router—A communications device between networks that determines the best path between them for optimal performance. Routers are used in complex networks of networks such as enterprise-wide networks and the internet.

RSS—See *Really Simple Syndication.*

scalability—Ability to expand the number of users or increase the capabilities of a computing solution without making major changes to the systems or application software.

search engine—A retrieval tool on the Web that matches keywords input by a user to words found at a website.

secure electronic transaction (SET)—A security standard that ensures privacy and protection for conducting credit card transactions over the internet. Rather than a credit card number, a digital signature is employed.

Secure Sockets Layer (SSL)—A protocol for transmitting private documents via the internet. SSL works by using a private key to encrypt data that transferred over the SSL connection. Most web browsers support SSL.

security software—Computer software installed on a computer network or individual workstation that protects it from a hacker attack. Typically, security software includes firewall and antivirus software.

***see* or *see also* reference**—Directions in an index or catalog to look under another term or a related term, respectively.

Serial Line IP (SLIP)—Allows a computer to connect to the internet using a telephone line and a high-speed modem. SLIP is being superseded by the PPP protocol.

server—The computer on a local area network that often acts as a data and application repository and controls an application's access to workstations, printers, and other parts of the network.

server-based computing—A server-based approach to delivering business-critical applications to end-user devices, whereby an application's logic executes on the server, and only the user interface is transmitted across a network to the client. Its benefits include single-point management, universal application access, bandwidth-independent performance, and improved security for business applications.

service-level agreement (SLA)—A binding contract or agreement between an end-user organization and an application serviced provider (ASP). It details the specifics of your partnership, including customer service and data security.

servlet—An applet that runs on a web server. A servlet is persistent—it stays in memory and can fulfill multiple requests.

SFX—SFX is an OpenURL link resolver developed and maintained by Ex Libris.

shelf list—A record of materials in a library arranged in call number order, the order in which they are placed on the shelves.

short message service (SMS)—A service for sending text messages of up to 160 characters to mobile phones that use global system for mobile (GSM). The cell phone can receive the message even if the phone is being used.

Simple Mail Transfer Protocol (SMTP)—A TCP/IP-based standard for sending email messages between servers on the internet. Once received, the messages are stored using either Internet Message Access Protocol (IMAP) or point of presence (POP).

Simple Object Access Protocol (SOAP)—A common format for exchanging data stored in diverse formats and databases. Approved by the World Wide Web Consortium, SOAP uses XML and HTTP to define a component interoperability standard on the Web. Microsoft's implementation of SOAP is called BizTalk, and IBM's is WebSphere.

smartphone—A combination of a mobile phone and a PDA that is able to access the internet, store contact information, take photos, send and receive emails, and use a variety of apps.

source code—Program instructions in their original form using a specific programming language.

spider—A simple software program used by a search engine to scan the Web. Spiders are bots that crawl from link to link, searching for new sites.

Standard Generalized Markup Language (SGML)—SGML is an international standard for organizing and tagging elements of a document. SGML is the basis for HTML and a precursor to XML.

static IP address—An IP address that never changes and is typically used in businesses rather than with consumers.

stickiness—The degree to which a website retains its users.

streaming—The end user sees video or hears an audio file as a continuous stream as it arrives, rather than waiting for the entire file to be received.

Structured Query Language (SQL)—SQL (pronounced "SEE-kwell") is a standardized query language for requesting information from a relational database.

SUSHI—Standardized Usage Harvesting Initiative is a NISO initiative to develop a protocol to facilitate the automated harvesting and consolidation of usage statistics from different vendors.

T-1 line—Data communications circuit capable of transmitting data at 1.5 Mbps.

T-3 line—A digital carrier facility used for transmitting data through the telephone system at 44.7 Mbps (its like thirty T-1s put together).

Tagged Image File Format (TIFF)—Format for storing bit-mapped images. Files typically end in a .tif extension.

telephony—The technology associated with the electronic transmission of voice, fax, or other information between two parties, historically associated with the telephone. A telephony application is a programming interface that helps provide these services. Using the internet, three new services are now available:

- Ability to make a normal telephone call
- Ability to make a normal telephon
- Ability to make a normal telephone callnic trane-mail

thin client—A low-cost computing device that accesses applications and/or data from a central server over a network. Categories of thin clients include Windows-based terminals (which comprise the largest segment), X-terminals, and network computers (NCs).

topologies—A network topology refers to the architecture of how network nodes are connected.

total cost of ownership (TCO)—A model that helps IT professionals understand and manage the budgeted (direct) and unbudgeted (indirect) costs incurred for acquiring, maintaining, and using an application or a computing system. TCO normally includes training, upgrades, and administration, as well as the purchase price. Lowering TCO through single-point control is a key benefit of server-based computing.

Transmission Control Protocol (TCP)—The transport layer protocol built on top of the Internet Protocol (IP) in a TCP/IP network. The IP deals only with moving packets of information; TCP enables servers to establish a connection and exchange data streams. It guarantees the data packets will be delivered in the same order in which they were sent.

Transmission Control Protocol/Internet Protocol (TCP/IP)—A suite of network protocols that allow computers with different architectures and operating system software to communicate with other computers on the internet. It is the de facto standard for communicating data over the internet.

tunneling—A technology that enables one network to send its data via another network's connections; sometimes called IP tunneling.

unicode—A standard for representing characters as integers. Two integers or bytes are used to represent each character.

universal description, discovery, and integration (UDDI)—A DNS-like distributed web directory that would enable services to discover one another and define how they can interact and share information. The end result is expected to be a standards-based internet directory of business information.

universal resource identifier (URI)—The string of characters (often starting with http://) that is used to identify anything on the Web.

uniform resource locator (URL)—A term used sometimes for certain URIs to indicate that they might change. The URL appears in the address line in the web browser window, for example, http://www.wiley.com.

universal resource name (URN)—A historic name for a uniform resource identifier (URI) that is a string of characters used to identify a web resource.

unshielded twisted pair (UTP)—A form of cooper telephone wiring in which two insulated copper wires are twisted around each other to reduce cross talk or interference.

uptime—The amount of time your system is working; the ideal is 100 percent of the time.

user interface—The part of an application that the end user sees on the screen and works with to operate the application, such as menus, forms, and "buttons."

user name—A name used to gain access to a computer system. In most systems, users can choose their own usernames and passwords.

UTP—See *unshielded twisted pair*.

value-added network (VAN)—A private network provider that facilitates electronic data interchange (EDI) or provides other network services. Before the arrival of the World Wide Web, some organizations hired value-added networks to move data from their location to other locations. With the arrival of the World Wide Web, many companies found it more cost efficient to move their data over the internet instead of paying the minimum monthly fees and per-character charges found in typical VAN contracts.

very high data rate digital subscriber line (VDSL)—An evolving form of DSL that can deliver data at a rate of 13 to 52 Mbps downstream and 1.5 to 2.3 Mbps upstream over a single copper twisted-pair line. The operating range of VDSL is up to 4,500 feet from the local telephone company office.

virtual private network (VPN)—A secure, encrypted private internet connection. Data is encrypted before being sent and decrypted at the receiving end to maintain privacy and security. A set of communication rules has been created, called Point-to-Point Tunneling Protocol (PPTP), to create VPNs.

virus—A software program that is loaded onto your computer without your knowledge and runs against your wishes. Most viruses can also replicate themselves. A simple virus that can make a copy of itself over and over again is dangerous because it will quickly use all available memory and bring the system to a halt. An even more dangerous type of virus is one capable of transmitting itself across networks and bypassing security systems. Antivirus programs periodically check your computer for the best-known viruses.

Voice Extensible Markup Language (VXML)—VXML or VoiceXML allows a user to interact with the internet using voice-recognition technology.

Voice over Internet Protocol (VoIP)—The delivery of voice information in the language of the internet (i.e., as digital packets instead of the current circuit protocols of the copper-based phone networks). In VoIP systems, analog voice messages are digitized and transmitted as a stream of data (not sound) packets that are reassembled and converted back into a voice signal at their destination. The killer idea is that VoIP allows telephony users to bypass long-distance carrier charges by transporting those data packets just like other internet information. With VoIP, your PC becomes your phone and you can call anywhere in the world for the cost of a local call.

Web—Refers to the World Wide Web (WWW) and is what the internet became with the introduction of HTML.

web browser—A software application used to locate and display web pages. The two most popular browsers are Netscape Navigator and Microsoft Internet Explorer.

web hosting—Placing an organization's web page or website on a server that can be accessed via the internet.

web services—A family of tools involved in transmitting data stripped of formatting and layout requirements between domains.

wide area network (WAN)—Local area networks linked together across a large geographic area.

WiFi—WiFi (wireless fidelity) is an IEEE standard for wireless connectivity to the internet by way of a broadcast signal.

Windows-based terminal—Thin clients with the lowest cost of ownership, as there are no local applications running on the device.

Wireless Applications Protocol (WAP)—WAP is a specification that allows wireless devices to access interactive information services and applications from screens of mobile phones.

wireless local loop (WLL)—A broadband connection system that uses high- frequency radio links to deliver voice and data without the problems of gaining right of way for a fiber-optic cable installation or finding adequate copper connections for DSL. Also known as fixed-point wireless.

wireless markup language (WML)—WML is an XML language used to specify content and user interface for WAP devices; the WAP forum provides a DTD for WML. Almost every mobile phone browser around the world supports WML. WML pages are requested and served in the same way as HDML pages.

World Wide Web Consortium (W3C)—An entity composed of many organizations that work on developing common standards for the evolution of the Web.

XDSL—This term refers to the assorted flavors of the DSL connections including, but not limited to, ADSL (asymmetric digital subscriber line), HDSL (high bit-rate DSL) and RADSL (rate adaptive asymmetric digital subscriber line).

XML—See *eXtensible Markup Language.*

Z39.2—A standard for encoding information in machine-readable form. Often referred to as a MARC record.

Z39.50—A standard protocol that allows one computer to query another computer and transfer search results without the user needing to know the search commands or the remote computer.

> **Tip!** Excellent online resources for keeping abreast of technical terms and acronyms include https://www.whatis.com and https://www.webopedia.com.

Index

Note: Page numbers followed by *t* indicate tables and *f* indicate figures.

About the Authors

JOSEPH R. MATTHEWS has provided consulting assistance to numerous academic, public, and special libraries and local governments. Previously an instructor at the School of Library Information Science (SLIS) at San Jose State University, Matthews has taught evaluation of library services, library information systems, strategic planning, management, and research methods. In 2010, he was honored as the SLIS Outstanding Scholar. In addition to numerous articles, he is the author of more than thirty books, including *Managing with Data: Using ACRLMetrics and PLAmetrics, Getting Started with Evaluation, Reflecting on the Future of Academic and Public Libraries, Listening to the Customer, Library Assessment in Higher Education, The Customer-Focused Library: Re-Inventing the Public Library from the Outside-In, The Evaluation and Measurement of Library Services,* and *Strategic Planning and Management for Library Managers.* Matthews is an invited conference speaker and is active in the American Library Association (ALA) and the Association of College & Research Libraries.

CARSON BLOCK has been a library technologist for more than twenty-five years—as a library worker, IT director, and now a library technology consultant. As a consultant with Carson Block Consulting Inc., Carson is often brought in to help solve complex institutional issues and to help align the library's public service mission with its technology efforts to serve the needs of patrons and staff. Past president of the Colorado division of the Public Library Association, he has also served in leadership positions in the ALA, the Association of Specialized and Cooperative Library Agencies (ASCLA), the Colorado Public Library Association (PLA), and others. Carson is also a member of the Future of Libraries advisory group to ALA's Office of Information Technology Policy. His publications include *Managing Library Technology: A LITA Guide* (2017).